ALSO IN THE
Amistad Literary Series

LANGSTON HUGHES
ZORA NEALE HURSTON
TONI MORRISON
GLORIA NAYLOR
RICHARD WRIGHT

Also by Henry Louis Gates, Jr.

Figures in Black: Words, Signs, and the "Racial" Self
Signifying Monkey: Toward a Theory of Afro-American Literary Criticism
Loose Canons: Notes on the Culture Wars
Black Literature and Literary Theory (editor)
The Classic Slave Narratives (editor)
Reading Black, Reading Feminist (editor)

Also by K. A. Appiah

Assertion and Conditions
For Truth in Semantics
Necessary Questions: An Introduction to Philosophy
Avenging Angel (fiction)
In My Father's House: Africa in the Philosophy of Culture
Early African-American Classics (editor)

AMISTAD LITERARY SERIES

ALICE WALKER

Critical Perspectives
Past and Present

EDITED BY
Henry Louis Gates, Jr., and K. A. Appiah

Amistad

NEW YORK, NEW YORK

Critical Perspectives Past and Present

MICHAEL C. VAZQUEZ, *Project Coordinator*

WAYNE L. APONTE
LISA GATES
SONJA OKUN

Amistad Press, Inc.
1271 Avenue of the Americas
New York, NY 10020

Distributed by:
Penguin USA
375 Hudson Street
New York, NY 10014

Designed by Stanley S. Drate/Folio Graphics Company, Inc.
Produced by March Tenth, Inc.

1 2 3 4 5 6 7 8 9 10

Library of Congress Cataloging-in-Publication Data

Alice Walker : critical perspectives past and present / edited by
    Henry L. Gates, Jr. and K. A. Appiah.
        p.   cm. — (Amistad literary series)
    Includes bibliographical references and index.
    ISBN 1-56743-013-9 : $24.95. — ISBN 1-56743-026-0 (pbk.) : $14.95
    1. Walker, Alice, 1944– —Criticism and interpretation.   2. Afro-
American women in literature.   I. Gates, Henry Louis.   II. Appiah,
Anthony.   III. Series.
PS3573.A425Z54   1993
813'.54—dc20   92-45754
                                                                    CIP

Contents

INTERVIEWS

Preface

◆◆◆◆◆◆◆◆◆◆◆◆◆◆
Alice Walker
(1944–   )

More than any other Black author at work today, Alice Walker has been concerned about grounding her work in a matrilineal tradition of black writing, paying particular homage to the exuberant imagination of Zora Neale Hurston. It was Walker who located Hurston's resting place and set a monument there. And it was Walker who, more than anyone except her biographer, Robert Hemenway, resurrected Hurston's work and reputation from the burial grounds of obscurity. Walker's patient work established Hurston at the structural center of a tradition of African-American women's writing, and indeed, within a larger tradition of Black letters, as a counterpoint to the naturalist art of Richard Wright. To be sure, Walker's construction of her own progenitors need not be shared by her attentive readers; hers is a self-conscious and complex contribution to contemporary writing that lends itself to a variety of approaches and perspectives.

Alice Walker was born in Eatonton, Georgia, the daughter of Willie Lee and Minnie Tallulah Grant Walker. Educated at Spelman and Sarah Lawrence colleges, Walker was an active participant in the civil rights movement, working on voter registration in Georgia and for the Head Start program in Mississippi, as well as for the department of welfare in New York City. She has taught at Jackson State College in the sixties, and at Tougaloo College, Wellesley College, the University of Massachusetts at Amherst, the University of California at Berkeley, and Brandeis University for varied intervals in the 1970s. She has won several awards for her work, most notably the Pulitzer Prize for fiction and the National Book Award, both for *The Color Purple* in 1983.

Walker has published five novels, and it is her novels that have secured her reputation for the larger public: *The Third Life of Grange Copeland* (1970), *Meridian* (1976), *The Color Purple* (1982), *The Temple of My Familiar* (1989), and *Posessing the Secret of Joy* (1992). Her short stories have been collected in two volumes—*In Love & Trouble* (1973) and *You Can't Keep a Good Woman Down* (1982). Walker's publication of poetry has kept pace with her novels: Her collections are *Once* (1968),

Five Poems (1972), *Revolutionary Petunias & Other Poems* (1973), *Good Night, Willie Lee, I'll See You in the Morning* (1979), and *Horses Make a Landscape Look More Beautiful* (1984). She has also published two important collections of her own essays—*In Search of Our Mother's Gardens* (1983) and *Living by the Word* (1988); a significant collection of the writings of Zora Neale Hurston; and a young adult biography of Langston Hughes.

Plainly, her achievements as a writer are characterized by an astonishing versatility. She is equally at home with poetry and fiction—it is worth remembering her first appearance in book form was as a poet, not as a novelist or fiction writer. Indeed, as an essayist alone she would be a noteworthy presence in American letters. And, of course, the rigorous sensibility that she designates "womanism" in her expository prose, one that seeks to transcend the failings she decries in some mainstream feminisms, suffuses her larger oeuvre as well.

But it is her novels for which she is best known, and it is her novels in which the full complexity of her vision is most evident. Like Hurston, she incorporates elements of traditional folklore into her fiction, but elements of the Gothic, of the Southern black migration novel, of the romance, and of the nineteenth-century sentimental novel also appear in her fiction. Deeply informed by the evolving 1960s' discourse of civil rights, she chafes against the confinements of the doctrinally correct— a theme pursued in such poems as "Revolutionary Petunias" as well as in her fiction. Perhaps inevitably, some black intellectuals—generally male—would castigate her for her doctrinal heresies, propagating a highly reductive account of her literary concerns.

Certainly the unsparing nature of her vision was apparent from her first novel. Grounded in an agrarian black community of the South, *The Third Life of Grange Copeland* refuses ever to sentimentalize or idealize it. And while *Meridian* is propelled by the revolutionary discourse of the civil rights and Black Power eras, Walker demonstrates a keen eye for hypocrisy and cruelty under the cover of correctness. Ambivalent allegiances and divided loyalties are Walker's preoccupation here, as elsewhere.

Walker had, by this time, established herself as one of the two central figures in the nascent renaissance of Black women's writing. In fact, some scholars date the birth of this movement to the publication in 1970 of Walker's *The Third Life of Grange Copeland* and Toni Morrison's *The Bluest Eye*. It was, after all, through the success of her fictional prose that Walker had established the authority to canonize Hurston. By doing so, she contributed enormously to the construction of the idea of a Black woman's "tradition" out of which she and a host of others could write, could ground and revise their fiction. It would be difficult to overestimate the signal importance of this foundational gesture.

As epistolary novel, *The Color Purple* was, of course, Walker's breakthrough book, winning a wide public through its formally ingenious and dramatically gripping account of Celie's trials and eventual triumph. Lamentably, its very success exposed its author to changes of male-bashing by those who would prefer that the varied forms of violence against women be discreetly ignored by the Black literary record.

In fact, while the theme of oppression has been one of the great concerns of Black fiction since the novel form was first employed by William Wells Brown and Harriet E. Wilson, the oppression of Blacks by Blacks does not have a long history as a subject for representation. While Bigger Thomas's senseless and brutal murder of his girlfriend, Bessie, might suggest itself as an exception, Richard Wright's *Native Son* is not concerned with telling Bessie's story—even in relation to Bigger—in any particular detail. She is a narrative supplement, her tale the shadow narrative to Mary Dalton's murder.

Celie's tale, "told" in the epistolary form, charts the triumph of sheer will over oppressive forces, forces that would seem initially to be omnipotent, irresistible. White racism, with a notable exception, does not take center stage. Male over female, Black male over Black females, these are the axes of domination that structure *The Color Purple*. Celie's resistance to and eventual triumph over this oppression is connected to a growing self-consciousness embodied in the letters she is writing (and which we are reading over her shoulder, as it were). Walker was determined that Celie "speak" in her own voice, to counter Robert Stepto's argument that *Their Eyes* is flawed because its narrative frame is rendered in the third person. Each sentence of Celie's successive letters registers her growth in self-awareness and strength.

The Temple of My Familiar, a large-scale work of mythopoesis spanning half a million years, can also be read as a book about storytelling and the role such stories have in fashioning our collective identities. Most recently, Walker's fascination with divided loyalties as much as double consciousness is trenchantly dramatized in *Possessing the Secret of Joy*, a tortured indictment of clitoridectomy that centers on the interplay between modern and traditional identities and cultural practices and the price that patriarchy may extract in the passage from one to the other.

Often misread as simply a didactic or moralistic voice in contemporary fiction, Walker's moral imagination is in fact most fully engaged when exploring cultural dualities and dilemmas, the ineradicable tensions and ambivalences of our own modernity. Indeed, it is precisely her ability to postpone any facile resolution of such conflicts that continues to discomfit and intrigue a devoted readership.

The sequence of reviews that opens the volume documents the evolving critical response to Walker's novels, widely considered to represent her essential contribution to American letters. Drawn from newspapers and popular magazines, they show Walker's accomplishments in the eyes of her literary contemporaries.

The sixteen essays that follow chart the range of scholarly response to Walker's writing. In an encompassing essay, Mary Helen Washington describes Walker's ambition to be an "apologist and chronicler" of Black women's lives. Her works—short fictions, poems, essays, novels—reveal the complexity of moral decision-making and the tattered fabric of life in the day-to-day existence of Black women. Barbara Christian performs extensive readings of Walker's first two novels, noting broad themes of degeneration and regeneration. Walker's work frames the possibility of meaningful change, of an escape from the abusive patterns of past history. Christian further describes how Walker encumbers stereotypes about Black life with the full living weight of social reality, the better to dramatize the complexity of the choices faced by human actors living in poverty or ignorance.

Elliot Butler-Evans examines the gendered production of history in the first two novels. He describes a dual process, in which a generalized narrative of racial history is doubled (and displaced) by a feminine counternarrative, a historical struggle which mirrors the personal struggles of the protagonists. The passage from *The Third Life of Grange Copeland* to *Meridian* is shown to consist in the eruption of this second, female narrative or historical voice.

Theodore Q. Mason, Jr., examines the play of space and the sense of enclosure in *The Third Life of Grange Copeland*. He notes the often deleterious, sometimes enabling varieties of enclosed space in the novel.

Michael Cooke's reading of *Meridian* focuses on Walker's treatment of the struggle for intimacy in the context of the revolutionary aspirations of the 1960s. Set against a series of standardized, mock intimacies, real intimacy is shown to be a *project*, the result of a spiritual work of renunciation.

Alan Nadel's account of *Meridian* describes how the process of self-creation is inscribed in the body of Meridian herself. Nadel argues that this process takes place in the encounter with artifacts from the past, in the struggle to make the past live in the present. The political implications of this model of the self are shown to be one of the novel's subtexts. In a similar vein, Deborah E. McDowell's essay charts the Emersonian ambition of the title character, whose struggle to forge an autonomous self results in a revisionary embrace of the rural, Southern past—symbolized by the newly militant Black church.

In an affirmative essay, Hanna Nowak recounts the engaging simplicity of Walker's poetry, noting themes of love, death, and tradition. Adopting a more skeptical view, Alice Hall Petry registers discontent with what she describes as the mixed results of Walker's short-fiction writing.

Lauren Berlant's theoretically engaged reading of *The Color Purple* traces the complex interplay of gender, race, and capital on the lives and identities of the novel's characters. Berlant argues that Walker's euphoric treatment of the mythic spirit of American capitalism and her insistence on voice as a nondiscursive medium foreclose the possibility of an Afro-American national consciousness. In my own essay I consider the problem of writing and voice—exemplified by what I call the "speakerly text"—in Walker's revision of Zora Neale Hurston.

In a sweeping essay, Wendy Wall examines the relationship between writing and the body in *The Color Purple*. In her interpretation, the violence Celie initially sustains is transformed into a textual inscription in her letters to God; writing serves as a strategy for psychic survival by creating a second body, unmarred by physical force. Wall further elaborates on the consequences of the epistolary structure of much of the novel.

Thadious Davis reads Walker's poetry in the context of her other fiction and nonfiction work. Davis detects the resonance of her poetic concerns in all of Walker's artistic works.

bell hooks's contribution initiates a critique of Walker's narrative strategies in *The Color Purple*. Like Laura Berlant, hooks discerns the triumph of fantasy over imagination, as Walker divorces social acts from their contexts and consequences in her affirmative "Black woman's" capitalism and, most notably, in her portrayal of a homosexuality that is neither challenged by the dominant culture nor even subversive of heterosexuality.

Linda Abbandonato, in a provocative reading of *The Color Purple*, maintains that its form (Hurstean vernacular) and its content (Black lesbian triumph), undermines white patriarchal political and linguistic structures. In the volume's final essay, Houston A. Baker, Jr., and Charlotte Pierce-Baker situate Alice Walker's writing in the context of quilt-making in Afro-America. Both represent, they argue, a specifically female craft of confronting chaos and ordering it through the skillful arrangement of patches, the literary art of bricolage.

The volume concludes with two interviews, in which Alice Walker discusses her literary craft from a highly personal perspective.

—Henry Louis Gates, Jr.

REVIEWS

THE THIRD LIFE OF GRANGE COPELAND (1970)

◆◆◆◆◆◆◆◆◆◆◆◆◆

JOSEPHINE HENDIN

Saturday Review, August 22, 1970

Can one still shed tears for blacks of the lower middle class? Is their misery too ordinary, their suffering too quiet to arouse the compassion of an age addicted to extremes of violence? Can we, after our adulation of Eldridge Cleaver, still feel that Uncle Tom was human, too; had a tragedy of his own inviting more than contempt? These four black writers would quietly say yes. Their novels explore the agony of the respectable and reveal those forces that give decency a horror all its own.

When the Fire Reaches Us is set in Detroit during the summer of the great riot. But, even in flames, Barbara Tinker's Detroit is like a quiet Southern town, filled with decent, gentle people. Even Maybelle, the prostitute, is a solid working girl: "Now I want to make it clear that Maybelle is not one of your trashy whores who hooks for the fun of it. She is in the business strictly as a way to make a living and she is a very ladylike individual." And indeed she is. In fact, all of Mrs. Tinker's characters are ladies and gentlemen who, though they feel themselves victims of white atrocities, never lose their Christian charity. "How come white folks hate us so much? We ain't never done nothing to them, has we?" is the closest one woman can come to outrage at the police's murder of a black child.

Clearly, the author meant to tell her story from the point of view of those who would not burn or loot, but instead cared for children displaced by the fires. The narrator-hero, Danny, and his wise old mentor, Uncle Ambrose, do not waste their lives in bitterness against whites. Ambrose has learned to live without "letting that Man get under his skin." He has also lived without letting a woman or his adopted son get under it either. In fact, Danny and Ambrose exist without any strong feeling at all. They are helpful and kind; they ask nothing for themselves from blacks or whites. And they are, in the most profound sense, alone.

* * *

3

A pall lies over this novel, a spell that turns all its characters into the living dead. Mrs. Tinker is so intent on establishing the good works of her heroes that she never sees how hard won is their goodness, or at what deep levels it was forged. Their very deadness suggests how dearly they have paid for their equanimity.

If emotional aridity is the price for living in Mrs. Tinker's Detroit, it is also the price Al Young's hero pays for getting along with his grandmother. *Snakes* starts out as the tale of how MC, a Detroit high school student, discovers jazz. But it quickly turns into a tedious success story of how "Snakes," a song MC wrote and recorded, becomes a local hit. Although Young's inert, stifling prose rarely conveys the rhythm or texture of the music MC tells you he loves, it is well suited to conveying MC's reaction to the grandmother who reared him, "the last person in the world [he] would want to hurt."

All this woman asks of MC is that he "mind her," finish high school, and "make something" of his life. But at the book's end, when MC gets on a bus for two weeks alone in New York, he realizes with great surprise: "For the first time in my life I don't feel trapped . . . and I'm going to try and make this feeling last for as long as I can." Had MC reached that state earlier in the novel, the book might have been less tepid. As it is, MC avoids conflict of any kind. In the process of "minding" his grandmother, but not letting her get under his skin, he becomes too thick-skinned even to sense how cramped he is.

Snakes and *When the Fire Reaches Us* are themselves in the throes of precisely that constriction which proves fatal to Uncle Ambrose. One suspects that, like MC, Mrs. Tinker and Young are "minding" some symbolic grandmother, some force of tradition that exerts a terrible pressure to be "correct" and "nice." But novels that are too "nice" to look searchingly at human conflict or passion are doomed to miss the point of both.

In contrast, Cyrus Colter, who began to write ten years ago at the age of fifty, makes brilliant fiction out of uptightness, exploring the disease with the awareness and precision of a first-rate clinician. *The Beach Umbrella* is a remarkable collection of stories about the isolation and emptiness of the lower-middle-class black, and of those who rise to wealth and social prominence only to find the same despair at the very center of themselves. Whether his characters are rich or poor, lusting after expensive clothes or unattainable women, all are crushed by a sense that some vital force is missing from their lives. And this consciousness of loss most affects those industrious family men for whom life is an endless series of obligations.

Elijah in the title story is a white-collar worker who is ridiculed by his wife for not taking a more lucrative factory job. The more she complains, the more he yearns for his Saturdays on a beach at the edge of Lake Michigan, where he finds "life": those laughing, joking people whom he observes from afar seem to contain all the world's mirth under their beach umbrellas. Chased away from their parties, Elijah takes money from his hard-working twelve-year-old son to buy a beach umbrella of his own, and the day a group gathers around his umbrella he comes as close as he can to joy.

Coltcr powerfully conveys the fervor of Elijah's longing, and the force with which his emotional tightness strangles his single day of fulfillment. This is a fine and tragic tale of how deadening are the ways of decency, and how hard it is to ward off gloom.

The depletion of love and the erosion of the sources of affection are the themes of Alice Walker's *The Third Life of Grange Copeland*, a powerful story about three generations of a black family in rural Georgia. This novel has heroes and villains. The villains are those who have a genius for hate, but no capacity for love. The heroes acquire the ability to care deeply for another human being.

Brownfield Copeland, whose mother kills herself in despair when his father abandons her, grows up hungry and unloved. Throughout his marriage his unsatisfied need for protection persists although for a while his wife passionately mothers him: "as the babies . . . sucked and nursed at her bosom, so did he, and grew big and grew firm with love, and grew strong." But Brownfield's life has not made him able to care deeply for her. When babies become numerous, and debts grow faster than cotton, he begins to loathe her. "Every Saturday night he beat her, trying to pin the blame for his failure on her by imprinting it on her face . . ."

Miss Walker skillfully depicts Brownfield turning into a murderous, whining beast. Her sympathy, however, is plainly with his wife, with all black women, whom she sees as the victims of both whites and their own husband's rage. Women are not broken by poverty, the author seems to imply, but she never probes the impact of poverty on Brownfield's inner life, or the psychic starvation that makes him so unable to love. Brownfield appears to have an intense self-hatred; to him black is anything but beautiful. Miss Walker hates his self-hatred too much to dissect it.

At one time the self-hatred of Brownfield's father, Grange Copeland, was so intense that he could not bring himself to touch his son. But when he discovered in New York that he hated whites even more, that he could act on his hatred and preach it in the streets, Grange lost his self-loathing. By beating up as many whites as he could, he presumably glimpsed his own worth. Now an old man, he is able to return to Georgia and feel love for his granddaughter.

Miss Walker disappoints by explaining Grange's conversion in political clichés. Do militant slogans really cure a sense of failure so great it inhibits a man from touching his own son? Has any man's soul ever been healed by politics? Miss Walker's solution ignores the depth and force of the loveless agony she describes.

◆◆◆◆◆◆◆◆◆◆◆◆◆◆

ROBERT COLES

The New Yorker, February 27, 1971

We all know that America's cities are in trouble, especially because blacks have fled to them in mixed hope and fear. We know, because we are constantly told, that the whites don't understand the needs of the blacks, that we will go from bad to worse, that it is too late, because another apocalypse is at hand. But almost no one has tried to tell us about the early lives, the *inner* early lives, of black people, the particular ways that black children in a rural setting grow, only to leave and become the urban poor, the "social dynamite" we hear abstractly described again and again. The tragedy had to be documented, yet social documentation and political prescription can be static and flat and self-defeating when the men, women, and children involved become merely part of something called "a history of exploitation and oppression." And books and thinking that carry on in this fashion will not, unfortunately, really be counterbalanced by Alice Walker's "The Third Life of Grange Copeland" (Harcourt Brace Jovanovich). Novelists and poets (Miss Walker is a published poet, too) are not the people we look to for help about "ghetto children" and "racial violence in our cities." Moreover, Miss Walker was born in and has spent most of her life in the Southern countryside, and she is now a writer-in-residence at Tougaloo College, a black Mississippi school that is not in a city. What can she know of the crime and violence, the drug addiction and alcoholism and despair we have been told exist so significantly in our urban ghettos? What can she volunteer about the "attitudes" of black children or their "problems"?

In her own way, she has supplied some answers, but she has not written a social novel or a protest novel. Miss Walker is a storyteller. A black woman from the farmlands of Georgia, she knows her countryside well—so warm and fertile and unspoiled, so bleak and isolated and bloodsoaked—and especially she knows the cabins, far out of just about everyone's sight, where one encounters the habits of diet, the idioms of speech, the styles of clothing, the ways of prayer that contrast so strikingly with the customs of the rest of us. Fearful and vulnerable, rural blacks (and whites, too) can at the same time be exuberant, passionate, quick-witted, and as smartly self-displaying as the well-dressed and the well-educated. She knows, beyond that, what bounty sharecroppers must hand over to "bossmen," and how tenant farmers struggle with their landlords, and how subsistence farmers barely get by. But she does not exhort. In "The Third Life of Grange Copeland," the centuries of black life in America are virtually engraved on one's consciousness. Equally vivid is Grange Copeland, who is more than a representative of Georgia's black field hands, more than someone scarred by what has been called "the mark of oppression." In him Miss Walker has turned dry sociological facts into a whole and alive particular person rather than a bundle of problems and attitudes. Character portrayal is what she has accomplished, and character portrayal is not to be confused with "motivational analysis."

Grange Copeland is a proud, sturdy black yeoman who has the white man on his back. He picks cotton, lowers his head when "they" appear, goes through the required postures a segregationist society demands—the evasions, duplicities, and pretenses that degrade black men and make moral cowards out of white men. Underneath, he is strong enough to hate, and without a rage a man like him might well become the ingratiating lackey he has to pretend to be. His anger is not really political or ideological. He sulks, lashes out at his wife, his young son Brownfield, and her illegitimate infant. He sees too much, feels too much, dreams too much; he is like an actor who has long ago stopped trying to estimate where "he" begins and his "roles" end. He works backbreaking days in the field, comes home saddened and hungry for sleep, but tense and truculent. ("By Thursday, Grange's gloominess reached its peak and he grimaced respectfully, with veiled eyes, at the jokes told by the man who drove the truck. On Thursday nights he stalked the house from room to room and pulled himself up and swung from the rafters of the porch.") He is nearly consumed by his contempt for the white landowners, the bossmen, but he and his wife struggle tenaciously for the little integrity and self-respect they can find. Eventually they conclude that they are losers and take to drink and promiscuity, followed by hysterical efforts at atonement on Sunday mornings. Then Grange abandons his wife, and she poisons herself and her illegitimate infant. Brownfield, the child of their hope and love, is left to wander across the land, left to learn how much a child has to pay for the hurt and pain his parents live with and convey.

I suppose it can be said that "The Third Life of Grange Copeland" is concerned with the directions a suffering people can take. His first life ends in flight, and his wandering son takes flight, too, becoming in time a ruined and thus ruinous man, bent on undermining everyone who feels worthwhile and has a sense of pride and dignity. For a while, the lives of father and son converge on the establishment run by Josie, a sensual, canny, generous, possessive madam whose café and "rooms" full of women feed off the frustrations men like Grange and Brownfield try to subdue. There are complications, accidents, sudden and surprising developments. And always there is the unpredictable and potentially violent "atmosphere" of the small Georgia towns and the dusty, rutted roads that lead from them into the countryside.

Grange's second life, in Harlem, is equally disastrous. He becomes slick, manipulative, unfeeling—the thief and confidence man our respectable world (which has its own deceptions and cruelties) is shocked to find and quick to condemn—yet not wholly unfeeling: he tries to help a white woman in distress and is rebuffed. His hatred of whites presses more relentlessly, and so he goes South, to find escape from them at any cost. Josie is waiting for him. Brownfield has married her niece, a charming girl, "above" her husband in intelligence and education and sensitivity, but step by step he goes down, systematically destroying his wife and daughters. Yet Grange finds at last—in his third life, as an exile returned home—the freedom he has asked for. The whites are everywhere still powerful, so it is not political and economic freedom he achieves. But he does take care of his son's youngest daughter after her mother is killed by her drunken husband, and, finally, he can say to his beloved grand-daughter, "I know the danger of putting all the blame on somebody else for the mess you make out of your life. I fell into the trap myself. And I'm bound to believe that that's the way the white folks can corrupt you even when you done held up before. 'Cause when they got you thinking that they're to blame for *every*thing they have you thinking they's some kind of gods!"

Brownfield tries to get his daughter back, and to prevent that Grange kills him. What goes on between that duaghter, that growing child, and her grandfather is told with particular grace; it is as if one were reading a long and touching poem. But Alice Walker is a fighter as well as a meditative poet and a lyrical novelist. She has taken part in the struggles her people have waged, and she knows the struggles they must yet face in this greatest of the world's democracies. She also knows that not even ample bread and wine or power and the applause of one's countrymen can give anyone the calm, the freedom that comes with a mind's acceptance of its own worth. Toward the end of his third life, Grange Copeland can at last stop being hard on himself and look with kindness upon himself—and one wonders whether any achievement can be more revolutionary.

MERIDIAN (1976)

◆◆◆◆◆◆◆◆◆◆◆◆◆

MARGE PIERCY

Liberty Journal, May 1976

In *Meridian*, Alice Walker has written a fine, taut novel that accomplishes a remarkable amount. The issues she is concerned with are massive. Events are strung over 25 years, although most occur between the height of the civil rights movement and the present. However, her method of compression through selection of telling moments and her freedom from chronology create a lean book that finishes in 228 pages and goes down like clean water.

Although this is only Alice Walker's second novel, it is her sixth book. She has published poetry, short stories and a study of Langston Hughes. She writes with a sharp critical sense as she deals with the issues of tactics and strategy in the civil rights movement, with the nature of commitment, the possibility of interracial love and communication, the vital and lethal strands in American and black experience, with violence and non-violence and self-hatred.

In spite of many sharply sketched minor characters (for instance, the young woman dying of a kidney ailment who says "Don't sit there . . . You blocks my view of my husband"), there are only four important characters: Meridian's mother, Mrs. Hill, dour, narrowly religious, frightened and unloving; Lynne, a Jewish civil rights worker who marries and loses Truman, a painter, who shifts and slides with the times; and Meridian herself, a black woman who cannot lie and for whom ideas are simply real and to be acted upon with her life.

What Walker wants to say about history and choice she works out through a 10-year-long triangle, of Meridian, Truman, and Lynne—their misadventures, their ability and inability to love or forgive each other, the dreadful believability of how they flay and feed and comfort by turns. Meridian has been passionately in love with Truman, who leaves her for Lynne, whom he later abandons along with their daughter Camara. By the time he wants Meridian, she no longer wants him because her life of total commitment to struggle in the black small towns of the South is meaningless to him, an increasingly commercial artist. Lynne cannot go back to where she came from and she does not belong in the black community either.

Meridian, the protagonist, is the most interesting, an attempt to make real in contemporary terms the notion of holiness and commitment. Is it possible to write a novel about the progress of a saint? Apparently, yes. With great skill and care to make Meridian believeable at every stage of her development, Walker also shows us the cost. For every exemplary act of bravery for the black community (standing up to a tank so black children can see a peepshow), she pays an immediate price in her body. Asked by a group of temporary revolutionaries if she can kill for the revolution, she infuriates her friends because she cannot say an easy yes and spends a decade worrying about the question.

Walker has put "Meridian" together carefully, on every level. For instance, the lost dead black child is a motif running throughout. In ignorance Meridian got pregnant and had to leave high school. When she is offered a college scholarship for her work in civil rights, she gives her baby away to relatives and goes. She feels that giving up her child is a sin and a shame, and after aborting Truman's baby, she is sterilized. She is haunted by having failed to win her mother's love, by the great lack of mothering and nurture; and by her own failure as a mother. Her inability to forgive cripples her. At the same time she is aware that without that harsh choice, she would have accomplished nothing. Her life would have been wasted and she would have taken out her emptiness and frustration on her baby, whom she could not love.

That theme is played out in the story of a child of 13 who bears a baby and kills it, after she has bitten its cheek like an apple, and is put in prison. Lynne, whose daughter Camara is raped and murdered, loses her child and almost her reason. One of Meridian's acts on behalf of the black community in a small town in Alabama is to force the end of the flooding that menaces the children. The city has closed the swimming pools sooner than integrate them. In the hot weather, black children wade in the ditches behind their houses, where the city without warning flushes the reservoir of excess water.

> It was Meridian who led them to the mayor's office, bearing in her arms the bloated figure of a five-year-old boy who had been stuck in the sewer for two days before he was raked out with a grappling hook . . . To the people who followed Meridian, it was as if she carried a large bouquet of long-stemmed roses. The body might have smelled just that sweet, from the serene, set expression on her face. They had followed her into a town meeting over which the white-haired, bespectacled mayor presided, and she had place the child, whose body was beginning to decompose, beside his gavel.

I do not find the ending successful. Walker consciously rejects death. Meridian's political commitment is not to end in martyrdom: there have been too many martyrs to her cause. Still, we need some other equivalent of death or marriage to round off a tale, and Walker has not found one here. We are told that Meridian has brought off a successful change from victim to fully responsible protagonist: that she no longer need punish herself physically, have fits, go blind because she acts for her people and herself, and that she believes she could kill if she must to prevent more martyrdom. But telling is not enough. She has ceased to be one sort of committed person and become another. Some act is needed to make real the change and it isn't there; but that's a minor failure in a tight fascinating novel.

◆◆◆◆◆◆◆◆◆◆◆◆◆

GREIL MARCUS

The New Yorker, June 7, 1976

Alice Walker's second novel, "Meridian" (Harcourt Brace Jovanovich), appears twenty-five years after Albert Camus's "The Rebel," a book that grew from Camus's conviction that in the modern world every political act leads directly to murder. Camus sought a way out through the idea of rebellion. Rebellion, he argued—the act of one who says no, who says, "There is a limit beyond which you shall not go"—brought the idea "We are" into the world. This was so, Camus said, because the rebel ultimately takes his stand not merely out of personal suffering but in the name of "right": in the name of something larger than himself. Thus the act of rebellion implies—philosophically, it calls into being—the human community, and reveals a common good. But the recognition of a common good invalidates the means that may be necessary to defend it: murder.

> For it is now a question of deciding if it is possible to kill someone, whose resemblance to ourselves we have at last recognized and whose identity we have just sanctified. When we have only just conquered solitude, must we then re-establish it definitively by legitimizing the act which isolates everything? To force solitude on a man who has just come to understand that he is not alone, is that not the definitive crime against man?

Those lines come from the final chapter of "The Rebel," which Camus called "Thought at the Meridian." Its subject is moderation: action with limits. Murder has a limit: if the rebel commits murder, it is implicit that he must then sacrifice his own life, to show that even though murder is sometimes necessary, it can never be justified. "He who does not know everything cannot kill everything." The ethic of rebellion, in other words, means that murder, even in defense of that "right" which links all men and women, cannot be permitted to survive itself. Camus, dead and superseded by more "radical" thinkers like Sartre, has long been out of fashion, but it is perhaps not a coincidence that Alice Walker's novel shares a title with him. The questions he raises are at the heart of "Meridian," a story about the civil-rights movement, and a spiritual and political biography of the character for whom it is named—Meridian Hill, a black woman who determines to live out the movement long after it has faded away.

Alice Walker, a black writer born in Georgia in 1944, has herself been a civil-rights worker. Her first novel, "The Third Life of Grange Copeland," appeared in 1970, and she has also published two books of poetry, a collection of short stories, and much nonfiction. She reminds us, with a page of definitions, that the word "meridian" has varied meanings. The most striking recalls both Camus's concept of moderation and the clarity on which he always insisted: "meridian" as it refers to the sun at noon, in the middle of the day, when the light is brightest and there are no shadows. (This recalls as well the quote from Camus with which Miss Walker opened "Once," her first book of poems: "Poverty was not a calamity for me. It was always balanced by the richness of light . . . circumstances helped me. To correct a natural indifference I was placed halfway between misery and the sun. Misery kept me from believing that all was well under the sun, and the sun taught me that history wasn't everything.") The word "meridian" also refers, in a "definition" Miss Walker does not give but in a connection that cannot be coincidental, to a specific place: Meridian, Mississippi, the home of James Chaney, one of three civil-rights workers murdered by the White Knights of the Ku Klux Klan in nearby Neshoba County, Mississippi, in June of 1964.

One begins to get a sense of Meridian Hill a few pages into the novel, with a scene set perhaps two years after that triple murder—an event that, along with others like it, forced the civil-rights movement beyond the limits it had set for itself. In New York, a group of black women, veterans of marches and voter-registration campaigns in the South, are recommitting themselves to their rebellion, putting rebellion as they had understood it behind them. The question each must answer is whether she will kill for the revolution. It seems like an easy, necessary question: Anne-Marion, Meridian's friend from their days at a black women's college in Atlanta, presses Meridian to say yes, but Meridian can't get the word out. She doesn't really know why; there is some depth of knowledge she lacks, will perhaps always lack, which she senses is a prerequisite to murder.

What kind of knowledge? She thinks back to herself as a girl in church, with her steadfast but cold and stolid mother urging her, as she revelled in gospel music, to accept Jesus as her Saviour, which she could never do. (Couldn't she just listen to the music? Did she have to believe to really hear it? Or earn the right to listen?) She thinks about her father, who, as a Georgia farmer, is obsessed by what America—not "the white man" but America, of which he thinks he is a part—has done to the Indians, some of whom once lived on his land. Her father is consumed by debts owed to the dead which he will never find a way to pay. And there is the history of the women her mother came from: a great-great-grandmother who, as a slave, repeatedly stole back her children each time they were sold away from her, and who, when finally allowed to keep them, starved to death trying to feed them; a great-grandmother, also a slave, who painted faces on barns across Georgia; Meridian's grandmother, who killed herself working to get her daughter through school; and her mother herself, who got through school and helped four of her brothers and sisters do the same.

And more still. On her college campus, there was a giant magnolia tree that Meridian loved (and, in a campus riot, her fellow-students destroyed). There was a story behind it. When the campus was a plantation, a slave named Louvinie, born in West Africa, would entertain the children, black and white, with horror stories. In the midst of one such story, the youngest child of the plantation owner dropped dead.

> Louvinie's tongue was clipped out at the root. Choking on blood, she saw her tongue ground under the heel of Master Saxon. Mutely, she pleaded for it, because she knew the curse of her native land: Without one's tongue in one's mouth or in a special spot of one's own choosing, the singer in one's soul was lost forever, to grunt and snort through eternity like a pig.

The master kicked Louvinie's tongue to her. Later, during an eclipse, "she buried it under a scrawny magnolia tree on the Saxon plantation."

If the question of murder is a question of knowledge, and if experience is knowledge, then inherent in Meridian's genealogy and in the legends to which she has attached herself is a knowledge she cannot match. All this, along with the connections that her parents have made and the connections that Meridian is being asked to make—connections to the grace of gospel music, to damnation by the crimes of history, to the purgatory of committing oneself to murder—is out of her reach. She says no to her group, and the group expels her.

The group, in a sense, expels Meridian from history, which she has made along with its members. It cuts off the road she has been following since the movement first came to her town, when she was a seventeen-year-old child-mother with a boy-husband, apparently trapped in dull, cramped rhythms of social and economic poverty—rhythms she barely perceived. The movement gave her a chance to start life over again; there was a quality of intelligence in it, a refusal to accept most of what she took for granted, that attracted her. And she was more than fit for the work that was being done. She gave up her baby, divorced her husband, went to college, demonstrated, was beaten and arrested, took risks. In New York, out of the movement, stranded by her co-workers and estranged from the momentum of events she had helped to set in motion, she begins a third time, deciding to go back South and live with the people there. "Like Civil Rights workers used to do," she says, in a plain and tragic line, as if she were speaking of a lost civilization and not a way of life that had made sense two or three years before. That "used to do" echoes through the novel, like some half-remembered fairy tale, as Meridian proceeds to live it out. "You're not serious," says her friend Anne-Marion. "Yes," she says, "I am serious."

At its best, that is the tone of the book: flat, direct, measured, deliberate, with a distinct lack of drama. (As in Miss Walker's telling of the Louvinie story, which she refuses to overplay.) And the tone is right; it's not the plot that carries the novel forward but Meridian's attempt to resolve, or preserve the reality of, the questions of knowledge, history, and murder that Miss Walker introduces early on. The astonishing dramatic intensity that Walker brought to "The Third Life of Grange Copeland" would in "Meridian" blow those questions apart.

But such questions lead all too easily to high-flown language and to pretensions that fictional characters cannot support, which is why most "philosophical" novels are impossible to reread. Miss Walker does not always avoid this trap; though her tendency is to insist on the prosaic, to bring philosophy down to earth, Meridian at times seems to be floating straight to Heaven. The book tries to make itself a parable—more than a mere novel—or trades the prosaic for an inert symbolism that would seem to be intended to elevate the story but instead collapses it. In an early chapter, Meridian, age seven, finds a gold bar and rushes with it to her parents; they ignore her. She buries the gold (her unrecognized gifts) and finally forgets about it (and it will be years until she finds her gifts again). In college, as Meridian lies sick in bed, a halo forms around her head. Back in the South after the meeting in New York, she works alone persuading people, one at a time, to register to vote, organizing neighborhoods around local issues, and staging symbolic protests, which she calls, wonderfully, her "performances." This is beautifully presented and utterly convincing; each incident is memorable, shaped as a story in itself. But after every "performance" Meridian falls to the ground, paralyzed, and must be carried like a corpse back to wherever she is living. A hundred years ago, an author would simply have made Meridian an epileptic if we were meant to guess that she was sainted. The problem is more than melodrama: if Meridian is a saint, the profound questions that Camus raised, which have gone out of style, and which Walker is forcefully resurrecting, are made instantly irrelevant to the rest of us. If only saints can bear such questions, we can forget them.

Meridian is interesting enough without all this—without symbolism and "higher meanings" that are one-dimensional and fixed. There is no mystery in these symbols—as there is in Meridian's ability to get through to Southern blacks, or in the questions of the rebel, murder, and limits— and a symbol without mystery, without suggestive power, is not really a symbol at all. But most of the book's scenes have the power its symbols lack, and its last chapters rescue Meridian's questions from a holy oblivion. For they are resolved, after a fashion, and passed on. Ten years after leaving the group of women in New York, Meridian discovers, in church, that she can kill. It's a strange church; the minister acts out—arrogantly, it seems—the role of Martin Luther King, Jr., long after his death, but nobody is put off.

> It struck Meridian that he was deliberately imitating King, that he and all his congregation *knew* he was consciously keeping that voice alive. It was like a *play*.

Meridian touches, as she had not been able to touch, or live up to, the knowledge that she'd sensed, thinking back over her ancestors, when she said no in New York. For what else had she been doing with her life ever since but, like this minister and his congregation, keeping something alive, by acting it out, which everyone else had managed to put behind him?

An old man comes before the congregation, the father of a young man who, like James Chaney, was murdered in the struggle years before. Half-crazed, he lives as a hermit in the ruins of the house he destroyed when he was told his son was dead. Every year, on the anniversary of that day, he stands up for his son and for the people who want to be reminded of him. That quality of pain, the insistence on a history without gaps, and her own recognition of her well-earned place in that history, is what Meridian can kill for.

> To boast about this new capacity to kill—which she did not, after all, admire—would be to destroy the understanding she had acquired with it. Namely, this: that even the contemplation of murder required incredible delicacy as it required incredible spiritual work, and the historical background and present setting must be right. Only in a church surrounded by the righteous guardians of the people's memories could she even approach the concept of retaliatory murder. Only among the pious could this idea both comfort and uplift.

It seems clear, as Meridian makes this connection and, as time goes on, loses it, regains it, loses it again, that the spiritual necessities that make it posible for her to say yes to murder will be negated should she ever commit murder; that should she kill, her life would be over. As in that extraordinary image from Louvinie's story, her soul would "grunt and snort through eternity like a pig." And it might be a price worth paying. The question, crude in the form in which it opens the novel, takes on something like a final shape—a final ambiguity—at the end. In that sense, it is passed on, not only to the book's other characters, who share Meridian's life, but perhaps to the reader as well. Meridian's role in the play she has devised for herself within a larger history—the speech her actions give—stands out with great tension. "Does the end justify the means?" Camus wrote in "Thought at the Meridian." "That is possible. But what will justify the end? To that question, which historical thought leaves pending, rebellion replies: the means."

THE COLOR PURPLE (1982)

◆◆◆◆◆◆◆◆◆◆◆◆◆

MEL WATKINS

The *New York Times Book Review*, July 25, 1982

Without doubt, Alice Walker's latest novel is her most impressive. No mean accomplishment, since her previous books—which in addition to several collections of poetry and two collections of short stories, include two novels (*The Third Life of Grange Copeland* and *Merdian*)—have elicited almost unanimous praise for Miss Walker as a lavishly gifted writer. *The Color Purple*, while easily satisfying that claim, brings into sharper focus many of the diverse themes that threaded their way through her past work.

The Color Purple is foremost the story of Celie, a poor, barely literate Southern black woman who struggles to escape the brutality and degradation of her treatment by men. The tale is told primarily through her own letters, which, out of isolation and despair, she initially addresses to God. As a teenager she is repeatedly raped and beaten by her stepfather, then forced by him into a loveless marriage to Albert, a widower with four children. To Albert, who is in love with a vivacious and determinedly independent blues singer named Shug Avery, Celie is merely a servant and an occasional sexual convenience. When his oldest son, Harpo, asks Albert why he beats Celie, he says simply, "Cause she my wife." For a time Celie accepts the abuse stoically: "He beat me like he beat the children. Cept he don't never hardly beat them. He say, Celie, get the belt . . . It all I can do not to cry. I make myself wood. I say to myself, Celie, you a tree. That's how come I know trees fear men."

But during the course of the novel, which begins in the early 1900's and ends in the mid-1940's, Celie frees herself from her husband's repressive control. Bolstered by her contacts with other women and by her affection for her younger sister, Netti—who with Celie's help has fled to Africa with a missionary group—Celie eventually leaves Albert and moves to Memphis, where she starts a business designing and making clothes. Ironically, it is Albert's real love and sometime mistress, Shug Avery, and his rebellious daughter-in-law, Sofia, who provide the emotional support for Celie's personal evolution. And, in turn, it is Celie's new understanding of an acceptance of herself that eventually lead to Albert's evaluation of his own life and a reconciliation among the novel's major characters. As the book ends, Albert and Shug sit with Celie on Celie's front porch, "rocking and fanning flies," waiting for the arrival of Netti and her family.

This plot summary reflects neither the density of subtle interactions among the characters nor the novel's intense emotional impact. It does, however, suggest some of the book's major themes. Most prominent is the estrangement and violence that mark the relationships between Miss Walker's black men and women. Although this subject has been raised in the fiction of earlier American writers, such as Zora Neale Hurston, and in comic caricatures of the Frankie and Johnny variety, it was largely ignored by most black writers until the early 1960's; at that point, the strongly felt need for a more open scrutiny of black life led writers to challenge longstanding black middle-class proscriptions against dramatizing and thereby exposing anything that might reinforce damaging racial stereotypes. Notable among the novels that have explored the theme since then are James Baldwin's "Another Country" (1962) and Carlene Hatcher Polite's acidulous "The Flagellants" (1967). More recently, such writers as Toni Morrison, Toni Cade Bambara and Gayl Jones have produced powerful novels that, among other things, dramatize the theme of conflict between black men and women.

Alice Walker has dealt with the subject before. In her collection *You Can't Keep a Good Woman Down*, two stories ("Porn" and "Coming Apart") assess the sexual disaffection among black couples. And the saintly heroine of the novel *Meridian* is deserted by a black lover who then marries a white civil-rights worker, whom he also later abandons. In *Meridian*, however, the friction between the black men and women is merely one of several themes; in *The Color Purple* the role of male domination in the frustration of black women's struggle for independence is clearly the focus.

Miss Walker explores the estrangement of her men and women through a triangular love affair. It is Shug Avery who forces Albert to stop brutalizing Celie, and it is Shug with whom Celie first consummates a satisfying and reciprocally loving relationship. "It don't surprise me you love Shug Avery," Albert tells Celie. "I have love Shug Avery all my life . . . I told Shug it was true that I beat you cause you was you and not her . . . some womens would have just love to hear they man say he beat his wife cause she wan't them. . . . But Shug spoke right up for you, Celie. She say, Albert, you been mistreating somebody I love. So as far as you concern, I'm gone."

What makes Miss Walker's exploration so indelibly affecting is the choice of a narrative style that, without the intrusion of the author, forces intimate identification with the heroine. Most of the letters that comprise this epistolary novel are written by Celie, although correspondence from Netti is included in the latter part of the book. Initially, some readers may be put off by Celie's knothole view of the world, particularly since her letters are written in dialect and from the perspective of a naive, uneducated adolescent: "Last spring after little Lucious come I heard them fussing. He was pulling on her arm. She say it too soon, Fonso, I ain't well. Finally he leave her alone. A week go by, he pulling on her arm again. She say Naw, I ain't gonna. Can't you see I'm already half dead, an all these children."

As the novel progresses, however, and as Celie grows in experience, her observations become sharper and more informed; the letters take on authority and the dialect, once accepted, assumes a lyrical cadence of its own:

"After all the evil he done, I know you wonder why I don't hate him. I don't hate him for two reasons. One, he love Shug. And two, Shug used to love him. Plus, look like he trying to make something out himself. I don't mean just that he work and he clean up after himself and he appreciate some to the things God was playful enough to make. I mean when you talk to him now he really listen, and one time, out of nowhere in the conversation us was having, he said Celie, I'm satisfied this the first time I ever live on Earth as a natural man."

The cumulative effect is a novel that is convincing because of the authenticity of its folk voice. And, refreshingly, it is not just the two narrator-correspondents who come vividly alive in this tale. A number of memorable female characters emerge. There is Shug Avery, whose pride, independence and appetite for living act as a catalyst for Celie and others, and Sofia, whose rebellious spirit leads her not only to desert her overbearing husband but also to challenge the social order of the racist community in which she lives.

If there is a weakness in this novel—besides the somewhat pallid portraits of the males—it is Netti's correspondence from Africa. While Netti's letters broaden and reinforce the theme of female oppression by describing customs of the Olinka tribe that parallel some found in the American South, they are often mere monologues on African history. Appearing, as they do, after Celie's intensely subjective voice has been established, they seem lackluster and intrusive.

These are only quibbles, however, about a striking and consummately well-written novel. Alice Walker's choice and effective handling of the epistolary style has enabled her to tell a poignant tale of women's struggle for equality and independence without either the emotional excess of her previous novel *Meridian* or the polemical excess of her short story collection *You Can't Keep a Good Woman Down*.

◆◆◆◆◆◆◆◆◆◆◆◆◆

DINITIA SMITH

The Nation, September 4, 1982

As admirers of *The Third Life of Grange Copeland* and *Meridian* already know, to read an Alice Walker novel is to enter the country of surprise. It is to be admitted to the world of rural black women, a world long neglected by most whites, perhaps out of ignorance, perhaps out of willed indifference. The loss is ours, for the lives of these women are so extraordinary in their tragedy, their culture, their humor and their courage that we are immediately gripped by them.

Witness the opening passage of *The Color Purple*, a tale of violence, incest and redemption that starts out in Georgia in the 1900s and goes on for about thirty years. Beginning when her mother is laid up in childbirth, skinny, "ugly" 14-year-old Celie is repeatedly raped by the man she believes to be her father:

> Dear God,
> I am fourteen years old. I ~~am~~ I have always been a good girl. Maybe you can give me a sign letting me know what is happening to me.

Celie, who retreats into an emotional numbness that will last for years, has two babies by her "father"; he gives them away. They end up in Africa with Celie's sister Nettie, who works for the missionary family that adopted them. (The novel is a series of letters, first from Celie to God, and then back and forth between Celie and Nettie.)

Celie is married off to Mr. _____, a downtrodden farmer who beats her. At night, she parts her legs for him and forces all thought and feeling from her body: "I make myself wood. I say to myself, Celie, you a tree. That's how come I know trees fear man."

Along comes Shug Avery, a blues singer of legendary beauty. Mr. _____ has been in love with her for years, and when she falls sick, he brings her home to Celie to nurse. Celie and Shug become friends and then lovers. Through Shug, Celie discovers that Mr. _____ has been intercepting Nettie's letters for several years. And from the letters, which Shug helps her obtain, she learns that the man who raped her wasn't her real father. Her real father had been lynched. With the stigma of incest removed, Celie finally stands up to Mr. _____:

> You lowdown dog. . . . It's time to leave you and enter into Creation. And you dead body just the welcome mat I need.

I wanted to cheer.

Celie goes with Shug to Memphis, and there she learns to live and love. When her "father" dies, she inherits his farm and returns to Georgia, where she sleeps in a room painted purple—for Walker, the color of radiance and majesty (and also the emblematic color of lesbianism). She is reunited with her children and Nettie, and, surprisingly, she befriends Mr. _____, who has been broken and humbled by Shug and Celie's joint departure. The end of the book finds Celie and her erstwhile tormentor sitting companionably on the front porch smoking their pipes, "two old fools left over from love, keeping each other company under the stars."

Walker can be a pungent writer. When Celie's father-in-law, Old Mr. _____, criticizes Shug, Celie, who has been sent to get the man a glass of water, overhears him:

> I drop little spit in Old Mr. _____ water. . . . I twirl the spit round with my finger. . . . Next time he come I put a little Shug Avery pee in his glass. See how he like that.

And sometimes she can break our hearts. When the aging Shug wants to have one last fling with a young man, Celie is so devastated she cannot speak. She can only talk to Shug in writing:

> He's nineteen. A baby. How long can it last? [Shug says.]
>   He's a man. I write on the paper.
>   Yeah, she say . . . but some mens can be lots of fun.
>   Spare me, I write.

No writer has made the intimate hurt of racism more palpable than Walker. In one of the novel's most rending scenes, Celie's step-daughter-in-law, Sofia, is sentenced to work as a maid in the white mayor's house for "sassing" the mayor's wife. In a fit of magnanimity, the mayor's wife offers to drive Sofia home to see her children, whom she hasn't laid eyes on in five years. The reunion lasts only fifteen minutes—then the mayor's wife insists that Sofia drive her home.

The Color Purple is about the struggle between redemption and revenge. And the chief agency of redemption Walker is saying, is the strength of the relationships between women: their friendships, their love, their shared oppression. Even the white mayor's family is redeemed when his daughter cares for Sofia's sick daughter.

There is a note of tendentiousness here, though. The men in this book change *only* when their women join together and rebel—and then, the change is so complete as to be unrealistic. It was hard for me to believe that a person as violent, brooding and just plain nasty as Mr. _____ could ever become that sweet, quiet man smoking and chatting on the porch.

Walker's didacticism is especially evident in Nettie's letters from Africa which make up a large portion of the book. Nettie relates the story of the Olinka tribe, particularly of one girl Tashi, as a kind of feminist fable:

> The Olinka do not believe girls should be educated. When I asked a mother what she thought of this, she said: A girl is nothing to herself; only to her husband can she become something.

What can she become? I asked.

Why, she said, the mother of his children.

But I am not the mother of anybody's children. I said, and I am something.

Later, Nettie tells Tashi's parents that "the world is changing. . . . It is no longer a world just for boys and men, and we wince at the ponderousness, the obviousness of the message. At times the message is confusing, too. The white rubber planters who disrupt Olinka society also destroy the old (and presumably bad) tribal patriarchy. Does this mean the white man's coming is good thing? I doubt it, but I was puzzled.

Walker's politics are not the problem—*of course* sexism and racism are terrible, *of course* women should band together to help each other. But the politics have to be incarnated complex, contradictory characters, characters to whom the novelist grants the freedom to act, as it were, on their own.

I wish Walker had let herself be carried along more by her language, with all its vivid figures of speech, Biblical cadences, distinctive grammar and true-to-life starts and stops. The pithy, direct black folk idiom of *The Color Purple,* in the end its greatest strength, reminding us that if Walker is sometimes ideologue, she is also a poet.

Despite its occasional preachiness, *The Color Purple* marks a major advance for Walker's art. At its best, and at least half the book is superb, it places her in the company of Faulkner, from whom she appears to have learned a great deal: the use of a shifting first-person narrator, for instance, and the presentation of a complex story from a naïve point of view, like that of 14-year-old Celie. Walker has not turned her back on the Southern fictional tradition. She has absorbed it and made it her own. By infusing the black experience into the Southern novel, she enriches both it and us.

THE TEMPLE OF MY FAMILIAR (1989)

◆◆◆◆◆◆◆◆◆◆◆◆◆

URSULA K. LE GUIN

The *San Francisco Review of Books,* Summer 1989

The richness of Alice Walker's new novel is amazing, overwhelming. A hundred themes and subjects spin through it, dozens of characters, a whirl of times and places. None is touched superficially: all the people are passionate actors and sufferers, and everything they talk about is urgent, a matter truly of life and death. They're like Dostoyevsky's characters, relentlessly raising the great moral questions and pushing one another towards self-knowledge, honesty, engagement.

The one we get to know best is Suwelo, a professor of American history. Suwelo was married to Fanny Nzingha, daughter of Olivia, daughter of Celie—yes, Celie of *The Color Purple,* and we get to hear from Shug, too, which is a treat. Suwelo took up also with a woman named Carlotta, daughter of a South American exile, Zedé, and both Carlotta and Zedé have a lover, Arveyda, a musician. Zedé saved and was saved by a white women, Mary Jane, who then went to Africa, where she knew Ola, father of an African daughter, Nzingha, and also of an African-American daughter, Olivia's Fanny Nzingha—and so the circles interlock, and all these major characters and many minor ones round-dance and swing-your-partners from South America to North America to Africa and back. And then there's Hal and Lissie, who take Suwelo's neglected education in hand. Since Lissie remembers her previous incarnations all the way back, she's a whole cast of characters by herself. It's Miss Lissie who tells the tremendous story of being taken and transported as a slave, and hers too is the central image of the book: her dream of the temple, of the brilliantly feathered fish-lizard-bird familiar, and of what happens when the soul is betrayed.

> It looked at me with pity as it passed. Then, using wings it had never used before, it flew away. And I was left with only you and the rest of your people on the steps of a cold stone building, the color of cheap false teeth, in a different world from my own, in a century that I would never understand.

As I read *The Temple of My Familiar,* the kaleidoscope of people and relationships occasionally daunted and confused me. I wanted just to slow down and get to know somebody better. There were times I felt like saying, "Dear Genius, please—you don't have to get it *all* into one book!" But it's her book, and she gets it all in. It isn't a novel of observation or of meditation, it's a story of transformation, and the essence of transformation is that it goes on. It's not a matter of "conflict" and "resolution" as in the laboratory-novel, but of urging, asserting, and recording *change*. Every character in the book bears witness that if we don't change, we perish.

The characters all tell one another fiercely, tenderly, how the world is and why and who they are and who they ought to be. Often they lecture. The book would go stiff, go dead, at these points, except that even the lectures are borne and buoyed by the current of passion and sympathy. The anger is great but not rigid, not self-righteous. It explodes. It unbuilds. Some of the characters are more mouthpiece than person, but even if they're all talk, their talk is powerful, vivid, funny, and also what one says another may contradict just as vehemently. They are all trying (as Shug puts it) "to keep their feet on the goddam Path." Here are some of their voices:

"'If your work exists, you exist,' she huffed. 'Ask God.'"

"If you tear out the tongue of another, you have a tongue in your hand the rest of your life. You are responsible, therefore, for all that person might have said."

"Black is a color the sun loves."

"She was someone who could not be rushed. This seems a small thing. But it is actually a very amazing quality, a very ancient one."

"There was a greeting that habitués of our house used on encountering each other: 'All those at the banquet!' they'd say, and shake hands or hug. Sometimes they said this laughing, sometimes they said it in tears. But that they were still at the banquet of life was always affirmed."

A banquet it is—everybody eating together and talking together across the table, across the oceans, across the centuries. Rich food for mind and soul!

Lissie's memories carry us back several times to prehistoric lives, Africa of the human dawn, lovingly and fearfully imagined. So many women are writing such imaginations now that it is surely a communal undertaking responding to a communal need. Those whose minds are locked in the conservatism of "growth," and even "higher" technology based on unlimited exploitation, see these tribal societies (real and imagined) only as escapist regressions; they cannot understand that women are studying such societies in a radical and subversive effort to think back to before things went wrong. What went wrong, they say, was Civilization—Western Civ—The White Man's World. (By the way, Asia is notably lacking from this book; it's Africa, Europe, and the Americas, and I don't think one of all the many characters is East or West Asian.

But now here I am asking her to get it all in!) To get away from or back before all that takes a long mental journey, and a hard one, since the evidence of what went before white patriarchy has been systematically defiled and destroyed. But the women writing these books are going back so we can go forward, so we can realistically try to get our feet on the goddam Path. No more temples, they say, built on the bones of our children: we are trying to get down to the sacred earth, and build right. Not easy, and anything but a simplification. The complexity of Alice Walker's book—a rainforest tangle, the front and back of the tapestry seen all at once—perfectly embodies its vision of life, not alienated, rigid, hierarchized, bleached, "the color of cheap false teeth," but life interlocked, multiple, multiplying, endless, desirous, vociferous, and gorgeously peacock-colored.

Virginia Woolf said that "the words ride on the back of the rhythm." The rhythms of Alice Walker's prose are beautiful and characteristic, flexible, vigorous, easy, the gait of a hunting lion. Even when the pace of the story crowds and races and the words are choked with meaning and intent, the rhythms never falter. The lion goes her way.

◆◆◆◆◆◆◆◆◆◆◆◆◆

J. M. COETZEE

The New York Times Book Review, 1989

Readers of *The Color Purple* will remember that part of the book—the less convincing part—consists of letters from Miss Celie's missionary sister about her life in Africa.

The Temple of My Familiar again bears a message from Africa, but this time in a far more determined manner. The message reaches us via Miss Lissie, an ancient goddess who has been incarnated hundreds of times, usually as a woman, sometimes as a man, once even as a lion. Less a character than a narrative device, Lissie enables Alice Walker to range back in time to the beginnings of (wo)man.

Here are just three of the ages in human evolution that Lissie lives through:

First, an age just after the invention of fire, when humanfolk live in separate male and female tribes, at peace with their animal "familiars." Here Lissie is incarnated as the first white-skinned creature, a man with insufficient melanin, who flees the heat of Africa for Europe. Hating the sun, he [invents] an alternative god in his own image, cold and filled with rage.

Next, an age of pygmies, when the man tribe and the woman tribe visit back and forth with each other and with the apes. This peaceful, happy age ends when men invent warfare, attack the apes and impose themselves on women as their sole familiars. Thus, says Ms. Walker (rewriting Rousseau and others), do patriarchy and the notion of private property come into being.

Third, the time of the war waged by Europe and monotheistic Islam against the Great Goddess of Africa. The instrument of the warfare is the slave trade (Lissie lives several slave lives). Its emblem is the Gorgon's head, the head of the Goddess, still crowned with the serpents of wisdom, cut off by the white hero-warrior Perseus.

These episodes from the past of (wo)mankind give some idea of the sweep of the myth Alice Walker recounts, a myth that inverts the places assigned to man and woman, Europe and Africa, in the male-invented myth called history. In Ms. Walker's counter-myth, Africa is the cradle of true religions and civilization, and man a funny, misbegotten creature with no breasts and an elongated clitoris.

The impact of Lissie's revelations upon modern black consciousness is traced in the lives of Fanny (Celie's granddaughter) and her ex-husband, Suwelo, a middle-class academic. Suwelo finds his authentic self by absorbing Lissie's message; Fanny finds hers by opening herself to her dreams—her archetypal memories—and by journeying back to meet her African kinfolk.

Suwelo learns that there are better things than philandering and watching football on television. By the end of the book he has rejoined Fanny and lives with her in a house shaped like a bird, in which they have separate wings. As for Fanny: "The woman in her consciousness-raising group had taught her how to masturbate. Sexually free, for the first time in her life. At the same time, she was learning to meditate, and was throwing off the last clinging vestiges of organized religion. She was soon meditating and masturbating and finding herself dissolved into the cosmic All. Delicious."

Such cliche-ridden prose is not representative of the best of *The Temple of My Familiar*, but there is enough of it to give one pause. How deep can one's liberation run when its very language is secondhand? At another level, how seriously can we take Lissie's Europe, whose aboriginal "dark peoples" have been exterminated by white invaders, or her Africa, which reads like an overlay of South Africa over a vaguely realized Nigeria?

The immediate answer is that we betray the book by demanding this kind of realism. We should read it, rather, as a fable of recovered origins, as an exploration of the inner lives of contemporary black Americans as these are penetrated by fabulous stories.

But this answer strikes me as too easy. History is certainly written by people in positions of power, and therefore principally by men. The history of the world—including Africa—is by and large a story made up by white males. Nevertheless, history is not just storytelling. There are certain brute realities that cannot be ignored. Africa has a past that neither the white male historian nor Ms. Walker can simply invent. No doubt the world would be a better place if, like Fanny and Suwelo, we could live in bird-shaped houses and devote ourselves to bread making and massage, and generally adopt Fanny's mother's gospel: "We are all of us in heaven already!" Furthermore, I readily concede that inventing a better world between the covers of a book is as much as even the most gifted of us can hope to do to bring about a better real world. But whatever new worlds and new histories we invent must carry conviction: they must be possible worlds, possible histories, not untethered fantasies; and they must be born of creative energy, not dreamy fads.

There is an element of the book I have neglected thus far. In many ways its most serious element. Fanny's crisis is the crisis of an oppressed woman, but also the crisis of a black person living in the gunsights of white racism who does not want to turn into a hate-filled racist herself. "What do you think of white people?" asks her therapist. In reply, she recounts a terrible recurring dream. A feast is going on at which white people are endlessly eating. Sometimes she is present at their feast as an emaciated, chained slave. Sometimes she is the one being devoured. And sometimes she sees herself participate in the joyless eating.

Whether as victim or horrified participant, Fanny cannot escape racism: "It had become like a scale or a web over her eyes. Everywhere she looked, she saw it. Racism turned her thoughts to violence. Violence made her sick."

Revulsion against the death feast of the West and equal revulsion against a countervailing black violence—this is the agony at the root of "The Temple of My Familiar." Its fierceness erupts at many places in the text. It is an agony experienced by all too many black people across the world. But the brand of salvation discovered by Fanny and Suwelo will help few of them. The words of Fanny's father, in whom there are elements of Wole Soyinka and Nelson Mandela, carry a greater if more chilling conviction: "I have been responsible for the deaths of whites. It did not 'liberate' me psychologically, as Fanon suggested it might. It did not oppress me further, either. I was simply freeing myself from the jail that they had become for me, and making a space in the world, also, for my children."

The Temple of My Familiar is a novel only in a loose sense. Rather, it is a mixture of mythic fantasy, revisionary history, exemplary biography and sermon. It is short on narrative tension, long on inspirational message.

POSSESSING THE SECRET OF JOY
(1992)

CHARLES R. LARSON

Washington Post Book World, July 5, 1992

Fiction and conviction make strange bedfellows. Nor am I convinced that novels that resurrect characters from a writer's earlier work are likely to be as imaginative and as artful as the result of the initial inspiration. But one does not have to read many pages of *Possessing the Secret of Joy* to realize that Alice Walker has not foisted her subject—female circumcision—upon us; instead, this writer of bold artistry challenges us to feel and to think. Here is a novel—and a subject—whose time has surely come.

In a note to the reader, Walker explains the genesis of the novel. During the filming of *The Color Purple* the young African woman who played Tashi—now the heroine of *Possessing the Secret of Joy*—made Walker think more thoroughly about Tashi and the still-widespread cultural practice of female circumcision. Tashi also appears in Walker's *The Temple of My Familiar,* and the writer admits to taking certain liberties with her own earlier novels: "The storyteller's prerogative [is] to recast or slightly change events . . . in order to emphasize and enhance the meaning of the present tale." Walker has taken a compelling character and placed her in an outrageous situation, yet it is impossible to have anything but admiration for the result.

The novel's ironic beginning is patently romantic. There is joy in Tashi and Adam's initial lovemaking, in spite of their conflicting backgrounds. Because of her conversion to Christianity, Tashi has not been traditionally circumcised. And Adam, the African-American missionary's son, appears not to harbor the Puritan layers of guilt typical of missionaries at the time—though Walker uses no dates, apparently the 1920s or '30s—the story begins. What, in fact, can possibly diminish their happiness? The marriage appears destined to become a union of their complementary spirits and yearnings for togetherness.

But then Tashi wavers. As Adam's future wife, in America, shouldn't she attempt to retain as much of her African culture as possible? Shouldn't she be circumcised? The operation, she feels, will join her to her sisters, "whom she envisioned as strong, invincible. Completely woman. Completely African."

The description of the excision itself and its aftereffect is graphic enough to make one gag, yet I am convinced that Walker has not intended to make her story sensational. A fact is, after all, only a fact. Like millions of other Third World woman, Tashi undergoes a procedure that is often less ritualistic (a clipping of a tiny portion of the clitoris) than desexualizing: genital mutilation. Walker and many others rationally believe that the cultural intent of such mutilation is absolutely clear: the denial of pleasure for women from all sexual activity.

The events that I have described are painfully revealed during the several stages of Tashi's madness as an adult and subsequent psychotherapy. Renamed Evelyn in America, Tashi undergoes a fundamental personality change. It is difficult to determine which is worse—the physical or the psychological changes resulting from her excision. The Tashi/Evelyn split hints at the complexity of the problem, for she no longer knows who she is or what her liberation, if any, will be. Sexually dead, she retreats into her imagination, her fantasy world, the domain of the storyteller.

When her analysis leads her to realize that Dura, her favorite sister, bled to death because of her circumcision, Tashi begins to formulate a goal for her own escape from her living hell. How is it possible, she asks herself, that the person who administered her own excision (and Dura's) could be a woman? The question takes her back to Africa, to her Olinka people, and to the resolution of her fate. Though it would be unfair to reveal the end of her story—Tashi's final act of defiance—a part of her understanding of her ordeal can be noted: "The connection between mutilation and enslavement that is at the root of the domination of women in the world." It's a chilling realization, not simply related to Tashi's own culture, but central to images of female victimization worldwide. Tashi says: "It's in all the movies that terrorize women . . . The man who breaks in. The man with the knife . . . But those of us whose chastity belt was made of leather, or of silk and diamonds, or of fear and not of our own flesh . . . we worry. We are the perfect audience, mesmerized by our unconscious knowledge of what men, with the collaboration of our mothers, do to us."

Toward the end of her novel, Walker explains the meaning of her title by having her heroine quote a European writer who wrote of Africans, "Black people are natural . . . they possess the secret of joy, which is why they can survive the suffering and humiliation inflicted upon them." By the time readers come to this passage, they have also encountered the contemporary sections of the narrative dealing with the AIDS epidemic across the African continent. The situation, especially for African women, would appear to be hopeless.

But that is not what Alice Walker believes. Like Tashi, Walker believes that if women wait for men to act, they may have to wait forever. Even Adam, as sympathetic as he is to Tashi's condition, refuses to discuss the question of her mutilation publicly because he is ashamed to do so. It's a matter of getting the taboo in the consciousness of those who are unaware of the practice. As Tashi concludes, "If we do not, Africa may well be depopulated of black people in our grandchildren's lifetime, and the worldwide suffering of our children will continue to be our curse."

It's the suffering of children, the wholesale mutilation of little girls, that finally haunts us in Walker's daring novel. I hope that *Possessing the Secret of Joy*, already on the best-seller lists, will be the most talked about book of the season.

◆◆◆◆◆◆◆◆◆◆◆◆◆

JANETTE TURNER HOSPITAL

The *New York Times Book Review*, June 28, 1992

"**B**lack people are natural, they possess the secret of joy," proclaims the epigraph to Alice Walker's new novel. These are the words of Mirellia Ricciardi, identified by Ms. Walker as a "white colonialist author" whose book, *African Saga*, was published in 1982, and they are used here with bitter irony. "With the added experience of my safaris behind me," Ms. Ricciardi writes, apparently without any postcolonial self-consciousness, "I had begun to understand the code of 'birth, copulation and death' by which [the Africans] lived" and why they could "survive the suffering and humiliation inflicted upon them."

"But what *is* it? This secret of joy of which she writes," demands Tashi, Ms. Walker's protagonist, when, toward the end of the novel, she herself reads Ms. Ricciardi's book. And what, the novel asks, is the secret of Tashi's pain?

Tashi, a black African woman who has spent most of her adult life in the United States, has made peripheral appearances in Ms. Walker's previous books *The Color Purple* and *The Temple of My Familiar*, but she occupies center stage in this one. She has indeed survived "suffering and humiliation," though only narrowly, and she cannot speak of them. "They've made the telling of the suffering itself taboo," says her husband, Adam, a black American.

Possessing the Secret of Joy is about the "telling" of suffering and the breaking of taboos. And when taboos are broken, new forms and modes of discourse must evolve to contain that which has previously been unspeakable Predictable outrage—moral, political, cultural and esthetic—ensues, and the breakers of taboos are both vilified and deified. Alice Walker tackles all these developments head-on in a work that is part myth, part polemic, part drama. It is a work that sits uneasily within the category of "the novel," though the breakers of taboos must always redefine the terms and the rules of the game. Indeed, Ms. Walker's book is a literary enterprise whose ancestry runs closer to the Greek chorus and the medieval miracle play than to the modern novel. Its subject matter is ritual clitoridectomy and the genital mutilation of young women.

Because her mother was influenced by black American missionaries (by that family, in fact, whose history occupies the second half of *The Color Purple*), Tashi herself was not circumcised at puberty. As a young child, however, she did hear the screams of her older sister, who died bloodily in a botched initiation in the tribal village. Tashi repressed this memory and "forgot why the sight of her own blood terrified her." Subsequently, in a voluntary act of identification with Pan-African aspirations, the teen-age Tashi submits herself to the *tsunga's* knife.

Olivia (that same Olivia who was a major presence in *The Color Purple*, a black American, Tashi's childhood playmate and lifelong friend) tries to dissuade her, and in the argument between Tashi and Olivia Ms. Walker is able to suggest some of the explosive issues that surround her subject, issues that pit the victims of gender imperialism against the victims of cultural imperialism.

"All I care about now is the struggle for our people," Tashi tells Olivia. "You are a foreigner. Any day you like, you and your family can ship yourselves back home." She puts the case for cultural autonomy passionately: "I saw the children, potbellied and with dying eyes, which made them look very wise. I saw the old people laid out in the shade of the rocks, barely moving on their piles of rags. I saw the women making stew out of bones. We had been stripped of everything but our black skins. Here and there a defiant cheek bore the mark of our withered tribe. These marks gave me courage. I wanted such a mark for myself."

But the receiving of the mark almost destroys Tashi, physically and emotionally. Adam rescues her, marries her, brings her to the United States. The novel catalogues her descent into madness, her long fight to salvage and reconstruct a self, her return to Africa, her final costly liberation and her discovery that "resistance is the secret of joy."

Along the way, Ms. Walker probes the various arguments in an extremely complex debate. She airs such unresolved moral problems as the idealization and deification of liberation leaders, the easy acceptance of corruption in a "good" political cause and the collusion that exists between oppressor and oppressed—a collusion on which the oppressor's tyranny relies.

The people in Ms. Walker's book are archetypes rather than characters as we have come to expect them in the 20th-century novel, and this is by defiant intention. One character, a white man, speaks of "an ancient self that thirsts for knowledge of the experiences of its ancient kin. . . . A self that is horrified at what was done to [Tashi], but recognizes it as something that is also done to me. A truly universal self."

When the novel is operating genuinely on this archetypal level, it has a mythic strength. Its many voices are not rendered as stream-of-consciousness monologues, nor are they made to belong to distinct individuals. Instead, they are highly stylized, operatic, prophetic—and powerfully poetic. The characters speak as Jason and Medea speak in Greek drama, as Greed and Sloth and Grief speak in the medieval plays.

Such a framework can successfully contain many disparate and disturbing elements: the grotesque techniques of clitoridectomy, after which the raw wound is fastened with thorns, so that only a tiny aperture is left when the flesh heals; the use of a hunting knife on the wedding night, when the bride is again cut open, this time to fit her husband; the self-mutilation that often follows in the wake of such trauma. Ms. Walker's narrative also encompasses the grim routine of an African prison and the tension of a politically charged trial. It even manages to bring Carl Jung into the story, to offer solace to Tashi. But there are other elements of the book (the jargon of West Coast therapists, for example) that fit far less successfully with the others, and the narrative voice can suddenly sound trite and irritating, even rather silly, when it makes such pronouncements as "I felt negated by the realization that even my psychiatrist could not see I was African."

At such times, one wishes Ms. Walker had opted for a different literary form, a new kind of polemic rather than a variation on the traditional novel—perhaps something akin to Pascal's *Pensées*, an episodic collage of documentary fact, scholarly opinion and lyrical monologue. For the book's power resides in those moments when polemic intention and mythopoeic voice are in balance, when Tashi—who is also Medea, who is also Everywoman and Everyman in violation and crisis—cries out:

"I studied the white rinds of my mother's heels, and felt in my own heart the weight of [my sister's] death settling upon her spirit, like the groundnuts that bent her back. As she staggered under her load, I half expected her footprints, into which I was careful to step, to stain my own feet with tears and blood. . . .

"And I was like a crow, flapping my wings unceasingly in my own head, cawing mutely across an empty sky. And I wore black, and black and black."

◆◆◆◆◆◆◆◆◆◆◆◆◆

TINA MCELROY ANSA

The *Los Angeles Times Book Review,* July 5, 1992

Black people can speak volumes with a gesture.

Months ago, I heard an African-American male scholar/writer say in the manner of a comic throwing away a line. "Hey, did you hear that Alice Walker dedicated her latest novel to "the innocent *vulva?*"

He sort of pursed his lips and looked slowly around the room. Then, he raised one eyebrow, sort of chuckled and went on to another subject. As if to say, "'Nough said."

His gesture was part amusement, part embarrassment, part incredulity, part derision.

Having read the novel, I now know why my literary associate reacted as he did, why he made it clear no discussion was necessary. Female circumcision and infibulation—an initiation rite usually performed on a girl before age 11 in which the clitoris and the inner and outer lips of the vagina are cut off and scraped away, and the wound sewn up tightly—is a difficult subject to face head-on without the armor of humor or derision or disbelief. In many societies where this rite is still performed, it has always been taboo to speak of it.

But once again, as she did so stunningly and accessibly in "The Color Purple," Alice Walker takes her readers into formerly taboo territory— areas of the human soul usually shrouded in silence and shame and fear and anguish. She insists that we look at what we would rather pretend doesn't exist, that we hear what we want to close our ears to.

As in her previous works, she asks the big questions (What is the secret of joy? How is the sewing up a child's vagina linked with property and inheritance?) and the small ones (Why is the child crying?). In the process of answering them, Walker proves that the smaller questions are as prodigious as the big ones. This time, Walker skillfully weaves the answers through the life of one 20th-Century African woman—Tashi-Evelyn Johnson, a born storyteller, a griot who knows she will never get to write her story.

Readers of Walker's works will remember Tashi from "The Color Purple" as the African child of the Olinkian village where Nettie, Olivia, Adam and the black missionaries come to evangelize. Caught in the clash of religions, cultures, continents, Tashi grows up hearing stories from her playmates Olivia and Adam of a pristine America, while watching her slow-gaited mother, herself a "gelded woman," move about her stooping, laborious African life.

It is, in part, the missionaries' presence that suspends the ritual mutilations for a while. But then, as a teen-ager, surrounded by the fervor of revolution in her country and struck by the loss of her people's land, livelihood, power and culture, she makes a defiant act: Spurred on by the words of the Olinkas' imprisoned leader that "no Olinka man would even think of marrying a woman who was not circumcised," she defiantly decides to submit herself to the hands of the ancient honored *tsunga* M'Lisa, a woman who has severed the vulvae of hundreds of little girls, thrown the "insignificant morsel" out the door to the waiting chickens and sewn the girls back up.

Her American friend Adam finds her lying on a filthy mat in an Olinkan rebel camp, her legs bound, flies swarming around her fresh facial and genital wounds. He saves her and takes her back to America as his wife, but Tashi is no longer the graceful, quick impish sprite he knew. She is passive and slow. ("Her soul had been dealt a mortal blow.")

"It now took a quarter of an hour for her to pee. Her menstrual periods lasted ten days. She was incapacitated by cramps nearly half the month . . . cramps caused by the near impossibility of flow passing through so tiny an aperture as M'Lissa had left, after fastening together the raw side of Tashi's vagina with a couple of thorns and inserting a straw so that in healing the traumatized flesh might not grow together, shutting the opening completely. . . . There was the odor, too, of soured blood."

She not only has a scar between her legs, but one as deep on her psyche as well. The circumcision has not only cut away her clitoris and the possibility of lovemaking that is not painful and humiliating. It has also eradicated her sense of self and her ability to feel.

In her lifelong struggle with the concomitant madness that the clitorectomy brings, she comes with her nightmares, rages, self-mutilation and her terrifying vision of a dark tower to Carl Jung and his tower Bollingen on Lake Zurich, to an African-American woman therapist, even to her husband's son by his French friend and lover. But it is her own action, her resistance to rituals that mutilate body and soul in the name of tradition and culture, that leads to her healing.

There is a tendency for the reader to try to place this action, this genital mutilation, in a former time, in another century, to put some space between *us* in our own safe world and *them*, who would do this to a child, a human being. But Walker won't allow it. Characters read Newsweek; a floor of the Olinkan prison has been turned over to AIDS patients. This is going on right now, Walker keeps reminding the reader, and this is what it is like. Walker's novel with its wounded main character struggling for a healing and understanding of what has been done to her pulls the covers off a practice as old as the pyramids and as current as the AIDS epidemic.

Walker, who has called this her most difficult book to write, does not make it easy for the reader, either. In just the way that men instinctively reach to protect their genitals when they see someone kicked in the groin, parts of "Possessing" make a woman want to reach for her vagina and protect herself "down there": "The obstetrician broke two instruments trying to make an opening large enough for Benny's head. Then he used a scalpel. Then a pair of scissors used ordinarily to sever cartilage from bone."

The little-known fact of contemporary female circumcision in African, Far Eastern and Middle Eastern countries as well as its spread into the Western world through immigration is a stunning discovery. (Or rediscovery: I read about the procedure more than 20 years ago in African History class and promptly shuffled it aside because it was too painful to contemplate.) Walker's use of it in her fiction shows the depth of her ideas, the range of the subjects she is willing to tackle. The imagery of the procedure done on a dirt floor with a tin can, a shard of glass or a sharpened stone's edge is so graphic, so hurtful, so poignant, and still so obvious as a methaphor for women's silencing and manipulation and self-loathing.

The idea of female circumcision and Walker's handling of it is something that remains with one long after finishing Tashi's story. It is difficult to wash oneself without imagining Tashi's wound; to make love, to bend over comfortably in the garden, to sprint to the ringing telephone without thinking how labored, how painful, how nearly impossible all these quotidian actions would be if one's vulva was mutilated.

That is the power of "Possessing," that an image one would rather forget is impossible to put out of one's mind. Impossible to ponder and imagine and feel.

Alice Walker's dedication of her fifth novel—"With Tenderness and Respect to the Blameless Vulva"—is not only not enough said; it is only the beginning.

As Tashi makes clear, "It is only the cruelty of truth, speaking it, shouting it, that will save us now." Not nearly enough has been said about this topic.

"Possessing the Secret of Joy" is a stunning beginning.

ESSAYS

◆◆◆◆◆◆◆◆◆◆◆◆◆

An Essay on Alice Walker

MARY HELEN WASHINGTON

From whatever vantage point one investigates the work of Alice Walker—poet, novelist, short story writer, critic, essayist, and apologist for black women—it is clear that the special identifying mark of her writing is her concern for the lives of black women. In the two books of poetry, two novels, one short story collection, and many essays and reviews she has produced since she began publishing in 1966, her main preoccupation has been the souls of black women. Walker herself, writing about herself as writer, has declared herself committed to "exploring the oppressions, the insanities, the loyalties, and the triumphs of black women."[1] In her first four published works—*Once*,[2] her earliest book of poetry; *Revolutionary Petunias*,[3] also poetry; *The Third Life of Grange Copeland*,[4] her first novel; *In Love and Trouble*,[5] a collection of thirteen stories—and her latest novel, *Meridian*,[6] there are more than twenty-five characters from the slave woman to a revolutionary woman of the sixties. Within each of these roles Walker has examined the external realities facing these women as well as the internal world of each woman.

We might begin to understand Alice Walker, the apologist and spokeswoman for black women, by understanding the motivation for Walker's preoccupation with her subject. Obviously there is simply a personal identification. She says in her interview with John O'Brien, "I believe in listening—to a person, the sea, the wind, the trees, but especially to young black women whose rocky road 1 am still traveling."[7] Moreover her sense of personal identification with black women includes a sense of sharing in their peculiar oppression. In some length she describes her own attempts at suicide when she discovered herself pregnant in her last year of college and at the mercy of everything, especially her own body. Throughout the interview with this writer in 1973,[8] Ms. Walker spoke of her own awareness of and experiences with brutality and violence in the lives of black women, many of whom she had known as a girl growing up in Eatonton, Georgia, some in her own family. The recurrent theme running throughout that interview and in much of her other pieces on women is her belief that "Black women . . . are the most oppressed people in the world."[9]

In one of her earliest essays, "The Civil Rights Movement: What Good Was It?"[10] she herself recalls "being young and well-hidden among the slums,"[11] knowing that her dreams of being an author or scientist were unattainable for a black child growing up in the poorest section of rural Georgia, that no one would encourage a black girl from the backwoods to become an artist or writer. In the same essay she recounts an episode in her mother's life that underscores her sensitivity to the peculiar oppression of black women. She saw her mother, a woman of heavy body and swollen feet, a maid in the houses of white women for forty years, having raised eight children in Eatonton, Georgia, turn to the stories of white men and women on television soap operas to satisfy her yearnings for a better life:

> My mother, a truly great woman who raised eight children of her own and half a dozen of the neighbors' without a single complaint—was convinced that she did not exist compared to "them." She subordinated her soul to theirs and became a faithful and timid supporter of the "Beautiful White People." Once she asked me in a moment of vicarious pride and despair, if I didn't think that "they" were "jest naturally smarter, prettier, better."[12]

Walker understands that what W. E. B. Du Bois called double consciousness, "this sense of always looking at one's self through the eyes of others, of measuring one's soul by the tape of a world that looks on in amused contempt and pity,"[13] creates its own particular kind of disfigurement in the lives of black women, and that, far more than the external facts and figures of oppression, the true terror is within; the mutilation of the spirit *and* the body. Though Walker does not neglect to deal with the external *realities* of poverty, exploitation, and discrimination, her stories, novels, and poems most often focus on the intimate reaches of the inner lives of her characters; the landscape of her stories is the spiritual realm where the soul yearns for what it does not have.[14]

In the O'Brien interview Ms. Walker makes a statement about Elechi Amadi's *The Concubine*, a Nigerian novel, and in that statement there is an important revelation about Walker's own writings. She sees Amadi as unique among black writers because through his book he exposes the subconscious of a people; that is, he has written about the dreams, rituals, legends, and imaginings which contain the "accumulated collective reality of the people themselves."[15] It would be possible to apply that same description to Walker's writings about black women, particularly the stories in *In Love and Trouble*, through which we can see a conscious effort by Walker to explore the imaginings, dreams, and rituals of the subconscious of black women which contains their accumulated collective reality. We begin this analysis of Walker's writings with a discussion of her personal identification with the lives of black women because it is that internal personal sharing that has put Walker in touch with this selective reality. Speaking of her short story "The Revenge of Hannah Kemhuff," Walker says:

> In that story I gathered up the historical and psychological threads of the life some of my ancestors lived, and in the writing of it I felt joy and strength and my own continuity. I had that wonderful feeling writers get sometimes, not very often, of being *with* a great many people, ancient spirits, all very happy to see me consulting and acknowledging them, and eager to let me know, through the joy of their presence that indeed I am not alone.[16]

One vital link to those "historical and psychological threads" of her ancestors' lives is the stories passed on to her by her mother, stories which Walker absorbed through years of listening to her mother tell them. The oral stories are often the basis for her own stories, as are the lives and stories of people she grew up with in Eatonton, Georgia. Once when questioned about the violence and pain in the lives of so many of her women, she recounted an incident from her childhood which was the basis for the story of Mem in Walker's novel *The Third Life of Grange Copeland*. When she was thirteen, a friend's father killed his wife, and Walker, a curious child, saw the mother's body laid out on a slab in the funeral home:

> . . . there she was, hard working, large, overweight, Black, somebody's cook, lying on the slab with half her head shot off, and on her feet were those shoes that I describe—hole in the bottom, and she had stuffed paper in them . . . we used to have, every week, just such a murder as these (in my home town), and it was almost always the wife and sometimes the children.[17]

The true empathy Alice Walker has for the oppressed woman comes through in all her writings—stories, essays, poems, novels. Even in a very brief review of a book of poetry by a woman who calls herself "Ai," Ms. Walker exhibits, almost with conscious design, her instinctive concern for the experiences of women. The choice of *Ai* as a pen name appeals to Ms. Walker because of the images of women it suggests:

> And one is glad she chose "Ai" as her name because it is like a cry. If I close my eyes and say the word (the sound) to myself, it is to see a woman raising an ax, to see a woman crying out in childbirth or abortion, to see a woman surrendering to a man who is oblivious to the sound of her true—as opposed to given—name.

Raising an ax, crying out in childbirth or abortion, surrendering to a man who is oblivious to her real name—these are the kinds of images which most often appear in Ms. Walker's own writing and have prompted critic Carolyn Fowler to say that Walker has the true gift of revealing the authentic "Heart of Woman" in her stories.

What particularly distinguishes Alice Walker in her role as apologist[18] and chronicler for black women is her evolutionary treatment of black women; that is, she sees the experiences of black women as a series of movements from women totally victimized by society and by the men in their lives to the growing developing women whose consciousness allows them to have control over their lives.

In historical terms the women of the first cycle belong to the eighteenth and nineteenth centuries and the early decades of the twentieth century. Although only one of Walker's characters is a slave, the institution of slavery set up the conditions and environment for the period immediately following, extending from the end of the Reconstruction Era to the first two decades of the twentieth century. Borrowing the term first used by novelist Zora Neale Hurston, the black women of this period are "the mules of the world," carrying the burdens heaped upon them by society and by the family, the victims of both racial and sexual oppression. Walker calls them her "suspended" women: a concept she develops in an important historical essay entitled "In Search of Our Mothers' Gardens: The Creativity of the Black Woman in the South," published in *Ms.* magazine in May 1974. Walker explains this state of suspension as caused by pressures in society which made it impossible for the black women of this era to move forward:

> They were suspended in a time in history where the options for Black women were severely limited. . . . And they either kill themselves or they are used up by the man, or by the children, or by . . . whatever the pressures against them. And they cannot go anywhere. I mean, you can't, you just can't move, until there is room for you to move *into*. And that's the way I see many of the women I have created in fiction. They are closer to my mother's generation than to mine. They had few choices.[19]

Suspended in time and place by a century, an era that only acknowledged them as laborers, these women were simply defeated in one way or another by the external circumstances of their lives. For such women— the great-grandmothers of the black women of contemporary times— pain, violence, poverty, and oppression were the essential content of their lives. Writer June Jordan calls them "black-eyed Susans—flowers of the blood-soaked American soil."

If these were the pressures and obstacles against the ordinary black woman who existed in the eighteenth and nineteenth centuries, what, then, did it mean for a black woman to be an artist, or want to be an artist in such times? Walker poses the question: "How was the creativity of the Black woman kept alive, year after year, century after century, when for the most of the years Black people have been in America, it was a punishable crime for a Black person to read or write?"[20] If the freedom to read and write, to paint, to sculpt, to experience one's creativity in any way did not exist, what became of the black woman artist? Walker says it is a question with an answer "cruel enough to stop the blood."

> For these grandmothers and mothers of ours were not "Saints," but Artists; driven to a numb and bleeding madness by the springs of creativity in them for which there was no release. They were Creators, who lived lives of spiritual waste, because they were so rich in spirituality—which is the basis of art—that the strain of enduring their unused and unwanted talent drove them insane. Throwing away this spirituality was their pathetic attempt to lighten the soul to a weight their work-worn, sexually abused bodies could bear.[21]

Of course, in spite of these many circumstances in which the art of the black woman was denied or stifled, some evidences of the creative genius of the black woman of that age still remain. Walker cites the poetry of Phillis Wheatley, the quilt making of so many anonymous black women of the South, the wise woman selling herbs and roots, as well as the brilliant and original gardens designed and cultivated by her own mother, as evidence that the creative spirit was nourished somehow and showed itself in wild and unlikely places. Though Ms. Walker is the first writer to define and develop the concept of the black women of the post-Reconstruction period as "suspended," as artists "hindered and thwarted by contrary instincts," the suspended black woman is a recurrent theme in the writers who deal with black women. Many of the black women characters in women writers from Frances Harper to Toni Morrison, as well as the women of Jean Toomer's *Cane*, are suspended women, artists without an outlet for their art or simply women of deep spirituality who "stumble blindly through their lives . . . abused and mutilated in body . . . dimmed and confused by pain, unaware of the richness of their gifts but nonetheless suffering as their gifts are denied."[22]

So we have part one of Walker's personal construct of the black woman's history—the woman suspended, artist thwarted and hindered in her desires to create, living through two centuries when her main role was to be a cheap source of cheap labor in the American society. This is the construct developed mainly in Walker's interviews and essays: How, then, does this construct fit in the fiction of Alice Walker?

Most of Walker's women characters belong to the first part of the cycle—the suspended woman. Three women from her first novel, *The Third Life of Grange Copeland*, and seven of the thirteen women from her short story collection, *In Love and Trouble*, are women who are cruelly exploited, spirits and bodies mutilated, relegated to the most narrow and confining lives, sometimes driven to madness. They are the contemporary counterparts of the crazy, pitiful women Jean Toomer saw in the South in the early 1920s.

In "Roselily," the opening story of *In Love and Trouble*, the main character, Roselily—young, black, poor, trapped in the southern backwoods, unmarried, the mother of three children, each by a different man—is about to give herself in marriage to a Muslim man. His religion requires a set of customs and beliefs that control women and subordinate them to men. She will have to wear her hair covered, sit apart from the men in church; her required place will be in the home. There will be more babies regardless of her wishes. She also senses another kind of oppression, dictated not by his religion, but by his condescension. He is annoyed by country black folk, their way of doing things, the country wedding. Roselily knows that in his eyes her three illegitimate children, not all by the same man, add to her lowliness. He makes her feel "ignorant, wrong, backward." But he offers her a chance that she must take. A chance for her children. A chance for her to be "respectable," "reclaimed," "renewed." And it is a chance she cannot afford to miss because marriage is perhaps her only way out of brutal poverty.

The excerpt from Elechi Amadi's *The Concubine*, a prefatory piece to *In Love and Trouble*, is a particularly interesting one for the light it throws on Roselily's situation. This excerpt depicts a woman named Ahurole who is given to unprovoked sobbing and fits of melancholia. An intelligent woman, Ahurole is generally cheerful and normal, so her parents blame her fits on the influence of an unlucky and troublesome personal spirit. At the end of the excerpt, it is revealed that "Ahurole was engaged to Ekwueme when she was *eight days old*." Walker sees Roselily, like Ahurole, as a woman trapped and cut down by archaic conventions, by superstition, by traditions that in every way cut women off from the right to life. Their personal and inner rebellion against the restrictions of their lives is reduced to the level of an unlucky spirit.

Roselily, too, has no way to explain her troubled and rebellious spirit. She has married off well, she will give her children a better life; but she is disturbed by what she senses will be an iron shackle around her life and her self. All of the fleeting images that inadvertently break through her consciousness are premonitions of what is to come: *quicksand, flowers choked to death, cotton being weighed, ropes, chains, handcuffs, cemeteries, a cornered rat*. The very robe and veil she is wearing are emblems of servitude that she yearns to be free of.

Mrs. Jerome Franklin Washington III, a beautician, another of Walker's suspended women, not unlike Roselily, is caught in a marriage that destroys her little by little. When she discovers how very little she means to her husband, she burns herself up.

Ms. Washington (we know her in this story only through her husband's name) is an unlovely, unloved woman: big, awkward, with rough skin, greasy, hard pressed hair. She is married, because of a small inheritance, to a quiet, "cute," dapper young schoolteacher whom she adores. She buys him clothes and cars, lavishly spending money on him, money she has earned in her beauty shop by standing many hours on her feet. It is not long before he is beating her and ridiculing her coarseness; for he considers himself one of the elite, the "black bourgeoisie," and his wife is so obviously, in spite of her hard-earned money, a woman of no learning, no elegance. In short, she is devoid of any black middle-class pretensions. Even her pretensions are clearly indicative of her lower class. She tells her customers as she does hair behind dark glasses, "'One thing my husband does not do, he don't beat me.'" She discovers Jerome's infidelity is his dedication to some sort of revolutionary cadre. He has hidden it from her no doubt because she is ignorant, but it is a revolution financed by her money and her devotion to him. She sets fire to their marriage bed, and she herself is caught in the blaze.

The physical and psychic brutality that are part of the lives of several other women in Walker's *In Love and Trouble* are almost always associated with poverty. Rannie Toomer, in "Strong Horse Tea," for example, struggling to get a doctor for her dying child, is handicapped by poverty and ignorance as well as by the racism of the southern rural area she lives in. No "real" doctor will come to see about her child, so she gives in to the "witche's" medicine of Aunt Sarah and goes out in the rain to catch horse urine, which is the "strong horse tea" the old rootworker has requested. Her child dies while she is out filling up her shoes with the tea. In his death, all of the elements seem to have conspired—the earth, the "nigger" magic of Aunt Sarah, the public and private racism of the South. One wonders what desperate hysteria allowed Rannie Toomer to stomach the taste and smell of horse urine.

In "The Child Who Favored Daughter," the father presides over the destruction of three women in his family: his own wife, whom he drives to suicide after beating and crippling her; his sister, named Daughter, whose suicide is the result of the punishment her family exacts after she has an affair with a white man; and his own daughter, whom he mutilates because she will not renounce her white lover. To understand the violence of this man toward these three women in his family, author Walker makes us know that it is the result of an immense chaos within—the components of which are his impotent rage against the white world which abuses him, his vulnerable love for his child and his sister, both of whom chose white lovers. He is so threatened by that inner chaos that the very act of violence is a form of control, a way of imposing order on his own world. By killing his daughter, he has at once shut out the image of Daughter which haunts him, he has murdered his own incest, and he has eliminated the last woman who has the power to hurt him. His brutality toward women foreshadows other Walker characters—Grange and Brownfield in *The Third Life of Grange Copeland,* the farmer who cripples his wife in "Really Doesn't Crime Pay?," Hannah Kemhuff's husband ("The Revenge of Hannah Kemhuff"), and Ruth's father in "A Sudden Trip Home in the Spring."

It is Walker's own documentation and analysis of the historical struggles of the black women that authenticates the terrible and chilling violence of these stories. These are stories about several generations of black women whose lives were severely limited by sexual and racial oppression. First slaves, then sharecroppers, then part of the vast army of the urban poor, their lives were lived out in slow motion, going nowhere, a future not yet within their grasp.[23]

Such were the women Jean Toomer discovered in *Cane,* and the similarity between Toomer's women and the women of Walker's first cycle (the suspended woman) is striking:

> To Toomer they lay vacant and fallow as Autumn fields, with harvest time never in sight: and he saw them enter loveless marriages, without joy; and

become prostitutes without resistance; and become mothers of children, without fulfillment.[24]

Both Toomer and Walker have explored the tragedies in the lives of Black women—the tragedy of poverty, abuse from men who are themselves abused, the physical deterioration—but there is greater depth in Walker's exploration because not only does she comprehend the past lives of these women but she has also questioned their fates and dared to see through to a time when black women would no longer live in suspension, when there would be a place for them to move into.

In the second cycle of Walker's personal construct of the history of black women are the women who belong to the decades of the forties and fifties, those decades when black people (then "Negroes") wanted most to be part of the mainstream of American life even though assimilation required total denial of one's ethnicity. Several literary critics have labeled this period in black literature a period of "mainstreaming" because of the indications in literature that writers such as Willard Motley and Frank Yerby and even one novel of Zora Neale Hurston were "raceless." And what of the black women during this period, particularly the woman who had some chance at education? Walker writes of her as a woman pushed and pulled by the larger world outside of her, urged to assimilate (to be "raceless") in order to overcome her background. In Walker's historical construct, these black women were, ironically, victims of what were ostensibly greater opportunities:

> I have this theory that Black women in the 50's, in the 40's—the late 40's and early 50's—got away from their roots much more than they will probably ever do again, because that was the time of greatest striving to get into White Society, and to erase all of the backgrounds of poverty. It was a time when you could be the Exception, could be the One, and my sister was The One. But I think she's not unique—so many, many, many Black families have a daughter or sister who was the one who escaped because, you see, that was what was set up for her; she was going to be the one who escaped, and the rest of us weren't supposed to escape, because we had given our One.[25]

The women in this cycle are also victims, not of physical violence, but of a kind of psychic violence that alienates them from their roots, cutting them off from real contact.

The woman named Molly from Walker's poem "For My Sister Molly Who in the Fifties" is the eldest sister in a poor rural family in Eatonton; she is, in fact, Alice Walker's sister and Walker is the child narrator of the poem mourning the loss of her talented and devoted "Molly." When Molly first comes home on vacation from college, she is very close to her brothers and sisters, teaching them what she has learned, reading to them about faraway places like Africa. The young narrator is enraptured by Molly, spellbound by the bright colorful sister who changes her drab life into beauty:

Who in the Fifties

Knew all the written things that made
Us laugh and stories by
The hour. Waking up the story buds
Like Fruit. Who walked among the flowers
And brought them inside the house
And smelled as good as they
And smelled as good as they
And looked as bright.
Who made dresses, braided
Hair. Moved chairs about
Hung things from walls
Ordered baths
Frowned on wasp bites
And seemed to know the endings
Of all the tales
I had forgot.[26]

As a writer especially concerned with the need for black people to acknowledge and respect their roots, Walker is sensitive to these women who are divorced from their heritage. As she describes them, the Chosen Ones were always the bright and talented ones in the family. They were the ones selected to go to college if the family could afford to send only one; they were meant to have the better life, the chance at success. And they learned early the important lesson that to be chosen required them to feel shame for their background, and to strive to be as different and removed as possible from those not chosen. But being a child, the narrator does not realize or suspect the growing signs of Molly's remoteness. Molly goes off to the university, travels abroad, becoming distant and cold and frowning upon the lives of the simple folks she comes from:

Who Found Another World

Another life   With gentlefolk
Far less trusting
And moved and moved and changed
Her name
And sounded precise
When she spoke   And frowned away
Our sloppishness[27]

From her superior position she can only see the negatives—the silent, fearful, barefoot, tongue-tied, ignorant brothers and sisters. She finds the past, her backward family, unbearable, and though she may have sensed their groping after life, she finally leaves the family for good. She has, of course, been leaving all along with her disapproval of their ways, her precise speech, her preference for another world. The tone of the last two lines suggests the finality about her leaving, as though Molly has become too alienated from her family to ever return:

> For My Sister Molly Who in the Fifties
>
> Left us.

The women of the second cycle are destroyed spiritually rather than physically, and yet there is still some movement forward, some hope that did not exist for the earlier generation of American black women. The women in this cycle are more aware of their condition and they have greater potential for shaping their lives, although they are still thwarted because they feel themselves coming to life before the necessary changes have been made in the political environment—before there is space for them to move into. The sense of "twoness" that Du Bois spoke of in *The Souls of Black Folk* is perhaps most evident in the lives of these women; they are the most aware of and burdened by the "double consciousness" that makes one measure one's soul by the tape of the other world.

In June of 1973 in an interview with this writer, Ms. Walker made one of the first statements about the direction and development of her black women characters into a third cycle:

> My women, in the future, will not burn themselves up—that's what I mean by coming to the end of a cycle, and understanding something to the end . . . now I am ready to look at women who have made the room larger for others to move in. . . . I think one reason I never stay away from the Southern Movement is because I realize how deeply political changes affect the choices and life-styles of people. The Movement of the Sixties, Black Power, the Muslims, the Panthers . . . have changed the options of Black people generally and of Black women in particular. So that my women characters won't all end the way they have been, because Black women now offer varied, live models of how it is possible to live. We have made a new place to move. . . .[28]

The women of the third cycle are, for the most part, women of the late sixties, although there are some older women in Walker's fiction who exhibit the qualities of the developing, emergent model. Greatly influenced by the political events of the sixties and the changes resulting from the freedom movement, they are women coming just to the edge of a new awareness and making the first tentative steps into an uncharted region. And although they are more fully conscious of their political and psychological oppression and more capable of creating new options for themselves, they must undergo a harsh initiation before they are ready to occupy and claim any new territory. Alice Walker, herself a real-life prototype of the emergent black woman, speaks of having been called to life by the civil rights movement of the sixties, as being called from the shadows of a world in which black people existed as statistics, problems, beasts of burden, a life that resembled death; for one was not aware of the possibilities within one's self or of possibilities in the larger world outside of the narrow restraints of the world black people inhabited before the struggles of the sixties. When Walker and other civil rights activists like Fannie Lou Hamer[20] began the fight for their lives, they were beaten, jailed, and, in Fannie Lou Hamer's case, widowed and made homeless, but they never lost the energy and courage for revolt. In the same way Walker's own characters, through suffering and struggle, lay the groundwork for a new type of woman to emerge.

The process of cyclical movement in the lives of Walker's black women is first evident in her first novel, *The Third Life of Grange Copeland*. The girl, Ruth, is the daughter of Mem Copeland and the granddaughter of Margaret Copeland—two women whose lives were lived out under the most extreme forms of oppression. Under the pressure of poverty and alienation from her husband, Margaret kills herself and her child; and Mem, wife of Brownfield Copeland, is brutally murdered by her husband in one of his drunken rages. Ruth is brought up by her grandfather, Grange, who in his "third life" attempts to salvage some of his own wasted life by protecting Ruth. Ruth emerges into a young woman at the same time as the civil rights movement, and there is just a glimpse at the end of the novel of how that movement will affect Ruth's life. We see her becoming aware, by watching the civil rights activists—both women and men—that it is possible to struggle against the abuses of oppression. Raised in the sixties, Ruth is the natural inheritor of the changes in a new order, struggling to be, this marking the transition of the women in her family from death to life.

Besides political activism, a fundamental activity the women in the third cycle engage in is the search for meaning in their roots and traditions. As they struggle to reclaim their past and to re-examine their relationship to the black community, there is a consequent reconciliation between themselves and black men.

In Sarah Davis, the main character of Walker's short story, "A Sudden Trip Home in the Spring,"[30] we have another witness to the end of the old cycles of confusion and despair. Her search begins when she returns home to the South from a northern white college to bury her father. She is an artist, but because of her alienation from her father, whom she blames for her mother's death, she is unable to paint the faces of black men, seeing in them only defeat. It is important for her, therefore, to answer the questions she is pondering: What is the duty of the child toward the parents after they are dead? What is the necessity of keeping alive in herself a sense of continuity with the past and a sense of community with her family? Through a series of events surrounding her father's funeral, Sarah rediscovers the courage and grace of her grandfather and re-establishes the vital link between her and her brother. Her resolve at the end of the story to do a sculpture of her grandfather ("I shall soon know how to make my grandpa up in stone") signifies the return to her roots and her own personal sense of liberation. This story, more than any other, indicates the contrast between the women of the second cycle who were determined to escape their roots in order to make it in a white world and the emergent women of the third cycle who demonstrate a sense of freedom by the drive to re-establish those vital links to their past.

In Walker's second novel, *Meridian*, the cyclical process is clearly defined in the life of the main character, Meridian Hill, who evolves from a woman trapped by racial and sexual oppression to a revolutionary figure, effecting action and strategy to bring freedom to herself and other poor disenfranchised blacks in the South. Again, as with other third-cycle women who are depicted in the short story collection, the characters in the two novels—*Grange Copeland* and *Meridian*—follow certain patterns: They begin existence in a numb state, deadened, insensible to a life beyond poverty and degradation; they are awakened to life by a powerful political force; in discovering and expanding their creativity, there is a consequent effort to reintegrate themselves into their culture in order to rediscover its value. Historically, the second novel, dealing with a woman who came of age during the sixties, brings Walker's women characters into the first few years of the seventies.

Notes

1. John O'Brien, ed., *Interviews with Black Writers* (New York: Liverwright, 1973), p. 192.
2. New York: Harcourt, Brace & World, 1968.
3. New York: Harcourt Brace Jovanovich, 1973.
4. New York: Harcourt Brace Jovanovich, 1970.
5. New York: Harcourt Brace Jovanovich, 1973.
6. New York: Harcourt Brace Jovanovich, 1976.
7. O'Brien, p. 211.
8. Interview with Mary Helen Washington, Jackson, Mississippi, June 17, 1973. I traveled to Jackson in June of 1973 in order to meet, talk with, and interview Ms. Walker.
9. "Interview with Mary Helen Washington," Part 1, p. 7.
10. *American Scholar,* Winter 1970–71.
11. Ibid., p. 551.
12. Ibid., p. 552.
13. W. E. B. Du Bois, *Souls of Black Folk* (New York: Blue Heron Press, 1953), pp. 16–17.
14. Carolyn Fowler, "Solid at the Core," *Freedomways* 14 (First Quarter, 1974), p. 60.
15. Alice Walker, "Interview," in O'Brien, p. 202.
16. Reid Lecture at Barnard College, November 11, 1975.
17. "Interview with Mary Helen Washington," p. 6.

18. *Apologist* is used here to mean one who speaks or writes in defense of a cause or a position.
19. "Interview with Mary Helen Washington," p. 6.
20. "In Search of Our Mothers' Gardens," *Ms.*, May 1974, p. 66.
21. Ibid.
22. Ibid., p. 69.
23. Ibid., p. 66.
24. Ibid.
25. "Interview with Mary Helen Washington," Part 1, p. 1.
26. *Revolutionary Petunias* (New York: Harcourt Brace Jovanovich, 1973), p. 17.
27. Ibid., p. 18.
28. "Interview with Mary Helen Washington," Part 2, p. 2.
29. The identification of Hamer as a model for the emergent woman is developed in Walker's review of a biography of Hamer by June Jordan. The review appeared in *The New York Times Book Review*, April 29, 1973.
30. In Mary Helen Washington, ed., *Black-eyed Susans: Classic Stories by and About Black Women* (Garden City, N.Y.: Doubleday & Company, 1975).

◆◆◆◆◆◆◆◆◆◆◆◆◆

Novels for Everyday Use

BARBARA CHRISTIAN

Alice Walker's works are quilts—bits and pieces of used material rescued from oblivion for everyday use. She takes seemingly ragged edges
and arranges them into works of functional though terrifying beauty.
She has published books of poetry, *Once* (1968), *Revolutionary Petunias*
(1973); *Good Night Willie Lee, I'll See You in the Morning* (1979); a book
of short stories, *In Love and Trouble, Stories for Black Women* (1973);
a children's book about Langston Hughes; ed. anthology on Zora Neale
Hurston (1979); and two novels, *The Third Life of Grange Copeland*
(1970) and *Meridian* (1976).

The bits and pieces are not random fabric. Like their quilter, they
originate in the South. The daughter of a Georgian sharecropper, Walker
is the significant black woman novelist of our generation to concentrate
on the sensibility of the South as a way of perceiving the perennial conflict between the human spirit and societal patterns. She has long insisted
that until the solids and prints of the South are sorted out and stitched
into clarity, the relationship in this country between men and women,
blacks and whites, will continue in disarray.

As a craftsman, Walker sorts out the throwaways, the seemingly
insignificant and hidden pieces of the lives of Southerners, particularly
black families, and stitches them into a tapestry of society. Who is to
blame for the waste in our lives, she asks? Ourselves? The society that
seems at every turn opposed to blossoming? The wrath of God? The
question of responsibility for personal action and societal change is one
recurrent motif in the complex quilts that Walker makes out of thrifty
sentences, knotted questions, tight metaphors, terse sections. Her novels continually stitch a fabric of the everyday violence that is committed
against her characters and that they commit upon one another in their
search for regeneration, and regeneration is what they as black people
desire.

The exploration, then, of the process of personal and social growth
out of horror and waste is a motif that characterizes Walker's works.
For her, the creativity of the black women is essential to this process.
In her classic essay, "In Our Mothers' Gardens" (1974), Walker asks,
"How was the creativity of the black woman kept alive, "when the freedom to read and write . . . sculpt, paint or expand the mind with action,
did not not exist." In searching for the means to her own artistic and
political freedom, Walker investigates the legacy of the past. To deepen
our understanding of the plight of her maternal ancestors, she not only
calls upon her own personal history but upon Jean Toomer, who perhaps

more than any other writer of the past had focused on the repressed creativity of black women:

> When the poet Jean Toomer walked through the South in the early twenties he discovered a curious thing: Black women whose spirituality was so intense, so deep, so *unconscious* that they were themselves unaware of the richness they held. They stumbled blindly through their lives: creatures so abused and mutilated in body, so dimmed and confused by pain, that they considered themselves unworthy even of hope. In the selfless abstractions their bodies became to the men who used them, they became more than "sexual objects," more even than mere women: they became Saints. Instead of being perceived as whole persons, their bodies became shrines: what was thought to be their minds became temples suitable for worship. These crazy "Saints" stared out at the world wildly like lunatics—or quietly, like suicides and the "God" that was in their gaze was as mute as a great stone.
>
> Who were these "Saints"? These crazy loony women? Some of them without a doubt were our mothers and grandmothers [author's emphasis].[1]

What Walker discovers is that some of these women were not "Saints," but "Artists," "who were driven to a numb and bleeding madness for which there was no release." In contrast to these mute women who were physically and psychologically abused, a few, like Phyllis Wheatley and Nella Larson were preened by black and white society to escape the horror. They, too, suffered, for they struggled in the mire of confused identity and were torn by what Walker calls "contrary instincts." As creative women, however, they struggled to sing even as they were denied the freedom to express their own voice and thus "kept alive, in so many of their ancestors, the *notion of song.*" Still others held onto the creative spark by using daily parts of their lives such as storytelling, singing in church, root working, quilt making, and, as Walker's mother did, their gardens as mediums for their creative expression. The artist Walker describes the impact that one of these everyday art forms had on her:

> For example: in the Smithsonian Institution in Washington, D.C. there hangs a quilt unlike any other in the world. In fanciful, inspired and yet simple and identifiable figures, it portrays the story of the Crucifixion. It is considered rare, beyond price. Though it follows no known pattern of quiltmaking and though it is made of bits and pieces of worthless rags, it is obviously the work of a person of powerful imagination and deep spiritual feeling. Below this quilt I saw a note that says it was made by "An anonymous Black woman in Alabama, a hundred years ago."
>
> If we could locate this "anonymous Black woman from Alabama", she would turn out to be one of our grandmothers, an artist who left her mark in the only materials she could afford, and in the only medium her position in society allowed her to use.[2]

In her search for our mothers' gardens, Walker describes a legacy from which the creativity of the contemporary black woman can flower. To develop further, the black women of her generation must garner wholeness from the bits and pieces of the past and recreate them in their own image. Walker then uses the often unheralded heritage of black women, the creative sparks as well as the history of restrictions, as the foundation of her artistic vision. A feminist, she explores the relationship between this tradition and societal change as crucial to the search for freedom—not only for woman, but for man, the child, the society, the culture, the land.

This theme, though, is never ostentatiously stated in Walker's works. Rather it is revealed through her skillful, often subtle narrative. She is at her best a storyteller. We can feel her delight, sheer delight, in telling stories, in mingling bits and pieces of hard reality and lyrical fantasy. Like a quilter, she is economical; her stories are thrifty; there are no bulges or long stretches of the same material, no waste. Her tales are marvelous themselves, intriguing the imagination with wondrous touches juxtaposed to the mundane; velvet pieces lie comfortably next to the most used flannel. Her craft of words, in fact, becomes a potential model for regeneration. Search for the bits of plain and fancy, the memories of pain and pleasure, and lay them out, examine them, rearrange them, and remake them. The pattern at first may be beautiful only in its terror, but until that terror is faced and explored, precarious contentment may be possible, but not rebirth.

PART I

The Third Life of Grange Copeland:
A Saga of Degeneration and Regeneration

The plot of Alice Walker's first novel, *The Third Life of Grange Copeland,* exposes the pattern of terror over a span of sixty years in the lives of one black family of sharecroppers. Grange Copeland abuses his wife, Margaret, and neglects his son, Brownfield, because he feels himself less than a man in a land where his entire life is indebted to the white boss. As he grows older, he feels trapped by his family, for they hold him to this life. Increasingly he feels guilt because he can neither protect his wife from the white hairy arms of Shipley nor make possible a better life for his son. As he drinks solace from the overflowing breasts and bar of Josie, the local whore, Margaret takes on lovers, reacting to Grange's abuse by abusing herself. When her husband leaves his life of indebtedness for the North, Margaret poisons herself and her young, illegitimate baby.

Deserted by his parents, Brownfield, a young man of sixteen, follows his father's path only to end up working for and sleeping with Josie. While he is employed at the Dew Drop Inn, Brownfield meets and falls in love with Mem, Josie's schoolteacher niece. In love and passion they marry—only to repeat the pattern of depression and abuse Grange and

Margaret had already drawn. In spite of Mem's efforts to better her life and the lives of her daughters Daphne, Ornette, and Ruth, Brownfield drags her down. Feeling less than a man, he, too, buries himself in Josie only to lose even her to the father that deserted him.

The pieces, slightly rearranged, remain essentially the same. Walker graphically tells the story of Brownfield and Mem's deterioration. In revenge for his father's rejection, Brownfield kills his newborn albino son, a white baby that looks like his father. In a moment of terrible strength, Mem threatens her husband with a gun and tears his defenses apart. In a clear drunken stupor, after years of mangling guilt and self-hatred, Brownfield murders Mem, leaving his own children, as his father had done before him, to fend for themselves.

Grange, who has returned from the North, takes on the responsibility of raising Ruth, his youngest grandchild, with the same vigor that he had shunned the responsibility of raising his own son. Ruth in her innocence gives Grange a new life. Jealous and angry, the imprisoned Brownfield plots with Josie, Grange's now neglected wife, to wrest the girl from her grandfather. After he leaves jail, Brownfield manages to have a white judge give the custody of the sixteen-year-old Ruth to him, her father but also the man who has killed her mother. Calmly, deliberately, Grange kills his son Brownfield in the court of justice to make life possible for Ruth. Grange, in turn, is shot at his home by the sheriff's men.

That is the plot. The story is marked throughout by the motif of physical and spiritual murder, by suicide and infanticide, by wife beating and killing, set against a background of the horror of racism in the South. The pervasive pattern of this quilt is kin killing.

Why is this novel saturated with murder and violence of all kinds? Isn't Walker substantiating the pervasive myth that black people, particularly black men, are by their very nature violent and that they inflict the full range of their violence on their own blood? Doesn't Grange's neglect of Margaret and Brownfield's abuse of Mem give fuel to the idea that black men hate their women, and doesn't Mem's attack on Brownfield reinforce the covert fear of many black men that black women are always trembling with the desire to castrate them? In fact, doesn't *The Third Life of Grange Copeland* effectively prove the racist myths about Afro-Americans?

It is as if Walker consciously selects all the nasty bits and pieces about black people that they as well as white people believe. Then she examines each bit, lucidly arranges the pieces so we might see the savage nibblings of everyday oppression at the souls of black Southerners.

Of all the savage nibblings of racism, the most poisonous bite is the abnegation of responsibility for one's own soul. The novel, through its juxtaposition of parts, relates the monstrous ramifications that result from blacks believing what society, at every turn, teaches them—that they are not capable of being responsible for their own actions, that white folks are to blame for everything. This abnegation of responsibility is what it means to be a "nigger." All of the bits and pieces of violence in the book are arranged to reiterate this motif—a motif that Grange Copeland in his one true communication with his son Brownfield explores:

> By George, I *know* the danger of putting all the blame on somebody else for the mess you make out of your life. I fell into the trap myself! And I'm bound to believe that that's the way the white folks can corrupt you even when you done held up before. 'Cause when they got you thinking they're to blame for everything they have you thinking they're some kind of gods! You can't do nothing wrong without them being behind it. You gits just as weak as water, no feeling of doing *nothing* yourself. Then you begins to think up evil and begins to destroy everybody around you, and you blames it on the crackers. *Shit!* Nobody's as powerful as we make them out to be. We got our own *souls*, don't we?[3]

Yet the dilemma for poor black Southerners is not as simple as all that. In every corner of this novel, the reader feels the tight control the white bosses have over the black sharecroppers and how this control, although seemingly focused on a work relationship, fends its way into the relationships between black men, black women, and black children.

Through her graphic description of the Copelands' everyday lives, Walker illuminates a basic strategy of racism. Because it is so obvious, we often forget that the most effective way to control anyone is by confusing his or her sex definition according to the norms of society. The masculine thrust in this society manifests itself in forms of power and acquisition, phantom qualities to which neither Grange nor Brownfield Copeland have access. The female, according to southern norms, should present herself in images of passivity, chastity, and demure beauty and should receive from men the rewards of security, comfort, and respect, rewards that neither Margaret nor Mem Copeland can exhibit. Although physically grown, the black adults in this novel are never treated by the majority culture as men or women or even as boys or girls. They are seen as sexual beings without the human qualities necessary for sex definition, except in purely physical terms.

Because Walker covers three generations of the Copeland family, she is able to show us how consistent and deep-rooted this strategy of racism is. By having one figure, the figure of Grange Copeland, persist throughout this generational span, Walker dramatizes the possibilities of change. Throughout the eleven economical sections of this novel, however, the author refuses to let her readers forget society's insistent, often stolid, attempt to control the psychological as well as the material conditions under which black people struggle. She graphically lays out her patterns by tracing in the first half of the novel the degenerate effects of racism on the Copeland men, women, and children and by demonstrating the process of regeneration in the second half. Two elements, then—the need to accept responsibility for one's life, for self-definition, and the obvious fact that much of it, at least in this time and place, is beyond one's control—form the axis of the novel's cyclical patterns. This novel poses the question: In the grip of physical and psychological oppression, how do you "find a place in you where they can't come?" How do you hold onto self-love?

The obvious answer is to go somewhere else, to go North. That is why, I believe, Walker begins the novel with Brownfield's northern cousins' visit at his backwoods home. That is why we are first shown an escape route based on history. But the North, the promised land, has got its own sharecropping system as the death of Brownfield's northern uncle reveals. Still, the land up North is a dream of hope for the Copeland men, who at least are mobile if nothing else. Grange deserts Margaret to go north where he believes he will escape white people's control. The young Brownfield wants to go north with his cousins.

He wants to go, for the cycle of his father's days are fixed in hopelessness. Walker carefully stitches a square that will be repeated in this quilt, when she describes Grange Copeland's week, every week:

On Monday, suffering from a hangover and the aftereffects of a violent quarrel with his wife the night before, Grange was morose, sullen, reserved, deeply in pain under the hot early morning sun. Margaret was tense and hard, exceedingly nervous. Brownfield moved about the house like a mouse. On Tuesday, Grange was merely quiet. His wife and son began to relax. On Wednesday, as the day stretched out and the cotton rows stretched out even longer, Grange muttered and sighed. He sat outside in the night air longer before going to bed; he would speak of moving away, of going North. He might even try to figure out how much he owed the man who owned the fields. The man who drove the truck and who owned the shack they occupied. But these activities depressed him, and he said things on Wednesday nights that made his wife cry. By Thursday Grange's gloominess reached its peak and he grimaced respectfully, with veiled eyes, at the jokes told by the man who drove the truck. On Thursday nights he stalked the house from room to room and pulled himself up and swung from the rafters of the porch. Brownfield could hear his joints creaking against the sounds of the porch, for the whole porch shook when his father swung. By Friday Grange was so stupefied with the work and the sun he wanted nothing but rest the next two days before it started all over again.

On Saturday afternoon Grange shaved, bathed, put clean overalls and a shirt and took the wagon into town to buy groceries. While he was away his wife washed and straightened her hair. She dressed up and sat, all shining and pretty, in the open door, hoping anxiously for visitors, who never came.

. . . Late Saturday night Grange would come home lurching drunk, threatening to kill his wife and Brownfield, stumbling and shooting off his shotgun. He threatened Margaret and she ran and hid in the woods with Brownfield huddled at her feet. Then Grange would roll out the door and into the yard, crying like a child in big wrenching sobs and rubbing his whole head in the dirt. He would lie there until Sunday morning, when the chickens pecked around him, and the dog sniffed at him and neither his wife nor Brownfield went near him. Brownfield played instead on the other side of the house.

> Steady on his feet but still ashen by noon, Grange would make his way across the pasture and through the woods, headlong, like a blind man to the Baptist church, where his voice above all the others was raised in song and prayer. Margaret would be there too, Brownfield asleep on the bench beside her. Back home again after church, Grange and Margaret would begin a supper quarrel which launched them into another week just about like the one before.[4]

Although Brownfield had dreamed, had believed, that his life would be different from his fathers, twenty years later he finds himself caught in the same square.

> It was a year when endless sunup to sundown work on fifty rich bottom acres of cotton land and a good crop brought them two diseased shoats for winter meat, some dried potatoes and apples from the boss's cellar, and some cast-off clothes for his children from his boss's family. It was the summer that he watched, that he had to teach, his frail five-year old daughter the tricky, dangerous and disgusting business of handmopping the cotton bushes with arsenic to keep off boll weevils. His heart had actually started to hurt him, like an ache in the bones, when he watched her swinging the mop, stumbling over the clumps of hard clay, the hot tin bucket full of arsenic making a bloodied scrape against her small short leg. She stumbled and almost fell with her bucket, so much too large for her, and each time he saw it his stomach flinched. She was drenched with sweat, her tattered dress wringing wet with perspiration and arsenic; her large eyes reddened by the poison. She breathed with difficulty through the deadly smell. At the end of the day she trembled and vomited and looked beaten down like a tiny, asthmatic old lady; but she did not complain to her father, as afraid of him as she was of the white boss who occasionally deigned to drive by with friends to watch the lone little pickanniny, so tired she barely saw them, poisoning his cotton.
>
> That pickanniny was Brownfield's oldest child, Daphne, and that year of awakening roused him not from sleep but from hope that someday she would be a fine lady and carry parasols and wear light silks. That was the year he first saw how his own life was becoming a repetition of his father's. He could not save his children from slavery; they did not even belong to him.
>
> His indebtedness depressed him. Year after year the amount he owed continued to climb. He thought of suicide and never forgot it, even in Mem's arms. He prayed for help, for a caring President, for a listening Jesus. He prayed for a decent job in Mem's arms. But like all prayers sent up from there, it turned into another mouth to feed, another body to enslave to pay his debts. He felt himself destined to become no more than overseer, on the white man's plantation, of his own children.
>
> That was the year he accused Mem of being unfaithful to him, of being used by white men, his oppressors; a charge she tearfully and truthfully denied.[5]

Like his father before him, Brownfield at first dreams of going North, but even these dreams finally die. Imprisoned in his own life, he, like Grange, begins to see his wife as a trap and gives her the blame for this failure. Both Grange and Brownfield know inside themselves that Margaret and Mem are not to blame for the waste in all of their lives. But since they cannot get near the true cause of their poverty, their wives are accessible targets upon whom they can vent their frustration.

The true cause of their misery is the racist sharecropping system.

Thus, another figure that appears throughout this novel is the figure of the powerful white boss. Brownfield as a boy is puzzled at how the white man who drove the truck could turn his father into stone, and his young soul is filled with terror of this man who could by his presence alone transform his father into something "that might as well have been a pebble or a post or a piece of dirt, except for the sharp bitter odor of something whose source was forcibly contained in flesh." As if harnassed by that childhood memory, the man Brownfield does not even maintain his father's stony silence (in its way a form of protest) before the boss; for "he had no faith that any other place would be better," or that he could do anything about the restrictions on his life.

Again the bits and pieces are slightly different, but the pattern remains the same. It would be madness, Grange and Brownfield know, to bite the hands that feed them. It would be madness to believe that they could defeat the sharecropping system. Knowing what their society denies, that they are men, the Copeland males try to free themselves first by working hard. When this fails, they hate themselves for their impotence, their inability to fulfill the masculine urge to power. Finally, they use whatever power they feel they have, primarily their power over their women, in a destructive way. Their masculine urge is blocked and therefore turns in on itself. So Grange abandons his family and goes North where he learns the harshness of invisibility and Brownfield attacks the only vulnerable person available to him, his lovely wife.

The lives of their wives, too, follow a similar pattern. Both Grange and Brownfield marry sweet, virginal women who had had a girlhood brimming with hope. Margaret and Mem at first believe, as do their husbands, that through love, kindness, fortitude, orderliness, they can create and maintain a good home. The wives are programmed to be demure and pretty, to plant flowers, be chaste. If they do these things well, they believe they will receive their just rewards. Because they believe in the definition of woman dictated by society, neither Margaret nor Mem are emotionally prepared to understand, far less cope with, their reality. So when the rewards do not materialize, when in fact they are abused and blamed by their men for their failure, the wives believe they have not done their part well.

Depressed by their condition, Margaret and Grange fight as if to preserve some part of the feeling of being alive. Crushed by the deadly labor of her days, and the neglect of her husband, the kind, submissive Margaret becomes "a wild woman looking for frivolous things, her heart's good times in the transient embrace of strangers." But in spite of, even because of, her amorous adventures, she believes that she is at fault; she blames herself, without knowing what she can do, for everything, especially for not being able to deliver her husband from his lot in life. So when Grange leaves her, Margaret accepts the responsibility for his failure and the pain of her loss. "She was curled up in a lonely sort of way, away from her child, as if she had spent the last moments on her knees."

Brownfield chooses a wife, much like his memories of his mother before she became a wild woman. When he first meets her, Mem is a schoolteacher, plump and quiet, with demure slant eyes. In the beginning of their relationship she tries to teach Brownfield how to read; he feels she can help him to rise above his ignorance. At first she is for him a lady, "the pinnacle of his achievement in extricating himself from evil and the devil and aligning himself with love." In the fashion of hopeful young men, Brownfield tells Mem on their wedding day: "We ain't always going to be stuck down here, honey, don't you worry." She believes him. Walker tells us about their initial happiness, so we can see that they were originally passionate and hopeful. But unceasing labor with no chance of reward is a cesspool they cannot get out of:

> Over the years they reached, what they would have called when they were married, an impossible and *unbelievable* decline. Brownfield beat his once lovely wife now, regularly, because it made him feel, briefly, good. Every Saturday night he beat her, trying to pin the blame for his failure on her by imprinting it on her face; and she, inevitably, repaid him by becoming a haggard automatous witch, beside whom even Josie looked well-preserved.[6]

Mem's response to her husband's abuse is not quite the same as Margaret's. She begins to deteriorate; she loses the school speech and the plump beauty that Brownfield had coveted. "Her mildness became stupor; then her stupor became horror, desolation and at last hatred." Framed by the children she bears, those who live and the many who die, she wants to find a door but cannot. For most of the novel, we feel that she cannot act because she does not believe or understand what is happening to her. Eventually, she becomes so desperate that she must believe in, fight for, something. The goal she puts all her energy into, as do many women, is a house, a house that can become a home, because it is stable and comfortable and commands respect.

The woman's desire to have a house becomes the major conflict in the battle between the Copelands, as it had been between the Boyces in Paule Marshall's *Browngirl, Brownstones*. It is not the acquisition of a house that causes the conflict so much as the fact that the women in question find the inner as well as the financial resources to accomplish their goal while the men cannot. For their part, both Mem and Silla become so desperate in their struggle for survival and stability, in their engulfing desire to have a home for their children, that they are willing to confront their men and if necessary move them out of the way. In one bold stroke, they are forced to redefine their definition of themselves as women, thus inevitably assaulting the men's definition of themselves as men.

Mem's determination to have a house and Brownfield's fear of her growing strength is the dominant motif in Part Five. The way in which

Walker puts this section of her quilt together is a good illustration of her particular style. Part Five is divided into six short sections of tiny bits and slightly larger pieces, as the quilter sorts out the appropriate fabric for her pattern. Two pieces of fabric recur in this section: Brownfield's fear that Mem will find a house for *his* family when he could not and his equally powerful fear of his white boss, Captain Davis.

A lover of succinct units, Walker customarily begins each of her sections with a tight topical sentence. In this case, the first sentence of Part Five is: "Brownfield did not believe Mem would be able to find a house." The *be able* is crucial here, for Brownfield tells us that he *could not* find a decent house "the first and only time he had looked for one." One page long, chapter 19 shows the relationship between Brownfield's sense of his own inadequacy and the abuse Mem receives from him for her initiative.

Chapter 20, about one and one-half pages long, presents the other recurring piece of fabric in this square. Brownfield receives an "offer" from his white boss, Captain Davis, to go to work for his son, Mr. J. L., who of course would provide the sharecroppers with a shack. Brownfield does not want to work for Mr. J. L. but he cannot refuse Captain Davis: "Yassur," he said finally, hypnotized by the old man standing in the sun. One is reminded of Brownfield's first childhood experience of the white boss as the man who turned his father into stone.

Brownfield must of course tell his family that he has committed them to work for Mr. J. L. In the slightly longer chapter 21, he forces his weakness on them. This scene has as its focus the image of Brownfield as an animal. In being unable to refuse Captain Davis's offer, his wife and her children perceive him as less than human. In fact, Brownfield himself acts as if he, too, has come to believe this:

> When her father was eating Ornette could not think of him as anything but a hog.[7]

> A shiver of revulsion ran through his wife. "He's just like a old dog. . . ."[8]

> "I ain't never going to marry nobody like him," Daphne swore to herself, watching the big ugly hands that smell always of cows and sour milk."[9]

> "I already told you," she (Mem) said, "you ain't dragging me and these children through no more pigpens."[10]

> "If I was a man," she (Mem) thought, frowning later, scrubbing the dishes, "if I was a man I'd give every man in sight and that I ever met up with a beating, maybe even chop up a few with my knife, they so pig-headed and mean."[11]

The following chapter (chapter 22) is built on the tension caused by Mem's ability to find a house and Brownfield's refusal to accept that fact. Even after years of abuse, Mem apologizes to Brownfield for her accomplishment. In spite of what it has cost her, she still holds onto society's definition of Brownfield's and her respective roles:

> "I'm real sorry about it, Brownfield," said Mem, whose decision to let him be man of the house for nine years had cost her and him nine years of unrelenting misery. He had never admitted to her that he couldn't read well enough to sign a lease and she had been content to let him keep that small grain of pride. But now he was old and sick beyond his years and she had grown old and evil, wishing every day he'd just fall down and die. *Her generosity had shackled them both* [author's emphasis].[12]

Although apologetic, Mem is determined to make the move, not so much for herself but for her children who, she believes, must now be her primary concern. Brownfield may also want to believe this, but he is caught between his wife's determination and the wishes of his white boss. Walker emphasizes this internal conflict of his by placing two very short chapters next to each other. In chapter 23, Captain Davis informs Brownfield that the deal has been made. As usual, the white man treats Brownfield like chattel; as usual, Brownfield, although angry, responds obsequiously. In chapter 24, Mem informs Brownfield that not only has she got a house in town, but she has got a job there, too. In the space of one day, Brownfield's manhood has been insulted by his white boss and threatened, he feels, by his wife.

Brownfield is too afraid of his boss to challenge him in any way. So it is not surprising that in chapter 25, the climactic chapter of Part Five, he takes out his feelings of anger on Mem. In contrast to the rest of this section, this chapter is long, divided into two smaller parts: Brownfield's customary assault on Mem and her reaction. Strengthened by her recent victories, as well as by her determination to save her children, Mem's response is not her usual one:

> "You going to move where I says move, you hear me?" Brownfield yelled at her giving her a kick in the side with his foot. "We going to move to Mr. J. L.'s place or we ain't going nowhere at all!"[13]

> "Open your eyes?" Mem's voice was as even as a dammed-up river. Slowly he stopped turning and opened his eyes, squinting them stickily to keep out the light. Mem was propped up against the wall on her side of the bed, holding a shotgun. At first he saw only the handle, smooth and black and big, close to his head like that. One of Mem's long wrinkled fingers pressed against the trigger. He made a jump, half toward her, half away from her. He felt a sharp jab on his body down below the covers, the shooting pain caused him to wince and thrash on the bed.[14]

The struggle between the determined Mem and the frustrated Brownfield that is dramatized in this section is a compression of the dominant motifs of Part Five. In the bed that has caused her such agony, Mem recites the long year of hardship and abuse that she has endured because of their insistence on holding onto the South's definition of woman and of man. But Brownfield does not hear her words; he only sees himself as trapped between his crazy wife and his all powerful boss. In an attempt to get Mem to put down the gun, to get her to accept her state, he threatens her with his ultimate authority, the big white boss,

Captain Davis. Mem's insistence that Captain Davis does not see Brownfield or any other black man as a man, and her refusal to accept Brownfield's abnegation of his responsibility for his acts, assaults Brownfield's definition of himself.

Walker risks hell and brimstone when she stitches together the remnant of a black man's lost pride with the new cloth of a black woman's mounting strength. Although Brownfield has consistentlly brutalized Mem, to maintain his sense of his own manhood, her attack on him might be seen by many as a betrayal, as unwomanly. At the core of this scene is Mem's acknowledgment that Brownfield responds only to acts of a brutal castrating nature, that this is the way he relates to her and her children, and that this mode of action is the only one that commands his respect. And why shouldn't it be? All of his life he has had to respect the white boss's power and the castrating mode is the form that this power usually takes. Mem finally resorts to his mode of behavior in order to get her husband to act for his own benefit. In the process she challenges the double standard by which society judges her and her husband's actions. In order to help him regain his manhood, in order to force him to break away from the belief that says he is not responsible for his actions, she forcefully shows him his lack of manliness. Most importantly, she insists on being treated as a human being rather than an object. Mem has no choice. If she does not challenge Brownfield's definition of masculinity, she and her children will not survive. She must use her own skills, even if Brownfield feels diminished by them, or her entire family will be destroyed.

Part Five ends with Brownfield's "Yes ma'am." For the moment, Mem has begun to gather strength. But Part Six reminds us that she must maintain and develop her strength even further by redefining herself as a woman, for it begins, "Brownfield lay in wait for Mem's weakness." Brownfield's reaction to Mem's attempt to make him take responsibility for his actions reveals the source of his definition of himself as a man. Although his life is more human in their new house, he is willing to destroy it all, since he has not made it possible in the same way that white men are able to:

> "I done waited a long time for you to come down, Missy," he said when he came home, reeking of alcohol for the first time in almost three years. "This is what I can afford and this is what you going to have to make do with. . . .
>
> "You was going to have your house, straight and narrow and painted and scrubbed, like white folks. You was going to do this, you was going to do that. Shit," he said, "you thought I fucked you 'cause I wanted it? Josie better than you ever been. Your trouble is you just never learned how not to git pregnant. How long did you think you could keep going with your belly full of childrens?"[15]

Brownfield has been lying in wait for the weakness of the womb. Ironically, Mem's strength, her having children, is also her weakness.

Just as the male's inescapable need to take on the forms of masculinity in his society turns him against himself, so the female's distinctive quality, her womb, turns in on her. Even the indomitable strength that flows from motherhood undermines the definition of what her society tells her a woman should be. To save her children Mem must become aggressive rather than passive; she must be willing to create security and comfort for herself rather than have it delivered to her, and she must be willing to do it alone, without a man.

Having taken responsibility for her own actions, Mem's definition of herself as a woman changes. Although she is temporarily defeated by Brownfield, she intends to get well, leave her husband, and hold on to the life she had a glimpse of in her moment of strength. No longer does she plant flowers; no longer will she be the demure wife. But since Brownfield's definition of himself as a man does not change, is in fact assaulted by Mem's redefinition of herself, he must destroy her. No wonder that he kills her with the very gun with which she first proclaimed her recent independence. Tormented by his inability to change, he cannot allow her to. Mem dies violently as did Margaret, a generation before. Like Margaret, "her bloody repose had struck them instantly as a grotesque attitude of profound inevitable rest."

So much for the stereotypical strong black woman who conquers all. Walker calls up the other side of that strong black woman image, as well as the reason why it is emphasized so much in American mythology. That image is necessary because so many black women, like Margaret and Mem, have been crushed and utterly destroyed precisely because they are black and because they are women. Their blood flushes the Copeland quilt with the colors of violent death and with the threads of degeneration. Now the children are left to fend for themselves in a world that will naturally abuse them. Margaret and Mem are examples of Walker's first group of black women, the most abused of the abused. It is important to note that these women are destroyed when they begin to gather strength or to rebel.

Just as their husbands are defeated by an internal as well as an external disorder, both Margaret and Mem are destroyed not only by their husbands and their society but by their "stupid belief that kindness can convert the enemy." They have tried to be women in the traditional southern Christian sense. Margaret tries to rouse Grange to concern by abusing herself, and Mem believes that she can give her own strength and its rewards to Brownfield. Even as they rebel, these women lived and died with their husbands, rather than themselves, foremost on their minds. Brownfield, musing in his jail cell, fixes Mem's essence for us:

> If she had been able to maintain her dominance over him perhaps she would not stand now so finished, a miniature statue, in his mind, but her inherent weakness, covered over momentarily by the wretched muscular hag, had made her ashamed of her own seeming strength.[16]

Fat Josie is the one black woman in the book who is neither virginal nor wifely, and who does not depend on a man for her financial needs. In fact, her profession feeds on the despair of the men around her. But although she is economically independent, Josie's life is another example of the way in which the society's definition of woman and man conflict with one another.

At age sixteen, Josie becomes a whore because her father rejects her when she becomes pregnant. In an attempt to win back his love, she uses her body, her only asset, to earn money to buy him gifts. Walker's presentation of young Josie's fall as a woman is marked by her analysis of the difference between society's view of her lovers, who are encouraged to express their manhood through their sexuality, and its punishment of the woman who succumbs to them. Although the young Josie is expected to attract men through her body, she is also expected to be a virgin. This irresoluble conflict is powerfully dramatized when the very pregnant Josie literally falls at the birthday party she gives for her father:

> Her mother stood outside the ringed pack of men, how many of them knowledgeable of her daughter's swollen body she did not know, crying. The tears and the moans of the continually repentant were hers, as if she had caused the first love-making between her daughter and her daughter's teen-age beau, and the scarcely disguised rape of her child that followed from everyone else. Such were her cries that the men, as if caught standing naked, were embarrassed and they stooped, still in the ring of the pack, to lift up the frightened girl, whose whiskied mind had cleared and who now lay like an exhausted, overturned pregnant turtle underneath her father's foot. He pressed his foot into her shoulder and dared them to touch her. It seemed to them that Josie's stomach moved and they were afraid of their guilt suddenly falling on the floor before them wailing out their names . . . "let'er be," growled her father. "I hear she can do tricks on her back like that."[17]

Forevermore, in her dreams that foot continues to ride Josie. Her father, whom she calls a witch, continues to haunt her. The relish with which Josie does her job, then, is partly based on the anger towards her father, laced with an insatiable desire for the love she never had. Throughout the novel she is presented as a devouring cat, voracious and sly.

Ironically, Josie the whore is also the continuing thread between the various generations of Copelands. As a whore, she is indispensable to the system of sexual and racial conflict within which the frustrated husbands and the anguished wives suffer. She is both Grange and Brownfield's whore, later Grange's wife, and finally Brownfield's co-conspirator. She feels Margaret has taken Grange away from her and hates her. Since Mem is her niece, it is through her that Brownfield meets the budding schoolgirl. But Josie is also angry at Mem for taking Brownfield away from her and feels obligated to wreck his marriage. Years later, Josie the fat whore is replaced by Ruth Copeland, her innocent stepgranddaughter, in Grange's affections. If there is any character in this novel who finds her way into the innards of all the principals, it is Josie. She is the destructive link between father and son. But in using men, Josie is used by them for purposes beyond her single-minded desires. Continually living her father's judgment of her, Josie "felt somehow she was the biggest curse in her life and that it was her fate to be an everlasting blunderer into misery."

So much for the stereotypical loose black woman who gets what she wants through sex. Unlike the stereotype, Josie not only fucks but feels. Although men are encouraged by the society to release their frustrated manhood through her and others like her, she is seen by them as an object to be used rather than a person. In the final analysis she gets nothing but sleepless nights and perhaps a long, wasted life. She sleeps with Grange and then Brownfield, conspires against their wives and children, and finally helps to cause the death of Grange, the man she wants. She ends up as Brownfield had begun, "mumbling what had become for her the answer to everything: 'the white folks is the cause of everything.'"

The children of this book, though, do not conceive of white folks as the source of *their* problems. Trapped by their youth, they are the ones most affected by their parents' patterns of self-hatred. In their prepubescent period they catch this disease by abhorring their parents, and then as their sexuality begins to manifest itself and they become parents, that hatred turns in on them. The children of Brownfield—Daphne, Ornette, and Ruth—delineate the complexity of cause and effect. Who is responsible for their condition—their parents, who are themselves victims, or are their parents victims only because they allow themselves to be? At what point does their responsibility end and the inevitability of fate begin. Is their condition fixed, no matter what they do? Is it too much to ask of a human being that he or she keep the spirit intact in spite of a barrage of attacks?

Throughout the novel, children give us their feeling, their sense of confusion about their parents and the life imposed on them. In fact, one way in which the novel could be described is as a two-child narrative. The first narrative flows through the consciousness of the child Brownfield who never really grows up, who never believes he is a man. The second is concerned with the child Ruth as she struggles into adulthood. At the center of each of these narratives is the figure of Grange, first as the daddy that Brownfield never had and then as the transformed Grange who is Ruth's father in place of her real daddy, Brownfield. Certainly the child point of view is recurrent in Walker's quilting, particularly the point of view of the child who feels rejected or abandoned by the father.

In this novel, as in her short stories, Walker puts much emphasis on the relationship between the fathers and their children. Since the society in which the children develop their sense of values is patriarchal, their belief in their own worth is very much related to the ways their fathers judge them.

Thus the novel begins with a child, Brownfield, as he tries to understand his father. At ten he loves his mother; already his father seems unreachable. Grange hardly ever talks to his son, hardly ever admits his existence. Practically the only words we hear him speak directly to Brownfield when he is a child are, "I ought to throw you down the goddam well," words Brownfield tells us that are not spoken in anger but with pity and regret. Of course, Brownfield is too young to understand that Grange sees in his son the continuation of a life of slavery. Unable to free his son from bondage, he regrets that Brownfield exists at all.

At ten, Brownfield gets a headache, like any child would, trying to comprehend his parents' actions. By fifteen, he has given up trying. By now even his mother eludes him, for her attentions are riveted on securing some small, if fleeting, happiness for herself. Enveloped by the depression of their lives, his parents no longer see him. Even when Grange leaves her home forever, he cannot bear to touch Brownfield or acknowledge any feelings of tenderness for him:

> Brownfield pretended to be asleep, though his heart was pounding so loudly he was sure his father would hear it. He saw Grange bend over him to inspect his head and face. He saw him reach down to touch him. He saw his hand stop, just before it reached his cheek. Brownfield was crying silently and wanted his father to touch the tears. He moved toward his father's hand, as if moving unconsciously in his sleep. He saw his father's hand draw back, without touching him. He saw him turn sharply and leave the room. He heard him leave the house. And he knew, even before he realized his father would never be back, that he hated him for everything and always would. And he most hated him because even in private and in the dark and with Brownfield presumably asleep, Grange could not bear to touch his son with his hand.[18]

Forevermore, Brownfield will repeat to himself and to everyone else that Grange was never a daddy to him, as indeed he was not. When Margaret kills herself, the son realizes that even she would prefer to die for the father rather than live for the son.

In tune with his father's despair, Brownfield begins his abuse of his own children when he realizes that he is caught in the same square of life that his father before him had been caught in. So Daphne, his first child, receives love and tenderness from him until he realizes that he cannot free her from a life of slavery. Also, Brownfield himself never grows up, so it is difficult for him to give the love that he never received. He is forever seeking his father's love even as he hates him. The only way that he can resolve that emotional contradiction is in some way to destroy his father.

Many of the characters in this novel waver between an intense love for the father and an equally intense self-hatred engendered by the rejection of the father. The father's rejection of his child is very much related to his view of that child's future as man or woman. So Grange rejects

Brownfield because he belives he cannot give his son the qualities of power that will fit the society's definition of a man. Brownfield becomes an abusive father when he realizes he cannot give his daughters the gifts that will allow them to be ladies. Josie's father rejects her because she loses her virginity before marriage and therefore can never, in his eyes, be a lady. The society's definition of a person's worth as man or woman distorts the love between father and child.

In the course of the novel, Walker stitches together squares that grotesquely reveal how dependent the children are on the humaneness or inhumaneness of their father. One of these squares, perhaps more than any other in the book, lays out the damage done to Brownfield by his father and by his own inability to accept responsibility for his soul. Brownfield tells Josie that his last child, a boy, was white, not real white but an albino baby who looked just like Grange. In his insanity, the figures that have controlled his life—the daddy who rejected him and the white man—seem to mesh in this baby. Brownfield deliberately kills his only son:

> "An' one night when that baby was 'bout three months old, and it was in January and there was ice on the ground, I takes 'im by the arm when he was sleeping, and like putting out the cat I jest set 'im outdoors on the do' steps. Then I turned in and went to sleep. . . . I never slept so soundly before in my life—and when I woke up it was because of her (Mem) moaning and carrying on in front of the fire. She was jest rubbing that baby what wasn't no more then than a block of ice. Dark as he'd *ever* been though, sorta *blue* looking."[19] . . .

Brownfield explains his action. He killed his son, his future, because he doesn't believe there is any future. The instinct in all living things to see their offspring as the future is reversed in Brownfield's mind. For him his son is despair not hope: "I jest didn't *feel* like going on over my own baby who didn't have a chance in the world whether I went on over him or no." In Brownfield's twisted mind, his despair, his futility, meshes with his hatred of his father and his hatred of himself, for his father's blood flows through him to his son: "I got sick of keeping up the strain." His act is the essence of self-hatred.

The bereft children of the book—Brownfield, Daphne, Ornette, and Ruth—invent ways of ameliorating their pain. Left with no vessel for their trust and faith or the experience to understand what is happening to them, fantasy, particularly about fatherhood, becomes their outlet. The child Brownfield's persistent daydream, a fantasy that he first has after his northern cousins' visit, lasts for five years. Dreaming this dream becomes his favorite occupation:

> He saw himself grown-up, twenty-one or so, arriving home at sunset in the snow. In this daydream there was always snow. . . . In his daydream he pulled up to his house, a stately mansion with cherry-red brick chimneys and

matching brick porch and steps, in a long chauffeur-driven car. The chauffeur glided out of the car first and opened the back door, where Brownfield sat puffing on a cigar. Then the chauffeur vanished around the back of the house, where his wife waited for him on the kitchen steps. She was the beloved and very respected cook and had been with the house and the chauffeur and Brownfield's family for many years. Brownfield's wife and children—two children, a girl and a boy—waited anxiously for him just inside the door in the foyer. They jumped all over him, showering him with kisses. While he told his wife of the big deals he'd pushed through that day she fixed him a mint julep. After a splendid dinner, presided over by the cook, dressed in black uniform and white starched cap, he and his wife, their arms around each other, tucked the children in bed and spent the rest of the evening discussing her day (which she had spent walking in her garden), and making love.

There was one thing that was odd about the daydream. The face of Brownfield's wife and that of the cook constantly interchanged. So that his wife was first black and glistening from cooking and then white and powdery to his touch; his dreaming self could not make up its mind. His children's faces were never in focus. He recognized them by their angelic presence alone, two bright spots of warmth; they hovered about calling him "Daddy" endearingly, while he stroked the empty air, assuming it to be their heads."[20]

At age ten, Brownfield's first daughter Daphne calls herself the Copeland Family Secret Keeper and makes her childhood days bearable by telling her younger sisters stories about the good old days when Brownfield had been a good daddy. In the only way she knows how, the older daughter tries to sow in the younger ones the seeds for regeneration. But the memories are not enough; in fact, they help to make Daphne a nervous child:

> She tried so hard to retain some love for him, perhaps because of her memories of an earlier time, that she became very nervous.[21]

In spite of her efforts to remain whole, Brownfield's attitudes condition Daphne and her sisters' development. His nickname for the nervous Daphne is "Daffy", as an adult she would become a mental patient. Ornette, Brownfield's second daughter, who has no memory of her father's tenderness, is jolly and tough by the age of eight. By the age of four, Ruth, the third daughter, tells her father: "You nothing but a sonnabit."

Ruth, who is the focus of the second half of the book, is born at the same time in the midst of degeneration and regeneration. From her birth, Brownfield does not relate to her as a father. Her mother delivers her herself because her father is too drunk to get the midwife; and on the morning that she is born, Grange, her grandfather rather than Brownfield, builds a fire, cooks stew for the weak Mem, and takes care of the older children. He, rather than Brownfield, takes on the responsibility of the father mainly because he feels guilt about his neglect of his own son. Ruth's benevolent father image is, from her very beginnings, the figure of Grange. When Mem is killed, "Ruth alone could not be pried loose from her grandfather's arms." Rather than going North with her mother's father, she insists on that gloomy Christmas Day that she remain with her father's father, an insistence that results in a bond that will transform the oldest and the youngest of the Copelands.

Part One to Part Seven of this quilt continually reiterates the cyclical motifs of spiritual and physical degeneration within the Copeland family, the most bloody motif being Brownfield's murder of his wife in the presence of their children. Given that climactic act, one would expect the hopeless Copeland pattern to continue. But ironically, Brownfield's murder of Mem breaks the pattern, at least for Ruth. Hope creeps into her life when her grandfather, Grange, resolves to be a father to her, as he never was to Brownfield.

From Part Seven through Part Eleven, about one-half of the book, the grandfather and the granddaughter give each other new life. A new pattern evolves as Grange, the impotent, rejecting father, becomes an involved, caring human being, and as the young child Ruth both seeks her identity through her elder and yet helps him to understand his own life.

Certainly a change in texture is one of the vivid differences between the first and the second half of the book. The first half is gray in its desperation, sharp in its bleakness, tense in its rhythm; the second half, although not without intense tensions or murders, has splashes of golden days, some laughter, and much tenderness. At Grange's farm, ambrosia-making days are mellow marathons, spiced with color and tales, as this section of the book reminds us that there is another side to black life in the South. In helping her to grow, Grange gives Ruth a feeling for her peoples' lore, history, and culture. And he teaches her to dance, for in the dance is the essence of black folk:

> They danced best when they danced alone. And dancing taught Ruth she had a body. And she could see that her grandfather had one too and she could respect what he was able to do with it. Grange taught her untaught history through his dance; she glimpsed a homeland she had never known and felt the pattering of the drum. Dancing was a warm electricity that stretched, connecting them with other dancers moving across the seas. Through her grandfather's old and beautifully supple limbs she learned how marvelous was the grace with which she moved.[22]

Almost always, though, even in the good times, there is an undercurrent of questioning in Walker's stories. In this novel, this undercurrent is the difficult questions that children ask themselves about their ancestors and the world, the answers to which are often complicated and terrifying. Just as the ten-year-old Brownfield wondered about his parents' actions, his father's silence, and his mother's submission, Ruth wonders about her father and mother, about her grandfather's relationship with her father, and about her grandfather's life before she came to live with him. Brownfield could not penetrate his father's stony silence, and Grange gives Ruth not so much answers but the knowledge he has learned in his three, maybe four, lives.

In the talks Grange and Ruth have about themselves and the world, teacher becomes student and student, teacher. At first, precisely because he loves her, Grange wants Ruth to understand the nature of her world, how white folk have caused the misery of black folk and how she must learn to hate them, better still, to avoid them:

> "They are evil."
> "They are blue-eyed devils."
> "They are your natural enemy."
> "Stay away from them hypocrites or they will destroy you."
> "They killed your father and your mother."[23]

But Ruth will not believe that white folks killed her mother, for she had seen her father do it. More than anything, she wants to understand how her father got the way he did: "Ruth turned her father's image over and over in her mind as if he was a great conundrum." In her innocence she knows what she had seen but cannot comprehend its complexity. Can she forgive her father for killing her mother even if she understands that he is a victim? Grange wants his granddaughter to understand the world's cruelty so she might survive and she, at her young age, wants to know love so she can be whole.

Even as Grange instructs his granddaughter in the ways of the cruel world and in understanding how racism affects her life, Ruth's love and her questions lead him into self-examination and reflection. Through the clarity of the third life she gives him, his first and second lives begin to make some sense:

> "The white folks hated me and I hated myself until I started hating them in return and loving myself. Then I tried just loving me, and then you, and ignoring them much as I could. You're special to me because you're a part of me; a part of me I didn't even used to want. I want you to go on a long time, have a heap of children. Let them know what you made me see, that it ain't no use in seeing at all, if you don't see *straight!*"[24]

Old patterns may be torn apart, but they leave old scraps, untied ends. The structure of the first half of the novel is continuous with the second, for although the pattern of Ruth and Grange's life together is new, Brownfield's pattern remains the same. The chapters in which Grange and Ruth are transforming their souls set next to sections in which Brownfield, along with Josie, Grange's now-neglected wife, conspire against his family. Like a ragged but necessary piece of cloth, Brownfield's schemes to hurt Grange interrupt the new pattern. Although Grange feels that "his one duty in the world was (is) to prepare Ruth for some great and herculean task, some magnificent and deadly struggle, some harsh and foreboding reality, . . . It maddened Brownfield that his father should presume to try to raise his child."

What Brownfield feels most in prison is aloneness, the same intense aloneness he had experienced when his parents deserted him. The repetition of this traumatic feeling verifies for him the reasons behind his tragic life:

> "Yeah," said Brownfield, "you'd think more peoples would think about how they ain't got no more say about what goes on with 'em than a pair of shoes or a little black piece of writing in a newspaper that con't move no matter what it stands for. How come we the only ones that knowed we was men?"[25]

The *was* is important, for certainly Brownfield no longer looks at himself as a man but as a force, a force to bring down his father, for Grange's neglect of him represents to Brownfield his father's inability to preserve his own humanity and defend it from the all powerful white man. Brownfield so intensely hates himself that he must hate the one who gave him, if nothing else, existence.

When he leaves prison, nine years of aloneness later, he is clear about what he wants to accomplish in his worthless life. He intends to take Ruth away from his father. He intends to continue the pattern of kin killing. His strategy in pursuing his goal reveals his essence; at his center is the need to be destructive because he feels sorry that he exists at all. More complex than mere self-hatred, his self-pity verifies his own total involvement with himself while denying him any capacity for regeneration.

In the last section of the novel, it is almost as if we are at its beginning. In pursuing his goal, Brownfield confronts his father, only to find that Grange is finally capable of relating to him as a father. In giving his son the sum of the wisdom he had acquired in his three lives, Grange tries to transform the old pattern. In admitting to his son grave errors, the old man insists that Brownfield be a man, that he take some responsibility for his life:

> "I'm talking to you, Brownfield," said Grange, "and most of what I'm saying is *you got to hold tight a place in you where they con't come.* You can't take this young girl here and make her wish she was dead just to git back at some white folks that you don't even *know.* We keep killing ourselves for peoples that don't even mean nothing *to* us!"[26]

But Brownfield is no longer a receptive ten-year-old; his soul has hardened into a changeless stump, for he so hates and pities himself that he cannot reach out to others. In his one meeting with his daughter Ruth, he reveals his inability to change. Although he feels some grief and guilt about the pain he has inflicted on his family, he is unwilling to allow his daughter her life. When Ruth says, "If you love me leave me alone!" he exclaims: "No, I can't do that. I'm a *man*. And a *man's* got to have *some* thing of his own." Brownfield's concept of love is based on his definition of manhood that he has learned from the white folks, the acquisition and the possession of things.

Ruth's innocence, though, does have some impact on Brownfield. It causes him to think about what love might be. He is surprised that "Ruth still ran toward something. This annoyed Brownfield. What did she see in the world that made her even want to grow up?" For a brief moment he sees himself as a human being capable of loving and being loved. But he cannot sustain that moment, for his soul has accepted the fixed nature of reality as he has known it—"The changelessness was now all he had— . . . . He must continue hard as he had begun." Brownfield continues hard, lives the old pattern out until the quilt of kin killing is completed. When he succeeds in having a white judge give Ruth to him, he feels he has triumphed over his father. He has kept the saga of degeneration intact. In effect, he becomes like the white man whom he hates.

But new patterns exist as well. In the one grand, ironic twist of the novel, the new mode of existence takes on the tactics of the old to survive. Grange kills Brownfield, his only son, in the presence of the white judge, to save Ruth, his granddaughter. All of the elements of the novel coexist in this act. Grange kills his son—the old pattern of kin killing; but he spills the blood of his son to save his granddaughter, the new pattern. He does this not only to thwart the power of the white folks that Brownfield has enlisted but also in the very presence of the white judge, the symbol of racist disorder in the South. Grange knows, of course, that in sacrificing his unregenerative son to his granddaughter in the presence of white law, he has also killed himself. The sheriff's men follow him to the home he had vowed to hold inviolate against the white man and there they kill him, gun in hand. He dies as if he were a motherless child, "rocking himself in his own arms to a final sleep."

We know that Grange in killing his son reverted to the old pattern so Ruth, the new pattern, might not just survive but live. His act is based on his vision of what life could be for her:

> And still, in all her living there must be joy, laughter, contentment in being a woman; someday there must be happiness in enjoying a man, and children. Each day must be spent, in a sense, apart from any other; on each day there would be sun and cheerfulness or rain and sorrow or quiet contemplation of life. Each day must be past, present and future, with dancing and winemaking and drinking and as few regrets as possible. Her future must be the day she lived in. . . . Survival was not everything. *He* had survived. But to survive *whole* was what he wanted for Ruth.[27]

We know, too, that Grange's bloody act is necessary if Ruth is to survive whole. It is as if he uses up all of the cloth intended for the old quilt so a new one might be started. Yet in killing Brownfield and himself, Grange has left Ruth alone. Can she avoid the unworkable definition of woman by which her mother and her grandmother were trapped? Must she confront and be defeated by the self-hatred of a man like her father, a self-hatred that is a result of the racist fabric of the South? Can she, as a woman survive whole?

Because Alice Walker's quilt is so compactly made, we cannot help but ask questions that go beyond the Copelands's specific history. To what extent can individuals within a deranged society overcome the destructive male and female definitions that are thrust upon them? What is the relationship between responsibility for one's actions and the hardships that society imposes on us? Does the knowledge of the attacks on the spirit suffice in our struggle to hold onto our souls? The paradox of death-giving-life remains. We wonder if it must be so.

PART II

Meridian: **The Quest of Wholeness**

Alice Walker's second novel, *Meridian,* proceeds naturally from *The Life of Grange Copeland,* as the younger generation from the older. Again, her illumination of the potent process of personal change unifies the bits and pieces of southern life as was true in *The Third Life of Grange Copeland.* Again, the image of the child as a continuing possibility is one of the dominant motifs of the novel. Again, the black woman's struggle is focal to the novel's theme. Whereas Walker's first novel is deep in its penetrating concentration on the Copeland family, her second novel expands the theme of a procession of generations to the history of black people in the South up to a peak period in the 1960s. Like Paule Marshall's second novel, *The Chosen Place, The Timeless People,* Walker's *Meridian* is more inclusive in its scope without losing the depth that comes from concentration on one family at a particular time.

In this story so like a quilt of complex and multiple pieces, Walker gives a vibrant and connected personal and collective history rather than a generalized and sterilized account of the sixties. Meridian, the major character in this book, is a black woman who allows "an idea—no matter where it came from—to penetrate her life." The question that permeates this book and her life is the nature of social change and its relationship to the past and the future, a question that is at the crux of the Civil Rights Movement. In other words, what does one take from the past, which is still often present, to create a new future? What does one throw away? This question is specific in the novel to black people in America as they acknowledge a past born in suffering, fed by violence, conditioned by powerlessness—as they try to create a future, a glowing child out of the past. Again, the intersection of degeneration and regeneration co-exist in this novel as they did in *The Third Life of Grange Copeland.* How do you change the pattern of life without destroying what is essential and good in it? Grange Copeland's last bloody act, killing his son to save his granddaughter, haunts *Meridian.* At the vortex of the book's many strivings is the relationship of violence to change. Is it necessary, is it right, or when is it right to kill to create? Meridian wonders if she could kill for the revolution? And if she could, would she be destroying what she is trying to recreate—the respect and love for life in a society that does not value the lives of every one of its children.

Although both Walker novels examine the impact that social conditions have on personal growth, the difference between the two is as instructive as the similarities. The emphasis in *The Third Life of Grange Copeland* is on the necessity to accept responsibility for one's life, despite overwhelming social restrictions. *Meridian*, however, specifically explores the relationship between a movement for social change and the personal growth of its participants. *Meridian* is a novel of ideas, for Walker attempts to let its constructive elements develop out of her analysis of the history and philosophy of southern blacks, who were the foundation of that movement.

The difference in emphasis between the first novel and the second is crystallized in the difference between their major female characters. Certainly Mem is one of those pitiful "Saints" that Walker described in her essay, *In Our Mothers' Gardens*, for the author's presentation of this character emphasizes the oppression that eventually destroys her rather than the creative sparks that would enable her to hold on. The major character of the novel *Meridian*, on the other hand, is a combination of the three types of black women that Walker described in her essay. Like some of her ancestors, Meridian is a "looney" woman who is physically and psychologically abused. Like Phyllis Wheatley and Nella Larsen, she is given the opportunity to become an exception, torn by "contrary instincts." And like the contemporary black woman that Walker envisions, Meridian becomes an artist by "expanding her mind with action." In *Meridian*, Walker encompassed the past, the present, and the future as her major character uses her heritage to change her society, even as she seeks her own expression. Meridian then is not only a character, she is the embodiment of the novel's major concept, the relationship between personal and social change.

However, since a novel by definition contains its elements through a causal flow of events, one major problem that a writer who is primarily interested in analyzing an idea must solve is the way in which this flow will take place. That is, the structure of the novel must be organic to the ideas, lest the peculiar ability of the novel, its ability to put flesh on ideas, give way to abstract analysis. This problem is heightened when the major idea to be embodied is how the characteristics of an individual human personality relate to the political, racial, and sexual composition of a peculiar society. As a novelist, Walker cannot give us the entire history of this country, in relation to the issues of sexism and racism. As a writer who clearly prefers succinct units, she would not want to. She attempted to solve this problem by using each of the major elements—

its plot movement, its motifs, and its characters—as an economic way of adding specific dimensions to the novel.

Walker's presentation of the plot is integrally connected to *Meridian's* central idea. The novel tells us the story of a black woman, Meridian Hill, who grows up in a small southern town. After an early marriage and divorce, she gives up her child to accept a scholarship to go to college. While in college she is an active participant in the Civil Rights Movement. She falls in love with Truman Held, a black political activist from the North with whom she become pregnant. But when he becomes involved with Lynne Rabinowitz, a Jewish civil rights volunteer, Meridian aborts her baby and has her tubes tied. Truman later marries Lynn, and the relationship between these three characters continue even when the Civil Rights Movement gives way to the idea of violent revolution. Meridian, who is not sure that she can kill, even for the revolution, continues to practice nonviolent resistance in a world that no longer respects it. In her quest for an answer to her questions about the relationship between violence and change, she undergoes a personal transformation and is able to absolve her feelings of guilt about her inability to be a mother. At the end of her quest, she passes on her struggle for wholeness to Truman Held.

This may be an outline of the major events that take place in *Meridian*. But it certainly is not the movement of the plot. The sequence of events is itself a visual representation of the term *revolution*, the moving backward to move forward beyond the point at which you began. Walker indicated her order of presentation to the reader by calling the book and her major character *Meridian* (an echo of Jean Toomer's prophetic poem about America, *The Blue Meridian*) and by listing at the beginning of the novel its many definitions, the essence of which is an ascending series of intersecting circles toward the highest point.

The first chapter, which follows this list, acts as an additional clue to the reader, for it is an outline of the sequence of events as they will be presented in the rest of the novel. Even its name, "The Last Return," suggests the movement backward to move forward. In spite of the fact that the book will largely be occupied with the period of the sixties, it begins with a point of time in the seventies when the strategy of nonviolent resistance is no longer widespread, at a time when the dramatic demonstrations of the Civil Rights Movement have ended, and when most observers would say that the Movement was over. Thus we are invited to see the sixties as history. But the character Meridian continues to practice nonviolent resistance as if it were the present rather than the past. Because of her intransigence, this initial scene invites us to question her sanity or at least the inappropriateness of her actions in time and space.

Because of its tone of slapstick absurdity and its lightning quick movement, this chapter may be a shock to some readers as Walker presents to us the major ideas of her novel in the form of American rituals elongated to such an extent that the absurdity of their essence leaves us unsettled.

It begins with Truman's return to the South. He is seeking Meridian and finds her in Chicokema, a small southern town whose Indian heritage lingers only in its name. Dominated now by white interests, the town is distinguished by its possession of an old army tank bought during the sixties to defend its white inhabitants against outside agitators. In more recent times, its folksy nature has been enhanced by "Marilene O'Shay, One of the Twelve Human Wonders of the World: Dead for Twenty-Five Years Preserved in Lifelike Condition." This dead white woman is presented as the epitome of Southern Womanhood—"A Goddess," "Obedient," "Pure," "Beautiful." In fact, her husband had killed her when she betrayed him with another man. According to the mores of the South, he had been forgiven by family, as well as the civil authorities, because his victim was female and had committed adultery. Piling necromancy upon murder, he has put together this replica of his wife to make money. In keeping with the reality of southern life, "Blacks cannot look at this human wonder, except on their day, Thursday."

With biting surreal stitches, Walker satirizes the lavish trademarks of the South—the white woman protected, indeed mummified, by the sanctimonious rhetoric of her society, but losing even these questionable privileges when she exercises any sexual freedom; the white man using even his kin to make money; the sanctification of violence in the pursuit of protection; the exclusion of black folk even from participating in the lunatic activities of their white counterparts; the preservation of Indian culture in the town's name even after the conquering race has extinguished the original natives. The absurdity of this scene is heightened even more when we watch Meridian employ the weapon of nonviolent resistance against the fortress of values that protects Marilene O'Shay's preserved dead body.

When Truman finally talks to Meridian, our curiosity is further piqued by his assertion that Meridian, who after all lives in America, owns nothing, that she becomes paralyzed from time to time but lives a life of wandering, and that she has "volunteered to suffer." As if daring us to pass judgment on the outmoded and crazy actions of her major character, Walker sardonically smiles at the absurdity of Truman Held, a decidedly nonrevolutionary painter, dressed as he is in a Che Gueverra hairdo and Mao jacket, but whose objections to Meridian's life-style sound practical and sane. The contrast between Truman's pragmatic point of view and Meridian's insistent struggle is crucial to this book's inquiries.

Truman watched her struggle to regain the use of her body.

"I grieve in a different way," he said.

"I know," Meridian panted.

"What do you know?"

"I know you grieve by running away. By pretending you were never
there."

"When things are finished it is best to leave."

"And pretend they were never started?"

"Yes."

"But that's not possible."[28]

Both Truman and Meridian grieve for the Movement, for the idea
that nonviolent action could change the "absurdity" of the Chickemas
all over the South. They grieve in their own way for the collective action
that thrived for a few years in the blood-soiled soil of the South, only to
be replaced by an equally blood-soaked idea. The new idea was to change
their personal lives, as well as the history of the South. Walker juxtaposes the intransigence of Chicokema to the intransigence of Meridian,
while juxtaposing that critical moment in the North when the action of
nonviolent protest is replaced by the idea of violent revolution.

Mentally we find ourselves no longer listening to Truman and Meridian talk in a small southern town in the seventies. Now we are sitting
with Meridian, her best friend Anne-Marion, and other black students
in a New York apartment ten years before Truman will make his last
return to the South. Meridian is confronted with the question. "Will you
kill for the Revolution?" A positive answer to this query meant entry
into or exclusion from many circles. We know that this scene occurred
among black students and intellectuals after the major protest demonstrations had caused do many of them to wonder if allowing oneself to
be hit on the head accomplished very much, if volunteering to suffer was
not a weak posture. We have lived this history. Meridian's essential
characteristic, her resistance to accepting the easy solution, her refusal
to speak the word without living its meaning, reminds us of the many
who succumbed to group pressure whether or not they believed what
they were saying, and the many who simply would not, could not, say
yes without fussing, fighting, questioning.

In creating this historic scene, Walker announces her major motifs.
What Meridian is held by is her past: the children of the South; the face
of her mother in church as she insists that Meridian say the word and
be saved; her father's perennial conversation about the plight of the
Indian; the collective soul of her people that she hears in the music. Held
by these memories, she cannot say yes. Instead, she goes back to the
South to remain close to the people until she can make such a decision
and mean it. She resolves to stay within the action of the sixties until
she can formulate effective action for the seventies.

The New York scene together with our experience in Chicokema formulate the basic idea of the book: the way in which political movements
affect personal lives and how personal lives are the marrow of political
movements. So it follows logically that we find ourselves back in Chico-

kema as Truman and Meridian speak of their personal past; of Lynne, Truman's wife; of his dead child Camara; of Anne-Marion, Meridian's former best friend who still writes her letters of anger and fury. In fusing dream, action, counterpuntal times and places, and motifs and characters, Walker shows us the way to her pattern, a pattern that will be arranged and rearranged as we question Meridian's way of life, her persistent identification of her body with her soul, her past with her present. This insistence is both her strength and her weakness:

> *Truman:* I've never understood your illness, the paralysis, the breaking down
> . . . the way you can face a tank with absoluted calm one minute
> and the next be unable to move. I always think of you as so strong,
> but look at you.[29]

As an embryo, the first chapter presents us with the whole, the rest of the novel will give flesh to Meridian's essence. The book is an unraveling of the reasons for her continued nonviolent protest, as conditioned by her own past and the history of the South, a history that has led her to ask impossible questions and pursue seemingly absurd paths. But Walker's sensitive analysis of Meridian's essence will not move forward in a straight line. As in "The Last Return," Part I, called "Meridian," will travel from a time in the seventies backward beyond Meridian's specific existence to the lives of her mother, grandmother, and great grandmother and then forward to the seventies. Like Part I, the section called "Truman Held," will also proceed from a time outside the drama of the sixties and will go backward only to move forward to the time of the book's beginning. Only the last section, "Ending," will move forward beyond Chicokema to that moment when Meridian resolves her quest. But even then Truman replaces her in the search for wholeness, a search with which the novel begins.

By using time as a circular movement rather than a chronological pattern, the author is able to connect the parts of Meridian's life that are related to her cultural milieu, as well as to the nature of the Civil Rights Movement of which she is a part. Thus the particular events that Walker chooses in her dramatization of the reasons for Meridian's recalcitrance are not random. They are selected with great care so we might understand the influences on Meridian as she develops from a sensitive black girl-child who feels her mother's undercurrents of frustration and resentment to a pensive woman who continues despite the apparent ineffectiveness of the act to use her body to manifest her spirit. In describing Meridian's development, Walker is always taking great pains to heighten those threads that run throughout the life of any young girl in Meridian's particular cultural milieu: the discovery of sex as sordid, the importance of a man in one's life, the possibility of vision, the emptiness of a premature marriage, the hassles of "happy motherhood." Because of the author's resistance to the easy road of generalization, Meridian's development is most specific, but because her pattern exists within the history and culture of her milieu, it intersects with the rhythmic patterns of many others. So when Walker describes Meridian's relationship with Eddie, her boyfriend who would later become her husband, she is not only analyzing Meridian's personal history but prevailing cultural patterns as well:

> Being with him did a number of things for her. Mainly, it saved her from the strain of responding to other boys or even noting the whole category of Men. This was worth a great deal, because she was afraid of men . . . and was always afraid until she was taken under the wing of whoever wandered across her defenses to become—in a remarkably quick time—her lover. This, then was probably what sex meant to her; not pleasure but a sanctuary in which her mind was freed of any consideration for all the other males in the universe who might want anything of her. It was resting from pursuit.
>
> Once in her "sanctuary," she could, as it were look out at the male world with something approaching equanimity, even charity; even friendship. For she could make male friends only when she was sexually involved with a lover who was always near—if only in the way the new male friends thought of her as "So-an-So's girl."[30]

What we begin to see as we examine Walker's quilting is that personal history is an index to cultural history. Her analysis of Meridian's lapse into an early marriage is as much history as the Saxon students' reaction to President Kennedy's funeral on television, an event that involved millions of viewers. Throughout the novel, our quilter composes patterns of events that show how personal and public history mesh to make up the collective process of the sixties. At every turn, every personal experience is selected for emphasis as an indication of the personal history of many, and every public experience is given personal dimensions.

Just as the movement of the plot embodies the concept of revolution in relation to Meridian's personal and social milieu, so recurrent motifs add a philosophical dimension to the novel. As if they were the common threads of a fabric, Walker uses the images of black children and black mothers, of nature and music, and of the relationship between the body and the spirit in every chapter. She is able to use them as compressed images precisely because she concentrates on one of them in each chapter as indicated by its title.

At the crux of all of these images is the concept of animism, which Walker insists is one thing that Afro-Americans have retained of their African heritage. She defines *animism* as "a belief that makes it possible to view all creation as living, as inhabited by spirit"[31] and in so doing stresses the oneness of the natural and the human world. In *Meridian*, Walker attributes this view of the world not only to Afro-Americans but to the original inhabitants of America, the Native Americans. They are, throughout the novel, the motif that stands for the union of the land and its people. So the book begins with a quotation from Black Elk, which fuses the dominant motifs of the novel, even as it presents the dream of Nature's wholeness destroyed:

> I did not know then how much was ended. When I look back now I can still see the butchered women and children lying and scattered all along the crooked gulch as plain as when I saw them with eyes still young. And I can see that something else died there in the bloody mud, and was buried in the blizzard. A People's dream died there. It was a beautiful dream . . . the nation's hope is broken and scattered. There is no center any longer, and the sacred tree is dead.[32]

As this quotation suggests, Walker uses motifs that illuminate the concepts of wholeness and fragmentation, both of which are related not only to Meridian's past and present but also to the Civil Rights Movement. By describing her quest as a search for health, Meridian insists that to be whole, there must be a unity of body and mind. So, too, the central action of the Civil Rights Movement, body resistance to manifest the protest of the mind, attempted to demonstrate this oneness. The process of putting one's body on the line, of resisting oppression without inflicting violence, is crucial to the Movement's spirit—the desire to change without destroying, to maintain the integration of body and spirit, to resist separation and alienation.

The image in the novel that most fully expresses the concept of animism is *music*, which for Walker is itself "the unselfconscious sense of collective oneness."[33] The texture of *Meridian* is punctuated with the expression of the people's collective soul, music—not only music as an individual or extraordinary accomplishment, but as a part of the flow of life at parties, in church, while working, with friends and lovers, in civil rights demonstrations, in social action. In practically every chapter of the book, there is some music, except in the "Lynne" chapters where Walker seems consciously to replace it with art and poetry. Even the book's structure is naturally based on music. Like a circular rhythmic pattern, short chapters follow long ones, creating syncopated beats. There are starts and stops within every chapter, melodious outpourings, and dissonant sharps. Meridian, as the character who is at the foundation of the book's structure, articulates her most important doubts and revelation in images of music:

> Meridian alone was holding onto something the others had let go. If not completely, then partially—by their words today, their deeds tomorrow. But what none of them seemed to understand was that she felt herself to be, not holding onto something from the past, but *held*—by something in the past: by the memory of old black men in the South, who caught, by surprise in the eye of a camera never shifted their position but looked directly by; by the sight of young girls singing in a country choir, their hair shining with brushings and grease, their voices the voices of angels. When she was transformed in church, it was always by the purity of the singers' souls, which she could actually *hear* the purity that lifted their songs like a flight of doves above her music-

drunken head. If they committed murder—and to her even revolutionary murder was murder—*what would the music be like?* She had once jokingly asked Ann-Marion to imagine the Mafia as a singing group.[34]

The emphasis on music in the novel is of course partially based on its central position in black culture. But Walker does not merely rest on this often stated truism, for she shows us that the reason why music is so central to the culture is because it is the deepest connective between the creative force in human beings and nature itself. Through the makings of music, nature is renewed despite man's attacks on it, just as the ripped out tongue of the slave Louvenia becomes the seeds for Sojourner, the Music Tree, the most beautiful magnolia tree in the land.

Meridian's quest reaches its peak when she understands that "it is the song of the people, transformed by the experience of each generation that holds them together, and if any part of it is lost the people suffer and are without soul." It is significant that this realization of Meridian's takes place within the context of social change, as the people come together to honor and remember one of their sons who had struggled for their collective freedom.

> There was a reason for the ceremony she had witnessed in the church. And, as she pursued this reason in her thoughts, it came to her. The people in this church were saying to the red-eyed man that his son had not died for nothing, and that if his son should come again they would protect his life with their own. "Look," they were saying, "we are slow to awaken to the notion that we are only as other women and men, and even slow to move in anger, but we are gathering ourselves to fight for and protect what your son fought for on behalf of us. If you will let us weave your story and your son's life and death into what we already know—into the songs, the sermons, the "brother and sister"—we will soon be so angry we cannot help but move. Understand this, they were saying, "the church (and Meridian knew they did not mean simply "church" as in Baptist, Methodist or what not, but rather communal spirit, togetherness, righteous convergence), "the music, the form of worship that has always sustained us, the kind of ritual you share with us, there are the ways to transformation that we know. We want to take this with us as far as we can."[35]

In this small country church, Meridian sees the totality of experiences that the Civil Rights Movement had been for black folk. As they have always done, the folk have incorporated into their ritual the history of the movement, outward signs that indicate the depth of their experience, the measure of their transformation. So the words of the old songs have changed: the minister speaks in a voice like Martin Luther King about the politics of the nation rather than the omnipotence of God; the traditional painting of Jesus is replaced by a painting of an angered black man called B. B. with sword. The music, the music rises, incorporating all, articulating that which cannot be articulated, manifesting the continuing constancy of the entire tradition.

It is through the black ritual of constancy and change that Meridian comes to know that "she would kill, before she allowed anyone to murder the man's son again," for she realizes that in this hallowed setting, the contemplation of murder would receive the incredible spiritual work necessary to transform it into righteousness. Her realization not only frees her, it gives her health. Her body and spirit are fused in this moment of vision, a moment in which she is no longer apart, no longer alone, but part of a whole that fuses the personal, the political, the spiritual. Such a vision, rooted in ritual, is given only to those who would pass through the terror of conflict to see that the life of all is their life and that their life is the life of all.

The section called "Camara" answers the question Meridian had asked in the first chapter, "The Last Return": "If they committed murder—and to her even revolutionary murder was murder—what would the music be like?" In the ritual, the forces of conservatism and revolution and constancy and change join hands, as the essence of the heritage of black people, the music that articulates their history, is affected by secular and spiritual changes in the present.

Just as the image of music connects the motifs of wholeness that Walker uses throughout the novel, so the concept of guilt encompasses the motifs of fragmentation. Because as Black Elk put it, "the sacred tree is dead," because the mind and the body, the land and its people, are separated from each other; natural basic human relationships are poisoned by the thorns of guilt. Throughout the novel, the relationship between mother and child, man and woman, are distorted by the inability of society to see all life as sacred.

The wondrous fragility of life is compressed into the faces of the many black children, who like mist appear and reappear through the book. Their melodic faces connect the bits and pieces of the South's complexity. What all of these children have in common is the precariousness of their existence. They may be aborted before they even have a chance to live; they may be given away; they may be assaulted or killed. Like The Wild Child, they may be motherless children, or like the child-mother in "Ending," they may be children who kill their own children. Alongside their tentative child bodies stand the seemingly substantial figures of black mothers buttressed by the monumental myth of black motherhood, a myth that is based on the true stories of sacrifice black mothers had had to commit for their children. Walker chronicled the history of the mothers, and their history in turn organizes her analysis of the southern milieu. The history, then, of black Southerners is an essential piece of fabric in this quilt but not as dates of battles or even the accomplishment of singular important black figures but as the natural process of generation and regeneration inherent in all forms of life.

Ironically, however, Walker suggested that the fruits of this struggle may not only be strength or even extraordinary accomplishment but guilt; that we cannot reap the benefits of strength unless we acknowledge the limitations of guilt. Throughout the book we are reminded that the sense of shame develops in the living, not necessarily because they have done something wrong, but also because they know, feel, that others have given up their lives for them. As a hated people living in a land opposed to their regeneration, blacks by their very existence elicited monumental suffering and sacrifices from each other. At the peak of this sacrificial hierarchy stands the relationship between the parent and child, the paradox of life-giving guilt. In giving life to children who were both unwanted and unappreciated by society, Walker's mothers also had to give up much of their own lives to sustain their children's. The children know they survive only because their parents committed acts of extraordinary suffering. In the novel, the relationship among Meridian, her mother, and her maternal ancestors is the major, although not the only, extension through which the motif of guilt is explored:

> Meridian found, when she was not preoccupied with the Movement that her thoughts turned with regularity and necessity to her mother, on whose account she endured wave after wave of an almost primeval guilt. She imagined her mother in church, in which she had invested all that was still energetic in her life, praying for her daughter's soul, and yet, having no concern, no understanding of her daughter's *life* whatsoever; but Meridian did not condemn her for this. Away from her mother, Meridian thought of her as Black Motherhood personified, and of that great institution she was in terrible awe, comprehending as she did the horror, the narrowing of perspective, for mother and for child, it had invariably meant.[36]

Meridian feels that her mother is truly great because she "had persisted in bringing them all (the children, the husband, the family, the race) to a point beyond where she, in her mother's place, her grandmother's place, her great-grandmother's place, would have stopped." Along with life, then, the children receive from their ancestors a heritage of sacrifice and suffering, a heritage that they feel they cannot always maintain.

Since life demands such extraordinary sacrifices, sex, which is its cause, is rife with danger, particularly for the women. Throughout the novel, the role that sex plays in the development of girl-children into women and boy-children into men is at best static, at worst tragic. The body as sensual is almost always problematic. Often too late the girls realize that it is through the fecundity of their bodies their lives can be limited or even ruined. The only worth they find in themselves much of their early life is to make their bodies appealing to men, only to find that the fruits of that appeal come to them before they have even realized who they are:

> For all their bodies assertion, the girls moved protected in a dream. A dream that had little to do with the real boys galloping past them. For they did not perceive them clearly but as they might become in a different world from the one they lived in.[37]

Like the seventeen-year-old Meridian, many girls are dropouts from high school, divorced wives, and young mothers; like her husband, Eddie, many of the men are destined always to be boys, "fetching and carrying, courteously awaiting orders from someone above." Or if they resist, as many would in the civil rights demonstrations, they might be pummeled, kicked, or even killed in their attempt to hold onto their spirit. Given the precariousness of life, the body, as the means through which one's life may be ruined or taken away, is almost always "malingering," its usefulness maintained only through the strict tenets of the Baptist Church, lest everything be lost.

Just as the body can become the tomb of the mind, the mind's anguish can diminish the body, for these two entities are not separate but one. Violence to one is violence to the other. Mental states, particularly the flaccid bubble of guilt, induce dreams and hallucinations, visions that in turn affect the body. The guilt that Meridian feels in not living up to her mother's expectations about motherhood is expressed first in her recurring dream of death and then in her neglect of her own body, later in her "blue spells," in her temporary loss of sight, and finally in her occasional bouts with paralysis. Her body state reveals her spirit, just as the act of nonviolent resistance expresses the spiritual position of the demonstrators.

The thorns of guilt are woven not only into the fabric of Meridian's life but into the heritage of black people as well. That heritage contains within it the quality of powerlessness as well as strength. Thus many would erase aspects of their history from their memory even before they would understand them. In the novel, Walker uses the story of the tree Sojourner to amplify this point. Legend has it that this tree was planted on the ripped-out tongue of the slave storyteller Louvenia:

> Louvenia's tongue was clipped out at the root. Choking on blood, she saw her tongue grounded under the heel of Master Saxon. Mutely, she pleaded for it, because she knew the curse of her native land. Without one's tongue in one's mouth or in a special spot of one's own choosing, the singer in one's soul was lost forever, to grunt and snort through eternity like a pig.
>
> Louvenia's was kicked toward her in a hail of sand. It was like a thick pink rose petal, bloody at the root. In her own cabin she smoked it until it was as soft and pliable as leather. On a certain day, when the sun turned briefly black, she buried it under a scrawny magnolia tree on the Saxon plantation.
>
> Even before her death, forty years later the tree had outgrown all the others around it. Other slaves believed it possessed magic. They claimed the tree could talk, make music, was sacred to birds and possessed the power to obscure vision. Once in its branches, a hiding slave could not be seen.[38]

Louvenia's tragedy is transformed, through the process of Nature, into beauty, for although the Sojourner stands as a reminder of brutal slavery, it stands nevertheless resplendent in its flowering. That the tree is the only thing Meridian's fellow students would destroy in their first social protest at Saxon College illustrates how little they understand and accept their heritage, one of suffering as well as resistance. Although cut to the ground, years later the tree would begin to grow, its tiny sprouts a message of hope.

Like the mystery of the Sojourner, the Civil Rights Movement would transform the agony of black existence into a measure of its persistence. By using the technique of nonviolent resistance, the movement changed the quality of powerlessness into a powerful weapon of protest without doing violence to the spirit. In "volunteering to suffer," the participants of this social revolution confronted the totality of black people's heritage—the strength, the wisdom, and the shame. By insisting that all creation is inhabited by the spirit, the movement harkened back not to a Western Christian tradition, which its enemies also embraced, but to a deeper source, the African concept of animism.

The pervasive feelings of guilt as well as its cause, the philosophical perception of the universe as fragmented, are countered by the attempts of the person Meridian and by a social force, the Civil Rights Movement, to seek wholeness. Meridian is able to pursue her quest, is able to understand the necessity for it because she has been intensely affected by the Movement, and paradoxically, that thrust for social change existed precisely because persons like Meridian, who made it up, came from a tradition that saw creation as one, as inhabited with spirit. The truth that Meridian learns through her quest, the message that she passes unto Truman, at the end of the novel, fuses the motifs of guilt and animism:

> there is water in the world for us
> brought by our friends
> through the rock of mother and god
> vanishes into sand
> and we, cast out alone
> to heal
> and re-create
> ourselves
>
> i want to put an end to guilt
> i want to put an end to shame
> whatever you have done my sister
> (my brother)
> know i wish to forgive you
> love you
> it is not the crystal stone
> of our innocence
> that circles us
> not the tooth of our purity
> that bites bloody our hearts.[39]

Just as the movement of the plot is a symbol of revolution and the motifs of the novel reiterate the concepts of wholeness and fragmentation, so the characters add another dimension to the novel. The relationship between Meridian Hill, a black woman, Truman Held, a black man, and Lynne Rabinowitz, a white woman, set as it is within the context of a social revolution, is an exploration of the ways in which sexism and racism have affected the people of America. In addition, Walker's analysis of their personal lives indicates why the black woman, the black man, and the white woman were major actors in the Civil Rights Movement.

The units of this novel are in themselves a graph of their relationship. The novel is divided into three parts in which a mind-voice directs the flow of thought and action: "Meridian," which flows through the past and present consciousness of Meridian; "Truman Held," which is dominated by the mind-voice of his wife, Lynne, as well as by his own; and "Ending" in which the voices of Truman and Meridian play with and against one another.

Lest we see these characters primarily as types, however, Walker emphasizes their individuality by introducing other characters who are similar to Meridian, Truman, and Lynne, yet who react differently to similar situations. The most important of these is Anne-Marion, for she persists throughout the novel. Like Meridian she is black and intelligent and is involved in the Civil Rights Movement. She and Meridian are best friends in college and share many political activities. But although Meridian is always groping for meaning, even to the point of illness, Anne-Marion is confident, practical, unquestioning. Meridian is compelled to seek the answer to the dilemma of human beings' injustice to each other, but Anne-Marion is content with being the victor rather than the victim. Throughout the novel, her voice and Meridian's will counterpoint each other. Similarly, other black men like Tommy Odds, and white women like Margaret, will help define Truman and Lynne's particular personalities as well as extend the meaning of their struggle. The novel's characters, major and minor, intersect with each other and are a part of but yet distinct from each other. In unison they all illuminate Meridian's search for wholeness, for their particular actions are alternatives to her distinctly difficult quest. Eventually all of their paths lead back to her, as well as to the ideas that penetrate her existence, the questions that lie unanswered at the core of the movement for human justice.

Why does Walker choose Meridian, a lower-middle-class, southern black woman who could have escaped from her modest condition to be the character compelled to pursue this difficult although illuminating quest? The novel supplies us with the author's reasons, for they are as significant as Meridian's quest.

Meridian's own traditions allow her to be that pilgrim. As a black woman, her antecedents, by their very existence, were deviants of the society—female, in that they had breasts, vaginas, and wombs but non-women according to the mores of American society, which defined women as nonworkers, asexual, and fair. From Meridian's own personal ancestors, her great-grandmother who had literally starved herself to death to sustain her children, to her racial ancestors, women like Harriet Tubman and Sojourner Truth, Meridian's legacy from the past embodies the idea of personal suffering for a greater good. Within that tradition ". . . black women were always imitating Harriet Tubman escaping to become something unheard of. . . . Outrageous, if even in a more conventional way black women struck out for the unknown." Often that striking out took the form of steadfast devotion to a goal for which one suffered in the ascent to the top, like Langston Hughes's "Mother" whose life "wasn't no crystal staircase," but one of arduous climbing and climbing for the welfare of her children.

Yet black women had not only struck out for the unknown in the territory of suffering for they, as deviants, also sought bodily pleasure, that particular form of ecstasy denied to women in American culture. Clearly, Feather Mae, Meridian's outrageous great-grandmother, had also struck out for the unknown—the pleasure, the ecstasy of the body, she experienced in Indian religion. In either version of the quest, the note is one of unconventionality. Deviants at birth, black women could more easily assume the efficacy of the unknown, test forbidden waters, than other American women who were believed to be normal.

That, however, is not the whole story, for the deviant in any society pays a price, the price of uncertainty, the denial of their experience as valid. So even as black women struck out for the unknown or suffered for a goal, they did so often because they had no choice. Their "extreme purity of life was compelled by necessity" so when they could choose, they naturally chose the norm, sometimes with a vengeance that underscored their long years of suffering. Buttressed by the knowledge that the abysm of hardship was one-half step behind them, many of them galloped to security, girded their loins, starched their homes, and swallowed wholesale the feminine mythology from which they had been excluded. Often they found, like Meridian's mother, that they had exchanged sheer hardship for sheer frustration. Before they *knew* their lives were not their own; later they believed if they improved themselves they would have life, only to find that they were no longer trapped by being outside the norm but by being inside it. Applauded as strong, assailed by the weight of frustration, these women felt themselves caught between the heroism of their past and the mundane boredom of their existence. In both cases, either without or within the norm, the common denominator in their lives was their role as mother. Whether they were slave-women for whom "freedom meant that they could keep their own children," or women like Mrs. Hill who could declare, "I have six children, though I never wanted to have any and I have raised everyone myself," the ones for whom these women sacrificed their lives were their children.

Through Meridian's experiences, Walker examines one of the society's major contradictions about black women. The primary role to which they have been assigned and for which they are perpetually praised is also, paradoxically, the means by which they are cut off from life. Since, in principle, society places motherhood on a pedestal, while, in reality, it rejects individual mothers as human beings with needs and desires, mothers must both love their role as they are penalized for it. True for all mothers, this double-edged dilemma is heightened for black women because society does not value their children. As they are praised for being mothers, they are also damned as baby machines who spew out their products indiscriminately upon the society.

It is no wonder that Meridian, a sensitive girl-child who understands she had shattered her mother's emerging self, would break the pattern by giving her own child away not only because she wants to go to college (and of course mothers are not permitted there), but also because she knows she will do to her own son as her mother had done to her—poison his growth with thorns of guilt. "When she gave him away, she did so with a light heart. She did not look back, believing that she had saved a small person's life." But in keeping with the long tradition that preceded her, Meridian cannot forget her child as Gwendolyn Brooks' "mother" cannot forget her abortions. Meridian's quest is certainly intensified by the search for her child in the faces of all the young children she encounters in the book. Her guilt about her inability to live up to the standards of motherhood that had gone before her shatters her health and propels her on the search for salvation.

Her college years are filled with abortive attempts to give some part of herself as a mother. The first is her encounter with The Wild Child, "a young girl who had managed to live without parents, relatives or friends for all of her thirteen years." Meridian's reaction to this child when she first sees her is the beginning of a pattern in her life:

> The day Meridian saw The Wild Child she withdrew to her room in the honors house for a long time. When the other students looked into her room they were surprised to see her lying like a corpse on the floor beside her bed, eyes closed and hands limp at her sides. While lying there she did not respond to anything; not the call to lunch, not the phone, nothing.[40]

Meridian captures The Wild Child and tries to civilize her only to have her killed by a speeder as she tries to escape. Despite her first failure, Meridian is compelled to try again. Her abortive attempt at motherhood is repeated in her encounter with Anne, the young girl she had called to join her in a Civil Rights demonstration but whose screams Meridian believes she heard in one of the cells after they were arrested. The climax of her abortive mother syndrome is the abortion she must have after Truman Held sleeps with her once and leaves her for Lynne.

Ironically, Truman leaves Meridian because he finds out that she had been married, had had a child, and had given it away. "Yet had she approached him on the street dragging her child with her by the hand he would never have glanced at her." But Meridian does not know this. Believing that she cannot sustain motherhood beyond conception and giving birth, she gives it up. She has her tubes tied, an act that intensifies rather than eradicates her guilt.

Meridian is caught between her own tradition, her own personal desire to become a mother, and the fact that motherhood seems to cut her off from the possibilities of life and love. Paradoxically, it is this contradiction that precipitates her quest. In her pilgrimage toward wholeness, she becomes a mother not in the biological sense but in her insistence on nurturing life rather than destroying it. Her philosophical stance is symbolized in the novel by the actions of nonviolent resistance that she commits for the sake of the children in "Ending." By enlarging the concept of motherhood, she is able to absolve her guilt about her inability to live up to the society's standards. She passes on this struggle, the struggle to defend life to Truman, so he, too, may understand that all life is sacred.

Through Meridian's conflicts with society's concept of motherhood, Walker also explores the effects that this view has on the relationship between black men and women. At the core of society's criticism—that all black women are good for is having babies—festers the slightly hidden accusation that they are driven by sexual impulses they cannot control. The criticism of their continuous fecundity is in reality a judgment upon their promiscuity. Yet being a sexual partner to a man, preferably one man, is all society expects of them. No serious attention is given to the development of their minds or imagination, since all girls, particularly black girls, will grow up to be mothers. This line of reasoning is held tautly in place even as society presents sex as sordid.

Due to the ambivalence surrounding sex and its result, motherhood, Meridian's community never instructs her about it. On the one hand, she is told to "keep your panties up and your dress down," and on the other hand, her entire worth as she grows older resides in her ability to get a boyfriend and keep him. Her first sexual experiences, then, take place within the realm of secrecy and sordidness. As a result, Meridian realizes that what was expected of her in sex was not love or mutual affection but "giving in." But "as much as she wanted to—her body, that is— never had any intention of *giving in*. She was suspicious of pleasure. She might approach it, might gaze on it with longing but retreat was inevitable." Since sexual pleasure becomes associated in her mind with giving in rather than sharing, she cannot experience it, for the urge to self-protection is even more instinctive than body pleasure. Yet Meridian knows that her worth is determined by her position as "so-and-so's girlfriend," so she indulges in it.

Sex, as the act of "giving in" for the woman and conquering for the man, characterizes Meridian's relationship with men in this novel. Her deepest involvement with a man, her friendship with Truman Held, develops from a sexual game-play into a truly intense and complex sharing, but only after sex and the possibility of children have been eliminated from it. The nature of their friendship is anticipated by the mystical experience Meridian shares with her father in the Sacred Serpent burial grounds, a sharing that gives them a tangible connection to the past as well as the sensation of body ecstasy.

Meridian's spiritual communion with her father is exceptional, however, for she soon discovers that the men she meets believe it their duty or right to conquer her body. Whether they are the hot-blooded lovers of her teenage years, or professionals like the doctor who punctuates her abortion with the exclamation, "I could tie your tubes if you'll let me in on some of all this extracurricular activity," their stance is always the same. Nor does their age or intellectual development make any difference in their approach to her. Mr. Raymonds, the old university professor for whom Meridian works during her college years, spends much of his time chasing her around his desk in spite of the fact that he is "very emotional about protecting the virtue of black women from white men."

This old-fashioned "race man" is a foil for Truman Held, an activist and artist in the Civil Rights Movement. As a black man who is consciously struggling for social change, we would think that he should not need, like Eddie, to conquer women. Meridian first meets him when she goes to volunteer for the movement and their relationship initially forms in the crucible of the struggle for social justice:

> Within minutes they had been beaten inside, where the sheriff and his deputies waited to finish them. And she realized why Truman was limping. When the sheriff grabbed her by the hair and someone else began punching her and kicking her in the back, she did not even scream, except very intensely in her own mind, and the scream was Truman's name. And what she meant by it was not even that she was in love with him: What she meant by it was that they were at a time and a place in History that forced the trivial to fall away—and they were absolutely together.[41]

Truman seems to Meridian "unlike any other black man she had known. He was a man who fought against obstacles, a man who could become anything, a man whose words were unintelligible without considerable thought." This was in contrast to her husband, Eddie, who "she thought would always be a boy," and "who was not interested in education but in finishing school." Here certainly is a man, we would think, who has the sensitivity, the desire, to know Meridian, a man who would appreciate her spirit, as well as her body. But although Truman may struggle with Meridian for social change, he is primarily interested in sleeping with her.

It is especially significant that during her pilgrimage, Meridian does not relate to Truman or any other man in a sexual way. Left unresolved in the novel is the way in which men and women may be able creatively to relate to each other if they are sexually involved. Rather Walker provides us with some reasons why such a union is difficult to achieve, for her analysis of Truman's character is set within the context of his understanding of his own heritage as filtered through his relationship with women.

Truman's view of the opposite sex, which is prevalent, reveals the fragmentation that society fosters between men and women. On the one hand, Truman is conditioned to pursue women, but on the other hand, he reveres virginity. Because he is an intellectual as well as a man, he expects his mate to be wordly as well as virginal—that is, to be a woman who is well-to-do enough to know the world without having to endure its hard knocks. The veneer of the world must be there without its messy experiences. Thus he can tell Meridian that the reason why he is interested in the white exchange students is "because they read the New York Times." His wife must be knowledgeable although not sullied; she can be romantically idealistic because she has not had to deal with reality; thus she will admire him as a hero.

Such requirements cannot be met by most southern black women, who, like Meridian, grew up in the confines of a small community in which the women were governed only by the laws of survival and the necessities of motherhood. Because these black women had to be heroic for generations, they would be more informed by reality and less likely to be carried away by waves of adoration. Certainly not as mobile as black men, their provincial background, as well as their contact with sex (reality for a woman), would make them unsuitable for men like Truman who, day-by-day, expected more from life.

The fluid contradiction that Truman and many other black intellectuals like him faced was that the people they sought to save were too narrow, too ordinary, too provincial, for them to live with. As black, he is also seen by American society as a deviant, for in contrast to the prevailing definition that a man is worldly, powerful, and clever, the black man is seen in terms of his penis and his propensity to violence. Truman, however, is a thinker, an activist, an artist, who not only rejects society's definition of him but the lot in life it assigns him. One way in which he can transform the world's definition of him is by being as unlike Afro-American men as he can be, while being the epitome of the group— hence his continuous mouthing of the French language, his playing on the thrill that his blackness, his difference, evokes in liberal whites. It is as if Truman falls in love with his deviancy in society because it makes him exceptional when that uniqueness can be cast in a positive or at least a glamourous glow rather than in the stark light of racism. He does not want to be white, nor does he want to be like ordinary black men. Hence he rejects aspects of black culture like religion (which he calls fanatical) and black women because he wants, as any man would, "a woman perfect in the eyes of the world," a woman who would be the measure of his own worth. He wants to be seen as an exception, as heroic, as the conquering prince, as a man.

Although Truman shares political struggle with Meridian, as black men always have with black women, he wants a woman who knows less than he about reality, a woman who can see him as a prince.

> At times she [Meridian] thought of herself as an adventurer. It thrilled her to think she belonged to the people who produced Harriet Tubman, the only American woman who'd led troops in battle.
> But Truman, alas, did not want a general beside him. He did not want a woman, who tried, however encumbered by guilts, and fears and remorse, to claim her own life. She knew Truman would have liked her better as she had been as Eddie's wife for all that he admired the flash of her face across a picket line—an attractive woman, but asleep.[42]

He leaves her for Lynne who has had the time to read everything, the leisure to be idealistic, and the training to adore him, for Lynne sees her role not as claiming her own life but his life as her own.

Paradoxically, Truman and Meridian both see themselves as exceptional, Meridian because she does not measure up to the standards of her tradition and Truman because he cannot accept much of his tradition. Until their discomfort with themselves is eased, they cannot love each other. Appropriately in the novel, it is left to Lynne in her irrepressible way to describe their emotional condition without really understanding it:

> What's between you is everything that could have happened and didn't because you were both scared to death of each other, you knew. Not your *average* black man and woman, of course who accept each other as natural, but people like you and Truman who have to keep analyzing each other's problems.[43]

Truman Held's section in the novel is primarily concerned with his unraveling of the effects of sexism and racism upon him. Because he does marry Lynne, he grows increasingly aware of his own discomfort with himself, for he is forced to do so by the many challenges America presents to any "deviant" couple. But before he can look at himself, the South rivets his attention on Lynne as white and as woman. The chapter "Of Bitches and Wives" is one of the most lucid although complex analyses in the literature of interracial love and marriage. Although Truman is uncomfortable in his relationship with Lynne, he has no context in which to put it until Tommy Odds, one of his friends, loses his arm in a demonstration. Tommy Odds's loss gives him vision: "All white people are motherfuckers." The leap that Truman could now make is that Lynne is unworthy, is guilty, because she is white. But Walker does not let her character off so easily, for Truman knows that to be guilty of a color would necessarily end in racism, which is precisely what he is against.

So he moves to the next logical step: "Was Lynne guilty because she was a white woman? Because she was a route to Death? Because she had power over them?" But this Truman feels would be to deny Lynne her humanity and to see her as "some kind of large mysterious doll." Yet his friends, even the movement, begin to now exclude her from their trust, precisely for this reason.

As he muses, Truman comes closer and closer to the thorn that is really troubling him. It is not whether Lynne is guilty but whether *he* is guilty—of loving a white bitch. Yet would his rejection of Lynne on these grounds mean that he loved black people? His circlings around this question cover much ground:

> He had read in a magazine just the day before that Lamumba Katurim had gotten rid of his. She was his wife, true but apparently she was even in that disguise perceived as evil, a cast off. And people admired Lamumba for his perception. It proved his love of his own people they said. But he was not sure. Perhaps it proved only that Lamumba was fickle. That he married his wife in the first place for shallow reasons. Perhaps he was considering marrying a black woman (as the article said he was) for reasons just as shallow. For how could he state so assuredly that he would marry a black woman next when he did not appear to have any specific black woman in mind?
>
> If his own sister told him of her upcoming marriage to Lamumba he would have to know some answers before the nuptial celebration. Like, how many times would Lamumba require her to appear on television with him, or how many times would he parade her before his friends as proof of his blackness.[44]

Certainly the reasons must go deeper than that. In attempting to assuage the terrible feeling of rising guilt within him, Truman asks the pivotal question: Is it possible to love the wrong person? When is loving anyone an error?

Tommy Odd's accusations make Truman twist and turn because he knows that his feeling for Lynne had been undergoing subtle changes for some time. Why were they? Was it because of the pressure he was receiving from his friends in the Movement about his loving a white woman? Was it his own guilt that perhaps he did not truly love his own people? Walker amplified his initial analysis in "Of Bitches and Wives," when years later Truman thinks about the differences between Lynne and Meridian:

> Truman had felt hemmed in and pressed down by Lynne's intelligence. Her inability to curb herself, her imagination, her wishes and dreams. It came to her, this lack of restraint, which he so admired at first and had been so refreshed by, because she had never been refused the exercise of it. She assumed that nothing she could discover was capable of destroying her.[45]

So Truman's feeling for Lynne changes for precisely the same reasons it had begun: his desire to have a wife who is both worldly and idealistic, a wife whose intense idealism is based on freedom and security. Truman rejects the part of his heritage that had developed because it was not cradled in freedom and cuts himself off from the strength and control that accompanies such restrictions. In desiring a woman "who is perfection in the eyes of the world," he overlooks the galling fact that *his* world is not perfect in the eyes of the world. From what books was Lynne to learn the specific tradition of strength and poise, that precarious balancing that he identifies with Meridian. Meridian, as she always does in the novel, brings this point home when he tells her years later he loves her:

> "For Lynne's sake alone I couldn't do it," she had said languidly, rocking slowly in her yellow chair. . . .
> "How can you take her side?"
> "Her side? I'm sure she's already taken it. I'm trying to make the acquaintance of my side in all this. What side is mine? . . ."
> "Loving you is different—"
> "Because I'm black?"
> "You make me feel healthy, purposeful—"
> "Because I'm black?"
> "Because you're *you*, damn it! The woman I should have married and didn't!"
> "Should have loved and didn't," she murmured. And Truman sank back staring, as if at a lifeboat receding in the distance.[46]

Truman is unable to love Meridian because she embodies the many aspects of his tradition: the suffering, the lack of freedom, the impotency, the promiscuity, the provinciality, the restrictions. To survive, she, as many others, has to struggle to create beauty out of those limits, a beauty that cannot simply be given but must be earned.

In his attempt to understand this quality, Truman feels compelled to pursue Meridian on her "looney" sojourn through the South. As his teacher in "Ending," she asks him the questions about mother and child, woman and man, the principle of struggle, and the limits of pragmatism that he must confront to be whole. Although she can guide him to the source of his strength and his pain, as a black man he must unravel his own knots. He must pursue his own quest:

> "I meant it when I said it sets you free. You are free to be whichever way you like, to be with whoever, or whatever color or sex you like—and what you risk in being truly yourself, the way you want to be, is not the loss of me."[47]

The other major character that is affected by Meridian's quest is Lynne. At first the relationship among the three characters seems to follow the traditional pattern of a romantic love triangle. But this novel's trio of lovers is not usual, for the emphasis in their relationship is on their respective discovery of self rather than one person's possession of another. Each one of them is illuminated by the others and helps to bring the others closer to self-knowledge. That is why the relationship between Truman and Lynne is presented from Lynne's perspective as well as Truman's and why Lynne reflects on her life with Truman in the presence of Meridian. Each of them has been changed by the other.

Because the subject of a white woman married to a black man is so ridden with stereotypical responses in both the black and white world, Walker's presentation of the character Lynne is done gradually and from varying points of view. We first see her through the eyes of Meridian as she tells Truman about her initial reaction to this northern white woman. Appropriately, the setting is the context of social change. While out together on a register-to-vote drive, the two women encountered Mrs. Mabel Turner, "who is like everybody's grandmother." After feeding the civil rights workers, the old woman informs them, "I don't believe in voting," and insists that "the good lord he takes care of most of my problems." Although Meridian realizes that "Mrs. Turner was well beyond the boundaries of politics," Lynne wants to argue "and alienates Mrs. Turner forevermore." By having Truman, as well as Meridian and Lynne, react to Mrs. Turner's attitude, Walker outlines the relationship that will form these three characters. Meridian respects the tradition Mrs. Turner represents, but Truman rejects it as backward, and Lynne counters it with pragmatic logic. Although Meridian can tolerate what she perceives as Lynne's ignorance, she cannot abide Truman's disrespect. Truman, on the other hand, is drawn to Lynne's audacious behavior although he has not yet met her. In a sense the northern white woman's response embodies his rebellion against the provincial sounds of Mrs. Turner and her like.

Meridian sees Lynne initially as a white woman, not as a particular person. As a black woman growing up in the South, she has received from her community specific information about the nature of white women:

> But what had her mother said about white women? She could actually remember very little, but her impression had been that they were frivolous, helpless creatures, lazy and without ingenuity. Occasionally, one would rise to the level of bitchery, and this one would be carefully set aside when the "collective Others were discussed. Her grandmother—an erect former maid who was now a midwife—held strong opinions, which she expressed in this way: 1. She had never known a white woman she liked after the age of twelve. 2. White women were useless except as baby machines which would continue to produce little white people who would grow up to oppress her. 3. Without servants all of them would live in pigsties.
>
> Who would dream, in her hometown, of kissing a white girl? Who would want to? What were they good for? What did they do? They only seemed to hang about laughing, after school, until they were sixteen or seventeen they got married. Their pictures appeared in the society column, you saw them pregnant a couple of times, then you were no longer able to recognize them as girls you once "Knew." They sank into a permanent oblivion. One never heard of them *doing* anything that was interesting.[48]

Unlike black women who did "outrageous things," white women, in general, did nothing but produce babies. Ironically, the black female community appropriates to white women the stereotype that had been imposed on them—that all they were good for was having babies—although they took great care to erase from their judgment of white women any trace of sexuality: "White women were like clear dead water." In effect, Meridian's mother and grandmother accept the picture of white women that white society had projected, only they see the emptiness of this image rather than its attractiveness. White women *are* "helpless frivolous creatures," just as they had been billed, Meridian's community seems to say, and who wants to be like that? That is why Meridian is so "bewildered," "embarrassed," when Truman starts dating Lynne. It is incomprehensible to her that a man like Truman would prefer a white woman, a "helpless frivolous creature," to a "woman who claims her own life." When Meridian is trying to figure out Truman's behavior, we have yet to meet Lynne. Nor do we or Meridian know that Truman has rejected Meridian because she is a mother.

When we encounter Lynne again, we see her through the eyes of Truman, first as a white woman who romanticizes black people in the chapter "Truman and Lynne: Time in the South" and then as his white wife for whom his feelings are undergoing subtle changes in the chapter "Of Bitches and Wives." Lynne as a character is beginning to take on flesh; still, she has yet to speak for herself. She does not emerge in the book as her own character, until Meridian strips bare the reasons why Truman is attracted to Lynne, not until Truman tries to come back to Meridian, not until Meridian finally and uncategorically rejects Truman as a lover. Only then does Lynne appear not as a generalization in Meridian's mind or as an extension of Truman but as herself. When she does emerge, she is trying to define herself in relation to Truman and to Meridian, that is, she is trying to define herself as a white woman living in a black world. In keeping with Walker's pattern of inter-related illumination, Lynne muses about her life with Truman in Meridian's house.

Lynne first presents herself as an embittered woman who has been ruined by her husband—for the same reason that he initially desired her, because she is white. By now she has given up her own middle-class Jewish world for her husband and has lost him as well as their child. But Truman is not her only target. She assaults Meridian also, for she believes Truman now pursues her rival because she is black, an attribute that Lynne cannot ever acquire. What is closer to the truth is that Lynne believes she is unworthy because she is white. Thus she respects Meridian because she has what Lynne wants more than anything: blackness and the strength and grace she attributes to that state of grace:

> Even when Truman was leaving her she had been conscious of her size, her body, from years of knowing how he compared it to the bodies of black women, "Black women let themselves go," he said, even as he painted them as magnificent giants, breeding forth the warriors of the new universe. "They are so *fat*," he would say, even as he sculptured a "Big Bessie Smith" in so soft marble, caressing her monstrous and lovely flanks with an admiring hand.

Her figure then, supple from dancing, was like a straw in the wind, he said, her long hair, a song of lightness—untangled, glistening and free. And yet in the end he had stopped saying those things, at least out loud. It was as if the voluptuous black bodies with breast like melons and hair like a crown of thorns, reached out—creatures of his own creation—and silenced his tongue. They began to claim him. When she walked into a room where he painted a black woman and her heaving, pulsating, fecund body, he turned his work from her, or covered it up, or ordered her out of the room.

She had loved the figures at first—especially the paintings of women in the South—the sculptures, enduring and triumphant in spite of everything. But when Truman changed, she had, too. Until she did not want to look at the women, although many of them she knew, and loved. And by then she was willing to let him go. Almost. So worthless did the painted and sculptured women make her feel, so sure was she that Truman, having fought through his art to the reality of his own mother, aunts, sisters, lovers, to their beauty, their greatness, would naturally seek them again in the flesh.[49]

Lynne does not want to be a white woman, a member of that delicate group for whose benefit the most violent acts of racism are performed. It is supposedly to protect her virtue that white men systematically deny black men their freedom, for the white woman in southern mythology is the white man's most valuable possession. Because of this deeply entrenched societal value, Lynne cannot merely be a person; she is a white woman not only in the minds of white Southerners, but necessarily in the mind of the black community and increasingly in her own mind. She cannot escape her caste, for too much blood has been spilled over it. She leaves her young innocent room in her mother's house to confront reality through her involvement with Truman and the Civil Rights Movement. The reality she discovers, begins to experience, is racism, not only as it affects black people but also as it affects her. She is as much defined by the philosophy of racism as they are. In her desire to be worthy, to be on the side of righteousness, she allies herself with black people, sees them as the ultimate perfection. But she cannot erase her own history or the history of America by merely making a personal choice. In fact, by making that choice, she becomes the white woman who has stepped outside the confines of decency. By marrying a black man and living in Mississippi, Lynne gives up the protection of the white man and therefore becomes in the eyes of the world a slut. As a woman, her righteousness lies not in her intellectual or her political activity but in her sexual choices.

When she allows Tommy Odds to rape her, because she feels the guilt of being a white woman, Lynne strips herself of any romantic illusions she might have had about her connection with black men. In forgiving him the rape, she responds to his manhood by taking away *its* essence— the responsibility he has for his own actions. Instead, she validates society's beliefs that her only worth lies in her pussy. She reduces him and herself to a one-dimensional stereotype, as much as the southern racists who shot off his arm. Appropriately, Odds reacts to her forgiveness with rage, as if he had attempted to rape her to verify what he already knew, but wanted to disprove:

> "Black men get preferential treatment, man, to make up for all we been denied. She ain't been fucking you, she's been atoning for her sins."
>
> "That's not true," said Truman, sounding weak, even to himself.
>
> "She felt sorry for me because I'm black, man," said Tommy Odds and for the first time there was dejection in his voice. "The one thing that gives me some consolation in this stupid world, and she thinks she has to make up for it out of the bountifulness of her pussy." His voice hardened. "I should have killed her."[50]

Truman responds to Tommy Odds's assessment of Lynne's love for him by leaving her to herself, to become what she really is. Exposed both physically and psychologically, Lynne loses the sense of her own worth and gives herself up to the image the South has constructed for her. She sees her relationship to black men and women only in terms of sexuality—her only source of power. She sleeps with black men, tantalizes black women with her power to waylay their men—only to discover that she is not seen as a powerful person but as an object of pity or hate. Ironically, she steps down from her shaky pedestal only to put black men on it, although she knows through her own personal experiences that a pedestal does not lift; rather it dehumanizes. Finally, the only viable connection she has to the community she reveres is her and Truman's child.

Lynne's experience of the effects that the long tradition of American racism has on her illustrates how deep the connection is between racism and sexism. She cannot be what she wants to be because she is perceived by society as a White Woman, a person whose value lies in the preciousness of her pussy. One of the most consistent ways in which black people are made to understand that they are not valued in this country is the vehemence with which this precious object is denied them, whether or not they desire it. Like Marilene O'Shay in the first chapter of this novel, Lynne as a white woman who betrays her own "divinity" must be reduced to the opposite. As a white woman who does not guard her precious possession from all unworthy intruders, who, in fact, gives it away as if it has no value, she becomes a slut, a female devil, in the eyes of the South.

It is thematically as well as structurally significant that the only time Truman, Lynne, and Meridian come together is in their groping attempts to mourn the death of their child. Camara joins the long line of children in this book whose existence is snuffed out by society's violence. Together these three persons whose lives had so passionately affected each other unite to ask forgiveness of each other. Meridian is finally able to feel again for Truman: "with a love totally free of possessiveness or contempt, a love that is forgiveness." She and Lynne become sisters, not over their wrangling about Truman but in their desire for the freedom of, in their love for, the land and the people, of the South.

> There was a scene on the television of a long, shady river bank and people—mothers and fathers, children, grandparents—almost elegantly fishing, and then the face, close up of a beautiful young black man with eyes as deceptively bright as dying stars. Now that he had just won the vote, he was saying, where was he to get the money to pay for his food? Looks like this whole Movement for the vote and to get into motels was just to teach them that everything in this country from the vote to motels, has to be changed. In fact, he said, looks like what he needed was a gun.
> To them both this was obvious. That the country was owned by the rich and that the rich must be relieved of this ownership before "Freedom" meant anything was something so basic to their understanding of America they felt naive even discussing it. Still, the face got to them. It was the kind of face they had seen only in the South. A face in which the fever of suffering had left an immense warmth, and the heat of pain had lighted a candle behind the eyes. It sought to understand, to encompass everything, and the struggle to live honorably and understand everything at the same time, to allow for every inconsistency in nature, every weird possibility and personality had given it a weary serenity that was so entrenched and stable it could be mistaken for stupidity. It made them want to love. It made them want to weep. It made them want to cry out to the young man to run away, or at least warn him about how deeply he would be hurt. It made them homesick.[51]

It is only after this coming together through the land that Walker has Lynne reflect on her own tradition, her own Jewishness. Ironically, the land she loves has taught her that she, too, is part of a tradition that it will not accept. The South would not tolerate blacks, Indians, or Jews, seeing their difference as deviancy, a threat to the established order. Lynne's experience in the South, her relationship with Truman and Meridian, with black men and women within the context of the Civil Rights Movement, has helped her to discover an aspect of her own heritage that her blood relatives erroneously turn away from—the quality of struggle rather than accommodation. In discovering her own history and reinterpreting her life in the face of her own family, her own sex, as well as her minglings with the black South, Lynne begins to understand her own humanity:

> "Black folks aren't so special," she said. "I hate to admit it. But they're not."
> "Maybe," said Meridian, as if she had been wide awake all along, "the time for being special has passed." . . , "Good God, this is depressing," said Lynne. "It's even more depressing than knowing I want Truman back." "That is depressing," said Meridian. "Oh, I know he's not much." she said. "But he saved me from a fate worse than death. Because of him, I can never be as dumb as my mother was. Even if I practiced not knowing what the world was like, even if I lived in Scarsdale or some other weird place, and never had to eat welfare food in my life. I'd still *know*. By nature I'm not cut out to be a member of the oppressors. I don't like them; they make me feel guilty all the time. They're ugly and don't know poor people laugh at them and are just waiting to drag them out." "No, Truman isn't much, but he is *instructional*,"

said Lynne. "Besides," she continued, "nobody's perfect." "Except white women," said Meridian, and winked. "Yes," said Lynne, "but their time will come."[52]

These are the last words Lynne speaks in the novel. Her words reiterate the concept that white women too must accept a struggle that will rid them of their pedestal, their "perfection," and allow them to be human without risk or rebuke, without the scent of blood rising from mutilated bodies and souls at their feet. To give up the aura of perfection, the cloak of perfection, may seem a loss until one glimpses the wonder of one's own humanity. Until the assertion of that humanity is seen as a most precious gift, a most valuable responsibility, either perfection at the price of human blood or wantonness at the price of guilt will keep the pedestal and the foundation upon which it rests intact.

Lynne's discovery of the preciousness of her own humanity has come as much through her engagement in social struggle as through psychological searching. In bringing together individuals like Meridian, Lynne, and Truman, the Civil Rights Movement is the impetus for personal change and therefore deep and lasting social change. Whatever Lynne might become beyond the space of this novel, she cannot be, as she was before she went to Georgia or Mississippi, ignorant of the restrictions that this society's attitude toward black people and women have placed on her life. She knows, too, that she is a victim as well as a part of the wheels of oppression. What she will do to extricate herself from these restrictions is yet unknown. But she knows that no matter what her relationships are, she is not black. She knows that she is no missionary, no appreciator of the art in the lives of the oppressed. She cannot give what she does not have.

Nor can Meridian or Truman. The major characters in this novel all discover that they cannot give what they do not have. That in order to transform their society, they must understand their own heritage and transform themselves. And that, paradoxically, it is in the process of attempting social change that they discover their own personal and cultural paths. This discovery is itself the core of the novel, the essence of its focal idea.

The major elements of *Meridian* the circular plot movement, the use of motifs that delineate the spirit within all living things, the focus on the black woman in her struggle for social and personal transformation, and the relationship between its major characters and the Civil Rights Movement reiterate the novel's theme that the personal and societal quests for health and freedom are interrelated; that it is a continuing process rather than an adventure that ends in a neat resolution.

Thus the book ends with Truman replacing Meridian as that part of the pattern who must understand and try to change the entire pattern so he might be whole. Although Meridian has restored herself to health for the moment, Walker's ending suggests that even *her* dearly won salvation is not sure unless we others sort out the tangled roots of our past and pursue our own health. In other words, until the pattern of this society is transformed, no part of it is free, though the whole society will not change unless each of us pursue our own wholeness. By making the end of the novel the beginning of another such quest, Walker invites us to use the novel as a contemplative and analytical tool in our own individual search. For the questions that she gives flesh to in this novel, questions that are rooted in this country's past, persist in the present.

PART III

The Third Life of Grange Copeland and Meridian: Patterns for Change

> To acknowledge our ancestors means
> we are aware that we did not make ourselves, that the line
>   stretches
> all the way back, perhaps to God:
> or to Gods. We remember them
> because it is an easy thing to forget: that we are not the first
> to suffer, rebel, fight, love and die: The grace with which we
> embrace life, in spite of the pain, the sorrows, is always a measure
> of what has gone before.[53]

Alice Walker is a poet, short-story writer, and essayist, as well as a novelist. Because her works in these different genre complement each other and contain many of the same thematic and structural elements, they can be discussed as a whole. Her book of poetry, *Revolutionary Petunias*, for example, can be read as a companion piece to *Meridian*. Nevertheless, I think that her first two novels, *The Third Life of Grange Copeland* and *Meridian* are peculiarly characterized in thematic and structural terms by their emphasis on the possibilities of change.

In both novels, the focal ideas are similar, although from the first to the second, there is a progression in theme and structure. Grange Copeland is a man who experiences three lives, one in which he hates himself, one in which he hates his oppressor, and the final one in which he is able to love his granddaughter and, therefore, himself. The pattern of Grange's life is a series of psychological stages brought on by the oppression that is inflicted upon him and his family. Although much of the Copeland history is painful and horrible, the novel itself is optimistic, for in spite of all this, Grange is able to change. By taking responsibility for his own life, he is able to love himself and pass on the possibility of "surviving whole" to his granddaughter.

Similarly, *Meridian* is about personal change. Its major characters—Meridian, Truman, and Lynne—all attain some measure of self-discovery. Meridian, as the character in the novel who is compelled to pursue wholeness, transforms herself even as she affects the other major characters. She also passes on the possibility of "surviving whole" to Truman. But although *The Third Life of Grange Copeland* remains primarily within the context of the Copeland family, *Meridian* encompasses the history of oppression of black people in America, as well as the possibility of change on a societal level. The analysis of societal forces and their philosophical underpinnings that are implicit in the first novel are explicitly explored in the second. Thus Meridian, the character, is a synthesis of the many aspects of black southern heritage. The change that she undergoes is not only personal. It is set within the tradition of resistance (in this particular instance, the Civil Rights Movement) that is as much a part of that heritage as is oppression. Like many of her ancestors, Meridian takes responsibility for the injustices in her society. Because of this emphasis, *Meridian* is a novel about the relationship between personal change and movements for social change.

Both Walker novels also focus on the major characters' perception of their past as crucial to their personal transformation in the present and the possibility of change in the future. In *The Third Life of Grange Copeland*, Walker accomplishes this by having her major character live through three generations. By reflecting on his past, he is able to understand the nature of his own existence in relation to the world in which he lives. In sorting out the repetition of tragedy in his family as it extends through a period of sixty years, Grange is able to effect his own personal change, which in turn may change the future of his descendants. In *Meridian*, the concept of the present as "a measure of what has gone before" is not limited to one family. It is extended to the history of black women in the South as reflected through Meridian Hill's maternal ancestors. In concentrating on the "mothers" of the people, their suffering, wisdom, and triumphs, Walker illuminates the heritage of the folk. The character Meridian embraces that past so she might attain grace in the present and help to effect change in the future. In both novels, Walker's use of time as circular and progressive is central to her major character's capacity for change.

Walker's use of the past is also reflected in her characterizations of black women. The significant development of this theme from her first novel to her second is especially dramatic. In both novels, the way in which the women are treated and the way in which they define themselves are related to the possibility of change. Grange and Brownfield participate in their own degeneration through their assault on their wives. Because Margaret, Mem, and Josie accept society's definition of woman as a passive wife, or a manipulative whore, they are unable to call on the wisdom and strength that is a part of their ancestral tradition. As a result, their family is in continual danger of being destroyed. Only when Grange is able to define his own manhood for himself rather than in societal terms is the process of degeneration halted and regeneration a possibility. None of the adult women, however, is able to withstand the assaults that are inflicted upon them. Only Ruth may be able to "survive whole," primarily because of Grange's personal change. But she, too, must, in the final analysis, define herself for herself.

That is what the character Meridian does do in Walker's second novel. Like Margaret and Mem, Meridian at first accepts society's definition of a woman. But her understanding of the past, her involvement in the Civil Rights Movement, and her willingness to use her traditions helps her redefine herself in her own terms as a woman and as a mother. In her first novel Walker emphasized the oppression that has destroyed many black women; in her second novel, she shows the relationship between that oppression and the creative sparks that have enabled black women to define themselves.

Paradoxically, although both novels show how the past is related to the possibility of change, they also focus on how the past is an obstacle to change. In *The Third Life of Grange Copeland*, Brownfield is incapable of growth because he cannot reach beyond the pain of his past. He destroys much of his family and himself because he comes to believe in his oppressor and in the inevitability of his oppression. Interestingly, Mem falls somewhere between Brownfield's inability to change and his father's realization of his right to grow, for she is destroyed by her husband, precisely because she has gotten a glimpse of her own possibilities. Similarly, although many of the characters in *Meridian* are affected by the Civil Rights Movement, society remains recalcitrant because its past is so rooted in violence.

In both novels, then, Walker emphasizes the element of struggle, which she sees as a prerequisite to real and lasting change. The persons who do achieve wholeness are beacons of this possibility within human beings. Both Grange and Meridian commit acts that they perceive as destructive. It is in their struggle to transcend their own violations against life that they come to the vision they achieve. In *Meridian*, the emphasis is not only on the ordeal that the individual person must endure, but on how that struggle is intimately connected to the collective struggle that society must bear.

Although there is a progression in theme from *The Third Life of Grange Copeland* to *Meridian*, these two novels reveal Walker's insistence on penetrating the essence of her characters rather than creating types who stand for a political or philosophical idea. Although *Meridian* concentrates on the conflict between two philosophical views of the world, Walker embodies this conflict in the actions of her characters rather than in extraneous asides. Above all, Walker is, in both novels, a storyteller. The telling of the story is as important as what she tells; the structuring of her tales are themselves possible patterns for change.

In *The Third Life of Grange Copeland*, Walker lays out, arranges and examines bits and pieces of waste in the lives of the Copelands so we might see the overall design. Then she remakes these very same pieces into a different pattern, one of rebirth. Her use of thrifty units, much like the compression of poetry, enables her economically to develop her overall design so the major elements could be clearly seen and intensely felt. By using these same elements to create a new pattern, she suggests that the pain in life must be understood and used, if the new pattern is to endure.

In *Meridian*, the quilt that Walker creates is more intricate, for she uses the elements of pain and strength of an entire tradition as the bases for her design. Nevertheless, she again uses economical units and the repetition of motifs in creating her pattern. But because she is demonstrating the relationship between personal and societal change, between the past and the present of the South, and between the conflicting philosophies of animism and fragmentation, her major structural elements are strongly outlined. In charting a pattern for change she creates a design of circles that are continually intersecting with each other but that also move forward and upward toward the highest spiritual point. Ascension is impossible, she suggests, without the struggle to go backward in order to come forward. Nor is spiritual growth possible unless all life is seen as interdependent, as a circle of wholeness.

In creating this design, Walker also indicates that focus is as important as movement. Meridian, a sensitive black woman, is the median point of the circular patterns in the novel, for she has experienced sexism and racism, major obstacles to societal wholeness. For this author, the black woman, as a result of her history and her experience, must be in struggle against these two distortions of life. Until she is free, her people cannot be free, and until her people are free, she cannot be free. Walker stresses the interrelatedness of these two obstacles to wholeness, for the struggle against them is not merely a question of replacing whoever is in power; rather it is a struggle to release the spirit that inhabits all life. Walker's quilts reiterate the basic concept that "the greatest value a person can attain is full humanity which is a state of oneness with all things,"[54] and that until this is possible for all living beings, those of us who seek wholeness must be willing to struggle toward that end.

Notes

1. Alice Walker, "In Our Mothers' Gardens," *Ms.* 2 (May 1974): 65.
2. Ibid., p. 70.
3. Alice Walker, *The Third Life of Grange Copeland* (New York: Harcourt Brace Jovanovich, 1970), p. 207.
4. Ibid., pp. 11–13.
5. Ibid., pp. 53–54.

 6. Ibid., p. 55.
 7. Ibid., p. 82.
 8. Ibid., p. 83.
 9. Ibid.
10. Ibid.
11. Ibid., p. 84.
12. Ibid., p. 86.
13. Ibid., p. 91.
14. Ibid., p. 92.
15. Ibid., p. 107.
16. Ibid., p. 162.
17. Ibid., p. 40.
18. Ibid., p. 21.
19. Ibid., pp. 224–25.
20. Ibid., pp. 17–18.
21. Ibid., p. 111.
22. Ibid., pp. 133–34.
23. Ibid., pp. 138–39.
24. Ibid., p. 196.
25. Ibid., p. 166.
26. Ibid., p. 209.
27. Ibid., p. 214.
28. Alice Walker, *Meridian* (New York: Harcourt Brace Jovanovich, 1976), pp. 13–14.
29. Ibid., p. 19.
30. Ibid., pp. 54–55.
31. John O'Brien, ed. *Interviews with Black Writers* (New York: Liveright, 1973), p. 193.
32. Black Elk, *Black Elk Speaks; Being the Life Story of a Holy Man of the Oalala Sioux*, as told through John G. Neihardt [Flaming Rainbow] (Lincoln: University of Nebraska Press, 1961).
33. O'Brien, *Interviews with Black Writers*, p. 204.
34. Walker, *Meridian*, pp. 14–15.
35. Ibid., p. 204.
36. Ibid., pp. 92–93.
37. Ibid., p. 70.
38. Ibid., pp. 33–34.
39. Ibid., p. 219.
40. Ibid., p. 24.
41. Ibid., p. 80.
42. Ibid., pp. 106–7.
43. Ibid., p. 145.
44. Ibid., pp. 133–34.
45. Ibid., p. 138.
46. Ibid., pp. 137–38.
47. Ibid., p. 223.
48. Ibid., pp. 104–5.
49. Ibid., pp. 170–71.
50. Ibid., pp. 165–66.
51. Ibid., pp. 176–77.
52. Ibid., p. 185.
53. Alice Walker, "Fundamental Difference," in *Revolutionary Petunias*, by Alice Walker (New York: Harcourt Brace Jovanovich, 1973), p. 1.
54. O'Brien, *Interviews with Black Writers*, p. 205.

◆◆◆◆◆◆◆◆◆◆◆◆◆◆

History and Genealogy in Walker's *The Third Life of Grange Copeland* and *Meridian*

ELLIOTT BUTLER-EVANS

Alice Walker's ideological position stresses rebellion and liberation. Whether drawing on her involvement in the civil rights movement (an activity she views as "revolutionary"), or arguing that her fiction must speak to the "survival of the race," or advancing her program for a "womanist" ideology, her works address specific social and political issues. She succinctly stated her position in an interview reprinted in *In Search of Our Mothers' Gardens:*

> I am preoccupied with the spiritual survival, the *whole* of my people. But beyond that, I am committed to exploring the oppressions, the insanities, the loyalties, and the triumphs of black women. . . . For me, black women are the most fascinating creations in the world.
>
> Next to them, I place the old people—male and female—who persist in their beauty in spite of everything. How do they do this, knowing what they do? Having lived what they have lived? It is a mystery, and so it lures me into their lives.[1]

For Walker, a commitment to writing must be combined with social and political activism if it is to be of significance. Like Toni Cade Bambara, Walker views the role of the Black artist as multifaceted:

> My major advice to young black artists would be that they shut themselves up somewhere away from all debates about who they are and what color they are and just turn out paintings and poems and stories and novels. Of course the kind of artist we are required to be cannot do this. Our people are waiting. *But there must be an awareness of what is Bull and what is Truth,* what is practical and what is designed ultimately to paralyze our talents. For example, it is unfair to the people we expect to reach to give them a beautiful poem if they are unable to read it.
>
> *The real revolution is always concerned with the least glamorous stuff.* With raising a reading level from second grade to third. With simplifying history and writing it down (or reciting it) for the old folks. With helping illiterates fill out food-stamp forms. . . . The dull, frustrating work with our people is the work of the black revolutionary artist. It means, most of all, staying close enough to them to be there whenever they need you.[2]

In this chapter I focus on Walker's project of "simplifying history," particularly the semiotic representation of history in fictional discourse. Her first two novels, *The Third Life of Grange Copeland* and *Meridian*, are structured by their inscription of two historical narratives: one focuses on the broad racial experiences of American Blacks, without regard to gender issues; the other more specifically focuses on the histories of Black women. Walker's text constantly oscillates between these two discourses. The framing narrative, generally grounded in racial history, is often disrupted and subverted by the subordinate discourse that addresses the experiences of Black women.

An argument can be advanced that would challenge the reading of fiction as history, but modern scholarship has illustrated that such divisions are largely artificial. Hayden White, for example, has convincingly argued that the textual strategies—modes of emplotment, tropological strategies, and the like—are the same in the production of historiography and the novel.[3] White clearly has shown the relationship between history and fiction in his argument that "as verbal artifacts histories and novels are indistinguishable from one another."

> We cannot distinguish between them on formal grounds unless we approach them with specific preconceptions about the kinds of truths that each is supposed to deal in. But the aim of the writer of a novel must be the same as that of the writer of a history. Both wish to provide a verbal image of "reality." The novelist may present this reality indirectly, that is to say, by figurative techniques, rather than directly, which is to say, by registering a series of propositions which are supposed to correspond point by point to some extra-textual domain of occurrence or happening, as the historian claims to do. But the image of reality which the novelist thus constructs is meant to correspond in its general outline to some domain of human experience which is no less "real" than that referred to by the historian.[4]

White's description of the strategies employed by the novelist is directly relevant to Alice Walker's work. Generally covering four or more decades in her novels, Walker evokes specific historical events and personages, and her metaphorical and metonymical representations of the experiences of Blacks as oppressed people reflect historical consciousness. This focus on a general racial history locates her work within the tradition of Black male fiction. Yet that tradition cannot entirely accommodate Walker's narrative, for she is also concerned with the specific experiences of Black women, a focus that demands a feminist genealogy. Gayle Greene and Coppelia Kahn's description of the limitations of conventional historiography are relevant to the task Walker undertakes.

> What has been designated historically significant has been deemed so according to a valuation of power and activity in the public world. History has been written primarily from the perspective of the authoritative male subject—the single triumphant consciousness—with a view to justifying the politically dominant west—individualism, progress, conquest—i.e., to providing pedigrees for individuals, rising classes, nations, cultures and ideologies. As long as the "transmission and experience of power" are its primary focus, as long as war and politics are seen as more significant to the history of humankind than child-rearing, women remain marginalized or invisible. Its androcentric framework . . . has excluded from its consideration not only women but the poor, the anonymous, and the illiterate.[5]

Inscriptions of the feminine in Walker's novels are marked by their difference from the racial history she invokes. Quite often, they become alternative narratives that disrupt or address, directly or indirectly, the omissions of the framing historical discourse. The peremptory movement of a feminine-feminist counterdiscourse becomes the dominant textual activity. These historical narratives of women, while contained within the framework of the racial historical narratives, become signifiers of sexual difference.

Greene and Kahn's critique of historiography is arguably focused on Eurocentric historical discourse, but Afro-American representations of history share characteristics of that discourse. The stress on outer-world/inner-world conflict, the emphasis on the public over the private and the political over the personal, and the elision of existential modalities within the inner world characterize the Afro-American novel in general as largely male centered. What one encounters in Walker's early works in particular is an inscription of that discourse, but one that is persistently challenged by a feminine counterdiscourse.

The challenge, then, for any examination of Walker's narratives is to explore the manner in which the two discourses are inscribed in the text, marking their points of intersection and divergence. Moreover, one needs to examine the manner in which the racial historical discourse becomes increasingly marginalized and is often displaced by alternative narratives of feminist desire. Central to these concerns is the role of the reader. How is the reader's subjectivity influenced by a text that oscillates between two contending discourses? How is the reader actively implicated in the construction of those discourses? To what extent can the reader infer a cohesive ideological project in Walker's fiction? I address these issues in my readings of *The Third Life of Grange Copeland* and *Meridian*.

The Third Life of Grange Copeland

Alice Walker has described *The Third Life of Grange Copeland* as "a novel that is chronological in structure, or one devoted, more or less, to rigorous realism."[6] That purpose is undercut by ruptures generated by the narration of competing histories. Although one might expect Grange to be the primary focus of the novel, he becomes largely a vehicle through which the broader racial experience is narrated[7] and is then displaced and challenged by previously subordinate narratives that focus specifically on the experiences of Black women.[8] In addition to inscribing the narratives of Grange and Brownfield, the novel commits itself to the stories of Mem, Margaret, Josie, and communities of anonymous women. The personal histories of Brownfield and Grange remain the dominant focus of the narrative, but the women's stories serve significant textual and ideological functions. I return to this issue in a detailed treatment of those narratives, but at the moment I wish to focus on the Grange-Brownfield narrative frame.

The ideological enterprise that the novel undertakes may be viewed as having two dimensions: Through her symbolic use of Grange and Brownfield, Walker advances the argument that the culture of poverty, with its racial underpinnings, is essentially dehumanizing. At the same time, she asserts that one has a responsibility to transcend that dehumanization. What is involved is not merely a symbolic representation of dehumanization but the constant intervention of an external narrator who comments and interprets for the reader, keeping Walker's argument in the foreground. The narrative, by shifting the centers of consciousness throughout the novel, aids her in this strategy.

Grange's "first life" is viewed by the child Brownfield, whose perceptions are refined and transmitted by the narrator. A congeries of details invites the reader to construct a picture of the sharecropper's life. The single image is integrated into a pattern that ultimately forms a delineation of the culture of poverty. Brownfield develops sores because of poor nutrition; Margaret is forced to work in a bait factory as her husband labors as a sharecropper; at age six, Brownfield begins working in the fields; the family lives in grossly substandard housing. A significant manner in which this Gestalt is constructed is having the sharecropping experience viewed through Brownfield's eyes. The scene in which the narrator tells of Brownfield's reaction to Grange's fear of Mister Shipley, the white foreman for whom he works, illustrates this:

> Once the man touched [Brownfield] on the hand with the handle of his cane . . . and said, "You're Grange Copeland's boy, ain't you?" And Brownfield had answered, "Uh huh," chewing on his lip and recoiling from the enormous pile of gray-black hair that lay matted on the man's upper chest and throat. While he stared at the hair one of the workers—not his father who was standing beside him as if he didn't know he was there—said to him softly, "Say 'Yessir' to Mr. Shipley," and Brownfield looked up before he said anything and scanned his father's face. The mask was as tight and still as if his father had coated himself with wax. And Brownfield smelled for the first time an odor of sweat, fear, and something indefinite. Something smothered and tense (which was of his father and of the other workers . . .) that came from his father's body. His father said nothing. Brownfield, trembling, said "Yessir," filled with terror of this man who could, by his presence alone, turn his father into something that might as well have been a pebble or post or a piece of dirt, except for the sharp odor of something whose source was forcibly contained in flesh.[9]

Brownfield's reaction to this incident, reinforced by the narrator's interpretation of it, places the episode in a broader context, in what Hayden White has called the "domain of human experience." The reader's response goes beyond the particular experience of Grange to the larger issue of racial oppression. Grange's response is filtered through Brownfield's mind, and references to the other workers speak to its broader implications.

This strategy of employing a single image to make a broad ideological statement characterizes most of the novel. Grange's total impotence is conveyed through physical description; the reader must invoke a cultural code to interpret it. These descriptions may involve objects or persons, as can be seen by the juxtaposition of a description of the Copeland house with the physical description of Grange. The house has "rotting gray wood shingles" and is marked by a pervasive grayness. It resembles "a sway back animal turned out to pasture," and the surrounding area is marked by "a litter of tree trunks, slivers of carcass bones deposited by the dog and discarded braces and bits that had pained the jaws and teeth of a hard-driven mule." This bleak image is then reinforced in the description of Grange:

> He was a tall, thin brooding man, slightly stooped from plowing, with skin the deep glossy brown of pecans. He was thirty-five but seemed much older. His face and eyes had a dispassionate vacancy and sadness, as if a great fire had been extinguished within him and was just recently missed. He seemed devoid of any emotion, while Brownfield watched him, except that of bewilderment. A bewilderment so complete he did not really appear to know what he saw, although his hand continued to gesture, more or less aimlessly, and his lips moved, shaping unintelligible words.[10]

The two descriptions make up the broad picture of exploitation and dehumanization that the reader is invited to construct. The description of Grange illuminates that oppression, and it is made more poignant by having it filtered through the mind of the child. The reader can respond sympathetically to both of them and can experience rage at the conditions under which they live.

At the same time, an alternative narrative, centered on the oppression of the Black woman, is subtly introduced. Again, the reader experiences Margaret Copeland only through the eyes of Brownfield in a narration that is then mediated by the narrator. The reader is forced to construct a more complete narrative.

Margaret's oppressive situation is revealed early in the novel when she agrees with Grange during a family dispute. Brownfield's response is as follows: "His mother agreed with his father whenever possible. And though he was only ten Brownfield wondered about this. He thought his mother was like their dog in some ways. She didn't have a thing to say that did not in some way show her submission to his father." References to Grange's infidelity, his drunkenness and the terror it instills, and his abandonment of his family follow. Because of his behavior, Margaret sinks into alcoholism and sexual promiscuity, resulting in her having a child out of wedlock. Her death is briefly described after Grange has abandoned the family:

> "Well. He's gone," his mother said without anger at the end of the third week. But the following week she and her poisoned baby went out into the dark of the clearing and in the morning Brownfield found them there. She was curled

up in a lonely sort of way, away from her child, as if she had spent the last moment on her knees.[11]

Margaret's story is largely contained within the dominant narrative frame. Her suffering is represented as part of the larger spiritual annihilation that is characteristic of the sharecropping system. The narrative strategy of having events filtered through the mind of Brownfield precludes a telling of Margaret's story, yet her story remains a disturbing presence embedded within the dominant narrative. Even at this early stage, the text moves toward its own decentering.

In earlier chapters, the focus on Brownfield allows the reader to sympathize with him. Brownfield the child is the one we see as the primary victim of racism and economic exploitation. This procedure is followed as Brownfield assumes the role that Grange had played before fleeing the South. The narrator invokes the same strategy of physical description to address Brownfield's plight:

> He had once been a handsome man, slender and tall with narrow beautiful hands. From trying to see in kerosene lamplight his once clear eyes were now red-veined and yellow with a permanent squint. From running after white folks' cows, he never tended much to his own, when he had any, and he'd developed severe athlete's foot that caused him to limp when the weather was hot or wet. From working in fields and with cows in all kinds of weather he developed a serious bronchitis aggravated by rashes and allergies.[12]

The physical description of Brownfield becomes the embodiment of the oppressive conditions under which the sharecroppers lived. Disease, illness, and dehumanization underscore these destructive conditions. The details are presented directly by the extradiegetic narrator and invite the reader to respond.

The argument that such treatment does not justify abusing others is given even stronger weight in this section. Therefore, the movement away from Brownfield as victim to Brownfield as oppressor requires a shifting of the narrative focus. The reader must respond to the verbal and physical violence inflicted on Mem by Brownfield with a shift in judgment of Brownfield's character.

What was largely suggested in the Margaret-Grange marriage is presented in graphic detail in the description of the union between Brownfield and Mem. The larger history is subordinated as domestic violence dominates. Individual scenes record Brownfield's increasing brutality: Mem beaten and dehumanized; the children Daphne, Ornette, and Ruth living in constant fear of their father; the gradual physical and moral destruction of Mem. Brownfield's behavior forces the reader to withdraw from him. As attention shifts to Brownfield's victims, pathos becomes the dominant representation of the household. The Brownfield children construct an imaginary narrative about a more generous and kind Brownfield; and Mem, in a moment of rebellion, threatens to kill

Brownfield unless his behavior changes. Whatever sympathies the reader might still have for Brownfield are eliminated in the narrator's description of Mem's murder (examined in more detail later in this chapter).

The focus on Mem as a victim of brutality and the responses of her children to that brutal treatment mark a move away from the original ideological purpose. As the text focuses more intensely on the domestic violence, the outer world recedes. The argument shifts its perspective— from Brownfield as victim to the women and children as the most victimized. At this point, the text reintroduces Grange, now older and wiser, as the antithesis of Brownfield.

The return of Grange, in his "second life," endows him with larger-than-life dimensions. He is protective of his niece, Ruth, to whom he seems to be totally devoted; he is now the storyteller, the person who has traveled far and returned to share his wisdom. The reader is led to believe that Grange has undergone a major conversion. (Omitted is any detailed treatment of Grange's earlier desertion of his family and his cruelty to Brownfield as a child.) This change in character presents Grange as the embodiment of human possibility. At the core of Grange's transformation is the novel's ideological statement that one cannot be so dehumanized by a system as to lose one's own humanity. In a heated argument with Brownfield, Grange articulates that philosophy:

> "By George, I know the danger of putting all the blame on somebody else for the mess you make out of your life. I fell into the trap myself! And I'm bound to believe that that's the way the white folks can corrupt you even when you done held up before. 'Cause when they got you thinking that they're to blame for *everything* they have you thinking they's some kind of gods! You can't do nothing wrong without them being behind it. You gits just as weak as water, no feeling of doing *nothing* yourself. Then you begins to think up evil and begins to destroy everybody around you, and you blames it on the crackers. *Shit!* Nobody's as powerful as we make them out to be. We got our own *souls* don't we?[13]

This statement, while addressed to Brownfield, forces the reader to modify his or her initial response. The destruction of Margaret and Mem can no longer be attributed solely to racism; it is also directly related to the moral failures of the men. In this respect, the novel follows a conventional plot development. Grange moves from a state of disequilibrium, characterized by his abuse of those around him, to a state of equilibrium, marked by a significant change in behavior. Conversely, Brownfield becomes increasingly dehumanized. The novel does not offer any reasons for these changes in the men's personalities; it merely presents them. What is important is that these reconstructions of the characters of Grange and Brownfield force a rereading and reinterpretation of the entire novel.

Near the end of the novel, Brownfield is placed in an even more odious light when he conspires with a racist judge to regain custody of his daughter Ruth. This pairing of the judge and Brownfield against Ruth and Grange further cements the case against Brownfield. The novel's violent ending, in which Grange kills Brownfield and then dies in a shootout with the police, heightens Grange's heroic stature, giving his death a certain nobility.

In the Grange and Brownfield episodes, then, readers participate in the production of meaning and the working out of an ideological position. The early stages of the novel are clearly focused on the dehumanizing aspects of racial and economic oppression. The novel then proceeds to focus on victims other than Black males. And the characterizations of Grange and Brownfield, two men marked by exaggerated qualities of good and evil, become signs of opposing ideological positions, with the narrator clearly on the side of Grange.

If the personal histories of Grange and Brownfield reflect some of the areas of conflict in Walker's ideology, the representation of Black women reveals even stronger ambivalences and ambiguities. Margaret's life, which is seen solely through the eyes of Brownfield as a child, leaves these ambiguities largely unresolved. Mem, although more directly represented, has her life viewed largely within the context of the abuse she suffers in her marriage to Brownfield. The most problematic representation is that of another female character, Josie. Here the narrator vacillates, at times sympathetic to Josie and at times not. For example, Josie's independence is both praised and derided in the text. All three women's narratives are part of the larger design of the novel, however, and their individuality is suppressed.

Margaret is largely delineated within the initial Grange-Brownfield narrative. Mem emerges not as a specific woman but as a repository of various traits and virtues. The narrator stresses Mem's formal education, her physical attractiveness, and her assertive approach to life. Although these things differentiate her from the other women in the novel and help provide a background for her in which her goodness stands in contrast to Brownfield's evil, Mem's personal history is not revealed. The reader experiences Mem solely through the intervention of the narrator; Mem's life, as depicted in the text, is one of omissions and gaps. For example, amid all the verbal and physical abuse that Mem suffers at the hands of Brownfield, *his* reaction is more fully delineated than hers. This can be seen in the episode in which Brownfield ridicules Mem because of her language:

> In company he embarrassed her. When she opened her mouth to speak he turned with a bow to their friends, who thankfully spoke a language a man could understand, and said "Hark, mah *lady* speaks, lets us dumb niggers listen," Mem would turn ashen with shame, and tried to keep her mouth closed thereafter. But silence was not what Brownfield was after, either. He wanted her to talk, but to talk like what she was, a hopeless nigger woman

who got her ass beat every Saturday night. He wanted her to sound like a woman who deserved him.[14]

The passage focuses on Brownfield. The simple image of Mem's face "ashen with shame" and her acquiescence in trying "to keep her mouth closed thereafter" are all that the reader knows of Mem's response. The focus is even more intensely on Brownfield through a narrative strategy that Paul Hernadi calls "substitutionary narration." In this technique, Hernadi argues, the point of view of the narrator is merged with that of the character so that the two become inseparable.[15] Hence, the description of "their friends, who thankfully spoke a language a man could understand" and the observation that Brownfield "wanted her to talk, but to talk like what she was, a hopeless nigger woman who got her ass beat every Saturday night," although attributed to the narrator, represent the perception and language of Brownfield, thereby placing the primary focus of the episode on him. The intensity of Mem's rage must be supplied by the reader from the isolated images in the text.

This strategy is reintroduced when the text purports to represent Mem's despair. The reader gains a largely elliptical view of Mem's feelings as the text shifts immediately to Brownfield's response:

> She wanted to leave him, but there was no place to go. She had no one but Josie and Josie despised her. She wrote to her father, whom she had never seen, and he never bothered to answer the letter. From a plump woman she became skinny. To Brownfield she didn't look like a woman at all. Even her wonderful breasts dried up and shrank; her hair fell out and the only good thing he could say for her was that she kept herself clean. He berated her for her cleanliness, but, because it was a small thing, and because at times she did seem to have so little, he did not hit her for it.[16]

The first three sentences sum up the isolation and despair that Mem feels, but the reader never knows the depth of her emotions. Speaking of Mem's isolation, this discourse rather hurriedly describes it, but provides no depth of feeling. Rather abruptly, beginning with the passage "From a plump woman she became skinny," the paragraph focuses on Brownfield's response.

This mode of narrative distancing from Mem's emotions is evident even in the scene in which Brownfield murders her. The entire episode is seen through the eyes of Brownfield and the children:

> She was carrying several packages, which she held in the crook of both arms, looking down at the ground to secure her footing. Ruth wanted to dash out of the chicken house to her, but she and Ornette sat frozen in their seats. They stared at her as she passed, hardly breathing as the light on the porch clicked on and the long shadow of Brownfield lurched out onto the porch waving his shotgun. Mem looked up at the porch and called a greeting. It was a cheerful greeting, although she sounded very tired, tired and out of breath. Brownfield began to curse and came and stood on the steps until Mem got within the circle of the light. Then he aimed the gun with drunken accuracy right into her face and fired.[17]

The paragraph that follows details the horror experienced by the children. Thus, except for an isolated comment on the "large frayed holes in the bottom of [Mem's] shoes," with the flat piece of paper protruding, there is no attempt to delineate Mem even at the moment of her death. She represents pathos in the text, functioning largely to highlight Brownfield's cruelty and dehumanization. Through reading about her situation, we are forced to reevaluate Brownfield and are seduced by Grange's argument on the need to maintain dignity even in a world of oppression. Such a textual strategy necessarily results in Mem's personal history remaining largely incomplete.

Josie's narrative is significantly more fleshed out than that of Mem or Margaret, but the ambivalence through which her character is constructed produces uncertainty in the reader's response. She is a composite of contradictions: Both independent and dependent, she exercises absolute freedom in the manner in which she conducts her life and at the same time is seen as eager to abandon that freedom; she is kind yet vindictive and petty; and she is both celebrated and despised.

A significant development in the narrative of Josie is the attempt to create a personal history. The narrator provides a context through which Josie can be understood, and the fragmentary pasts that characterized the narratives of Mem and Margaret make way for a more fully developed character in Josie. The physical and mental abuse she endures at the hands of her father and the men who exploit her sexually are graphically represented. The following scene presents a pregnant, drunken Josie lying on the ground, surrounded by her mother, her father, and men of the community:

> Her mother stood outside the ringed pack of men, how many of them knowledgeable of her daughter's swollen body she did not know, crying. . . . Such were her cries that the men, as if caught standing naked, were embarrassed and they stooped, still in the ring of the pack, to lift up the frightened girl, whose whiskied mind had cleared and who now lay like an exhausted, overturned pregnant turtle underneath her father's foot. He pressed his foot into her shoulder and dared them to touch her. It seemed to them that Josie's stomach moved and they were afraid of their guilt suddenly falling on the floor before them wailing out their names. But it was only that she was heaving and vomiting and choking on her own puke. . . .[18]
>
> "Let'er be," growled her father. "I hear she can do *tricks* on her back like that."

This representation of Josie as a potentially rebellious woman suggests the archetypal Blues woman we saw in the fiction of Morrison and Bambara. As a prostitute and the infamous owner of the Dew Drop Inn, Josie is the embodiment of rebellion.

> As it was she was born into a world peopled by her grandfather's male friends, all of whom frequented the little shack on Poontang Street where "fat Josie" (she grew large after the baby) did her job with a gusto that denied shame, and demanded her money with an authority that squelched all pity. And from

these old men, father's friends, Josie obtained the wherewithal to dress her-self well, and to eat well, and to own the Dew Drop Inn. When they became too old to "cut the mustard" anymore, she treated them with a jolly cruelty and sadistic kind of concern. She often did a strip tease in the center of their eagerly constructed semicircle, bumping and grinding, moaning to herself, charging them the last pennies of their meager old-age savings to watch her, but daring them to touch.[19]

This passage marks a significant turning away from the dominant focus. A woman's individual history is related outside the context of the Grange-Brownfield discourse. Moreover, the themes of woman as both victim and victor and of woman as rebel are inserted into the narrative, marking the eruption of feminine desire.

This desire is depicted as Josie's triumph over her social situation. She is alternately lover to both Grange and Brownfield, and is totally in control of her life. But the text downplays that position through its ambiguous representation of her. The reader views Josie through the eyes of Grange and Ruth. After Ruth is adopted by Grange, the narrator provides us with this interaction between the family members:

At the beginning Ruth was jealous of Josie, for she thought maybe Grange found her pretty. But Grange also thought his wife was not very nice, and he said so, often and loudly. He said she lived like a cat, stayed away from home too much. Josie was one of those fat yellow women with freckles and light colored eyes, and most people would have said she was goodlooking, *hand-some*, without even looking closely. But Ruth looked closely indeed, and what she saw was a fat yellow woman with sour breath, too much purple lipstick, and a voice that was wheedling and complaining: the voice of a spoiled littler fat girl who always wanted to pee after the car got moving.[20]

Although the narrator's position is indeterminate here (the passage seems to approach free indirect discourse or substitution narration after the first three sentences), the narrator's mediation of Grange's and Ruth's responses to Josie clearly preclude a positive reading of her char-acter. Grange and Ruth are the embodiments of virtue at this point in the narrative: Grange has been reconstructed as a sympathetic figure, and Ruth represents a mythologized future.

The undermining of Josie is directly related to establishing an opposi-tional relationship between Grange and Ruth and Brownfield and Josie. Grange, whose "one duty in the world was to prepare Ruth for a great and Herculean task, some magnificent and deadly struggle, some harsh and foreboding reality," and Ruth, the hope of the future, with her prob-ing mind and overall intelligence are meaningful only in terms of their difference from others in the text. Their positive values show forth through the shortcomings of others. Hence, the reader is forced to see Josie, not as autonomous and rebellious, but as weak, mercurial, and petty. The identification of her with Brownfield stresses their apparent similarity.

In *The Third Life of Grange Copeland*, then, the larger historical picture becomes a containment strategy for the subnarratives that constitute it. The novel's dominant theme—dehumanization and the "correct" responses to that dehumanization—totally structures the narrative and strategies of representation in the text. It is imperative to position the reader so that he or she will make the appropriate response to the history presented. Thus, the women become semiotic strategies, signs of suffering and oppression, rather than complex individuals with personal histories. With the characterizations of Margaret and Mem, pathos becomes the dominant trope, leaving limited space in which to comprehend their full personalities. With the representation of Josie, the text assumes a more radical pose, alternately presenting her as desirable and undesirable, depending on the exigencies of the text.

Meridian

Meridian, published in 1976, six years after *Grange*, signals a radical departure from the earlier work in its representations of history and its narrative strategies. Yet it is also largely a work in which an accurate reading depends on the active participation of the reader. Form becomes a signifier of a new consciousness. There are no chapters as such, and so the reader is confronted with mere descriptions of episodes: "The Last Return," "Have You Stolen Anything," "The Wild Child," "The New York Times." These episodes are generally not structured by any strict chronology, and it would be possible to alter the structure without affecting the meaning of the text. At least one episode, "The Recurring Dream," assumes a metafictional aspect:

> She dreamed she was a character in a novel and that her existence presented an insoluble problem, one that would be solved only by her death at the end.
> She dreamed she was a character in a novel and that her existence presented an insoluble problem, one that would be solved only by her death at the end.
> She dreamed she was a character in a novel and her existence presented an insoluble problem, one that would be solved only by her death at the end.
> Even when she gave up reading novels that encouraged such a solution—and nearly all of them did—the dream did not cease.[21]

This literary consciousness abruptly moves the narrative away from reality and draws attention to the textual process. By repeating the "She dreamed" sequences, coherent representation ceases and narrative development stops; the reader must construct meaning. Moreover, the text itself is ironic because Meridian, the presumptive *she* of this discourse, *is* a character in the novel. Thus the work as an act of writing and a particular mode of discourse is highlighted.

This strategy is one of many that mark the narrative's attempt to disrupt coherence, to declare its polysemous character and force the reader to construct meaning. Further indications of this occur in the fusion of genres. For example, the mythological story of the Wild Child and the Sojourner tree is placed within the framework of a narrative grounded in realism. This total disregard for chronology renders the passage of time at best a secondary concern. The shift in narrative focus, while always mediated by an external narrator, is never in the strict sense polyphonic. The passage from one episode to another, one situation to another, forces the reader to reevaluate his or her position constantly.

In its treatment of Afro-American history the novel is at its most radical. Meridian is the medium through which that history is largely revealed, and through her involvement in the civil rights movement history remains a theme of the text. Yet that history occupies a subordinate role in the narrative and is often placed on the margins. For example, the violence of the 1960s, marked by political assassinations, is simply entitled:

MEDGAR EVERS/JOHN F. KENNEDY/MALCOLM X/MARTIN LUTHER KING/CHE GUEVARA/PATRICE LUMUMBA/GEORGE JACKSON/CYNTHIA WESLEY/ADDIE MAE COLLINS/DENISE MCNAIR/CAROLE ROBERTSON/VIOLA LIUZZO

Following this recitation of names is a look at Meridian's specific response to the funeral of John Kennedy, and what is striking here is that, throughout the episode, the horror of Kennedy's death is experienced only through Meridian's reactions to it. The death also serves as the onset of the friendship between Ann-Marie and Meridian, which takes precedence over the larger event.

Presenting historical events in this manner constitutes a displacement of the larger public history by a privatized version of historical events. The strategy recalls Habermas's description of the relationship of modernity to historical discourse:

> Historical memory is replaced by the historical affinity of the present with the extremes of history: a sense of time wherein decadence immediately recognizes itself in the barbaric, the wild, and the primitive. We observe the anarchistic intention of blowing up the continuum of history, and we can account for it in terms of the subversive force of this new aesthetic consciousness. Modernity revolts against the normalizing functions of tradition; modernity lives on the experience of rebelling against all that is normative. . . . This aesthetic consciousness continuously stages a dialectical play between secrecy and public scandal; it is addicted to the fascination of that horror which accompanies the act of profaning, and is yet always in flight from the trivial results of profanation.[22]

Meridian moves away from the ambiguous characterizations of women found in *Grange* and heralds the rise of the feminine. Racial history in general is marginalized here, noted only in the fact that Meridian is a civil rights worker. As such, it is secondary to the main body of narratives that constitutes the text. Meridian is the character in whom these separate narratives are held together, but their meaning and coherence depend on the reader's interaction with the text. Basically, they are articulations of a nascent feminist consciousness. Each narrative, although essentially self-contained, contributes to a Gestalt. Among the issues the narratives explore are the celebration of the female as other within the context of a new mythology; the deconstruction of traditional social and moral values, particularly those governing women's sexuality and motherhood; and the problems that are central to Black-white feminism. The reader must see each of these themes as a manifestation of an implicit feminist consciousness.

The mythological dimensions of the novel appear rather early, in the form of embedded narratives. These stories have a surreal quality and seem irrelevant to the text's main thread. Marilene O'Shay, for example, seems merely to evoke the real, but minor details that place her in a different light. In the following scene, her husband has her body on display in a circus wagon:

> "Marilene O'Shay. One of the Twelve Human Wonders of the World: Dead for Twenty-five years, Preserved in Life-Like Condition." Below this, a smaller legend was scrawled in red paint on four large stars. "Obedient Daughter," read one, "Devoted Wife," said another. The third was "Adoring Mother" and the fourth was "Gone Wrong." Over the fourth a vertical line of progressively flickering light bulbs moved continually downward like a perpetually cascading tear.[23]

The episode ends with the response of her cuckold husband:

> The oddest thing about her dried-up body, according to Henry's flier, and the one that . . . bothered him most was that its exposure to salt had caused it to darken. And, though he had attempted to paint her original color from time to time, the paint always discolored. Viewers of her remains should be convinced of his wife's race, therefore, by the straightness and reddish color of her hair.[24]

Marilene's narrative ends at this point, and the novel returns to an encounter between Meridian, Truman, and the children. Yet as the novel progresses, Marilene assumes a different significance. The banal descriptions of her as "devoted wife," "obedient daughter," and "adoring mother" become descriptions that imprison other women in Meridian's world, and the racial ambiguity signified by Marilene's skin coloring signifies the cross-cultural oppression of women. Thus, Marilene becomes a dialectical metaphor, subsuming the major arguments of the text.

A similar embedded narrative concerns the Wild Child, an abandoned child, impregnated and thus removed from the moral values governing the lives of the young women attending Saxon College. Her antisocial behavior marks her as the antithesis of society's norms. That she becomes a symbol of rebellion for the girls in the college underscores her significance in the text. The coupling of her with the Sojourner tree, the third metaphor used in this early section, reinforces the meaning.

A story about the power of narrative, the Sojourner tree recalls the storytelling of a mythologized Louvinie whose art proved fatal to one of her young wards and resulted in her having her tongue cut out. After the narrator relates the incident, the fragment of Louvinie's original text is repeated in its entirety. The narrative then focuses on the historical relationship of the girls of Saxon College to the Sojourner tree, and the mythological significance of the tree is enhanced.

These episodes are digressions from the larger struggles of the civil rights movement and deliberately place the personal histories of women in the foreground. The reader must establish the relationship of these apparently disparate narratives to an implied feminist discourse. The cluster of narratives all focus on problems of women's empowerment or, more accurately, *dis*empowerment.[25]

These narratives signify the emergence of feminist themes in Walker's fiction. What we have here is myth as an alternative to history. This mythologizing, on the surface somewhat disruptive of the narration, becomes an integral part of the text. The reader must insert these myths into the text so that they are integrated into the total framework of the novel. The feminist discourse of *Meridian* unfolds through this insertion of myth and folklore in narratives that signify their difference from the framing text, with its emphasis on racial oppression and blind spots to Black women's oppressed condition.

The symbolic representations of disempowerment exemplified by the Marilene O'Shay, Wild Child, and Sojourner tree episodes invoke folklore; the deconstruction of motherhood, also central to feminist ideology, is pursued more directly. It involves the defamiliarization, or "making strange,"[26] of the ordinary situations of women's oppression. What is undertaken is a demystification of the Black matriarchy myth, resonant with the critique of the ideology of motherhood that generally characterizes nonfictional and fictional feminist discourse. That myth is revealed through the fusion of Meridian's narrative with that of her mother. Another myth, of romantic love, is even more radically cast aside through the antierotic construction of Meridian's story. In both episodes, the narrator directly intervenes, strongly reinforcing the theme of the text.

The reader does not experience Mrs. Hill's anguish directly—her voice is generally not heard in the text; the narrator interprets the significance of her life. The narrator not only describes the problem-filled life of Mrs. Hill but, by appropriating her point of view, reinforces it. Representing Mrs. Hill as a woman "who had known the freedom of thinking out the possibilities of life," the narrator points to the destructive nature of marriage and motherhood:

> She could never forgive her community, her family, his family, the whole world, for not warning her against children. For a year she had seen some increase in her happiness: She enjoyed joining her body to her husband's in sex, and enjoyed having someone with whom to share the minute occurrences of her day. But in her first pregnancy she became distracted from who she

was. As divided in her mind as her body was divided, between what part was herself and what part was not. Her frail independence gave way to the pressures of motherhood and she learned—much to her horror and amazement—that she was not even allowed to be resentful that she was "caught." That her personal life was over. There was no one else she could cry out to and say "It's not fair!" And in understanding this, she understood a look she saw in the other women's eyes. The mysterious inner life that she imagined gave them a secret joy was simply a knowledge of the fact that they were dead, living just enough for their children. They, too, had found no one to whom to shout "It's not fair!"[27]

Mrs. Hill retreats into "abstraction," a tragic woman whose life is marked by despair and paralysis. In that description, the text makes a declaration to which the reader can become passively receptive: that motherhood is inherently oppressive. Not only is this reinforced by the narrator's comments (e.g., "Her frail independence gave way to the pressures of motherhood") but in the identification of the narrator with Mrs. Hill's perspective. The broader implications of Mrs. Hill's state, its relationship to the plight of "other women," places the event within the general discourse on feminism.

Having constructed Mrs. Hill as a victim of her acceptance of the role of Black matriarch, a position reinforced by Christianity and general social practice, the novel shifts its focus to Meridian's rejection of motherhood. Again the point of view is that of the narrator who explores the intensity of Meridian's response to her plight. The banal scene of a mother affectionately embracing her child is totally defamiliarized in this depiction of Meridian and her child:

She sat in the rocker Eddie had bought and stroked her son's back, her fingers eager to scratch him out of her life. She realized he was even more helpless than herself, and yet she would diaper him roughly, yanking his fat brown legs in the air, because he looked like his father and because everyone who came to visit assumed she loved him, and because he did not feel like anything to her but a ball and chain.

The thought of murdering her own child eventually frightened her. To suppress it she conceived, quite consciously, of methods of killing herself. She found it pleasantly distracting to imagine herself stiff and oblivious, her head stuck in an oven. Or coolly out of it, a hole through the roof of her mouth. It seemed to her that the peace of the dead was truly blessed, and each day she planned a new way of approaching it.[28]

This joining of the motherhood myth with fantasies of murder and suicide heighten the argument against a romantic treatment of that institution and compel the reader to view it from a different angle. Thus, when Meridian decides to abandon her child in order to attend college, her mother's view of her as a "monster" for doing so is not sympathetically received by the reader. Inscribed in the text, then, is a historical examination of Black women's changing views on motherhood: Mrs. Hill embodies the traditional position, largely self-effacing and destructive; and Meridian represents the emergence of a feminist dialectic.

The third body of narratives through which the novel develops its views on feminism focuses on the relationship between Lynne and Meridian. Their relationship as women who nurture and support each other is the basis of the chapter "Two Women." In this scene, Lynne's mulatta [sic] daughter has been brutally raped and killed, and she has turned to Meridian for comfort while waiting for her husband, Truman, who is Meridian's former lover:

> As they sat they watched a television program. One of those Southern epics about the relationship of the Southern white man to madness, and the closeness of the Southern black man to the land. *It did not delve into women's problems, black or white.* They sat companionable and still in their bathrobes, watching the green fields of the South and the indestructible (their word) faces of black people much more than they watched the madness. For them, the madness was like a puzzle they had temporarily solved (Meridian would sometimes, in the afternoons, read poems to Lynne by Margaret Walker, and Lynne, in return, would attempt to cornrow Meridian's short patchy hair), they hungered after more intricate and enduring patterns. Sometimes they talked, intimately, like sisters, and when they did not they allowed the television to fill the silences.[29]

The idyllic relationship of these women, with its suggestion of the emergence of a feminist consciousness, is rendered problematic by Lynne's shifting characterization in the novel. Her whiteness becomes a signifier of her difference from Meridian and the Black community in which she has immersed herself; and she is variously presented as naive, coarse, and victimized. In one of two chapters entitled simply "Lynne," her view of Blacks approaches a romantic stereotype:

> To Lynne, the black people of the South were Art. This she begged forgiveness for and tried to hide, but it was no use . . . to her, nestled in a big chair made of white oak strips, under a quilt called The Turkey Walk, from Attapulsa, Georgia, in a little wooden Mississippi sharecropper bungalow that had never known paint, the South—and the black people living there—was Art. The songs, the dances, the food, the speech. Oh! She was such a romantic, so in love with the air she breathed, the honeysuckle that grew just beyond the door.[30]

This portrait of Lynne, coupled with her occasional expressions of disdain for Blacks in general and Black women in particular, creates an ambiguity in the characterization and makes the reader's response to her somewhat of a problem. The ambiguity is heightened when the narrator identifies with Truman's assessment of Lynne's guilt as a white person:

> By being white Lynne was guilty of whiteness. He could not reduce the logic any further in that direction. Then the question was is it possible to be guilty of a color? Of course for years black people were "guilty" of being black. Slavery was punishment for their "crime." But even if he abandoned his search for Lynne's guilt, because it ended logically enough in racism, he was forced to search through other levels for it. For bad or worse, and regardless of what this said about himself as a person, he could not—after [Tommy's] words—keep from thinking Lynne was, in fact, guilty.[31]

Had these reflections been rephrased so as to identify them with Truman, the narrator would have been distanced from them. But the fusion of Truman's perception and the narrator's reporting makes this impossible and, combined with other negative portraits of Lynne in the novel, clouds her characterization.

A significant episode occurs when Lynne is raped by Tommy Odds. While the rape scene primarily depicts the relationship between Lynne and Tommy—particularly Tommy's role as rapist and villain—it also evokes complex social issues. It alludes to the historical moment in which the Black consciousness movement displaced the civil rights movement, resulting in the marginalization of whites in the struggle for Black liberation. In exploring Tommy's behavior, it develops the ambivalent feelings that some Black men at the time experienced toward white women.

> He had wanted to make love to her. Because she was white, first of all, which meant she would assume she was in control, and because he wanted—at first—to force her to have him in ways that would disgust and thrill her. He thought of hanging her from a tree by her long hair and letting her weight gradually pull the hair from her scalp. He wondered if that would eventually happen to a person hung up in that way.[32]

In the context of Tommy's having had his arm shot off by racists, the rape of Lynne assumes special proportions. His attempt to invest the act of rape with a larger political significance reproduces some of the cruder positions assumed by nationalist extremists in the 1960s, and the image of hanging evokes the entire history of lynching. In exploring Tommy's motives, then, the novel juxtaposes two discourses: one focused on Blacks, particularly Black males, as victims of racist oppression; the other on women as victims of rape, one of the most extreme acts of sexist terrorism.

The victimization of women, particularly the act of rape, is an issue central to feminist discourse. If the novel's racial politics demands that it explore Tommy Odds's behavior within the context of racial oppression, it is also committed to investigating Lynne's status as victim. That issue is somewhat ambiguously presented through the graphic detail of the rape coupled with Lynne's commitment to the "correct" political attitude, even at the expense of her own welfare.

> There was a moment when she knew that she could force him from her. But it was a flash. She lay instead thinking of his feelings, his hardships, of the way he was black and belonged to people who lived without hope; she thought about the loss of his arm. She felt her own guilt. And he entered her and she did not any longer resist but tried instead to think of Tommy Odds as he was when he was her friend—and near the end her arms stole around his neck, and before he left she told him she forgave him and kissed his slick rounded stump that was the color of baked liver.[33]

The novel's depiction of the rape as an act to which Lynne's sole response is an abstraction from self, from her own degradation and humiliation to an "understanding" of the feelings of her rapist, destroys whatever feminist argument the text attempted to advance. Coupled with her reluctance to report the incident to the police because of fears of the terror that would be inflicted on Black males in the community in general and her acquiescence to the sexual demands of all the Black males around her, the response makes her significance of woman as victim problematic. This depiction of Lynne is consistent with the ambivalent feelings that characterize Walker's other attempts to explore the possible union of white and Black women.[34] One becomes aware of the tension generated by a text committed to both racial and gender politics. As a white woman, Lynne becomes a signifier of difference and sameness. Her representational status within the racial discourse is compromised by her whiteness, while her status as woman places her in a common sisterhood.

Walker's two early novels, then, mark a point of intersection and a struggle between two discourses: racist and economic oppression and the victimization of Black women. In *The Third Life of Grange Copeland*, the women's stories are contained within a narrative of the strategies of survival necessary in a social milieu of racial and economic oppression; as such, the reader experiences them as largely elliptical and fragmented. *Meridian*, on the other hand, disrupts narrative form and displaces that larger history to focus more intensely on women's issues. The full articulation of a distinct feminist position unfolds in *The Color Purple*, which I treat in the next chapter.

Notes

1. Walker, *In Search of Our Mothers' Gardens*, 250–251.
2. Ibid., 133–135.
3. See Hayden White, *Metahistory: The Historical Imagination in Nineteenth Century Europe* (Baltimore: Johns Hopkins University Press, 1973); and idem, "The Value of Narrativity in the Representation of Reality," in *The Content of the Form: Narrative Discourse and Historical Representation* (Baltimore: Johns Hopkins University Press, 1987).
4. Hayden White, "The Fictions of Factual Representation," in *Tropics of Discourse: Essays in Cultural Criticism* (Baltimore: Johns Hopkins University Press, 1978), 122. Another essay in the same collection cogently addresses these issues; it is "The Historical Text as Literary Artifact," 81d–100.
5. Gayle Greene and Coppelia Kahn, eds., *Making a Difference: Feminist Literary Criticism* (London: Metheun, 1985), 12–13.
6. See Walker's interview with Claudia Tate in Tate, *Black Women Writers*, 176.
7. While I would cautiously embrace the concept of character advanced by Joel

Weinsheimer, it seems to have some relevance here. Weinsheimer argues: "Under the aegis of semiotic criticism, characters lose their privilege, their central status, and their definition. . . . As segments of a closed text, characters at most are patterns of recurrence, motifs which are continually recontextualized in other motifs. In semiotic criticism, characters dissolve." Cited in Shlomith Rimmon-Kenan, *Narrative Fiction: Contemporary Poetics* (London: Methuen, 1983), 32. It is arguable that "characters dissolve" in fictive discourse, but what may happen, as in the case of Grange Copeland, is that the character traits become so clearly linked with the larger discourse (e.g., Grange's dehumanization and the sharecropping system in general) that character becomes essentially a medium for illuminating the major issue and thereby primarily a textual strategy.

8. The terminology here is again borrowed from Genette. The heterodiegetic narrator is a nonparticipant in the story he or she tells; the homodiegetic narrator is present as a character in his narrative. See Gerard Genette, *Narrative Discourse: An Essay in Method*, trans. Jane E. Lewin (Ithaca: Cornell University Press, 1980), 244–245.

9. Alice Walker, *The Third Life of Grange Copeland* (New York: Harcourt Brace Jovanovich, 1970), 9.

10. Walker, *Third Life*, op. cit., 13.

11. Ibid., 21.

12. Ibid., 83.

13. Ibid., 207.

14. Ibid., 56.

15. See Paul Hernadi, "Dual Perspective: Free Indirect Discourse and Related Techniques," *Comparative Literature* 24 (1972): 32–43. Dorrit Cohn's theorizing of a "psychonarration" in which the narrator appropriates the speech and the thought of the character of a fictive discourse also addresses this narrative strategy. See Dorrit Cohn, *Transparent Minds: Narrative Modes for Presenting Consciousness in Fiction* (Princeton: Princeton University Press, 1978), 11. While it is not my intention to explore the debate related to this narrative strategy, my primary interest is its relationship to the production of textual ideology. What I am arguing is that in *The Third Life of Grange Copeland*, substitutionary narration or psychonarration results in a suppression of the histories of women.

16. Walker, *Third Life*, 58.

17. Ibid., 122.

18. Ibid., 40–41.

19. Ibid., 41.

20. Ibid., 124.

21. Alice Walker, *Meridian* (New York: Washington Square Press, 1976), 117.

22. Jürgen Habermas, "Modernity Versus Postmodernity," *New German Critique* (Winter 1981): 5.

23. Walker, *Meridian*, op. cit., 19.

24. Ibid., 20.

25. For an interesting reading of this narrative as one of several that focus on the issues of women's language and representational status, see Margaret Homans, "'Her Very Own Howl': The Ambiguities of Representation in Recent Women's Fiction," *Signs: Journal of Women in Culture and Society* 9 (Winter 1983): 186–205.

26. I am working here with the description of defamiliarization advanced by the Russian formalist Victor Shlovsky: "Habitualization devours works, clothes, furniture, one's wife, and the fear of war. If the whole complex lives of many people go on unconsciously, then such lives are as if they had never been.

And art exists that one may recover the sensation of life; it exists to make one feel things, to make the stone *stony*. The purpose of art is to impart the sensation of things as they are perceived and not as they are known. The technique of art is to make objects 'unfamiliar,' to make forms difficult, to increase the difficulty and length of perception because the process of perception is an aesthetic end in itself and must be prolonged." See Victor Shlovsky, "Art as Technique," in *Russian Formalist Criticism: Four Essays*, ed. and trans. Lee T. Lemon and Marion J. Reis (Lincoln: University of Nebraska Press, 1965), 12. I have appropriated and modified this description of defamiliarization to argue that the unusual narrative strategies and frames Walker employs to represent motherhood place it as the site of oppression of women and force the reader to experience it in a different manner than he or she is accustomed to doing.

27. Walker, *Meridian*, op. cit., 50–51.
28. Ibid., 69–70.
29. Ibid., 173; italics added.
30. Ibid., 130.
31. Ibid., 149.
32. Ibid., 157.
33. Ibid., 159.
34. See, for example, "Advancing Luna—and Ida B. Wells," in Alice Walker, *You Can't Keep A Good Woman Down* (New York: Harcourt Brace Jovanovich, 1981), 85–104. In this narrative, the alleged rape of Luna by Freddie Pye provides the context for an extensive discussion of the responsibility of Black women to their race in general and to women as a class. It explores the terrors historically inflicted on Black men as the result of false accusations of rape and at the same time acknowledges that such acts sometimes occurred and were advocated by some extremists in the nationalist movements of the 1960s. The text assumes an interrogative modality, leaving the conclusion to the reader.

♦♦♦♦♦♦♦♦♦♦♦♦♦

The Dynamics of Enclosure

THEODORE O. MASON, JR.

Finally, and the blows were heavier, faster, now, she was striking at the white world which thrust black people into a walled enclosure from which there was no escape. . . .

—Ann Petry, *The Street*[1]

In two of her more frequently considered works, "Coming Apart" and *The Color Purple*, Alice Walker conspicuously employs metaphorical values of enclosure—a trope employed by black writers as different in time and temperament as Frederick Douglass and Ann Petry, or Harriet Jacobs and Richard Wright, just to name a few. This esthetic trope expresses in literary form the experience of marginalization and domination. In *The Color Purple* Celie finds herself enclosed within a series of related imprisoning structures—her illiteracy; the sexist role that Mr. constructs for her as his wife (and all that that role encompasses); and the entire racist political, economic, and social structure of the South, among others. In "Coming Apart," the wife finds herself imprisoned by her husband's pornographic fantasies.[2] These fantasies result from his addiction to pornography—*Jivers* and *Jiveboy*. But the magazines are themselves expressions of a larger enclosing structure—hegemonic fictions about black men and women specifically, and all men and women generally. Clearly the same comprehensive sense of enclosure obtains in *Color Purple*—all the characters in that novel (even the men) find themselves enclosed and constrained by prevailing fictions that condition who they are, how they view themselves, and how they act.

In both *Color Purple* and "Coming Apart," these fictive structures have physical analogues in the important interiors in each work—the home or the store for instance in *Color Purple* and the bathroom or the bedroom in "Coming Apart." In both works, domination becomes expressed figuratively as the enclosing effect of both physical spaces and "fictive" ones. Significantly, liberation and expansion also find expression as the result of more generative fictions: in the cumulative effects of Celie's letter writing (and reading) and in her increased literacy, or in the effect of the essays by Lorde, Teish, and Gardner on the husband in "Coming Apart." Both works rely on this interplay between expansion and enclosure voiced in the literary work as an opposition between different kinds of space and different kinds of fiction—a trope also shared by *The Third Life of Grange Copeland*.

In *Grange Copeland*, Walker uses the sharecropper's cabin as a charged metaphorical structure indicating the fundamental and irresistible entrapment of its occupants. Walker depicts the cabin in much the same fashion as DuBois in the central chapter of *Souls of Black Folk* (1903). There the living quarters of the black sharecropper become an emblem of his domination by Southern agricultural capitalism, an indication of his continued slavery.[3] From the very opening chapters of *The Third Life of Grange Copeland* Walker's echoing of this device becomes clear:

> Brownfield turned from watching the road and looked with hateful scrutiny at the house they lived in. It was a cabin of two rooms with a brick chimney at one end. The roof was of rotting gray wood shingles; the sides of the house were gray vertical slabs; the whole aspect of the house was gray. It was lower in the middle than at its ends, and resembled a sway-backed animal put out to pasture. A stone-based well sat functionally in the middle of the yard, its mossy wooden bucket dangling above it from some rusty chain and frazzled lengths of rope. Where water was dashed behind the well, wild morning-glories bloomed, their tendrils reaching as far as the woodpile, which was a litter of tree trunks, slivers of carcass bones deposited by the dog and discarded braces and bits that had pained the jaws and teeth of many a hard-driven mule.

As in many other of her works and in the Afro-American literary tradition generally, Walker takes potentially bucolic rural settings and encodes them with images of despair and decay.[4] The routinization of everyday life expressed in the monotony of the first Copeland house combines with the repeated images of decay and privation to express a nearly unavoidable sense of marginalization and hopelessness. The possibility of productive work, the fundamental illusion shared by sharecropping and more traditional forms of industrial labor, fails to materialize. In place of this illusion come crushing degradation and inescapable entrapment. From the structural weakness of the house itself, to the disorder of the woodpile, and to the use of tools as emblems of pain, Walker contextualizes the experience of the sharecropper with symbolic reminders of failure and mortality.

The description of Grange Copeland's cabin is the second emblematic structure used to indicate the possibilities of black life. The first is Uncle Silas's shiny 1920 Buick sedan that Walker uses to indicate the realm of possibility Brownfield imagines as being "up North." By starting the narrative with the emblem of the automobile, Walker engages one of the most powerful iconographic oppositions in the Afro-American narrative tradition—the play between North and South, freedom and slavery. By association with a similar "vertical" trope in Christian iconography (up toward the promise of heaven and down toward the punishment of hell), the opposition between high and low, up and down, and North and South, gains a doubly-reinforced significance in Afro-American narrative. Yet Walker problematizes this opposition by revealing the promise of the North to be false. The car modulates from an emblem of promise to an emblem of a more sophisticated form of entrapment with the news of Uncle Silas's drug addiction and ultimate death in the middle of an armed robbery. The North offers only the illusion of freedom that masks the reality of complete imprisonment.[5] By undermining the attractiveness of the North, Walker does not offer a concomitant revaluation of the South. Instead, she collapses the distinctions embodied by the different poles of this vertical axis, thereby removing any possibility of escape for her characters, lending even greater dramatic weight to the immediate setting of the novel.[6] By limiting significantly any dramatic and psychological options outside the enclosing structure of the house, Walker turns our attention to what happens inside this critical space.

Yet circumstances inside prove no better than those outside, for the house encloses a profound and crippling absence. Grange, the cabin's primary inhabitant, has been so worn down by his life in the shack that he is "thirty-five but seemed much older" at the start of the narrative. But more significantly,

> his face and eyes had a dispassionate vacancy and sadness, as if a great fire had been extinguished within him and was just recently missed. He seemed devoid of any emotion, while Brownfield watched him, except that of bewilderment. A bewilderment so complete he did not really appear to know what he saw, although his hand continued to gesture, more or less aimlessly, and his lips moved, shaping unintelligible words.

Grange's sole response to this complete deprivation can only be "the fatal shrug." Revealing here is Walker's use of absence as a profound signifier. Literally, there is *nothing* to Grange's life, so that he may recognize himself and his family merely as experiencing the inversion of what other people (mostly white) have. His life is so debilitating and lacking of substance that it propels him beyond speech for its expression. The shrug itself expresses another level of absence by communicating that no remedy exists that might relieve the persistent nothingness and vacancy.

Not so surprisingly in a novel dominated by the idea of cycle and repetition, Brownfield's several cabins bear the same stamp of failure and hopelessness as did his father's. The warmth associated in the novel with generative human relations never enlivens Brownfield's domicile:

> One look at the walls of the room they were in made it clear no one could be warm in it. The walls had been covered, probably neatly at one time, with paper bags. Bags cut open along one side and flattened out, sides overlapping. But the bags hung down now, here and there, in rustling flaps; the wind had pushed them loose. . . . In the window frames without cardboard panes someone had tried to put in neat square pieces of cardboard, but the rain coming down against these squares at a slant, made the bottom half of them wet and the same wind that pushed the flaps aside to reveal holes in the roof forced aside these pieces of cardboard, and puddles of icy water were collected on the bare grey floor.

The conditions of this house defeat the efforts of even the most diligent and resourceful. Grange, silent in the face of his own hopelessness, has a vantage point (a critical distance) on his son's despair. His sigh of "condemnation" is thoroughly unmistakable. Enlightened by his trip North, Grange can see Brownfield's complicity in his own failure in clear relief—the deadness of the cabin standing in contrast to the fruit Grange brings the children for Christmas.

Worse still is the site of Mem's final tragedy, the cabin on Mr. J. L.'s place that Brownfield has reserved for his triumph over Mem's affirmative self-assertion and her efforts to save her children from her husband's brutishness. Her final home is even more degraded and dismal than the previous shack, lacking even the pitiful gesture of cardboard window panes. "Mr. J. L. had promised that someone would clean it out, but it was still half full of wet hay. There were no panes in the windows, only wooden shutters. Rain poured into all three of the small rooms, and there was no real floor, only tin, like old roofing, spread out to keep the bottom of the hay bales from getting soggy." Walker emphasizes here the sense of enclosure and constriction characteristic of the cabin as a dwelling and as a signifier. The latest shack bears a "crippled abandoned look," emblematic not only of Brownfield (abandoned child and emotional cripple that he is), but also of the ultimate fate to which Brownfield has brought Mem, Daphne, and Ornette—a fate Ruth certainly would have shared but for Grange's efforts.

Throughout the course of the narrative the structures inhabited by Brownfield and his family obviously become more entrapping and more debilitating. We have already seen how the despair occasioned by Grange's cabin leads him into silence. The structures Brownfield secures for his family have the same kind of effect on all of them, but particularly on Mem, who drifts from literate articulateness to its opposite:

> The starch of her speech simply went out of her and what came out of her mouth sagged, just as what had come out of her ancestors sagged. Except that where their speech had been beautiful because it was all they knew and a part of them without thinking about it, hers came out flat and ugly, like a tongue broken and trying to mend itself from desperation.

A verbal analogue for the sharecropper's cabins in the novel, Mem's speech progressively loses its strength and resilience, failing ultimately to protect her from the force of the surrounding environment conditioned largely by Brownfield's willfulness. Over the course of the novel, except when they live for a brief period in the house in town, Mem loses her capacity for language that distinguishes her from nearly everyone else, especially from Brownfield and by extension from Josie and Lorene. Even the material signs of her literacy, the books themselves, come to have an ironic utility when she burns them for heat—sacrificing a significant part of her identity simply in order to survive the kind of life Brownfield has reduced her to.

Walker makes Mem's eventual reduction and defeat more dramatically telling by allowing her to gain momentary control of her family's fortunes when she signs the lease and moves them to "her" house. This significant shift Walker emphasizes by setting off a description of the apartment in a separate chapter. Chapter 27 of *Grange Copeland* underscores the difference between the city environment and the milieu of the shack by foregrounding details that indicate a significant improvement in class status for Mem, Brownfield, and their children. Brownfield now works in a factory. He and his family have indoor plumbing with its attendant value transformation. "Now he could shit, and rising, look at himself, at the way his eyes had cleared themselves of the hateful veins and yellow tigerish lines, without much odor or rain, and much like a gentlemen; or as he invariably thought of it, like a white man." The walls of the house, though "dingy," get painted; even though the wiring is occasionally faulty, they have electricity; and the kitchen has a refrigerator. The Copelands have progressed so far up the class ladder that they now receive catalogues in the mail—a sure sign of their entry into consumer society, even if they occupy only its lowest rung.

The catalogue acts as a significant emblem in at least two ways. It affirms the Copelands' new class status, but it also gives them a view of an economic universe from which they are barred. "The pictures of the new clothes and the guns and the boats and everything looked extra good in clear light." By phrasing this response to the catalogues in Brownfield's accents and from his perspective, Walker indicates the difference between the universe of pleasure boats and the universe of the Copelands. And in doing so, she also reveals how limited their horizon of expectations actually is. Although Brownfield and family have progressed morally and economically, their progress is still powerfully limited by the controlling assumptions and economic practices of white society. By and large this hegemony is exercised not by violence or physical force (though this is always a threat), but by the controlling power of implied narrative fictions, such as the catalogue. We only occasionally see or hear the explicit indications of its existence—for instance, though Brownfield's invocation of whites as the cause of his cruelty, or through instances such as Ruth's discovery of "nigger" as an annotation in her history book, or by way of the occasional appearance of Shipley. Yet nevertheless the white world and its attendant power (expressed as controlling fictions) act as a framing device for Walker's narrative, contextualizing the action.

It would be a mistake not to recognize along with Harold Hellenbrand that *The Third Life of Grange Copeland* is marked by a progressive movement from silence to speech, a movement indicative of Grange's growth and Ruth's increased horizon of possibility. Certainly Walker emphasizes the significant silences early in the novel as emblems of the Copelands' fundamental sense of helplessness, their inability to communicate with one another, and their absolute marginalization. Yet in another sense the novel moves less from silence to speech than it provides a narrative field dominated by competing fictions, some of them authored by even the most conventionally inarticulate of the characters. These fictions become enclosing structures themselves, just as clearly as Walker uses the sharecropper's shack as a signifier of a powerful dynamic of enclosure.

Silence certainly plays a role in the development of Brownfield's impulse toward the creation of the sort of narrative likely to inform his life. Early in the novel Brownfield meditates on the condition of his life as well as the lives of his parents. Walker phrases his meditation as a problem of knowledge and interpretation:

> Brownfield got a headache trying to grasp the meaning of what his cousins told him. The need to comprehend his parents' actions seeped into him with his cousins' laughter. The blood rushed to his head and he was sick. He thought feverishly of how their weeks were spent. . . . Of his mother's soft skin and clean milky breath; of his father's brooding, and of an onrushing inevitable knowledge, like a summer storm that comes with high wind and flash flooding, that would smash the silence finally and flatten them all mercilessly to the ground. One day he would know everything and be equal to his cousins and to his father and perhaps even to God.

Interwoven with the images of destruction and enclosure in this passage is a similar movement toward expansion and fulfillment by means of the acquisition of knowledge. In this projected vision of himself, Brownfield imagines that he will ascend some ladder of knowledge and capacity, acquiring greater creative power at each step. In doing so he will outstrip his cousins' power to tell a story he cannot comprehend and "smash" his father's enclosing silence. This silence acts as a kind of narrative fiction itself since it so thoroughly conditions who and *how* Grange is, as well as determining the contours of both Margaret's and Brownfield's existence. Gaining enough knowledge would allow Brownfield to break out of his father's narrative authority and ultimately lead him to usurp the creative powers of the God who has assigned him such a miserable role to play in this world.[7]

Becoming a creator would presumably allow Brownfield to break out of the silence that so thoroughly informs his early life by reinvigorating his capacity to dream, something he has never been able to do. The reinvigorated creative impulse might well help him escape the cyclical patterns that dominate his life. "Brownfield slid down from the truck knowing his face was the mask his father's had been. Because this frightened him and because he did not know why he should have inherited this fear, he studiedly brushed imaginary dust from the shoulders of a worn black suit Shipley had given him." Shipley has given Brownfield more than the suit, of course. He has cast him in a role once occupied by his father in a drama about the relationship between blacks and Shipley's version of white authority. When Brownfield first sees his father in this role he notices how different Grange seemed to act. "When the truck came his father's face froze into an unnaturally bland mask, curious and unsettling to see. It was as if his father became a stone or a robot. A grim stillness settled over his eyes and he became an object, a cipher, something that moved in tense jerks if it moved at all." The mechanical quality of Grange's movements and attitude signals his acquiesence to and his enclosure in a fiction Shipley creates. Brownfield repeats this role, though he would like nothing more than to break out of it by expressing his own creative and narrative impulses, "writing" his own story so that he might throw off the mask.

Yet for all his desires to become a creator of his own fictions, Brownfield is hopelessly derivative as an artist. All he can do is recapitulate and revoice the fictions in which he has been cast, fictions whose primary theme involves dominance and oppression and whose primary trope is enclosure. Brownfield weaves a narrative around Mem whose personal tragedy signals a triumph for its author. Sexuality and pregnancy become not only biological facts, but also narrative metaphors for enclosure, as well as plot devices by which Mem may be brought "down."

In the beginning Walker takes narrative control of the representations of sexuality and sexual activity. "They were passionate and careless, he and Mem, making love in the woods after the first leaves fell, making love in the corncrib to the clucking of the hens and the blasting of cocks, making love and babies urgently and with purest fire at the shady ends of cotton rows." Contextualized by Walker as a celebration of their marriage, Brownfield's and Mem's sexuality clearly has its unfortunate effects, since each act and subsequent child creates "another link in the chain that held him to the land and to a responsibility for her children." Sex for Brownfield also becomes a way of seeking relief from the marginalization and domination that make up so much of his psychological life. "He prayed for a decent job in Mem's arms. But like all prayers sent up from there, it turned into another mouth to feed, another body to enslave to pay his debts. He felt himself destined to become no more than overseer, on the white man's plantation, of his own children." Though this passage follows the section denoting the Copelands' sexual exuberance by only a very few pages, already the character of their sexual lives is being changed by the economic relations that condition their existence. In fact, Brownfield's characterization of himself as an overseer to his own children prefigures the fashion in which familial relations achieve a kind of instrumentality. This vision of himself also indicates Brownfield's revoicing of the fiction that informs life, since the only significant relations he knows are characterized by either abandonment (by Grange and Margaret) or dominance (by Shipley or Captain Davis).

As the novel progresses, the representations of sexuality become cast less as expressions of exuberance and freedom and more as expressions of orchestrated enclosure. Sexuality is depicted less from the perspective of a slightly distanced narrator and located more within Brownfield's consciousness. "Brownfield lay in wait for the return of Mem's weakness. The cycles of her months and years brought it. The first early morning heavings were a good sign. Her body would do to her what he could not, without the support of his old bravado. . . . She could not hold out against him with nausea, aching feet and teeth, swollen legs, bursting veins and head, or the grim and dizzying reality of her trapped self and her children's despair. He would bring her back to lowness she had not even guessed at before." In one sense, pregnancy here is cast as an accident of biology, the assault of Mem's body on her psyche.[8]

Yet ever foregrounded is Brownfield's use of impregnation as an instrument of domination and as the fundamental plot device in his narrative designed to precipitate and record Mem's fall. "What a sly and triumphant joy he felt when she could no longer keep her job. She was ill; the two pregnancies he forced on her in the new house, although they did not bear fruit, almost completely destroyed what was left of her health."[9] Slightly later Brownfield makes explicit the intentionality behind his narrative of enclosure. "'You was going to have your house, straight and narrow and painted and scrubbed, like white folks. You was going to do this, you was going to do that. Shit,' he said, 'you thought I fucked you 'cause I wanted it? Josie better than you ever been. Your trouble is you just never learned how not to git pregnant.'" Of course, the insanity of Brownfield's orchestration of Mem's tragedy is its self-destructiveness. Ironically, Brownfield achieves a sense of power and expansion, precisely as his narrative creates the sense of enclosure that destroys him as well as Mem.

Mem tries to create an alternative fiction of her own—one based on different principles. Her ten-point list represents an attempt to control and redirect Brownfield's behavior. Put "fictively," the list is her way of creating a character since it seeks to control how Brownfield acts toward her, her children, and the white world. It further works to determine Brownfield's character, since it amounts to a program that would change his image of himself as well, in large measure by forestalling the self-pity and self-hate that lead him to abuse both wife and children. Throughout the passage Mem asserts her "narrative" control. This she does explicitly by asserting her superior authority over and against the authority of the white world.

The new house will be a space conditioned by her intentions. "If you intend to come along I done made out me some rules for you, for make no mistake it's going to be my house and in my house what the white man expects us to act like ain't going to get no consideration!" This explicit declaration of control is anticipated slightly earlier when Walker has Brownfield raise the spectre of Captain Davis as an intervening and protecting power. "Brownfield thought irresistibly of Captain Davis; the tall old cracker just popped into his mind like he was God or somebody." Davis comes to Brownfield's mind when Mem admonishes him to "Call on the one you've let make you what you are." We can recognize here a potential conflict in narrative authority, insofar as Mem proposes to revise completely the dominant fiction of Brownfield's life, the one authored by men like Shipley and Davis. Significantly, in order to indicate that narrative shift, Mem borrows from the symbolism and the language of that earlier dominating fiction. *She* holds the shotgun, not a white man. *She,* and not anyone else, calls Brownfield "Boy." To indicate her complete control she "borrows" and transforms the emblems and language of the fiction that previously dominated Brownfield. This moment of dominance is Mem's finest in the novel; but despite his acquiescence Brownfield begins almost immediately to undermine Mem in such a way that her story can only end tragically.

Despite Mem's failure, we can see the possibility articulated by Walker that not all enclosures need to be destructive or deleteriously self-serving. After all, the fiction Mem weaves to control Brownfield and the enclosed space in which that fiction would occur (the house in town) are created to protect herself and her children, and clearly to protect Brownfield from his defective vision of himself. Mem's tragedy notwithstanding, Walker uses Grange as a vehicle for expressing the power of affirmative and empowering enclosures, spaces that act as fictions, narratively interpreting and configuring the universe of the characters. Oddly enough, these generative spaces result in part from a combination of the same emotions and psychological states that condition destructive space—hate and a profound sense of marginalization. Yet the overwhelming self-pity determining Brownfield's narrative gives way in Grange's story to a more ironic posture that recognizes each person's complicity in his or her victimization. Coupled with a profound sense of responsibility, the recognition of complicity makes Grange's narrative more clearly motivated by love and by care rather than by love's opposite.[10]

Grange's experience in New York teaches him much about the destructive aspects of enclosure. As he witnesses the exchange between the white couple in Central Park, especially the "haughty rigidity" of the young woman's face, Grange thinks,

> Somehow this settling into impenetrability, into a sanctuary from further pain, seemed more pathetic to him than her tears. At the same time her icy fortitude in the face of love's desertion struck him as peculiarly white American. No blues would ever come from such a saving of face. It showed a lack of self-pity (and Grange believed firmly that one's self was often in need of a little sympathetic pity) that also meant less sympathy for the basic tragedies that occurred in the human condition.

Both a lack of self-pity (and too much self-pity as in Brownfield's case) lead to protective masks, fictions so thoroughly sealed they fail to recognize the essential humanity in others. Though Grange imagines that "misery leveled all beings," allowing them to partake of a common story, a more human fiction, the woman in the park proves him wrong. Ironically, her death at Grange's hand reveals to him a vision of closeness and solidarity, born of his belief in the necessity of killing one's oppressors, yet being joined with them ultimately by the refusal to shun one's own death.

This sense of connection, responsibility, "tolerance and . . . strength" conditions Grange's desire to create affirmative enclosures for his granddaughter Ruth. As Grange and Ruth build the fence around the farm, Walker has Grange parody Frost's "Mending Wall." "'Good fences don't make neighbors.'" This fence will indicate the boundaries of the farm that in the final sections of the novel becomes the space in which Ruth finds the freedom to survive and then the chance to mature. "'The fence we put up around it will enclose freedom you can be sure of, long as you ain't scared of holding the gun. The gun is important. For I don't know that love works on everybody. A little love, a little buckshot, that's how I'd say handle yourself.'" This care for others combined with a sense of the real need for protection characterizes the space Grange creates for Ruth. These spaces keep things in (the growing intimacy between grandfather and granddaughter) and keep things out (the self-centered intrusions of Brownfield and Josie; the possible interference of the white world, too).

Significantly, Grange makes values of enclosure generative not only for Ruth; but he would like to do so for others, too, in this case Quincy and Helen, the freedom workers. Though he doubts the possibility of achieving their goals, Grange "felt a deep tenderness for the young couple. He felt about them as he felt about Dr. King; that if they'd just stay with him on his farm he'd shoot the first cracker that tried to bother them. He wanted to protect them, from themselves and from their dreams, as much as from the crackers." Protecting them from the dissolution of their political ideals becomes just as important as saving their lives. Within the boundaries of this farm (just as in Mem's house in town) human dreams and desires prosper.

The farm is clearly a physical space, but even more importantly an analogue for an imaginative space, a way of "reading" and constructing the world. This construction of reality depends upon a recognition of others and a humane openendedness. Unlike Brownfield's narrative universe, Grange's allows other consciousnesses (Ruth's principally, but others, too) entrance on a nearly equal footing. Grange closes off this universe, invoking the gun both as the symbol and as the real thing, only when the intrusive white world in the form of the Judge seeks to replace Grange's authority with Brownfield's (whose only motive for wanting Ruth is self-aggrandizing and entrapping).

The gun becomes transformed into an emblem of liberation in this "story" (as it does in Mem's drama) for it works in the service of affirmatively expansive motives. Brownfield's death opens a universe of freedom for Ruth, even if its price is Grange's death. Yet even in the moment of Grange's death Walker invokes an image of enclosure. "'Oh, you poor thing, your poor thing,' [Grange] murmured finally, desolate, but also for the sound of a human voice, bending over to the ground and then rearing back, rocking himself in his own arms to a final sleep." Symbolically Grange becomes his own protective parent, re-enacting his relationship to Ruth, gaining the comfort of the valuable self-pity whose lesson he learned in Central Park. The capacity to create ways of viewing the self that are comfortable and yet also allow for the reality of others is given its final statement here. Grange symbolically "revoices" that fictive trope by wrapping his arms about himself, becoming his own protective enclosure, performing for himself at the conclusion of his third life the offices performed for his granddaughter.

The use of enclosure as a dominant metaphor has applications in the realm of criticism and theory as well as in the realm of literature itself—especially in the sort of criticism and theory that conceives of itself as being oppositional. The critic Susan Willis has identified the three-woman household, in the work of Toni Morrison and of black women generally, as both a comment on the masculine dominance of women (both economic and sexual) and also as a utopian space where that dominance might be overturned. Although she refers to the male-dominated household as a "boxed-in atmosphere," clearly the three-woman household is no less an enclosing structure, even if it emphasizes freedom rather than dominance. Audre Lorde's now famous remarks about the impossibility of dismantling the master's house with the master's tools implies at the very least an alternative house constructed with better-suited instruments.

Walker herself has taken recourse in the dynamics of enclosure in her essay "In Search of Our Mothers' Gardens." There at least two sorts of enclosure obtain. The emphasized womanist solidarity creates one kind of affirmative enclosure—an enabling space. We can see this even in the pattern of allusion and reference Walker employs. By foregrounding explicitly a connection to Virginia Woolf's "Room of One's Own" and by establishing a network of reference to other black women artists and black women generally, Walker establishes a significant horizon or perimeter—the enclosed space within which productive work can be done.

> How they did it—those millions of black women who were not Phillis Wheatley, or Lucy Terry or Frances Harper or Zora Hurston or Nella Larsen or Bessie Smith; or Elizabeth Catlett, or Katherine Dunham, either—brings me to the title of this essay, . . . which is a personal account that is yet shared, in its theme and its meaning, by all of us. I found, while thinking about the far-reaching world of the creative black woman, that often the truest answer to a question that really matters can be found very close.

*   *   *

The serious work of women, both literary and non-literary, requires this enabling space. Simultaneously that serious work facilitates the creation of more similarly expansive spaces.

At the same time, the mothers' garden can act as a kind of disabling space—at least in fiction. The utopian impulses identified by Willis account for one of the weaknesses in Walker's work: a tendency toward premature and total narrative closure. The neatness (as well as the completeness) of Celie's deliverance at the conclusion of *Color Purple* may well be something the reader wishes for, but it seems to contradict the difficulty and the complexity of the rest of the novel. Similar conditions obtain in "Coming Apart," where the husband's exposure to the essays by Lorde, Teish, and Gardner leads to a transformation, that, though incomplete, seems a bit too unproblematic and hurried given the rest of the short story. Utopian works may well require this kind of totalizing vision, this kind of seamlessness, for their success, since they intentionally posit other worlds, ones completely different from our own. Yet this seamlessness can signal another kind of enclosure that becomes limiting itself. The more seamless a text becomes and the greater the distance between the world of the text and the world outside the text, the greater the difficulty of achieving a kind of critical referentiality—one of the hallmarks of black women's fiction and other oppositional sorts of literature.[11]

We might go so far as to argue that any oppositional movement in criticism, theory, or literature runs a profound risk of creating alternative forms of closure no less problematic and destructive than the hegemonic closure presumably identified and attacked. There the force of the ideological position acting as both the pretext and the subtext for the work of literature, of criticism, or of theory comes far too much to the fore, making a conflict drawn as complex and difficult far too simplistic and unproblematic. And while such conclusions warm the hearts of "true believers," for anyone else they can ring less than convincing.

In *The Third Life of Grange Copeland* Alice Walker successfully avoids this trap by maintaining a fruitful narrative openness—one sign of which is Grange's capacity to change his life and his "lives." Another is Grange's ability to allow others, notably Helen and Quincy, into the enclosing space he has created for Ruth. Further, the effectiveness of the novel's conclusion depends on our recognition of the dynamic state of enclosure—a function of the competition between fictions. Grange's death reminds us that no fiction is ever absolutely complete, all powerful, or all-determining. Walker's conclusion also leaves Ruth's fate suspended, undetermined, and unrevealed. Yet despite this openness, in fact because of this openness, the enclosing spaces created by Grange as well as the fictional enclosure created by Walker can be read only as particularly expansive and profoundly enabling.

Notes

1. (New York: Pyramid, 1961; orig pub. 1946): 266.
2. Clearly the husband is just as imprisoned as his wife. We discover at the story's conclusion that "Still, he does not know how to make love without the fantasies fed to him by movies and magazines" and that "For years he has been fucking himself" in masturbatory fantasies ("Coming Apart" 53). "Fucking himself" expresses perfectly the husband's isolation, enclosure, and entrapment, as well as his complicity in his own victimization.
3. This is DuBois's description of the sharecropper's cabin: "It is nearly always old and bare, built of rough boards and neither plastered or ceiled. Light and ventilation are supplied by the single door and by the square hole in the wall with its wooden shutter. There is no glass, porch, or ornamentation without. Within is a fireplace, black and smoky, and usually unsteady with age. A bed or two, a table, a wooden chest, and a few chairs compose the furniture; while a stray show-bill or newspaper makes up the decorations for the walls. Now and then one may find such a cabin kept scrupulously neat, with merry steaming fireplace and hospitable door; but the majority are dirty and dilapidated, smelling of eating and sleeping, poorly ventilated, and anything but homes" (*Souls* 304). In DuBois's version of this universe the economic condition of blacks is characterized by complete domination. This economic condition leads to a profound collapse in the black social structure indicated not by "prostitution" or "illegitimacy," but by "separation and desertion after the family group has been formed" (305).
4. Jean Toomer's *Cane* (1924), Zora Neale Hurston's *Their Eyes Were Watching God* (1937), and *Richard Wright's Uncle Tom's Children* (1936) are but three of the more well-known texts that invert and subvert traditionally "pastoral" literary values. In all three the landscape is not even a neutral ground uninfected by the effects of racism and domination. Instead, it displays metaphorically the same values of enclosure and entrapment more traditionally identified in the early twentieth century with urban fictive settings; see for instance the work of Theodore Dreiser, among others.
5. Of course Walker uses this incident to prefigure Grange's experience in New York that occasions his return for a "third life."

   For another contemporaneous use of the automobile as emblem, see Toni Morrison's depiction of Macon Dead's car in *Song of Solomon*, 32 and Theodore Mason's "The Novelist as Conservator: Stories and Comprehension in *Song of Solomon*," 573.
6. Walker is naturally not the first black writer to problematize life in the North. Since as early as Frederick Douglass's *Narrative* or Harriet Jacobs's *Incidents in the Life of a Slave Girl*, the North has been depicted symbolically as a place of only limited possibility. In slave narratives (and "abolitionist" fiction, too) the Fugitive Slave Law becomes a symbol of the persistent threat of Southern slavery aided by the North. Rather than a place of deliverance, the North becomes only another locus of danger.

   By the turn of the century the North still remains a place with its own special form of imprisonment, largely a function of industrial capitalism. See DuBois's comments on capitalism in *Souls of Black Folk*, esp. Chapter Six, "The Wings of Atalanta." A less frequently referenced text from the same period invokes a similar symbolic pattern—Paul Lawrence Dunbar's *Sport of the Gods* (1902). For later versions, see Attaway's *Blood on the Forge* (1941) and more generally the work of Chester Himes.

7. Hellenbrand is right to notice the affinities between *The Third Life of Grange Copeland* and Wright's "Big Boy Leaves Home" and *Native Son*. The emphasis on violence as potentially creative would at least lead us toward that conclusion. So too should Walker's use of "smashing" as an expression of violence—a trope that dominates not only *Native Son*, but also, for instance, *The Outsider*. Walker reveals her indebtedness to Wright by borrowing the wording from an important section of *Native Son*. In *The Third Life of Grange Copeland* she writes "Now when she guffawed hoarsely at some tiny joke, corralling the slight intensity of the funny to her innermost heart, he could see himself reflected in the twin mirrors of her eyeteeth; and he wanted one dark gigantic stroke, from himself and not the sky, to blot her out" (103). Walker's punning on "hoarsely" and "corralling" may well deflect attention from her indebtedness to Wright. The wording in Wright's narration of Bigger's ride with Jan and Mary reveals it to be Walker's likely source. "Suddenly [Bigger] wanted to seize some heavy object in his hand and grip it with all the strength of his body and in some strange way rise up and stand in naked space above the speeding car and with one final blow blot it out—with himself and them in it" (*Native Son* 70).

8. Certainly at other points in this and other texts Walker emphasizes the potentially entrapping effects of women's physiology. See *Grange Copeland* 193, where Walker expresses Ruth's emerging fear (after her first period) that she can now be "had" and "trapped in a condition that could only worsen." In an interview Walker herself advanced a similar argument (O'Brien 187). See also Walker, "In Search of Our Mothers' Gardens," 233, in the volume of the same title.

9. Although Brownfield cannot take the complete credit for their failure, pregnancies that fail to come to full term suit his narrative purposes. They weaken Mem without "forging" another link in that chain of responsibility.

10. Although he tends to overstate Walker's emphasis on Grange's individualism, see Klaus Ensslen, "Collective Experience and Individual Responsibility: Alice Walker's *The Third Life of Grange Copeland*," 213 and passim, for a full reading of the role of responsibility in the novel.

11. We should certainly add "oppositional theory" here, too.

◆◆◆◆◆◆◆◆◆◆◆◆◆◆

Walker: The Centering Self

MICHAEL COOKE

In recent years intimacy has established itself as an important if not a dominant modality in black literature. Hayden's achievement is not unaccompanied or even uncontested in excellence. What he does with intimacy in a lyrical vein Alice Walker, in *Meridian*, translates into the larger political sphere, with education, religion, social action, racial commitment, and personal love mixed in for good measure. It is Walker who illumines the inner struggle and public cost of genuine intimacy, and who unmasks the varieties of false intimacy among us. To her credit she does this without stridency, and indeed with a wry acknowledgment of the seductions of false intimacy in commercial and sexual and racial and political guises; they are Falstaff's "ginger . . . i' the mouth." And she does not squint before the fact that true intimacy in turn cannot even offer Poe's "ethereal dances" and "eternal streams." The would-be ecstatic moment of returning the land to the Indian fizzles and falls to earth. With unhurried and unexasperated resolution Walker carries us into the depths that are ours when the false bottom of forced intimacy gives beneath us, and shows us the new light of austere surprises and rewards. *Meridian* is a study of intimacy in the thick of the world, and a summons to an inimitable intimacy for a reluctant world. Both psychologically and politically it stands as one of America's most daring works of the imagination in this century.

It will be an advantage to set this novel in the context of social as well as literary preferences prevailing in the mid-1970s, when it appeared. Militancy was no longer on the sidewalks. H. Rap Brown had disappeared. Stokely Carmichael had withdrawn to Africa. And feminism had co-opted much of the firepower that women such as Nikki Giovanni and Sonia Sanchez and Audre Lorde had brought to the "black power movement." Andrew Young and Ralph Abernathy presented a new mode of leadership, not more sedate but less eruptive, less given to momentary protestations and satisfactions. The more dramatic personalities, Jesse Jackson and LeRoi Jones, for example, seemed to be taking a more analytical, expository, even philosophical stance. Under the direction of Roy Innis, CORE was renouncing integration and espousing self-determination and separatism as the road to racial equality, but no mass movement ensued; rather, Mr. Innis toured east and west African states and called for black Americans to invest in sub-Saharan Africa. Here militancy took a financial turn, very different from the volatile boycotts of the 1960s.

In a sense, militancy had gone indoors, and even into bureaucracy with Black Studies programs, affirmative action, and voter registration applying topical poultices where before a total cure had been sought throughout the society. What Walker does in *Meridian* effectively takes us through another aftermath of the massive public Civil Rights movement, wherein she penetrates not so much the new bureaucracy as the original spirit and force behind the movement. By focusing on an eccentric individual, she reminds us that the movement envisioned a fitter life for all individuals, and drew up organizations solely to that end. By focusing on a spare, astringent individual, at a time when the accoutrements of "blackness"—Afro hairdos,[1] dashikis, Swahili catch phrases— were in vogue, she reminds us that personal manners and possessions, like impersonal institutions, can smother as much as protect us. And by focusing on an individual marked with denial and defeat, and haunted by obscure images of love and justice, she reminds us of the fact that suffering need not be random and meaningless, nor a centripetal human purpose without humor, or hope, or mercy, or effect.

It is a stroke of remarkable finesse that Walker should have made her centripetal heroine an eccentric. Not to belong in any standard and comfortable way is to escape the limitation of that way. The motif of edifices, of places to occupy and identify with, sharply illustrates the case in *Meridian*. Political meeting-rooms, churches, and schools all hold out a promise of security and dignity to Meridian, if she will give herself and her convictions or instincts over in some self-diminishing way. She withstands these invitations, but oddly without clamor or assertion. She is an eccentric, as far as confining centers go; she is not an individualist, as far as the rest of society goes. To the contrary, Meridian is almost alarmingly honest in her efforts to secure human relations, and almost alarming, too, in the frankness of her personal humility. When she makes her personal edifice a sleeping bag, her life becomes unpretentious and unprotected, with the paradoxical effect of (a) attracting other people to her and (b) facilitating her approach to other people, most especially lucidly innocent children.

Meridian stands out as a major character in a major twentieth-century work with the force of spirit to break the dualistic division of institutionalist and individualist that George Bernard Shaw gave a modern form in *Heartbreak House*. In Boss Mangan, Shaw depicts the troglodytic form of what would become the institutional man. In Captain Shotover he depicts the tentative, wistful shoot of individualism springing paradoxically in the ground of institutionalism and growing, over the decades, into a defiant if still dependent gladiolus (the sword-plant). The fact that Boss Mangan is killed in the bombing that consummates the play's action, combined with the young and much-desired Ellie Dunn's decision to attach herself to Captain Shotover, might lead us to think that Shaw is setting up against industry and institutions, and coming out for spontaneity and individualism. But the bombing is bringing down the locus, the bastion, of spontaneity and individualism. Mangan's death will not retard instituionalism; he is a newcomer, an upstart in its scheme. By the same token, the union of Captain Shotover and Ellie Dunn is at best one of unsinewed and sterile nostalgia.

The full reverberations of the Shavian bombing in *Heartbreak House* do not come to us till more than six decades later, with Thomas Pynchon's *Gravity's Rainbow*. Pökler and Slothrop embody institutionalism and individualism, respectively, but by now the individual has an attitude of anticipation toward the effect of institutions, and that effect does not appear, as in Shaw, like a bolt from the blue, but as the painstaking and ineluctable product of a co-opted human agent. The fatal rocket comes not with sudden horror, but with slow inevitability, like the Fall in *Paradise Lost*. Only the Fall in Pynchon's work is a matter of a complex physics, and the law of physics is that thou shalt kill. Inertia brings it, more than a positive will, and it is received as though with a song, a hymn of fatal welcome. The last line of the hymn and of the novel runs: "And a Soul in ev'ry stone." Perhaps this should hark back to a primordial pantheism, but the scene is more fundamentally one of apocalypse, with unexpected pathos and with overtones of a funeral—the stone is a tombstone over the soul.[2]

The singing of hymns and the sense of ultimate forces is also associated with death in *Meridian*. But it is not associated with finality. The church scene into which Alice Walker takes Meridian uses death to focus the commemorative impulse, to express and salve grief, and to renew or inspire human solidarity and aspiration. Death is not, as in *Gravity's Rainbow*, the ultimate climax, but rather the radical challenge that confronts Meridian in politics (will she kill?), in school (the fate of the Wild Child), in personal life (will she take her child's life, or her own?), as well as here in a social-religious setting. In a sense *Meridian* makes death and institutionalism equivalent; both undo individuals and *human values*. The genius of the novel lies in its ability to set up a restorative reaction without sentimentality or evasion.

A good measure of Walker's ability to break into new ground and take command of it can be found in Marge Piercy's *Vida*, which is also a novel with a bifocal view of the revolutionary late 1960s. Like Walker, Piercy has a female protagonist who must come to terms with her old revolutionary activities and relationships and with her new life. But Vida Asch proves paradoxically conservative, clinging at once to her family and to the prolonged Movement. Moods and circumstances dictate her conduct. She does not come to a new vision and her way of life remains peculiarly passive, or at least reactive. Inflated petulance or circumscribed rebellion seem to characterize her, when she is not preoccupied with sexuality. In a sense the superficiality of her "revolution," when compared with Meridian's, is revealed in the fact that Vida dyes her hair, whereas Meridian loses hers. Meridian's experience is thoroughgoing, Vida's assumed. It is in keeping with this difference that Vida's life is passed in skulking, in spasmodic and ill-concerted activity, while Meridian's builds out into the open from her sleeping bag, and builds in power and clarity. Vida Asch (her name suggests a confusion of life and ashes) is smothered in the habit of revolution; Meridian Hill (her name speaks for itself) ascends from the revolutionary cell, as from the cell of her spiritual confusion, to lead erstwhile revolutionaries, and children and adults in the wider social sphere, to new hope and strength.

The opening scene of *Meridian* establishes the fact that rigid and foolish force, on the one hand, and sanctimonious greed, on the other, stand as the only operative values in the society. It suggests that such a state of affairs will not suffice, but without projecting anything like an alternative position. The novel sets out in an atmosphere of crisscrossing disgruntlements, oppositions, indecisions. Only a sense that something new is de rigueur emerges, as the reader is taken through various channels of ignorance and multiple layers of illusion. What is expected, or even possible, does not have any positive image.

The action is simple on the surface. Though it is not their "day," the children want to see the miraculously preserved woman, Marilene O'Shay, and so Meridian leads them, past the gun-waving, whitewashed army tank that is bedecked with ribbons in American red, white, and blue, and past the phalanx of rifle-bearing police, into the circus wagon. Walker uses a double perspective on the action, with the newcomer Truman Held and the jaundiced old street-sweeper ("I seen rights come and I seen 'em go") playing off each other, to set up questions of how and whether things change, how and whether people change, and how and whether it makes any difference either way. Then, given the intensity and frankness of Meridian's engagement, the question arises whether intimacy is possible or worthwhile. And finally, in view of the children's part in the action, the opening scene prompts us to ask if intimacy can be transmitted, and to what end.

To get at answers, we must look not only at the interplay of deed and witness—Meridian's deed, and jointly Truman's and the street-sweeper's witness—but also at the intricate correspondences between Meridian's open, active, voluntary conduct and Marilene O'Shay's passive, trumped-up, hugger-mugger presence. For Walker dares to set up O'Shay as a sort of devil's-advocate counterpart to Meridian; if Meridian can withstand that, she is ipso facto established as having singular merit and virtue (or power) in our eyes. Let us look at the salient points of correspondence, or say rather obligatory association, between Meridian and Marilene:

Meridian Hill	Marilene O'Shay
a. brought home "like a coffin," Meridian says of herself: "they're used to carrying corpses"	a. "risen" from the depths of the sea, "Preserved in life-like condition"

Meridian Hill	Marilene O'Shay
b. Truman refers to her with the phrase "believe it or not"	b. is billed as "a wonder of the world"
c. "she thinks *she's* God"	c. "an ideal woman, a goddess"
d. "looked so burnt-out and weird"	d. "dried-up body"
e. "this weird gal"	e. "you know how childrens is, love . . . anything that's weird"
f. said to have "failed to honor not just her parents, but anyone"	f. "Obedient Daughter, Devoted Wife, Adoring Mother, *Gone Wrong*" (italics added)
g. theatricality, chosen and sustained ("they always follow me home after I perform")	g. theatricality, contrived by opportunistic widower ("red and gold circus wagon," etc.)

None of these marks is especially prepossessing, for either woman. It could be argued that Meridian puts her theatricality to the good of the children and the lessening of oppression. Or that the sweeper is as ready to believe she "ain't all there" as to charge her with thinking she can run other people's lives (the source of his arguing that she thinks "she's God"). But even such an effort to defend or exculpate Meridian gives evidence of assumed weakness in her. A true recognition of Meridian requires us also to take into account a number of elements that dissociate her from Marilene O'Shay:

Meridian Hill	Marilene O'Shay
a. "the door to Meridian's house was not locked"	a. there's a strict schedule and a fee to see the "risen" Marilene
b. the light-colored, visored cap ("she had practically no hair")	b. "her long red hair"
c. the children follow her faithfully	c. the children spot a fraud, in that there's "no salt . . . in the crevices of her eyesockets or in her hair"
d. the absence of goods, the life "in a cell"	d. had owned a washing machine, furs, and her own car, and had a full-time housekeeper-cook
e. "how can you not love somebody like that!"	e. given everything "she *thought* she wanted," but killed for infidelity and her corpse(?) exploited for cash

Both the children, in a vein of collective spontaneity, and Truman Held, as an experienced and analytical individual, attest to something in Meridian that makes for faith and love. No palpable basis for this offers itself. In fact, ordinary values seem to be overturned by Meridian: the children should "be afraid of her," while Truman is in direct encounter both "alarmed" and "bitter" toward Meridian, and rebuffed by her extreme detachment. But it is precisely in her detachment that her power may reside. She is the living antithesis to the materialism that pervades the black psyche in early twentieth-century writing. What seems like self-cancellation in her—her deathliness—is self-abnegation and an approach to self-transcendence. When she calls herself "a woman in the process of changing her mind," she gives a valuable clue to her position, *as long as* we do not put a teleological construction on her words. She is letting go of the known for the unknown, the limited for the limitless self. It is of great moment that her loss of health and hair constitutes, as Kimberly Benston has remarked to me, a form of hibernation. For of all the figures in the tradition of black hibernation, so cogently discussed by Robert Stepto in *From Behind the Veil*, Meridian is the only one who can be said to grow a new skin. This all but literally. Hibernation is a pure and self-conscious metaphor for "Jack-the-Bear" in Ellison's *Invisible Man*. With Meridian, the metaphor comes home to the realm of natural, involuntary experience (we may recall that Jack-the-Bear is as busy as a beaver in his hideaway world.) But Nelda Henderson, who also loses her hair progressively and irreversibly with each of her pregnancies, enables us to see that Meridian's state is not merely physiological. Meridian's bodily decline represents a reaction to spiritual bafflement, and also gives a sign that her powers are being spent on the hidden struggle of the spirit. She experiences an ecstatic sense of continuity with nature and the universe, but it is a *natural* occurrence, in a scheme where nature takes on uncommon dynamism and dimension. Meridian is not a transcendent or mystical figure; rather, she is one who breaks through the habitual constrictions and definitions of available knowledge.

By the same token, what seems like solitude in Meridian amounts only to a separation from specific connections, from possessive or exhaustive ties that in effect hold her away from others. She is lashed to (and by) the demands of specific events and groups and persons, that is to say, the demands of making love to Truman, of the revolutionary goal of homicide, of a violated and vulnerable Lynne Rabinowitz Held. The difference between serving these *demands* and serving the *needs* of the children lies precisely in the fact that the children's needs are not self-oriented and exclusive. They are concrete, but not specific to person or place or time. They are in that regard universal. When Meridian keeps (or finds) herself in solitude vis-à-vis amorous life, revolutionary life, or a desperately clutching personality, the effect is to keep from being cut off from a larger, more complex world. The appearance of solitude is the foundation of catholicity.

It will be necessary to come back to the question of Meridian's "solitude" or "catholicity" in light of her final departure from the other characters'—and the reader's—line of vision. But it is appropriate here to say that Meridian refuses the appearance of intimacy where the act in question does not deepen her apprehension of herself *and* her relationship to other people. Not that she never compromises herself. With Truman Held she does so, and it is noticeable that the text refers to her in disparaging animal phraseology: she becomes a "beached fish." She compromises herself also with her college "mentor," Mr. Raymonds, in an effort to make her way through school.[3] It is striking that the patent contrasts between the two men disappear in their common willingness to exploit her while talking up "blackness." Mr. Raymonds further embodies the exhausted, impotent character of one whose approach to *identity* goes by rote (his certificates on the wall, his clichés concerning black womanhood) and whose approach to *intimacy* means preadolescent gifts of candy and adolescent gropings and pressings at Meridian's body. The phenomena of scholarship and love grow dreary and distasteful in his person. He is all gesture, mere gesture; he reduces the vocation of teaching to gesture, as well as the impulses of passion. There is no denying that Mr. Raymonds is on a footing of "intimacy" with Meridian, but it is a furtive and sterile intimacy, the reflective counterpart to Truman's impetuous and aborted intimacy with her. (The deathliness of this kind of intimacy is brought out when Mr. George Daxter, undertaker, courts Meridian's consent from her twelfth to her fifteenth year.)

If we take into account Tommy Odds's "intimacy"—by rape—with Lynne, we can recognize a major implication of *Meridian,* namely, that a standardized *form* of intimacy such as sex works as an impediment and even as an enemy to its intrinsic nature. Revolution here is an analog to sex. People sit around asking one another if they would kill, if they *will* kill for the revolution, treating this as the first question where it ought by its nature to be the last, the ultimate confrontation of the capacities and failings of one's nature under the worst pressure of principle and circumstances. To adopt such killing as a policy is the *ejaculatio praecox* of politics. Truman produces the literal equivalent in love, leaving Meridian's body with an unbearable pregnancy, as she knew her conscience would have had to bear the projected killing.

Yet a third form of standardized intimacy occurring in *Meridian* is grief. Now grief brief above all would seem little susceptible to tampering, to artificial formation in the interest of novelty or revenge (which sex and politics so readily lend themselves to). Its occasions are clear, and binding. And yet even here Walker brings out an alarming degree of isolation and egotism, a deep dislocation of social and personal response. With an incisive revision of the McLuhanesque theme of the global village, she notes that with modern technology making the occasions and the forms of grief (the cutting down of "Medgar Evers, John F. Kennedy, . . . Martin Luther King, . . . Viola Liuzzo") universally available, *"television became the repository of memory, and each on-*

looker grieved alone." The word *onlooker* alone is worth reams of criticism. The basic absence of other people, the denial of public presence and mutual influence, changes the individual from sharer to onlooker. The very idiom, to watch television, interposes the medium between person and event, arrogating attention to the medium. In this sense the medium is indeed the message. The point is not only that the fullness of the human event is cheated, but the human individual is cheated of his fullness.

The episode of the Wild Child, even as it follows directly upon the assassinations passage, brings its grim story of human discontinuity into ordinary life. Meridian has tried, by refusing to kill "politically," to maintain a barrier between the momentum of political madness and the movement of personal, imaginative action; she has tried to keep that discontinuity at bay. The Wild Child's life says her task is greater than she thinks, that discontinuity will fall upon her even if she won't bring it down upon herself. The sequence from assassinations to Wild Child is structurally jarring, but only because the surface movement follows the laws of straightforward narrative, when in fact the novel operates according to abstract clues of association and is rife with psychological complexity.

Let us note the disparity between action and expectation in both episodes. What *happens* gives evidence of a total absence of principle, a pervasive randomness in social behavior. One shoots, one seduces—not for a discernible purpose or within a discernible scheme, but out of raw, random impulse. But the *reaction* to what happens, the sense of crushing and maddening trauma, tacitly presumes that life has been proceeding as more than wanton starts and turns. The episode of the Wild Child domesticates and paradoxically magnifies the lawless world of the assassination. The Wild Child's presence says life is wanton from its inception, with no responsibility, no connection, no sympathy; her pregnancy and death say that we may deplore her fate but we cannot even identify the "low-down dirty dog" who might be made to set things right.

The fact that Meridian is able to make even a rudimentary contact with the Wild Child again signalizes some socializing, some healing and freeing power in her. Almost without exception a child is involved in the crucial, seminal, cardinal episodes of the novel, as though it were working out that simplest and most uncontrollable manifestation of human presence and continuity. If Meridian's own conduct seems to give the lie to this emphasis, it is because basically Meridian is a spirit-giving mother, rather than a body-making one, and each interferes with the other. That is why she leaves her first natural child and refuses to have the second. With the Wild Child, as with the children deprived of seeing Marilene O'Shay, Meridian comes to the healing position by separating herself from the merely standard connections of the honors house at Saxon College. In this solitude of prereconciliation she lies in her room "like a corpse"; it is difficult not to see an analogy between Meridian's spontaneous behavior and the Pauline notion of dying to the *vetus homo* so that the *novus homo* can be put on.

It would be misleading to read Meridian's character hagiographically, but she is unmistakably involved in the rediscovery of the spirit, after the excess of materialism and of materialistic credulity that has marked her world. That even the Wild Child is touched by materialistic lures— "cake and colored beads and . . . cigarettes"—does not weaken the point. We are matter; we must begin in matter, but matter is not the be-all or end-all of our nature. In fact, Meridian comes out of her "silence" in college to recommend the destruction of matter, in the form of the president's house, and the preservation of the spirit embodied in the Sojourner tree, which has become materially less convenient with the dismantling of its carpentered platforms, and which symbolizes growth in the face of oppression, hope, harmony, and the creative tradition. When the students, enraged and thwarted at not being allowed to give the Wild Child the funeral they see fit at Saxon College, vent their passions on the Sojourner and destroy it, all that the Sojourner symbolized is invoked, and pronounced hopeless.

The destruction of the Sojourner is the ultimate act of group dynamics in *Meridian*, and significantly it displays the group undoing the good of its members. A vicious paradox appears, for the members of the group proceed in the closest concert and yet are farthest from awareness of themselves, of one another or of one another's good. They are entranced, as Meridian is entranced before approaching the Wild Child, but they are entranced to no purpose, giving all the signs of a common intimacy when really caught in the sameness of automatons.

The life of action is brought into question equally by (a) the refined young women like cross-wired maenads tearing down the Sojourner tree; and (b) the revolutionaries trying to make themselves like programmed robots, to kill on call; and (c) Tommy Odds, forcing himself on Lynne Rabinowitz like a windup toy because he cannot bear to contemplate his physical and social handicaps. *Meridian* unfolds the life of passion-as-suffering, and shows that suffering is crucial to human development. In this regard the novel weaves itself into an important threat in recent Third World writing, other examples being Wole Soyinka, *Season of Anomie*, Camara Laye, *The Radiance of the King*, Wilson Harris, *The Palace of the Peacock*, and Francis Ebejer, *Leap of Malta Dolphins*. But it must also be remembered that suffering as revelatory and redemptive is a leit-motif of the work of Nikos Kazantzakis, and important in Saul Bellow's work from *The Victim* to *Henderson the Rain King*.

In *Meridian*, Walker seems to stress the enthusiastic above the millennial aspect of the concept of suffering. That is to say, she is mainly concerned with bringing the power of divinity into the human sphere (*enthusiasm* conveys etymologically "having the god within"); correspondingly, she neglects the kind of absorption of the human into the divine sphere that marks the climactic episode in *The Radiance of the King*. Meridian's coffinlike rigidity is, for example, akin to the state of possession experienced by the chief of the Thracian Anastenarides prior to visitation by the divinity.[4] Her extreme physical reduction, to a state verging on death, is matched too by an inner draining; she seems wholly impoverished. But the other characters reveal that much is mysteriously present to her when they react with adoration rather than pity or avoidance. Even the streetsweeper's jaundiced observation that "she thinks *she*'s God" may betray in him an envious sense of her approach to a god-related state. And we know in fact that she is anything but thinking of herself.

Nothing in the text suggests that Meridian is embarked on a mystical journey, but her adoption of the peripatetic life of poverty and chastity is reminiscent of mysticism, and her impact on the world in the state of poverty is reminiscent of Meister Eckhart's declaration that "God means absolute poverty."[5] At best, though, Meridian would make a reluctant and irascible mystic. Her initial refusal to hear Lynne's story and bear Lynne's burdens must be understood as a desire to preserve a precarious detachment, but she is not dogmatic about this; she does listen, and does involve herself, even to the extent of letting the soul-crushed Truman sleep with her after the loss of Lynne and Truman's child. Her detachment from the principle of killing also wavers. At sight of the father demented by the loss of his son in the Civil Rights struggle, she experiences a murderous rage, and it becomes clear that she might spontaneously kill but for the fact that she spontaneously sings, or attaches herself to song. She draws away from killing again, but not before we have seen depths of emotional struggle not apparent when she was merely under peer pressure and the pressure of political theory, as opposed to the force of human identification. The capacity to know and share the experience of people she glancingly meets links Meridian with "Pa Hayden" in "The Crystal Cave Elegy." It is not a mystical capacity, but one based on sympathy and intuition, bearing toward the intensest realism.

Meridian's trances, her approximations to death, are preludes to episodes of such realism. Thus we must see the trances themselves as militating against mysticism. The text in fact goes so far as to suggest that both the triumphant confrontations with reality and the trances are theatrical. "They [the people] always follow me home after I perform." But the word *perform*, along with its sense of deliberately carrying out a role for public effect, also means to bring off a difficult enterprise or to bring an idea to enactment with skill and power. Meridian is one who performs, where others have failed. And yet she is without a plan of action (or script, to glance back at the question of her theatricality). In effect, by force of character Meridian corrects the mere passivity of the world of *Gravity's Rainbow*. And by dint of involvement she corrects the mere imagination of the dying world of *Pincher Martin*.

Meridian's life seeks to fuse ecstasy and justice. This is almost a distillation of her heredity: (a) of her great-grandmother Feather Mae's experience on the Sacred Serpent (repeated in her father and in her own person), and (b) of her father's insight into and attempt to live, like his alter ego, Walter Longknife, according to a "historical vision . . . as a just person." But she seeks to be more than a just person on a one-to-one basis (like her father giving his farm back to Longknife, a modern Cherokee, as ancestral land).[6] She seeks a just world. Ecstasy is not privilege, or even relief for her, but a burdensome, corpselike state of preparation. And justice is not the self-satisfied, shortsighted meting out of punishment for misdeeds that our society has simplistically made of it, but an intricate fitting together, with sensitivity and precision, of multiform elements habitually going athwart one another and at cross-purposes.

The slow, error-filled, even tragic manner in which Meridian comes to this position is well worth noting. Her life, in detail, is shocking enough: promiscuity, child-abandonment, abortion, disbelief in the rhetoric of "the Constitution and . . . the American Way of Life." But Meridian's life, in essence, is a fragile triumph of consciousness and choice over unconsciousness and brute obedience. When the text says that Meridian, "in the middle of her speech" on the Constitution, "stumbled and then was silent," it is recapitulating and rejecting the invisible man's rote performance at the degrading smoker, and at the same time signaling Meridian's dawning awareness of a possible, an integral, a necessary link between what she says and what she thinks and means. In effect, Meridian slowly gains intimacy with her true feelings, thoughts, interests, needs, capacities, and limitations by an empirical process, including the sympathetic empiricism of taking family history and national history to heart.

We need to look upon her career not as an arithmetic, but as an evolution. In the matter of her lovemaking and childbearing, for example, Meridian proceeds largely on a prevoluntary basis, as much an object or even victim as a participant. It is coming to consciousness that makes for the beginning of responsibility, and for her that coming to consciousness has a terrible candor and intimacy. She knows her willingness to kill her own child, and her own self, and yet retrieves her humanity without going over into Bigger Thomas's blind pit of action; she finds in herself the conviction that killing is the ultimate evil. She is seventeen years old; killing is meant to cope with unmanageable experience.

Walker had already taken up the question of motherhood and abortion in a short story that helps us to appraise Meridian's position here. In "The Abortion" *(You Can't Keep a Good Man Down)*, Imani is thinking only of her personal well-being ("I chose me"),[7] whereas Meridian is struggling through a complex of human values *as well as* trying to discover herself. Like *Meridian*, "The Abortion" has a decisive church scene/memorial service, where Imani decides to leave her husband, Clarence, because she thinks he is insensitive and unappreciative. There is an opportunistic inconsistency about Imani. Oddly, she does not sympathize with her husband's struggle in support of the first black mayor "in a small town in the South," while she indoctrinates her toddling daughter with anathema against the "kind of people" who "can kill a continent—people, trees, buffalo." Again, she does not basically wish to attend the fifth memorial service for someone she "had never seen;" in fact she wrenches the memorial toward herself, thinking of its subject as "herself . . . aborted on the eve of becoming herself," and believing that "respect, remembrance was for herself, and today herself needed rest." Her resentment of her husband's staying outside conducting politics with the mayor uses irreverence as a pretext. It is intrinsically based on concern for herself, whom Clarence has discommoded by (a) marrying, (b) impregnating, (c) bringing out to the service, and (d) distracting while she listens contentedly to the eulogy. In sum, Imani[8] seems relatively selfish and narrow beside Meridian, whose political and human sympathies enlarge in church.

Two things follow when Meridian knows that she can neither kill herself or her child, nor live with herself as a mother and her child as daughter: she gives up her child so that it may live better, and after the aborted relationship with Truman gives up sex so that she may live more truly and harmlessly in herself. These are stern decisions, the former out of line with traditional values,[9] the latter out of keeping with contemporary ones. But their unorthodoxy forms the basis of Meridian's honorable refusal to kill for the revolution and her amazing capacity to serve all children not as a somatic presence but as a spiritual force. It is through the most unsparing (and unexpected) intimacy with her own nature that Meridian is able, as no one else in the book is, to "belong" wherever she finds herself. She becomes intimate with others, experiencing what they experience, by way of renunciation: "she could [not] enjoy owning things others could not have."

Ultimately, the text suggests, to own is to destroy and to be destroyed. The great virtue Meridian attains is the willingness, or better, the will to "let . . . go" and be let go. Then, paradoxically, all things needful come to her, and she can be one with the children and with the old folk, and never a stranger, wherever she may turn. People give of themselves to her, and people come to her in search of themselves, the only limit to intimacy being set by her *on their behalf,* for to take over their lives or, alternatively, to die for them is to deny their right to live, and to die.

The lodestar and balancing agent of *Meridian* is "peace," not in the usage concurrent with the later stages of the Civil Rights movement, but in the sense of composure of spirit in an honorable reconciliation to the environment. The text enumerates the peace that comes from natural beauty, from metasexual cuddling, from death and the cessation of connection and responsibility, and finally from confidence in a living symbol, the Sojourner tree. Each fails, and is succeeded by the next: natural beauty because the land is given and wrested away; sex because it makes usurious demands on the future to pay for its passing moments; death because it necessitates infanticide or suicide, and Meridian, long before she has to defy her revolutionary cohorts on killing to order, has opted for life; and finally the Sojourner fails Meridian as a source of peace when in torment and confusion the girls destroy even that beacon and bulwark of faith.

Even so, peace does not fail in the novel. It merely ceases to be external to Meridian. Instead of taking it in from without, she gives it off, and is never without it. What she leaves Truman at the end is peace, and she is able to leave him—he is able to bear her leaving—because of that peace. The sleeping bag he takes over from her quickly takes on copulative and uterine valences; Truman is symbolically entering Meridian, or the womb. But more deeply he enters his own space, where he has nothing but himself; that is not only enough, but enough to help others from. He is a child again, renewed, as Meridian begins and concludes helping chidlren, rectifying life. Truman enters into Meridian's example and way of life. Here at the outset he is anxious, as she also had been, with psychosomatic symptoms of hair and weight loss. Those symptoms, we can see in retrospect, constitute a form of self-veiling that comes dangerously close to literal self-cancellation. But the probable end of experience for a Meridian is the peace that, if it does not pass understanding, is parallel to it.

Meridian faces death in the South, as the ex-colored man cannot do, and not only lives but shows others how to live better. She chooses solitude, as Bigger Thomas has no chance to do, and transforms it into catholicity. She takes the principle of kinship so deeply that she offends against its ordinary expression, leaving one child and aborting another where Harper almost goes mad at the natural death of his; but her devotion to her mother, her grandmother, her great-grandmother, and especially her father is luminous, and she not only makes the cause of all children, all weak and suffering people, her own but she mothers Lynne and Truman Held, separately, after the death of their daughter, because the necessity is there. In short, she transforms the crisis of self-veiling and even the threat of self-cancellation into intimacy, and solitude into intimacy, and kinship into a universal intimacy. She is one who can love, with deep human appreciation and understanding and protective compassion, a man whose face she sees in passing on television. She is one who can love a dead man, whose face she sees in a photograph during a memorial service long after his death. She is one who has the patience and courage to ask how she "could show her love," wanting to achieve what is "right" and not settle for what is "correct."

And yet, because that love (like "even the contemplation of murder") requires "incredible delicacy as it [requires] incredible spiritual work," and because "the historical background and present setting must be right," it is not actual but potential love, it is *faith* that Meridian disseminates. The ultimate intimacy she attains, or allows, is typically by renunciation, leaving Truman her cell, her sleeping bag and her role, in confidence that he too will be "free." In like manner, she achieves the greatest authority by self-effacement, divesting herself of all modesty and privacy in the telling of her story, so that reading becomes an act of intimacy for whoever enters the book. The terrible candor of the book makes this a difficult intimacy, but it is, strikingly, nowhere claustrophobic. This results in large part from the generosity Meridian exudes. She is not even possessive toward her own story. A remarkably high proportion of the text, of Meridian's text, is yielded to others, while she practices silence and abnegation. Her power is not that of being present, but of a serenely strenuous presence, in the spirit, in the minds of all she meets. The least insistent character in black American literature is the most independent, and the least orthodox the most deeply attached.

Notes

1. Supposed to be an authentic African style, the Afro sprang from a powerful intrariparian sense of beauty which some African states preferred to admire rather than to adopt. The Afro was banned in Tanzania.
2. In megalithic cultures, stones were taken as the dwelling-place of souls; that value seems not to operate here.
3. Perhaps her "adulterated" perseverance can be most sympathetically seen beside the swift turning aside of the ex-colored man when his dream of an education runs into some "harsh realities."
4. K. J. Kakouri, *Dionysiaka: Aspects of Popular Thracian Religion of To-Day*, trans. Helen Colaclides (Athens: G. C. Eleftheroudakis, 1965), p. 105.
5. For a penetrating study of mysticism and poverty, the reader may take up Louis Dupré's *Deeper Life: A Meditation on Christian Mysticism* (New York: Crossroad Publishing, 1981).
6. If this is not a glancing allusion to Isaac McCaslin's conviction, in *The Bear*, that the social fabric can only be mended by giving land back to the Negroes who had earned it through slavery and beyond, it is certainly an entry into that discourse. Walker seems to be saying that the impulse to social justice by restitution is untimely, even unwanted. The problem is deeper than property, the solution deeper than title deeds. It is the self, not its belongings, that must change allegiance.
7. By contrast, June Jordan in "Poem: From an Uprooted Condition" expresses

a veritable dread of abortion: "What / is the right way the womanly expression / of the infinitive that fights / infinity/ *to abort?*" (*New Days*, p. 70).

8. The choice of this name, especially when the husband and daughter (Clarence and Clarice) have Western names, seems purposeful, but the force of the character does not seem to chime with the purpose of the name, which LeRoi Jones, in *Raise Race Rays Raze: Essays Since 1965*, glosses this way: "IMANI (faith)—To believe with all our heart in our parents, our teachers, our leaders, our people and the righteousness and victory of our struggle."

9. There is about it a Dostoevskian starkness, a willingness to venture into uncharted ground; and of course the impregnation of the Wild Child is very akin to that of Stinking Lizaveta in *The Brothers Karamazov*. At least what Meridian does is preferable to Medea's course when driven to extremity, and not unlike the wife's behavior in "The Hill Wife" by Robert Frost.

◆◆◆◆◆◆◆◆◆◆◆◆◆

Reading the Body: *Meridian* and the Archeology of Self

ALAN NADEL

Alice Walker's writing presents a continually dichotomous world, the antecedents of which we can locate in a problem common to slave narratives—a problem emphasized in the Epilogue of Ralph Ellison's *Invisible Man*—that identity is a function of place: "If you don't know *where* you are," the invisible man informs Mr. Norton, "you probably don't know *who* you are." An underlying premise of the slave narrative was that a literal place existed that altered the definition of humanity for Blacks. When the North failed to fulfill its promise of being that place, the relationship of place to identity became one more dichotomy embedded in the language and activities of black American existence, one more dichotomy embodying the impossibility of assimilation and the impossibility of continued "apartheid."[1]

The problem is one as well of reconciling the individual and tradition, which means both finding a tradition *and* breaking with one, for "tradition," as it has been handed down, is the tradition of an enslaved or oppressed people who have had many of the direct connections to their native rituals, beliefs, and languages ruptured by violent racial and economic oppression. Under such circumstances, Walker has pondered, "how was the creativity of the black woman kept alive . . . when for most of the years black people have been in America, it was a punishable crime for a black person to read or write? And the freedom to paint, to sculpt, to expand the mind with action did not exist?" Walker concludes that this creativity often manifested itself anonymously, in folk arts and domestic activities. The "anonymity," of course, has made the tradition hard to identify, and Walker recalls longing for black anthropologists and collectors of folklore: "Where is the *black* person who took the time to travel the back roads of the South and collect the information I need . . . ?" It is not surprising, therefore, that in the fictional world Walker presents, Blacks as a result of this oppression often repress their desires and sublimate their frustrations in ways that enable them to accept the status quo and/or even adopt their oppressors' values.

With this in mind, *Meridian* can be read as an attempt to mend the ruptures and reconstruct an alternative black tradition from its contemporary American artifacts. The novel, in other words, conducts an historical search in that it tries to recontextualize the past. In so doing, I will argue, Walker treats narrative as archeology and thus provides instructions for reading Meridian's life as though it were inscribed on the archeological site of her body. Such a reading depends on recognizing the relationship between Meridian's body and the body politic, and it reveals the role of maternal history in the definition of self. This lesson in reading, Walker further suggests, is necessary to reconcile the conflicts between art and activism in black American life.

NARRATIVE AS ARCHEOLOGY

The first half of the book moves not only through Meridian's personal history and the history of her parents and grandparents but also through the history of her land and folklore. It moves almost in an archeological manner, less interested in chronological exposition than in a process of unearthing and reexplaining.

In many ways, this situation could be seen as a structuralist endeavor of the sort applied to cultural anthropology by Claude Lévi-Strauss, among others, in that it attempts to decode cultural phenomena by understanding the implicit system that gives them meaning.[2] "When one takes as object of study," Jonathan Culler explains, "not physical phenomena but artifacts or events with meaning, the defining qualities of the phenomena become the features which distinguish them from one another and enable them to bear meaning within the symbolic system from which they derive." These "defining qualities" only have meaning in terms of the single point of view from which they are gathered. To change the point of view is to restructure the investigation and change the meaning of the constituent phenomena—just as changing the rules of grammar would alter the meaning of specific words in specific sentences.[3]

The first chapter of *Meridian* exemplifies this archeological approach to narrative by examining Meridian's life and ancestry synchronically, as though it were the strata of one archeological site at which each unearthing of an antecedent redefines the structure of the whole. The chapter begins in the novel's present, then quickly jumps back ten years to a meeting in New York of revolutionary women taunting Meridian with the question: would she kill for the revolution? She is unable to answer because she recontextualizes the question in terms of a further past:

> what none of them seemed to understand was that she felt herself to be, not holding on to something from the past, but *held* by something in the past: by the memory of old black men in the South who, caught by surprise in the eye of the camera, never shifted their position but looked directly back; by the sight of young girls singing in a country choir, their hair shining with brushings and grease, their voices the voices of angels. . . . If they committed murder [Meridian wonders] *what would their music be like?*

Remembering this black southern Christianity of her childhood takes Meridian still further backward in time, as her father's singing makes her connect the church music with the pre-Chrisitan beliefs of American

Indians. The fruitful interaction of the music, her imagination, and her family thus have taken her to a past that had been distorted by centuries of cultural rape. From the pre-Christian past, Meridian's memory starts moving forward again. It returns to a moment when she sat in church beside her mother. Because she had recognized a sense of pre-Christian spiritualism—the sense that her father did not believe in the same God as her mother did—Meridian was unable to embrace Jesus and thereby forever alienated her mother. From Meridian's childhood, the chapter continues to move methodically toward the present: from the church where Meridian is unable to meet her mother's condition, to the apartment where she is unable to satisfy the revolutionaries', to her home (set in the novel's present) where she similarly acknowledges her unwillingness to meet Truman's needs.

The chapter works, then, so that the present is embedded with, and thus constantly informed by, various layers of "pastness."[4] It is important to recognize, therefore, that the conversation with Truman, which frames the chapter, is not dramatic in the sense that it engages in a conflict that will effect a change. Because at this point in their lives the relationship between Truman and Meridian is beyond change but not beyond understanding, the opening chapter changes the reader's understanding of the relationship by unearthing a succession of historical, cultural, and artistic contexts.[5]

The book as a whole functions similarly, locating black American experience in ultimately pre-American, pre-Christian contexts through a stratified examination of its presence in postcolonial, postbellum, Christian, and white art and artifacts.[6] In addition, the book explores the problem that, within the black community, the roles of oppressor and oppressed are reenacted between men and women, so that women must go through the same encoding and sublimation to cope with male oppression that Blacks go through to cope with racial oppression.[7] This leaves black women at double remove from power and makes them participants in a double encoding system. If black history forms a repressed, encoded, ruptured alternative to published American history, then maternal history—the chain between generations bound by maternal experience, genetic biases, and empathetic subjugation—is an encoded subtext within the black male cultural history.[8]

THE ROLE OF HISTORY

This chain of maternal history, marginalized and suppressed by white patriarchal history, connects Meridian, for example, with her great grandmother, who had had an ecstatic experience while sunning herself on the mound of the Indian Sacred Serpent burial ground. "Later [she] renounced all religion that was not based on the experience of physical ecstasy . . . and near the end of her life she loved walking nude about her yard and worshipped only the sun." Meridian had a similar experience at the same site and another at the ruin of a pre-Columbian altar in Mexico. But this experience connects her with her *paternal* great-grandmother, and, like the pre-Christian spirit in which her father believed, it is associated in the book with an independence rarely found by black women because of their enslavement to men and to maternity.

Meridian grew up, therefore, with the sense that she had stolen something from her mother: "It was for stealing her mother's serenity, for shattering her mother's emerging self, that Meridian felt guilty from the very first. . . ." In the same way, her own early pregnancy had stolen something from her: her capacity to be active in the emotional, intellectual, or physical world. She is awakened from her lethargy by the bombing of a civil rights worker's house in her neighborhood: "And so it was that one day in the middle of April in 1960 Meridian Hill became aware of the past and present of the larger world." To become part of that world, to become an activist, however, she has to relinquish her role as mother. When she gives up, moreover, not only her child but the history of her life so that she can enter college, she thinks of her decision in terms of maternal history: "[Meridian] thought of her mother as being worthy of this maternal history, and she herself as belonging to an unworthy minority, for which there was no precedent and of which she was, as far as she knew, the only member."[9]

The motion from private to public, from personal to political, from artificial to historical, in other words, entails the breaking down of barriers as well as the reconstituting of the existing fragments in a new context. To put it another way, the book presents the enterprise of discovering a synchronic reading that will restructure the contexts through which the artifacts of black American culture are read. Barthes has emphasized this principle of semiological research: "in principle, the corpus must eliminate diachronic elements to the utmost; it must coincide with a state of the system, a cross-section of history. . . . [F]rom an operative point of view, the corpus must keep as close as possible to the synchronic sets. A varied but temporally limited corpus will therefore be preferable to a narrow corpus stretched over a length of time. . . ."

MERIDIAN'S BODY

The unique quality of *Meridian,* and its uniquely feminist quality, is that these conflicts—the simultaneous breaking down and reconstructing—take place in the body of Meridian. The "corpus," in other words, that Barthes desires in principle—the "varied but temporally limited corpus"—is Meridian's corporal self. In this way, Walker engages in what has become popularized by French feminist theorists as *écriture féminine*, writing located in and authorized by fundamental female experience: "writing the body."[10] Ann Rosalind Jones's description of this principle, when applied specifically to *Meridian*, provides a very apt gloss on the novel's structure: "to the extent that the female body is seen as a direct source of female writing, a powerful alternative discourse seems possible: to write from the body is to recreate the world."

In regard to this principle, Elizabeth Meese has noted that the "body is the site where the political and the aesthetic interpret the material." This is certainly true of Meridian. The first chapter of the novel makes clear the connection between Meridian's body and the body politic when, after leading a successful protest (by staring down an armed tank), Meridian's body suffers a seizure of paralysis that necessitates her being carried home by four men, "exactly as they would carry a coffin, her eyes closed, barely breathing, arms folded across her chest, legs straight." The protest had been staged to enable some black children to see an ostensibly mummified white woman housed in a circus wagon. Because, as Deborah McDowell has noted, Meridian's paralyzed condition mirrors that of the freakish white woman made inaccessible to the eyes of black children by armed force, the book forces a comparison between Meridian and the mummy, one that suggests an alternative to the untenable roles of womanhood produced by white and male culture and replicated in the mummy-woman's alleged history.[11]

Truman, misunderstanding the relationship of Meridian's body to the events, thinks her seizure followed from the protest and asks: "Did they hurt you out there?" As Meridian makes clear, however, social conditions, not social protest, have caused her illness; the protest is part of the cure:

> "They didn't touch me," she said.
> "You're just sick then?"
> "Of course I'm sick," snapped Meridian. "Why else would I spend all this time trying to get well!"

In her encounter with the Wild Child, before Meridian can take any action, her body similarly responds to the initial circumstances. Approximately thirteen years old, "Wile Chile" had grown up without home or parents, haunting the outermost margins of poverty-level civilization. Because she signified not only the inadequacy of social agencies and the breakdown of the family but also the failure of all social codes including language itself, when she is seen pregnant, the neighbors in the slum surrounding Saxon college "could not imagine what to do. Wile Chile rummaged about as before, eating rancid food, dressing herself in cast-offs, cursing and bolting, and smoking her brown cigarettes." Upon first seeing Wile Chile, Meridian enters into a corpse-like coma on the floor of her bedroom (in Saxon College's honors house). Only after passing through this act of embodying literally all the social paralysis that Wile

Chile's presence signifies can Meridian emerge with a method to lure the child into the shelter of the honors house.

Meridian's body also provides the site for sexual conflicts that reflect not only the conflict between the personal and the political but also the conflicts between male and female roles, the mind and the body, the sacred and the profane. In her relationship with her teenaged husband, Eddie, for example,

> she—her body, that is—never had any intention of *giving in*. She was suspicious of pleasure. . . . Besides, Eddie did not seriously expect more than 'interest' from her. She perceived there might be something more; but for him it was enough that his pleasure should please her. Understanding this, they never discussed anything beyond her attitude.

Meridian's sexual relationship with Truman necessitates a similar recognition of the antagonism, for Meridian, between mind and body: "She decided to click her mind off, and her body seemed to move into his of its own accord."

Like her relationship with her men, Meridian's political consciousness is described in terms of a mind/body dichotomy, and only after freeing herself from her body does she first come to realize that the demands of the political world require she relinquish her maternal role:

> she attempted to meditate on her condition, unconscious at first, of what she did. At first it was like falling back into a time that never was, a time of complete rest, like a faint. Her senses were stopped while her body rested; only in her head did she feel something, and it was a sensation of lightness— a lightness like the inside of a drum. The air inside her head was pure of thought, at first.

As her meditation develops, she focuses on the bodies of young and teenage girls, as they grow from shame to "the beginning of pride in their bodies." Meditating free of her body, with a greater political consciousness, however, Meridian thinks "for all their bodies' assertion, the girls moved protected in a dream. A dream that had little to do with the real boys galloping past them. For they did not perceive them clearly but as they might become in a different world from the one they lived in."

Confronting that "world they lived in" has a profoundly different effect on the body of Meridian, a form of "battle fatigue" that manifests an array of symptoms, from initial uncontrollable crying to the "shaking of her hands, or the twitch in her left eye," and later to the loss of her hair and the paralytic fits. When Meridian admits publicly at Saxon that she is not sure there is a God, the near ostracism she suffers shows its effects on her body. "She began to have headaches that were so severe they caused her to stutter when she spoke."

Finally, her body reflects the conflict between her role as a mother and as a self-fulfilling woman. For motherhood, in Meridian's world, reflects the agnegation of personal freedom for the roles defined by men, race, and class, and for the responsibilities mandated by poverty and by children. Or, as it is summarized by Meridian's mother: "The answer to everything . . . is that we live in America and we're not rich." The fertile body, capable of turning a woman into a mother—and of allowing her child to "steal" her life—thus becomes Meridian's obstacle as it impels women out of womenhood and into motherhood: "[Meridian was] disgusted with the fecundity of her body that got pregnant on less screwing than anybody's she had ever heard of. It seemed doubly unfair that after all her sexual 'experience' and after one baby and one abortion she had not once been completely fulfilled by sex." If her fertile body at one extreme is at odds with sexual pleasure, at the other it wars with her spiritual satisfaction. For Meridian perceives it as the obstacle to her mother's acceptance, that is, to the religoius traditions and the chain of women's history her mother represents: "Meridian felt as if her body, growing frailer every day under the stress of her daily life, stood in the way between a reconciliation between her mother and that part of her own soul her mother could, perhaps love." Meridian's body, in other words, must bear the burden for having stolen her mother's life and for having failed to accept the role of her mother, having failed to replicate motherhood.[12]

In these ways, Meridian's body becomes the territory that measures and tests the distinctions between theft and ownership, not only of property but of life, hope, and ambition. In all of these tests, it functions both as subject and as object and thus presents itself as a medium for connecting the contexts rent by relegation to the realm of "oppressor" or "oppressed." This is why Meridian's development as a civil rights worker reflects an inverse relationship between possession and power. The more she is able to shed not only of her personal property but also of her person itself—the flesh of her body, the aborted fetus of her womb—the more power she has to control and heal those around her, most importantly because she turns these renunciations into lessons in reading.[13] For black Americans to read and hence rediscover their cultural ancestry, her story suggests, they must remove the anglicized surface, the framing context of white, Western distortion, in much the way an anthropologist or archeologist would, discovering from the artifacts the art of a lost culture.[14]

ART, ARTIFACT, AND ACTIVISM

Yet the novel also seems suspicious of its own endeavor, insofar as art has been—in the form of storytelling, for example, or jazz—one of the traditional ways that Blacks sublimated frustration and thus facilitated, however unintentionally, their own oppression. One of the central conflicts in the novel, therefore, is between art and politics. Although both are subversive acts, the question is: what is being subverted and how? Because art turns experience into artifact, in some ways it militates against change. For this reason, the novel does not endorse as revolutionary Truman's work as an artist. Furthermore, if we cannot trust art because it serves as a form of sublimation that ultimately removes the artifact from its context, then perhaps artifacts, especially of an oppressed or destroyed culture, should always be distrusted. They exist, after all, in a context created by the same dominant power that tried to destroy the culture.

The novel presents us with the problem, however, that the active—the revolutionary—is equally untrustworthy exactly *because* it is not stable or predictable. It also is subject to the influence of vested interets, and those interests, likewise, are subject to change. When the students protest, for example, because Saxon College will not permit them to hold the "Wile Chile's" funeral in the chapel, the event moves back in stages that first permit the anglicized black students of Saxon to connect with their slave and pre-Christian heritage and then lead them to destroy the very roots of that connection. At first they want to use the Christian chapel. Denied access, they stage a replica Christian funeral on the chapel steps, for which the people from the local black community wear their "Sunday best outfits." After the community people, intimidated by the austerity of Saxon, flee, the students cast off some of their learned decorum and solemnity: "For five minutes the air rang with shouts and polite curses." Next they move to the more primal responses of booing, stamping their feet, and sticking out "their tongues through their tears," after which they begin to shed their Western garb: "they began to take off their jewelry and fling it to the ground—the heavy three-strand cultured pearl necklaces, and the massive, circular gold-plated chastity pins. . . . They shook loose their straightened hair," all the while glaring at the locked chapel with "ferocity."

As their attire becomes less anglicized and their behavior changes from polite curses to ferocity, "as if by mutual agreement" they shift the site of the funeral to The Sojourner—the tree planted on the site of a slave's buried tongue. With its roots both figuratively and literally connected to antebellum black, African, and pre-Christian spiritual lore, the tree is believed to possess talismanic qualities. Yet after Wile Chile is buried, the students "rioted on Saxon campus for the first time in its long, placid, impeccable history, and the only thing they managed to destroy was The Sojourner." Once again, the novel shows the activist in conflict with the artifact in ways that destroy the latter and render the former suspect.

One reason that activists in *Meridian* are particularly suspect is that they operate under premises based on a distorted version of history. When Anne-Marion assists in chopping down The Sojourner because she associates it with the college that surrounds it, she ignores the fact that the tree predates its current context, that it sheltered Blacks long before Saxon College recontextualized it. Similarly, Anne-Marion employs a Marxist version of history to discredit the church. The church she discredits, however, is not one that conforms to traits upon which Marx based his assault. She ends up, therefore, as with The Sojourner, severing her ties to the native traditions that, although disguised with the trappings of white authority, connect her with her own identity.[15]

Anne-Marion's writing is also suspect, and, as with Truman's art, Meridian cannot endorse it as revolutionary. After Anne-Marion breaks with Meridian, she continues compulsively to write Meridian letters: "no one could have been more surprised and confounded than she, who sat down to write each letter as if some heavy object had been attached to her knees, forcing them under her desk, as she wrote with the most galling ferocity, out of guilt and denial and rage." At the same time that Meridian cannot embrace the contents of the letters, she cannot dismiss the anger that produced them or, more importantly, the history that anger signifies. Therefore, she neither reads the letters nor discards them; instead, she decorates her walls with them.

In many different ways, Meridian's treatment of the letters is an act of recontextualization. First, as she explains to Truman in the first chapter, she looks at them for their appearance, not their content: "I keep the letters because they contain the bitch's handwriting." Because they also contain, in a sense, an action—the hand *writing*—Meridian's perspective demonstrates the way that action becomes artifact; by putting the letters on the wall, she also demonstrates how artifact becomes decorative art. The act of using the limited materials at her disposal to decorate her sparse surroundings, furthermore, replicates an activity Walker ascribes to her anonymous ancestors, the oppressed black women "who literally covered the holes of our walls with sunflowers." In this way, Meridian makes the letters allusions to the heritage Anne-Marion and she share and, by virtue of Meridian's act, one in which they continue to participate. The letters thereby serve to connect not only Meridian but also Anne-Marion with their pre-Christian ancestry, a connection Walker makes explicit in her essay, "In Search of Our Mothers' Gardens":

> Guided by my heritage of a love of beauty and a respect for strength—in search of my mother's garden I found my own. . . .
> And perhaps in Africa over two hundred years ago, was just such a mother; perhaps she painted vivid and daring decorations in oranges and yellows and greens on the walls of her hut; perhaps she sang—in a voice like Roberta Flack's—*sweetly* over the compounds of her village; perhaps she wove the most stunning mats or told the most ingenious stories of all the village storytellers. Perhaps she was herself a poet—though only her daughter's name is signed to the poems that we know.

By converting action into artifact into art, Meridian moreover makes the process of this conversion clear so that the decoration cannot be divorced from the action, the anger, and the history that produced it. Anne-Marion's letters decorating Meridian's walls not only allude to their mothers' gardens but also signify the anger and oppression that produced those anonymous gardens. As such, they perform the archeological re-contextualizing, so prevalent in the novel, both by reconstructing a lost tradition out of the present and by subsuming the present in that tradition.

Finally, because they signify a problem not resolved, an anger not dispersed, Anne-Marion's letters point toward the future as well as the past. For Meridian, they become quite literally the handwriting on the wall, the reminder that there are people who believe they would kill for the revolution. And we must remember that it is Meridian who takes these personal diatribes and converts them into the handwriting on the wall in the same act that connects her with the anonymous artistry of her ancestors. It is Meridian, in other words, who gives these letters their significance. As their addressee, recipient, reader, interpreter, and, ultimately, artist, she becomes the cipher that connects artifact to heritage.[16]

In the same way, her body serves this ciphering function throughout the novel. By making it the receptacle of this unearthing as well as reader of the unearthed, Meridian assumes an androgynous role that makes her an object lesson in both the reading and the authorship of self—the living connection between art and artifact. In this role, she tries to create a context that will revive the rituals of her lost tradition, that will connect the artifactual with the active. The novel is full of stories that have the quality of folk or fairy tales; they possess talismanic qualities also, and they echo the supernatural and/or religious and/or magical. Into which of these categories they fit is a question of reading and an issue of hermeneutics. A folk tale can have roughly the same rhetorical structure as a parable, yet one is given sacred importance, which it can only have based on a preconception about its meaning and context.[17] This is a lesson in hermeneutics and in history. We need a cipher through which to read the lessons (or the absence of lesson) in a fable, a parable, a folk tale, a religious ceremony, or a history book. The cipher that the novel *Meridian* presents is the body of Meridian—the body of her sensations, experience, and language.

But if Meridian is a lesson in reading, she is not a simple one, or one that will lend one sanctioned reading to a text. Rather she is a lesson in alternatives, attitudes, and perspectives, made perhaps most evident by the divisions in the novel and the difference in narrative technique in the respective parts. Whereas the first section of the novel, which identifies Meridian and is named for her, moves backward and forward through a series of juxtaposed findings, unearthed bits of gold (or fool's gold, as one chapter suggests), the section named for Truman Held adheres more strongly to linear narrative. Because even in its temporal interpolations the section never incorporates the parable-like or folkloric details found in the "Meridian" section, Walker forces us to read not only one history against another but also one kind of writing—one way of attributing significance—against its alternatives. The short third section of the book, "Endings," more sharply contrasts Truman's mode of reading with Meridian's. In the book's penultimate chapter, Meridian tells Truman about a poor black woman who left her husband because he was in love with his dog and treated it better than his family. The story, rendered in an almost fairy-tale fashion reminiscent of portions of the "Meridian" section, ends with the woman's returning to her husband because "alone she could not feed her children. Of course she made her husband promise to kill the dog." Truman, interested in linear narrative, in what happens next, in what the man does, asks if he did kill the dog. Meridian, reflecting a different mode of reading, a concern not with the last act but with the context in which it takes place, the organization of power it reflects, shrugs: "'I suspect that is not the point,' she said."

Through Meridian, Walker tests the ways one gives meaning to activities and to objects, to self and to others. Meridian is a lesson in the power of language, the power to retain as well as to distort, to affect as well as to deny. All of these lessons, moreover, are implicit in the definition page at the outset of the book that presents not only the myriad ways one can read the word "meridian" but also the two basic contexts: as a noun, that is, as something defined in and of itself; and as an adjective, that is, as something that modifies another subject. The merging of the modifier and the noun in Meridian's name thus signifies the reconstituting of a self both personal and political. It is the matrix where cultural and national history meet, and it is the name for that body in which the magic of maternity is one with the patriarchal authority of communal faith.

Notes

1. As Sidonie Smith points out, the slave narrative "is apparently a narrative of success. But there is also another story implicit, if not actually explicit, within the slave narrative. That story is the story of the failure to find real freedom and acceptance within American society, a disturbing sequel to the successful story of the radical break away from southern society." Frances Smith Foster notes further that this implicit story created generic plot restrictions for the nineteenth-century slave narrative: "Once the protagonist achieves his freedom the . . . narrative terminates. . . . [F]or to continue the adventures of a black in the so-called free states or countries would be to expose the overwhelming prejudice and discrimination which existed therein. The problem would be revealed as more complex and pervasive than would be to the advantage of most narrators to expose, for it would necessar-

ily indict those from whom their narratives sought sympathy and aid." See also Phyllis Klotman.

2. Cf. Lévi-Strauss: "The social facts which we study are manifested in societies each of which is a *total entity, concrete and cohesive.* We never lose sight of the fact that existing societies are the result of great transformations occurring in mankind at certain moments in prehistory and at certain places on the globe, and that an uninterrupted chain of real events relates these facts to those which we can observe" (Anthropology 24). See also *The Savage Mind* (1–33).

3. Roland Barthes stresses this: "The aim of semiological research is to reconstitute the functioning of the systems of significations other than language in accordance with the process typical of any structuralist activity, which is to build a *simulacrum* of the objects under observation. To undertake this research, it is necessary frankly to accept from the beginning (and especially the beginning) a limiting principle. . . . [I]t is decided to describe the facts which have been gathered *from one point of view only,* and consequently to keep, from the heterogeneous mass of these facts, only the features associated with this point of view, to the exclusion of any others (these features are said to be *relevant*)."

4. Deborah E. McDowell notes that this chapter, "as it explores the tension between Stasis (Tradition) and change (Meridian), sets the stage for the flashback of events which form the story of Meridian's development . . ." ("Self" 266).

5. McDowell identifies this contextualizing as an approach "not only useful but necessary to Black feminist critics" ("New Directions" 192). In this light, we might also note Edward Said's insight that identifying any beginning means identifying a context embedded with intentions, and that the Western practice of constituting the other (a practice Said calls "orientalism") depends on creating specific contexts by creating specific beginnings.

6. Peter Erickson describes something like this when he talks of Walker's "ruminative style," which creates a "meandering, yet disciplined meditation" through which Walker "establishes a frame of reference in the present from which she can delve into the past." More than delve into the past, however, Walker uses the past to restructure our reading of the present.

7. In Walker's earlier novel, *The Third Life of Grange Copeland,* Copeland addresses this issue very directly in his long diatribe, in Chapter 45, against his son, Brownfield. In that novel, "ostensibly about a man and his son," Walker has said, "it is the women and how they are treated that colors everything" (*Gardens* 250–251). See also Bettye Parker-Smith.

8. We should also note, as Barbara Christian points out: "Alice Walker *also* writes of the unwillingness of many black women to acknowledge or address the problems of sexism that affect them because they feel they must protect black men. She asserts that if black women turn away from the women's movement, they turn away from women moving all over the world, not just in America. They betray their own tradition. . . ."

9. Christian stresses the implicit connection here with the tradition of slave narrative: "[Walker presents] in a succinct way the essence of Afro-American motherhood as it has been passed on. At the center of this construct is a truth that mothers during slavery did not have their natural right to their children and did everything, including giving up their lives, to save them. From this truth, however, a moral dictum has developed, a moral voice that demands that Afro-American mothers, whatever the changed circumstances of their lives, take on the sole responsibility of the children. One result of this rigid position is the guilt which permeates mother/child relationships."

10. The crucial text, in this regard, is Hélène Cixous' "The Laugh of Medusa"; see also Julia Kristeva and Luce Irigaray. Jane Gallop also suggests the close connection between the literal and figurative body, especially as it applies to the reinscription of self and other through naming, alluding, and referring: that is, to the attempt to contain difference.

11. In showing the ways in which Meridian rebels against tradition, McDowell astutely lists all of these roles: "Like the mummy woman, Meridian is, at various stages in the novel, a daughter, though not obedient; a wife, though not devoted; a mother, though not adoring. . . ."

12. Nancy Chodorow has argued with great influence that the reproduction of mothering is "a central and constituting element in the social organization and reproduction of gender." Meridian's androgyny, in this light, can be viewed as being represented by the body that has both mothered and not-mothered; her body, in other words, has physically replicated her social roles.

13. For a discussion of the ways all texts provide lessons in how they are to be read, see Wolfgang Iser.

14. See McDowell ("Self" 274–275).

15. Cf. Walker: "As a college student I came to reject the Christianity of my parents, and it took me years to realize that though they had been force-fed the white man's palliative, in the form of religion, they had made it into something at once simple and noble. True, even today, they can never successfully picture a God who is not white, and that is a major cruelty, but their lives testify to a greater comprehension of the teachings of Jesus than the lives of people who sincerely believe a God *must* have a color and that there can be such a phenomenon as a 'white' church" (*Gardens* 17–18).

16. Cf. Lévi-Strauss: "The painter is always mid-way between design and anecdote, and his genius consists in uniting internal and external knowledge, a 'being' and a 'becoming,' in producing with his brush an object which does not exist as such and which he is nevertheless able to create on his canvas. This is a nicely balanced synthesis of one or more artificial or natural structures and one or more natural or social events. The aesthetic emotion is the result of this union between the structural order and the order of events, which is brought about within a thing created by man and so also in effect by the observer who discovers the possibility of such a union through the work of art" (*Savage Mind* 25).

17. Frank Kermode explains this principle clearly and applies it fruitfully to an analysis of the Gospels. Paul de Man also indicates the ways in which the relationship between the grammatical and rhetorical functions in a text can organize a reading. Although I have not looked at the various "languages"—that is, the interplay of grammar and rhetoric—in this text, it is ripe for such a study, both in terms of the juxtapositions of rhetoric within the "Meridian" section and in the differences among the three sections. In viewing the body of Meridian as text, furthermore, we can see that it performs in an analogous manner, if we equate its appearance with its rhetoric and its action with its grammar—a fair equation, I think, based on a reasonable extrapolation from the way de Man uses the terms "grammar" and "rhetoric" in Chapter One ("Semiology and Rhetoric") of *Allegories of Reading.*

◆◆◆◆◆◆◆◆◆◆◆◆◆

The Self in Bloom: Walker's *Meridian*

DEBORAH E. MCDOWELL

And she had nothing to fall back on: not maleness, not whiteness, not lady-hood, not anything. And out of the profound desolation of her reality, she may very well have invented herself.

—Toni Morrison[1]

What are we talking about when we speak of revolution if not a free society made up of whole individuals? I'm not arguing the denial of manhood or womanhood, but rather a shifting of priorities, a call for Self-hood. . . .

—Toni Cade[2]

Central to any consideration of Alice Walker's fiction is her preoccupation with black womanhood and its myriad shadings.[3] Both *The Third Life of Grange Copeland* (1970) and *In Love and Trouble: Stories of Black Women* (1973) explore, to varying degrees, the dynamics of being a black woman. But in *Meridian* (1976), Walker's latest and probably most artistically mature work, she transcends the boundaries of the female gender to embrace more universal concerns about individual autonomy, self-reliance,[4] and self-realization. In the tradition of the *Bildungsroman*, or apprenticeship novel, the book chronicles the series of initiatory experiences which Meridian, the title character, undergoes in an effort to find her identity, or her own moral center, and develop a completeness of being. Jerome Buckley lists the principal elements of the *Bildungsroman:* "childhood, the conflict of generations, provinciality, the larger society, self-education, alienation, ordeal by love, the search for a vocation and a working philosophy. . . ."[5] Meridian's struggle for identity embraces most of these elements, not all of which can be addressed here. Hers is a formidable struggle, for she lives in a society that domesticates conformity, that censures individual expression, especially for women; but she flourishes notwithstanding and evolves into a prototype for psychic wholeness and individual autonomy.

There is much in the novel to recommend such a reading, particularly the motif of death and rebirth that runs throughout and that recalls the force in nature which transforms decay into growth, loss into gain. When the novel opens, Meridian is seemingly in a state of decay. She is suffering from fainting spells and her hair has fallen out. Her face is "wasted and rough, the skin a sallow, unhealthy brown, with pimples across her forehead and on her chin. Her eyes were glassy and yellow and did not seem to focus at once. Her breath, like her clothes, was sour."[6] At the end of the novel, however, she has reflourished. Her hair has grown back; she is strengthened and renewed.

Similarly, the flashback of events between the opening and closing chapters sustain the death/rebirth motif and are congruent with this evolutionary theme which I am suggesting. Meridian's most significant, most insightful experiences occur in the spring—archetypically a time of both death and rebirth. For example, her husband deserts her in the spring, an experience which triggers a period of "death-like" introspection, culminating in her decision to offer her child up for adoption. Replacing the "old skin" of marriage is the new one of social activism. Likewise, just before her graduation from Saxon College, she falls into a death-like coma only to emerge renewed in a fashion which borders on the mystical.

It is important to note that this idea of Meridian's "New Birth," her cyclical self-transmutation is psychological rather than theological, for Meridian exemplifies the Emersonian notion that true growth and change can occur only when the individual discovers the "god" or divinity in himself or herself.[7] Meridian makes this discovery gradually[8] and develops a reliance on the "sacredness and integrity" of her own mind, even though the gods of social authority would provide her with a "ready-made" set of female role patterns.

One of the most perpetually looming obstacles to Meridian's struggle for self-discovery is the god of American tradition.[9] But rather than cower and defer to its menacing force, she confronts it. Whether represented by people, institutions, established "truths," or time-worn abstractions, Meridian examines tradition with a critical eye and rejects those aspects which impinge upon her self-discovery.

That much of Meridian's growth process will entaill a confrontation with the god of tradition, or the "dead hand" of the past, is established in the richly symbolic, tightly compressed opening chapter in which two of America's most cherished institutions—racism and sexism—meet head-on in a skillful, simultaneous dramatization. The chapter recounts the circus show, conducted Jim Crow style, featuring the mummy woman, Marilene O'Shay, "one of the Twelve Wonders of the World: Preserved in Life-Like Condition." At the most fundamental level, Walker is satirizing the tenacious but untenable belief in tradition, which is at the bowels of American culture, for the preservation of the mummy woman is a metaphor for the preservation of dead, no longer viable traditions and institutions. Thus Meridian challenges this Southern town's "separate-but-equal" racial tradition by leading a group of black school children to the circus wagon on a day not authorized by the local government.

While defying the tradition of separate-but-equal race relations, Meridian, in her active social role, concurrently challenges traditional and synthetic images of women. She is in sharp contradistinction to the images presented of the mummy woman (which are, Walker suggests, images of all women). The marquee of the circus wagon flashes the captions

"Obedient Daughter," "Devoted Wife" and "Adoring Mother," the traditional stages of a woman's life. The circus bill (significantly written by
the mummy woman's husband) explains that she had been "an ideal
woman," a "goddess," who had been given "everythin," that is, "a wash-
ing machine, furs, her own car and a full-time housekeeper cook." Her
only duty was to "lay back and be pleasured." But the mummy woman
loses her fringe benefits and her life in the process. Her husband kills
her because she "had gone outside the home to seek her 'pleasuring,'
while still expecting him to foot the bills." This image of woman as passiv-
ist, as "a mindless body, a sex creature, something to hang false hair and
nails on," is actively challenged by Meridian in her role as a human rights
crusader.[10] It is not incidental that her physical features in this chapter
most resemble a male's. Most of her hair has fallen out and she wears
an old railroad cap and dungarees which have masculine suggestions. But
the fact that she is physically unattractive does not concern Meridian,
an unconcern contrary to conventional notions of womanhood. Not only
does Meridian look like a male, but she also acts like one. She is decidedly
out of her "place" as a woman in her demonstration of unwavering leadership qualities, those generally associated with the male. Although there
are armed policemen stationed in a "red-white and blue" army tank to
prevent Meridian from fulfilling her mission, she bravely marches on,
facing the tank aimed at her chest. "The silence as Meridian kicked open
the door, exploded in a mass exhalation of breaths, and the men who
were in the tank crawled sheepishly out again to stare." Thus a symbolic
inversion of roles occurs in this scene and Meridian can be said to triumph
over tradition and authority. Her achievement in this series of attacks
on tradition is a pointed commentary on America's role-dependency. She
exemplifies Toni Cade's assertion that

> You find your Self in destroying illusions, smashing myths . . . being respon-
> sible to some truth, to the struggle. That entails . . . cracking through the
> veneer of this sick society's definition of 'masculine' and 'feminine.'[11]

and striving towards creating an androgynous, fluid self.

Such fluidity of personality is necessary because rigid role definitions
are static; by their very nature, they deny human complexity and
thereby stifle growth, completeness of being.

This critical chapter, then, as it explores the tension between Stasis
(Tradition) and change (Meridian), sets the stage for the flashback of
events which form the story of Meridian's development, which give rise
to her self-discovery, to her obsession with finding her own distinctive
"step" amid a composite of imitative marchers.

Like the mummy woman, Meridian is, at various stages in the novel,
a daughter, though not obedient; a wife, though not devoted; and a
mother, though not adoring, for the demands of these roles are circum-
scriptive and stifling. It is in her role as daughter, particularly in her

stormy relationship with her mother, that Meridian's insurgent self-awareness and independence first surface. This conflict between the generations is a motif peculiar to the apprenticeship novel. It is imperative that the initiate come to terms with a parental figure to free himself or herself from that parent's possessive hold before personal development can proceed.[12] Although her mother's domination is powerful, Meridian is intent upon freeing herself from its strangling clutches. She regards her mother as a "willing know-nothing, a woman of ignorance," who blindly adheres to tradition in its most sacrosanct forms. The Christian religion is one such form. The mother has been critically victimized by the European's gift of Christianity as an opiate to the black slave, a comforting myth which dimmed the horrors and brutalities of oppression. The mother has relinquished all responsibility for her own welfare to God and, in turn, wants Meridian to do so as well. But even at age thirteen, in the "mourner's bench" ritual, suffered and misunderstood by many a black child, Meridian questions the rationality of her mother's Christian beliefs and refuses to submit to them. Her adamant refusal costs her her mother's love; it "was gone, withdrawn and there were conditions to be met before it would be returned. Conditions Meridian was never able to meet."

Not only does Meridian challenge her mother's blind devotion to an escapist religion, but she also challenges her equally blind and passive acceptance of the overlapping constraints of marriage and motherhood. She sees her mother as "Black Motherhood personified" in her self-sacrifice. Although once a school teacher, her mother had been brainwashed into believing that she was missing something as a single person, and that that "something" was marraige and motherhood. She buys this myth wholesale, and while she later discovers that her twin roles of wife and mother are stymying, she accepts them, albeit with consuming resentment. Meridian believes that by surrendering to the demands of these roles, her mother has collaborated in her own suffocation:

> Her mother was not a woman who should have had children. She was capable of thought and growth and action only if unfettered by the needs of dependents, or the demands, requirements of a husband.

Finally, Meridian challenges her mother's unquestioning acceptance of her secondary citizenship. Of Meridian's involvement in the civil rights movement, her mother responds:

> "As far I'm concerned . . . you've wasted a year of your life fooling around with those people [civil rights activists]. The papers say they're crazy. God separated the sheeps from the goats and the black folks from the white. And me from anybody that acts as foolish as they do. It never bothered me to sit in the back of the bus, you get just as good a view and you don't have all those nasty white asses passing you."

And later, on the subject of no restroom facilities downtown for blacks, her mother states, "If somebody thinks he'll have to pee when he gets to town, let him use his own toilet before he leaves home! That's what we did when I was coming up!"

In her mother's "blind, enduring, stumbling through life," then, Meridian sees an example of thwarted potential resulting from a capitulation to the demands of tradition. Her mother's only release from the frustrations which these traditions impose is making artificial flowers and prayer pillows "too small for kneeling. They would only fit one knee." The sterility and essential uselesness of these two activities markedly contrasts with Meridian's now flourishing sense of purpose and independence.

> It seemed to Meridian that her legacy from her mother's endurance, her unerring knowledge of rightness and her pursuit of it through all distractions, was one she would never be able to match. It never occurred to her that her mother's and her grandmother's extreme purity of life was compelled by necessity. They had not lived in an age of choice.

Because she *does* live in an age of choice, Meridian opts for the twin "ills" of ending her marriage and offering her child up for adoption, thus willfully abdicating her roles as Devoted Wife and Loving Mother. Likening her life as wife and mother to being "buried alive, walled away from . . . life, brick by brick," Meridian escapes and commits herself to the civil rights struggle, a commitment that earns her a scholarship to Saxon College (Anglo-Saxon?), which represents tradition in another guise, and thus, still another deterrent to her growing individuality. "The emphasis at Saxon was on form, and the preferred 'form' was that of the finishing school girl . . . [who] knew and practiced all the proper social rules" and was, thereby, "ushered nearer to Ladyhood every day." The school song at Saxon began:

> "We are as chaste and pure as the
>   driven snow.
> We watch our manners, speech and
>   dress just so."

But the twin concepts of Ladyhood and chastity form another set of growth-retarding mythical abstractions which Meridian must reject. And she must reject them, among other reasons, because they are inherently contradictory. Nowhere is this made more explicit than in her sexual relationship with Truman Held, the young black French-speaking, dashiki-wearing "revolutionary." Truman is a student at a men's school across the street from Saxon, and he and Meridian are romantically and sexually drawn together because of their common involvement in the voters' rights crusade. But their relationship and their sexual encounters are soon baffling for Meridian, their conversations about them even more so, for Truman represents the traditional male in his hypocritical separation between "good" girls and "bad" girls. Truman "had wanted a virgin, had been raised to expect and demand a virgin; and never once had he questioned this. He had been as predatory as the other young men he ran with, as eager to seduce and de-virginize as they. Where had he expected his virgin to come from? Heaven?" In Truman's failure to recognize the contradictions and inequities in his sexual ideology, he condemns himself to a spiritually tragic divisiveness.

Despite her disappointing affair with Truman, Meridian stays at Saxon, but she defies its "Zoo restrictions and keeper taboos" and distinguishes herself as a "willful, sinful girl."

The extent to which Saxon upholds tradition in its emphasis on form is pointedly dramatized in the account of the Wild Child, an uncivilized, pregnant, orphan girl whom Meridian brings to the honors dorm of Saxon to care for. Shortly afterwards, the Wild Child runs to her death and Meridian arranges a funeral to be held in the school's chapel. By order of the president, however, the chapel guards refuse to let the coffin in. Meridian, who knows the president well, imagines him

> coming up to the Wild Child's casket and saying, as if addressing a congregation: "We are sorry, young woman, but it is against the rules and regulations of this institution to allow you to conduct your funeral inside this chapel, which, as you may know, was donated to us by one of the finest robber baron families of New York. Besides, it is nearly time for Vespers, and you should have arranged for this affair *through the proper channels* much earlier."

The bureaucratic mentality epitomized by the president pervades the Saxon community, and Meridian becomes increasingly aware that her growing individuality cannot be nourished in such a convention-bound climate. Therefore, she intensified her search for an opposing set of values which would provide relief from the strictures of the Anglo-Saxon value system, a search which takes her into the realm of the mystical. This notion of mysticism is congruent with the evolutionary motif, for the idea of a New Birth, a remaking or transmutation of the self, inheres in mysticism.[13]

While still at Saxon, Meridian begins to neglect her body; "she hated its obstruction." She begins to bald. Continually forgetting to eat, she begins to suffer fainting spells and blurred vision, which result in a coma. This coma and its aftermath resemble mystical ecstasy,[14] described by Evelyn Underhill as a death-like trance lasting for hours or several days, during which "breathing and circulation are depressed. The body is more or less cold and rigid. . . ."[15] Underhill adds that the mystic emerges from ecstasy "marvellously strengthened," ready for "the struggles and hardships," for "the deliberate pain and sacrifice of Love."[16]

Meridian's experience strikingly parallels Underhill's description. She emerges from the coma after two days:

> As the days passed . . . and she attempted to nible at the dishes Anne-Marion brought—she discovered herself becoming more and more full, with no appetite whatsoever. And, to her complete surprise and astonished joy, she began to experience ecstasy.
> Sometimes, lying on her bed, not hungry, not cold, not worried . . . she

felt as if a warm, strong light bore her up and that she was a beloved part of the universe; that she was innocent even as the first waters. And when Anne-Marion sat beside the bed and scolded her for not eating, she was amazed that Anne-Marion could not see how happy she was.

What is described in these passages is a mystical "dying-into-life" which involves a repudiation of the body's claims for those of the spirit. This accounts for Meridian's stolid indifference to food and other physical concerns, and her phenomenal spiritedness and strength following the coma. More significantly, however, is the light which Anne-Marion notices around Meridian's head; "the spikes of her natural had learned to glow." It is suggested here that Meridian has emerged from the trance-like state a saint. She explains to Truman that she has volunteered to suffer until her people are delivered from oppression. Her suffering takes an extremely ascetic form congruent with her nascent sainthood. She restricts herself to the "gross necessaries" of life, to borrow from Thoreau.

Each time Truman visited Meridian he found her with less and less furniture, fewer and fewer pieces of clothing, less of a social position in the community—wherever it was—where she lived.

To Meridian, such concerns are negligible, alien to all that she has cultivated up to this point. Her cultivation of self has necessitated her weeding out many of the most cherished values and institutions of the Western tradition, and she is left, despite her deepened commitment to the racial struggle, with the existential alienation that is the mark of the twentieth-century individual. She is the archetypal "outsider." The last stage in her development, then, requires the formation of an alternate value system, a system outside the sterility and meaninglessness of the Western orbit. She finds this alternative system in psychically repatriating to the most viable aspects of the black cultural heritage. In other words, the continued progress of her search for identity requires that she go backward in order to move forward, and backward is the South. It is significant that much of the novel is set in coastal Georgia, where the survival of Africanisms—particularly of the oral, religious, and musical traditions—is said to be most salient. Echoing Jean Toomer, Walker sees the South, despite its history of racism and oppression, as regenerative, for it is the South that is the cradle of the black man's experience in the New World, and the South that has continued to shape his experience in this country.

It is in the South, then, that Meridian rediscovers the power of the black past, accepts it and draws strength from its vital traditions, most notably the symbiotic musical and religious traditions. While crusading among older black people, she "was constantly wanting to know about the songs. 'Where did such and such a one come from?' or 'How many years do you think black people have been singing this?'"

Concomitant with the rediscovery of the black musical tradition is her rediscovery of its counterpart—the black church, which is, according to E. Franklin Frazier, "the most important cultural institution created by Negroes."[17] It is important to note, however, that the church which Meridian finally accepts is not her mother's church, not the church of the white Christian tradition with its futuristic eschatology, not the church which severed the black man's attention from the exigencies of the "here and now" and riveted it to the putative rewards of the hereafter. It is rather the *restored* church of her slave ancestors that Meridian ultimately embraces, the Church of Nat Turner, of Denmark Vesey, the church rooted in the soil of protest against oppression, the church of "communal spirit, togetherness, righteous convergence."

The musical and religious traditions converge in the critical chapter entitled "Camera." Falling strategically near the end of the novel, the chapter renders a certain completion to Meridian's characterization, for it is in this chapter that she resolves some of the most besetting quandaries of her life. The chapter begins by likening Meridian to a camera (an image suggesting distance and detachment) as she watches a group of churchgoers assemble for Sunday service, but it ends with her reunion with kindred black souls in a communal purpose. Wandering into a church shortly after Martin Luther King's assassination, she notices a number of changes which trigger her reexamination of the function of the black church in the social and political struggle. What strike her at first are the church's physical changes. It was

> not like the ones of her childhood; it was not shabby or small. It was large, of brick, with stained-glass windows . . . an imposing structure; and yet *it did not reach for the sky*, as cathedrals did, *but settled firmly on the ground.* (my italics)

That the church is settled firmly on the ground suggests its temporal rather than compensatory concerns. Its outer transformations mirror its internal changes. A man is called on to pray, but his is a short prayer and, significantly, he doesn't kneel. "He said he would not pray any longer because there was a lot of work for the community to do."

Similarly, Meridian observes a change in the music. It now has a tone which urges her to quote Margaret Walker's lines, "Let the martial songs be written. . . . let the dirges disappear."

The sermon has even changed from those unintelligible ones she knew as a child. The minister, boldly reminiscent of Martin Luther King, has a decidedly political thrust to his sermon, which is punctuated by references to President Nixon, "whom he called 'Tricky Dick.'" He admonishes the young men in the audience not to participate in the Vietnam War and challenges the young women "to stop looking for husbands and try to get something useful in their heads. . . . God was not mentioned except as a reference."

But the most telling transformation in the church is the picture in the stained-glass window, not of the traditional pale Christ with stray lamb, but rather of "B. B. With a Sword," a picture of a tall, broad-shouldered black man with a guitar in one hand and a blood-dripping sword in the other. The reference to blues singer B. B. King is obvious. Here, Alice Walker, like a number of other black writers,[18] is using the black musician as a symbol of an enduring cultural tradition and as an exemplification of unity and community.[19]

It is this same sense of unity and community evoked by "B. B. With a Sword" that Meridian experiences as she contemplates the meaning of the picture. In an epiphany of sorts, she discovers that her identity is inextricably tied to her black people, that she is a mere particle of a much larger, more complex composite, and that "[her] existence extended beyond herself to those around her because, in fact, the years in America had created [black people into] one life."

Upon perceiving her essential Oneness with black humanity, Meridian reassesses her commitment to the racial struggle once again. This time she feels duty-bound to make a commitment that extends beyond registering black voters and integrating rest room facilities. She begins to contemplate the power of the sword; the sword of the picture begins to have meaning for her. Thus, while throughout the novel Meridian could not contemplate killing for the struggle, she now sees the necessity for it. Even though she vacillates in the belief that she herself can kill, she thinks,

> ". . . perhaps it will be my part to walk behind the real revolutionaries—those who know they must spill blood in order to help the poor and the black and therefore go right ahead—and when they stop to wash off the blood and find their throats too choked with the smell of murdered flesh to sing, I will come forward and sing from memory songs they will need once more to hear. For it is the song of the people, transformed by the experiences of each generation, that holds them together, and if any part of it is lost the people suffer and are without soul. If I can do that, my role will not have been a useless one after all."

Thus, the self has bloomed; Meridian has found her identity, an identity fashioned not from the Western tradition, but rather from the artifacts of her own heritage. Moreover, she, like Claude McKay's Bita Plant of *Banana Bottom*, has found a connecting link to that heritage which enables her to prevail in comparison to all of the other characters in the novel. At the end of the book, she receives from Anne-Marion a sheet of paper, in the center of which is a gigantic tree stump from which a tiny branch is growing. Anne-Marion has written: "Who would be happier than you that the Sojourner did not die?" The Sojourner was the tree, a symbol of both the black oral and musical traditions, planted during slavery on a plantation which later became Saxon College, the tree destroyed by a group of rioting students. Metaphorically speaking,

Meridian is that branch from The Sojourner and the clarion testimony that although systematic attempts have been made at its destruction as the nucleus of black life, it is not dead. Anne-Marion's "grotesquely small" handwriting on the note parallels her stunted and puny existence, pale in significance to Meridian's, pale because she has suffered a self-authored separation from the trunk, from her root source.

Truman, unlike Anne-Marion, gradually realizes the source of Meridian's vitality and the ultimate value of her life. When the novel ends, Meridian is leaving the town of Chickokema for still other crusades. She leaves behind her cap and sleeping bag, the articles that have identified her throughout the novel. More importantly, however, she leaves Truman behind struggling to experience self-discovery and rebirth. After Meridian leaves, Truman climbs into her sleeping bag and then dons her cap, almost in an effort to "become" Meridian, to experience, through osmosis, her vitality. But like Meridian, Truman and Anne-Marion must individually sift through the shards of their cultural past to heal and re-create themselves.

Notes

1. Epigraph used by Mary Helen Washington, ed., *Black-Eyed Susans* (Garden City, New York: Anchor Books, 1975).
2. Toni Cade, "On the Issue of Roles," in *The Black Woman: An Anthology*, ed. Toni Cade (New York: The New American Library, Inc., 1970), p. 105.
3. Walker has stated that her fictional preoccupation is "exploring the oppressions, the insanities, the loyalties, and the triumphs of black women" (John O'Brien, ed., *Interviews with Black Writers* [New York: Liveright, 1973], p. 192).
4. There are very clear echoes of Emersonian idealism in the novel. *Meridian* embodies many of the underlying assumptions of transcendentalism.
5. *Season of Youth: The Bildungsroman From Dickens to Golding* (Cambridge, Mass.: Harvard University Press, 1974), p.18. For a more detailed statement of the *Bildungsroman*, see Susanne Howe, *Wilhelm Meister and His English Kinsmen* (New York: Columbia Univ. Press, 1930).
6. Alice Walker, *Meridian* (New York: Pocket Books, 1977), p. 25.
7. For a discussion of this notion of the divinity within the individual, see Emerson's "The Divinity School Address," where he states that a "true conversion" takes place only when all individuals "[come] again to themselves, to the God in themselves . . ." (Ralph Waldo Emerson, *Nature Addresses and Lectures* [New York: Houghton Mifflin and Company, 1903], p. 132).
8. It is significant that the old sweeper in the opening chapter says that Meridian "thinks she's God. . . ."
9. American tradition assumes many forms in the novel, one such being the symbolic presence of guards. The frequency with which guards appear in the novel is not incidental, for their appearance suggests protection, preservation, in this case protection and preservation of tradition. The guards also appear at the circus wagon and at the door of the Saxon chapel.

10. See also Walker's short story, "Really, Doesn't Crime Pay?" in *In Love and Trouble* (New York: Harcourt, Brace, Jovanovich, 1973). Myrna, the protagonist, wants to prove to her husband that she is not "a womb without a brain that can be bought with Japanese bathtubs and shopping spress."
11. "On the Issue of Roles," p. 108.
12. Buckley, *Season of Youth*, pp. 65–66.
13. See Evelyn Underhill, *Mysticism* (New York: E. P. Dutton and Company, Inc., 1930), pp. 140–41.
14. The word "ecstasy" is used several times in the novel to describe Meridian's experience, and thus, it is fairly accurate to assume its connections with mysticism.
15. Underhill, *Mysticism*, pp. 359–60.
16. Ibid., p. 379.
17. *The Negro Church in America*. (New York: Schocken Books, 1969), p. 70.
18. See especially James Baldwin's short story "Sonny's Blues."
19. For similar discussions see Shirley Williams, *Give Birth to Brightness* (New York: The Dial Press, 1972), pp. 140–41. See also Ralph Ellison's "Blues People," in *Shadow and Act* (New York: Vintage Books, 1972).

◆◆◆◆◆◆◆◆◆◆◆◆◆◆

Poetry Celebrating Life

HANNA NOWAK

"**A**nd it was then that I knew that the healing / of all our wounds / is forgiveness / that permits a promise / of our return at the end": These concluding lines of Alice Walker's third book of poetry, *Good Night, Willie Lee, I'll See You in the Morning* (1979), appropriately set the tone of the poet's voice and contain her essential message: a deep concern for all human beings, optimism and affirmation of life, the feeling of continuity, and a highly personal vision. To call her poems "hopeful strategies for recapturing one's humanity"[1] is, therefore, entirely apposite. The whole title poem includes another typical feature: Walker draws on a personal experience. "Good Night, Willie Lee, I'll see you / in the morning"[2] is the solemn and faithful promise of her mother at her father's death.

Alice Walker is better known as a novelist, short story writer, and essayist, although she has published three books of poetry: *Once* (1968), *Revolutionary Petunias* (1973),[3] and *Good Night, Willie Lee, I'll See You in the Morning*. A glance at her poetry in its entirety will provide some reasons for its rather tepid reception among critics. Walker's emphasis on concrete, precise images, everyday themes and personal tone are in marked contrast to the overwhelming dependence of much contemporary black poetry upon rhetorical brilliance and formal experimentation. Her short poems usually appear surrounded by blank space. Only in *Once* does Alice Walker play with the stanza arrangements by indenting some lines or building a snake form, e.g., in "What Ovid Taught Me." The later poems are more complex, and elaborate, and often longer. Their surface simplicity, however, does not preclude sophistication. The poem "The Democratic Order" can easily be converted into prose: "My father (back blistered) beat me because I could not stop crying. He'd had enough 'fun' he said for one damn voting day." This incident, which could be seen as part of a longer narrative, is transformed into an image with transcending meaning. No longer is it the isolated experience of a single black father's rage at a violent voting day and of a child's bewilderment. The poetic rendering of this episode implies the poet's matured understanding and an instance of self-revelation (the subtitle accordingly runs "Such Things in Twenty Years I Understood").

In her poetry, Alice Walker talks about herself directly, without donning a mask to disguise her words; she does not need to muffle her voice as early black women writers, notably Phillis Wheatley, had to; she is not forced to wear "the mask that grins and lies."[4] The black woman poet is now confident of herself and of her audience. The ostensible purpose of her poetry is the celebration of life and of the black woman trying to come to terms with the American reality. Alice Walker described the process of composing poetry in relation to *Once* which was written at a difficult time of her life:

> Since that time, it seems to me that all of my poems—and I write groups of poems rather than singles—are written when I have successfully pulled myself out of a completely numbing despair, and stand again in the sunlight. Writing poems is my way of celebrating with the world that I have not committed suicide the evening before.[5]

To sit down and think of a poem is for her the most genuine way to get in touch with her real self. Conscious manipulation of thoughts never turns into good poetry. Walker says, "I realize that while I write poetry, I am so high as to feel invisible, and in that condition it is possible to write anything."[6] Knowing which poems did not grow out of sincere emotions, she expects to be haunted by them. Instinctively, she feels that her poems are most successful when she relies on personal experience. Her poetry, it can be argued consequently, is the best access to the personality of Alice Walker.

This may need some clarification. Alice Walker wrote almost all of the poems in *Once* when she was 21 years old (they were published later) and completed *Revolutionary Petunias* during her last years in Jackson, Mississippi. In 1974, at the age of thirty, she moved to New York. That year can be taken as the beginning of a new stage in her life. She says about the time she spent in Jackson: "I grew to adulthood in Mississippi."[7] It is no mere coincidence that her search for identity, her own growing into self-confidence should run parallel to the nation's search for new ways of living. With her move to New York, Alice Walker completes that process and, in the consequence, her poetry changes, too. In her interview with John O'Brien in 1973 and also in several autobiographical essays, she draws the connection between her life and specific poems. Among her poetic sources are, to name a few, her parents, her sister Molly, early love affairs, her travels to Africa, marriage, and childbirth. To a degree, one can justify, therefore, the equation of the poet with the persona in a number of poems.

Larry Neal's observation that in black literature one frequently comes across a "clash between the private and public aspects of literary performance"[8] is certainly true of Alice Walker. Her fiction and essays are no doubt written for a public purpose; her poetry, on the contrary, decidedly emphasizes the private aspects, although all along she considers herself a poet with publication in mind. The latent dichotomy of publicity vs. privacy allows a grouping of her poems into three classes for the purpose of discussion. In the first of these, Walker is concerned with the historical experiences of black people and her own participation in them, always seen from an individualistic standpoint. This blending of the public and the private sides is symbolized in the two words "revolutionary" and "petunia". The "revolutionary petunia"-poems are definitely "black" and mostly Southern in context. Secondly, Walker writes very private love poetry which—because of the two dominant images—could be called "heart and soul"-poems. The poet-persona is not so much black—as she is woman-centered. Thirdly, in *Good Night, Willie Lee*, she reveals a tendency towards more public poems. These "facing the way"-poems, as I would like to name them, are often directly feminist in tone.

Black life in the South and her own involvement in it serve as the common denominators of the "revolutionary petunia"-poems. The poet's experiences and impressions are treated as representative of the collective history of the American South. Thus, the very personal poem about her own birth as the eighth child of a sharecropper's family in Eatonton, Ga., is at the same time a depiction of the economic progress, albeit slow, of the Southern black family. Whereas the midwife picked out a pig for her brother's birth, she received cash for Walker's own delivery because, as her mother proudly recalls, "'We wasn't so country then'." A Southerner by birth and inclination, though no longer by residence, Alice Walker knows that growing up in the South gave her life a sense of purpose that she would not like to do without. Although the history of the South forced her to fight for even the option to stay there or leave it, she values the vitalizing energy of its life. She once summarized her debt to the region by calling it

> a compassion for the earth, a trust in humanity beyond our knowledge of evil, and an abiding love of justice. We inherit a great deal of responsibility as well, for we must give voice to centuries not only of silent bitterness and hate but also of neighborly kindness and sustaining love.

Walker's interest in the South is not restricted to the time after slavery was introduced: Just as her concern for her racial roots extends to Africa, so her compassion for the Southern earth extends to the remnants of the original Indian population. The ancient burial mound "Eagle Rock"—it also features in the novel *Meridian*—symbolizes for her oneness with nature, communication with one's body, and peace:

> I used to stop and
> Linger there
> Within the cleanswept tower stair
> Rock Eagle pinesounds
> Rush of stillness
> Lifting up my hair

Sensitive to the long suffering and eventual defeat of the Indians, the poet laments the exploitation of the sacred place as a mass tourist attraction:

The people come on tours.
And on surrounding National
Forest lakes the air rings
With cries
The silenced make.

Walker's love of the South as a region is, however, most strongly inspired by her love of its black inhabitants. As a child she learned to trust other black people completely; she felt protected within this community. For this reason, she has dedicated many poems, especially in the first part of *Revolutionary Petunias*, to the people she grew up with. She cherishes the memory of the old men at the funerals "More awkward / With the flowers / Than with the widow"; the uncles with "broken teeth / And billy club stars" who bring tidings from the north, and are "Always good / For a nickle / Sometimes a dime" for the children. She treasures the old people in their little gardens, the Sunday School teachers, the old women in church singing of Jesus, their good friend. Most of all, Alice Walker pays homage to women like her mother: supporters of their families, helpful friends to their daughters, important role-models. Alice Walker begins the often quoted poem which is part of her essay "In Search of Our Mothers' Gardens" with the words, "They were women then / My mama's generation / Husky of voice—Stout of / Step. . . ." She admires these "Headragged generals" because "they knew what we / *Must* know / Without knowing a page of it / Themselves." Characteristically, Walker avoids stereotypes and refrains from romanticizing or exalting them. She knows this kind of woman was "A hard / worker, with rough, moist hands" whose life consisted of everlasting toil. She characterizes the chores of her grandmother when she was a young woman:

Come to seven children.
To aprons and sweat.
Came to quilt making.
Came to canning and vegetable gardens
big as fields.
Came to fields to plow.
Cotton to chop.
Potatoes to dig.

The realization that she is part of a tradition of women who have tried to assert themselves, even while their creative needs never found public recognition, helps the poet to define herself.

A very immediate and striking influence on her life—again it proves the parallel between collective and personal history—is Walker's sister Molly, from whom she learned that Eatonton, Georgia, did not mean "the world," that she should know things beyond the Southern life. The story of Molly revealed to her the difficulties—the civil rights movement had not yet fully begun—in being satisfied with Southern life once you had left for other, freer regions. Alice suffered when she found out that her admired sister Molly was ashamed of her family's backwoods behavior. Her now well-known poem to her sister, which went through numerous drafts, was intended to be vicious and even to hurt. Yet in the end it offered understanding for that young woman for whom "the gap that separated us from the rest of the world was too wide . . . to keep trying to bridge."[9] While in the fifties, Molly did not find it possible to develop her personality and remain in the South, Alice, in the sixties, struggled to effect the changes that would allow the Southern black person to do both at the same time.

From these women of an earlier generation, and of her own, Alice Walker learned about the beauties of birth, the duties to the dead, familial love and support. No doubt her early experiences provided her with the sincerity and energy to engage actively in the civil rights struggle. Whereas Walker gives a rather factual record of revolutionary work in her essays, some of her novels and short stories, she provides fragmentory but enlightening glimpses of emotions and atmosphere in her poetry. Thus, the people who refuse to join the movement are described as

> Fat chested pigeons
> resplendent of prodigious riches
> reaped in body weight
> taking bewildered pecks
> at eagles
> as though *muck*
> were God.

Again the individual, personal, "petunia" side of the public cause most captures her imagination. The title poem in *Once* consists of scattered incidents combined into a poetic picture of the revolutionary mood. Walker favors the stanza about the young black man who wanted to crash all barriers at once by swimming nude at a white beach. To her, this stanza belongs to a series of poems "full of playfulness and whimsicality, an attraction to world families and the cosmic sea—full of a lot of naked people longing to swim free." To a large extent, the success of these poems resides in the use of telling, revelatory details. "Sammy Lou of Rue" is a forceful, evocative poem becaues it catches the spirit of the time: Sammy Lou becomes a folk heroine when she revenges her husband's murder and kills the white man "using a cultivator's hoe / with verve and skill." She is, however, a conventional, religious black woman, not a deliberate, radical revolutionary. On her way to the electric chair she leaves only a single message:

> "Don't yall forgit to *water*
> my purple petunias."

This one sentence contains the essence of Alice Walker's vision: a revolutionary without a love for the everyday is not a whole person. It is obvious that she found the material again in family history. On a journey, her mother once picked up a purple petunia in a deserted yard and kept it for years. She offered her daughter a blooming branch on the day *her* daughter was born. Inspired by that symbol of beauty and endurance, Alice Walker named her book after it: "In a way," she says, "the whole book is a celebration of people who will not cram themselves into any ideological or racial mold. They are all shouting Stop! I want to get that petunia!"[10]

The South, then, signifies for Walker a measure of humanity and of the importance of a life in which dreams bridge past and present. In "View from Rosehill Cemetery: Vicksburg" Walker evokes its spirit:

> Here we are not quick to disavow
> the pull of field and wood
> and stream;
> we are not quick to turn
> upon our dreams.

In later years, Walker has to acknowledge that the spirit of a black community united for a common goal was in danger of dissolution. She cannot conceal her disappointment at the lack of solidarity and trust she sometimes encountered among black people. In the section "Crucifixions" of *Revolutionary Petunias*, several poems bewail the lamentable fact:

> Be the first at the crucifixion
> Stand me (and them and her and him)
> where once we each together
> stood.

"Black Mail" is an appropriate title for that poem.

No doubt, Alice Walker's "revolutoinary petunia"-poems have black people, black life, and black experience at their care. They really are

> Rebellious. Living.
> Against the Elemental Crush.
> A Song of Color
> Blooming
> For Deserving Eyes.
> Blooming Gloriously
> For its Self.

In contrast to this "Song of Color," her love poetry is obviously more woman- than black-centered. This is not to say that gender predominates over race; of course, the experiences of "black" women are the bases of the poems, but the problems of womanhood are now emphasized. Sometimes love in extreme situations is depicted, as in "Johann," which sketches the possibility of loving a blond German. In several poems, race causes disappointment or misgivings in love (or leads to suicide because of "incorrect" racial relations). Yet, extraordinary love affairs are not the only problematic ones, the male-female relationship in general is likely to raise frustration. One poem runs:

> To love a man wholly
> love him
> feet first
>> head down
>> eyes cold
>> closed
> in depression.

To juxtapose this view, a more conventional love poem features a simple, uncomplicated image.

> Here we lie
> You and I—
> Your mind, unaccountable,
> My mind simply
> Stopped—
> Like a clock struck
> By the treachery
> Of time.

Outright statements without embellishments characterize Alice Walker's love poems. In *Once*, many of them are related to poems considering suicide as a solution for unhappy love. In an interview, Walker confesses that she wrote them after she wanted to commit suicide because of a pregnancy. She says, " . . . I felt I understood the part played in suicide by circumstances and fatigue. I also began to understand how alone woman is, because of her body."[11] One exemplary stanza is the following:

> to die before one
> wakes
> must be joyous
> full swing glorious
> (rebellion)
> (victory)
> unremarked triumph.

Affirmation of life is, however, the persistent image in these early love poems; then and later (there are several suicide poems in *Revolutionary Petunias* and *Good Night, Willie Lee*) it is the alternative to suicidal thoughts. Characteristically she concludes *Once* in an optimistic tone:

> My fear of burial
> is all tied up with
> how used I am
> to the spring. . . !

In *Revolutionary Petunias*, five years later, the expectations youthful love raised have mellowed. The attitude towards love is no longer always positive; sometimes resignation tinges the tone of a poem. Consider the following advice in "Expect Nothing": "Tame wild disappointment / With caress unmoved and cold. / Make it a parka / For Your Soul"; and: "But expect nothing. / Live frugally / On surprise." Or listen to the near sarcasm in "Be Nobody's Darling":

> Be nobody's darling;
> Be an outcast.
> Take the contradiction
> Of your life
> And wrap around
> You like a shawl,
> To parry stones
> To keep you warm.

Despite her continuing fascination with the mysteries of love ("Your eyes are widely open flowers. / Only their centers are darkly clenched / To conceal Mysteries") she cannot disregard its affiliation with violence and wounds: " . . . and his fingers peeled / the coolness off / her mind / his flower eyes crushed her / till / she bled." On the whole, however, one encounters a matured persona who values love even when it is unfashionable, as Walker once writes in a poem to her husband. A self-confident, relaxed attitude claims more and more importance.

> I have learned not to worry about love;
> but to honor its coming
> with all my heart.

The tone of the love poems in *Good Night, Willie Lee* is at first similar to that of *Revolutionary Petunias*. It starts with "I love a man who is not worth / my love"; it contains the lines "I thought love could be controlled. / It cannot"; or:

> My hand shakes before this killing.
> My stomach sits jumpy in my chest.
> My chest is the Grand Canyon
> sprawled empty
> over the world.

Whereas in the earlier poems, the words "heart" and "soul" appeared only occasionally, they recur constantly in *Good Night*. Walker's most original lines contains these two words: "Your soul shines / like the sides of a fish"; "until the end / he called me possessive / and held his soul / so tightly /it shrank / to fit his hand"; "Never offer your heart / to someone who eats hearts"; "My heart—which I feel / freezing a bit each day to this man." Heart and soul as the symbols of the capabilities of love show how completely a person can be numbed and possessed by it and how difficult it is to get accustomed to its waning or subsiding. Yet, the poet succeeds in overcoming adversities as a whole person. One poem may clarify her firm self-confidence:

> He said: I want you to be happy.
> He said: I love you so.
> Then he was gone.
> For two days I was happy.
> For two days, he loved me so.
> After that, I was on my own.

The strength of the matured poet derives in large part from the new maternal love towards her daughter. This love is free of possessiveness, full of forgiveness, aware of future parting:

> Even as I hold you
> I am letting go.

Notwithstanding many beautiful lines and deep emotional sincerity, Walker's numerous love poems can sound repetitive and too self-centered when read one after another. As a reader, one would like to leave out several stanzas or poems and concentrate instead, after careful selection, on individual lines or poems. By disregarding undecipherably personal allusions, one is rewarded with the insight into a genuine black female core.

With her celebration of black life, the South, the spirit of community and, most of all, of black womanhood, Alice Walker forms part of a tradition of black women writers. Her "They were women then / My mama's generation," for example, resembles Margaret Walker's "Lineage;" in many poems Gwendolyn Brooks, like Alice Walker, sings for the common black people ("The Birth in a Narrow Room," "The Bean Eaters," "The Mother"). Her sisterhood with Nikki Giovanni, Sonia Sanchez, June Jordan, or Mari Evans is also undeniable; they all share the praise of black womanhood as a common theme. Erlene Stetson, the editor of *Black Sister. Poetry by Black Women, 1746–1980*,[12] cites Alice Walker's flower imagery as part of a tradition. On the other hand, Alice Walker is not included in Stephen Henderson's anthology *Understanding the New Black Poetry* (1973),[13] in which he collects poems with an emphasis on formal innovation, and radical or politically conscious themes which all derive from the black oral tradition. If such an anthology were made today, perhaps it would contain some poems of *Good Night, Willie Lee,* namely her "facing the way"-poems.

By the time of publication of *Good Night, Willie Lee* in 1979, Alice Walker's poetry points towards a more radical vision of black life, a more public-oriented voice. Possibly, her growing public spirit has two sources: in 1970, she wrote in an article on the "Duties of the Black Revolutionary Artist" that "(t)he real revolutionary is always concerned with the least glamorous stuff." Following that credo, she wrote about the private, personal side of the revolutionary movement (cf. also the novel *Meridian*) while still considering herself a real revolutionary. However, after living seven years in Jackson, Mississippi, as an active civil rights participant, Walker suddenly realized that she was by nature not a violent or radical person. She felt guilty about that self-revelation: "The burden of a nonviolent, pacifist philosophy in a violent, nonpacifist society caused me to feel, almost always, as if I had not done enough." Now, she even "cringe(s) at the inappropriateness" of being referred to as an "activist" or "a 'veteran' of the Civil Rights Movement." Walker's haunting doubts about her position as a black person in the seventies have resulted in a number of poems which are more radical and provoking than the earlier civil rights poems. Sometimes it seems as if she wanted to compensate the lack of personal radicalism by writing about it; probably she now feels like the protagonist in *Meridian;* she has to keep up the song of the people at a time when the real revolutionaries are left to struggle on their own. This self-conflict is best expressed in the poem "facing the way," which deals with the problem of giving up one's comfort to the service of the poor. The atmosphere is one of guilt about pursuing and loving art instead of dedicating one's energy and spending one's money in helping the poor:

> it is shameful how hard it is for me to give
> them up!
> to cease this cowardly addiction
> to art that transcends time
> beauty that nourishes a ravenous spirit
> but drags on the mind whose sale would patch
> a roof
> heat the cold rooms of children, replace an eye.
> feed a life.

Having successfully published essays, novels, short stories, and poems Alice Walker is sure that the purpose of her life is to write; nevertheless, she cannot escape the conflict of "facing the way," of being torn between verbal concessions and active engagement.

The second source for this new trend towards the public is her growing feminism, or "womanism" as she prefers to call it. The womanist content of her most recent novel *The Color Purple* has its precedent in several poems. As a typical example consider the following stanza:

> I find my own
> small person
> a standing self
> against the world
> an equality of wills
> I finally understand.

More than before, Walker hails the individuality of the contemporary black woman who has finally achieved the right to write, to think, to do what she wants.

In *Good Night, Willie Lee,* Alice Walker definitely contributes to what Henderson defines as a unifying theme of black poetry: "the idea of Liberation."[14] In "Early Losses: a requiem," Walker depicts the woman's side of slavery and captures a woman's emotions, thus blending the public, personal, and feminist aspects of her voice. "Omunu," the magic word that symbolizes Africa, the past, freedom, happiness for the slave mother has lost its meaning for the child sold away from the mother:

> A sound like a small wind
> finding the door of a
> hollow reed
> my mother's farewell
> glocked up from the back
> of her throat
>
> *the sound itself is all*

Other poems, "facing the way," "The Abduction of Saints," "Light Baggage" or "January 10, 1973" ("i sit for hours staring at my own right hand / wondering if it would help me shoot the judge / who called us chimpanzees from behind the bench"), pay tribute to the leaders and the cause of the black revolution and to prominent black women writers. In contrast to "Once" and earlier poems, they are not written in an individualistic, personal, impressionistic vein; but neither are they the kind of experimental oral-aural poetry as Sarah Webster Fabio's "Tribute to Duke," Sonia Sanchez' "A Coltrane poem," or Carolyn Rogers' "Poem to Malcolm" for which indigenous black musical forms such as gospel songs, sermons, blues, ballads, chants, hollers have provided the stylistic features of rhythm, improvisation, and repetition. Alice Walker reveals a deep affinity to American blues, gospel or jazz singers: Shug Avery in *The Color Purple* is the prominent example; the short story "Nineteen Fifty-Five" deals with a singer. Yet in her poetry, black music is only occasionally alluded to, structurally, no poem tries to capture the timber of black music or, a second recurring feature in contemporary black poetry, black street talk. It has to be emphasized that to qualify Alice Walker's poetry as "personal" does not connote "a female/feminine devaluation or dismissal of her work." In that sense, it was applied to the black female poets during the Harlem Renaissance. As Gloria Hull says, their "aracial or quietly racial works in traditional forms"[15] did not gain public recognition. Today, Alice Walker's largely "personal" poems are representative of a major trend in black women's poetry that stretches back to Phillis Wheatley and comprises most contemporary black women poets.

Despite her many beautiful and successful single poems, Alice Walker's poetry as a whole fails to convince the critics that she is better a poet than fiction writer. Statements like "She is at her best a storyteller" or "Walker's most notable accomplishment . . . has been in fiction" abound.[16] Reviewers tend to take a generally, though not enthusiastically, positive line of criticism. The poems in *Once*, for example, are characterized as "pencil sketches which are all graven outline: no shaded areas, no embellishments. Wit and tenderness combine into humanity;"[17] those of *Revolutionary Petunias* are "poems of extraordinary grace, wisdom, and strength," admired for "richness of detail and a convicting concreteness."[18] Another scholar lauds Walker's "loving sense of the individual in history," and praises her for "(i)gnoring proscriptive calls for black art radically to reorder the Western cultural aesthetic."[19] Yet another critic laments Walker's "linguistic mediocrity" in *Good Night, Willie Lee* which sometimes "sinks to the level of a kind of wisdom-poetry" or becomes a "sad jumble of banalities;" yet this same critic also stresses that, "The majority . . . of her rather preachy love poems are self-critical, fair-minded, bent on a reasonable blend of compassion and independence."[20]

Generally, it seems that the critics appreciate Walker's originality of approach, as well as the vividness of her diction with its precise wording and subtly pleasing sounds. The careful structuring of *Revolutionary Petunias*, its division into five parts, with each part the sequence of the former, is also praised. Walker's poetry is often regarded, however, as not so important as her fiction because it does not capture the reader's imagination as much as her novels or short stories do. As a prose writer, Alice Walker has even become something of a cult-figure for black women's literature after the publication of *The Color Purple* in 1983. Yet, no doubt, Walker considers herself a poet, too. Poems appear at strategic points in many essays, novels, and short stories: one prominent poem in *Meridian*, for example, encapsulates the protagonist's main concerns in a few lines. Many essays use poems to clarify a point; Walker often quotes them at public lectures.

Again, as with Walker's love poetry, one feels that the average reader might like to leave out a few lines or stanzas. To be precise in my criticism: Why does such a good poem as "Once" include a stanza with the banal lines "In the morning / there was / a man in grey / but the sky was blue;" and why does the poem end with the detailed description of a small black girl waving the American flag "gingerly / with / the very / *tips* / of her / fingers?" The penultimate stanza would have been more forceful and evocative: in a few words it recounts the death of a little black girl, an episode that subtly depicts the cruelties of the time without any bland flag-waving. In more than one poem, one is disappointed with the last line that one expects to summarize or conclude the poem with a note that reaches beyond. The last line of "Excuse," the last stanza of "Never Offer Your Heart," "At First," and "facing the way"—to cite the most obvious examples—had better been left out. On the whole, *Once* is a book in which the poetry sometimes possesses an unevenness that was balanced out in the following two books. Despite some small flaws, *Good Night, Willie Lee* is a skillful, successful book that one treasures highly. The poem dedicated to the heroine of a Zora Neale Hurston novel epitomizes the central creed of all of Walker's poetry: celebrating the lives of black women:

> i love the way Janie Crawford
>
> left her husbands the one who wanted
> to change her into a mule
> and the other who tried to interest her
> in being a queen
> a woman unless she submits is neither a mule
> nor a queen
> though like a mule she may suffer
> and like a queen pace
> the floor

Notes

1. Jerry W. Ward, review of *Revolutionary Petunias and Other Poems* by Alice Walker, *College Language Association Journal* 17 (1973), p. 128.
2. Alice Walker, *Good Night, Willie Lee, I'll See You in the Morning*, New York: Dial Press, 1979, p. 53.
3. Alice Walker, *Once*, New York: Harcourt, Brace and World, 1968; *Revolutionary Petunias and Other Poems*, New York: Harcourt Brace Jovanovich, 1973.
4. This is the first line of Paul Lawrence Dunbar's poem "We Wear the Mask."

5. John O'Brien, "Alice Walker," in *Interviews with Black Writers*, New York: Liveright, 1973, p. 191.
6. Ibid., p. 192.
7. Alice Walker, "Recording the Seasons," in *In Search of Our Mothers' Gardens; Womanist Prose*, New York: Harcourt Brace Jovanovich, 1983, p. 224.
8. Larry Neal, "The Black Contribution to American Letters: Part II. The Writer as Activist—1960 and After," in Mabel M. Smythe (ed.), *The Black American Reference Book*, Englewood Cliffs, N.J.: Prentice-Hall, 1976, p. 767.
9. O'Brien, *Interviews with Black Writers*, p. 210.
10. O'Brien, *Interviews*, p. 208.
11. O'Brien, *Interviews*, p. 189.
12. Bloomington: Indiana University Press, 1981.
13. Henderson, *Understanding the New Black Poetry: Black Speech and Black Music as Poetic References*. New York: Morrow, 1973.
14. Henderson, *Understanding the New Black Poetry*, p. 18.
15. Both quotes from Gloria T. Hull, "Afro-American Women Poets: A Bio-Critical Survey," in Sandra M. Gilbert, Susan Gubar (eds.), *Shakespeare's Sisters. Feminist Essays on Women Poets*, Bloomington: Indiana Univ. Press, 1979, p. 174.
16. Barbara Christian, *Black Women Novelists. The Development of a Tradition, 1892–1976*, Westport, Ct.: Greenwood Press, 1980, p. 182 and O'Brien, *Interviews*, p. 186.
17. Lisel Mueller, review of *Once, Poetry*, 117 (1970/71), p. 328.
18. Jerry Ward, review of *Revolutionary Petunias, College Language Association Journal* 17 (1973), p. 127.
19. Duncan Kenworthy, "Contemporary Poetry: Six Touchstones," *The American Scholar* 42 (Summer 1973), p. 522.
20. Alan Williamson, review of *Good Night, Willie Lee, Poetry* 135 (1979/80), p. 353–354.

♦♦♦♦♦♦♦♦♦♦♦♦♦

Walker: The Achievement
of the Short Fiction

ALICE HALL PETRY

There's nothing quite like a Pulitzer Prize to draw attention to a little known writer. And for Alice Walker, one of the few black writers of the mid-'60s to remain steadily productive for the two ensuing decades, the enormous success of 1982's *The Color Purple* has generated critical interest in a literary career that has been, even if not widely noted, at the very least worthy of note. As a poet (*Once*, 1968; *Revolutionary Petunias*, 1973) and a novelist (*The Third Life of Grange Copeland*, 1970; *Meridian*, 1976), Walker has always had a small but enthusiastic following, while her many essays, published in black- and feminist-oriented magazines (e.g., *Essence, Ms.*), have likewise kept her name current, albeit in rather limited circles. The Pulitzer Prize has changed this situation qualitatively and perhaps permanently. Walker's name is now a household word, and a reconsideration of her literary canon, that all but inevitable Pulitzer perk, is well underway. An integral part of this phenomenon would be the reappraisal of her short fiction. Walker's two collections of short stories—1973's *In Love & Trouble* and 1981's *You Can't Keep a Good Woman Down*—are now available as attractive paperbacks and selling briskly, we are told. But a serious critical examination of her short stories—whether of particular tales, the individual volumes, or the entire canon—has yet to occur. Hence this essay. As a general over-view, it seeks to evaluate Walker's achievement as a short story writer while probing a fundamental question raised by so many reviewers of the two volumes: why is *You Can't Keep a Good Woman Down* so consistently less satisfying than the earlier *In Love & Trouble*? How has Alice Walker managed to undermine so completely that latest-and-best-formula so dear to book reviewers? The answer, as we shall see, is partly a matter of conception and partly one of technique; and it suggests further that Walker's unevenness thus far as a writer of short fiction—her capacity to produce stories that are sometimes extraordinarily good, at other times startlingly weak—places her at a career watershed. At this critical juncture, Alice Walker could so refine her art as to become one of the finest writers of American short fiction in this century.

She could just as easily not.

One key to understanding the disparate natures of *In Love & Trouble* and *You Can't Keep a Good Woman Down* is their epigraphs. *In Love & Trouble* offers two. The first epigraph, a page-long extract from *The*

Concubine by Elechi Amadi, depicts a girl, Ahurole, who is prone to fits of sobbing and "alarmingly irrational fits of argument": "From all this her parents easily guessed that she was being unduly influenced by agwu, her personal spirit." It is not until the end of the extract that Amadi mentions casually that "Ahurole was engaged to Ekwueme when she was eight days old."[1] In light of what follows in the collection, it is a most suitable epigraph: the women in this early volume truly are "in love and trouble" due in large measure to the roles, relationships, and self-images imposed upon them by a society which knows little and cares less about them as individuals. A marriage arrangd in infancy perfectly embodies this situation; and the shock engendered by Amadi's final sentence is only heightened as one reads *In Love & Trouble* and comes to realize that the concubinage depicted in his novel, far from being a bizarre, pagan, foreign phenomenon, is practiced in only slightly modified form in contemporary—especially black—America. In the opening story of *In Love & Trouble*, "Roselily," the overworked title character marries the unnamed Black Muslim from Chicago in part to give her three illegitimate children a better chance in life, and in part to obtain for herself some measure of social and economic security; but it is not really a relationship she chooses to enter freely, as is conveyed by her barely listening to her wedding ceremony—a service which triggers images not of romance but of bondage. Even ten-year-old Myop, the sole character of the vignette "The Flowers," has her childhood—and, ultimately, her attitudes towards her self and her world—shatterd by the blunt social reality of lynching: as much as she would love to spend her life all alone collecting flowers, from the movement she accidentally gets her heel caught in the skull of a decapitated lynching victim it is clear that, for their own survival, black females like Myop must be part of a group that includes males. Hence the plethora of bad marriages (whether legal unions or informal liaisons) in Walker's fiction; hence also the mental anguish suffered by most of her women characters, who engage in such unladylike acts as attacking their husbands with chain saws ("Really, *Doesn't* Crime Pay?," *IL&T*) or setting fire to themselves ("Her Sweet Jerome," *IL&T*). Must be that pesky agwu again—a diagnosis which is symptomatic of society's refusal to face the fact that women become homocidal/suicidal, or hire rootworkers to avenge social snubs ("The Revenge of Hannah Kemhuff," *IL&T*), or lock themselves up in convents ("The Diary of an African Nun," *IL&T*) not because of agwus, or because they are mentally or emotionally deficient, but because they are responding to the stress of situations not of their own making.[2] Certainly marriage offers these women nothing, and neither does religion, be it Christianity, the Black Muslim faith, or voodoo. That these traditional twin sources of comfort and stability cause nothing but "trouble" for Walker's character might lead one to expect a decidedly depressing volume of short stories; but in fact *In Love & Trouble* is very upbeat.

Walker manages to counterbalance the oppressive subject matter of virtually all these 13 stories by maintaining the undercurrent of hope first introduced in the volume's second epigraph, a passage from Rainer Maria Rilke's *Letters to a Young Poet:* ". . . we must hold to what is difficult; everything in Nature grows and defends itself in its own way and is characteristically and spontaneously itself, seeks at all costs to be so and against all opposition." For Walker as for Rilke, opposition is not necessarily insurmountable: struggles and crises can lead to growth, to the nurturing of the self; and indeed most of the women of *In Love & Trouble*, sensing this, do try desperately to face their situations and deal with them—even if to do so may make them insane, or ignorant, or antisocial.

The sole epigraph of *You Can't Keep* lacks the relevance and subtlety of those of *In Love & Trouble:* "It is harder to kill something that is spiritually alive than it is to bring the dead back to life."[3] Fine words from Herr Hesse, but unfortunately they don't have much to do with the fourteen stories in the collection. Few characters in *You Can't Keep* would qualify as "spiritually alive" according to most informed standards. We are shown a lot of self-absorbed artistes (the jazz-poet of "The Lover," the authoress of "Fame," the sculpture student of "A Sudden Trip Home in the Spring"), plus rather too many equally self-absorbed would-be radicals ("Advancing Luna—and Ida B. Wells," "Source," "Laurel,"), plus a series of women—usually referred to generically as "she"—who engage in seemingly interminable monologues on pornography, abortion, sadomasochism, and rape ("Coming Apart," "Porn," "A Letter of the Times, or Should This Sado-Masochism Be Saved?"). These women are dull. And, unlike the situation in *In Love & Trouble*, the blame can't really be placed on males, those perennial targets of Alice Walker's acid wit. No, the problem with the women of *You Can't Keep* is that they are successful. Unlike the ladies of *In Love & Trouble*, who seem always to be struggling, to be growing, those of *You Can't Keep* have all advanced to a higher plane, personally and socially; as Barbara Christian observes, there truly is a clear progression between the two volumes, from an emphasis on "trouble" to an emphasis on self-assertiveness.[4] The women of *You Can't Keep* embody the product, not the process: where a mother in *In Love & Trouble* ("Everyday Use") can only fantasize about appearing on *The Tonight Show*, a woman of *You Can't Keep* ("Nineteen Fifty-Five") actually does it! Gracie Mae Still meets Johnny! Similarly, a dying old lady in *In Love & Trouble* ("The Welcome Table") is literally thrown out of a segregated white church, but in *You Can't Keep* ("Source") two black women get to sit in an integrated Anchorage bar! With real Eskimos! Trudier Harris is quite correct that, compared to those of *In Love & Trouble*, the women of *You Can't Keep* seem superficial, static: "Free to make choices, they find themselves free to do nothing or to drift"[5]—and they do, with Walker apparently not realizing that in fiction (as in life) the journey, not the arrival, is what interests. Men and marriage, those two bugaboos of *In Love & Trouble* responsible for thwarting women's careers ("Really, *Doesn't* Crime Pay?"), mutilating hapless schoolgirls ("The Child Who Favored Daughter"), and advocating anti-white violence ("Her Sweet Jerome"), at least brought out the strength and imagination of the women they victimized, and the women's struggles engross the reader. In contrast, the men of *You Can't Keep* have declined, both as people and as fictional characters, in an inverse relationship to the women's success. Most of the volume's male characters barely materialize; the few who do appear are milquetoast, from the pudgy, racist lawyer/rapist/lover Bubba of "How Did I Get Away with Killing One of the Biggest Lawyers in the State? It Was Easy"; to Ellis, the Jewish gigolo from Brooklyn who inexplicably dazzles the supposedly cool jazz-poet heroine of "The Lover"; to Laurel, he of the giant pink ears who (again inexplicably) dazzles the black radical journalist in "Laurel." And many of the male characters in *You Can't Keep* meet sorry ends—not unlike the women of *In Love & Trouble:* Bubba is shot to death by his schoolgirl victim; the shopworn Ellis gets dumped; poor Laurel winds up in a coma, only to emerge brain-damaged. Curiously, we don't miss them; instead, we miss the kinds of conflicts and personal/social revelations which fully-realized, reasonably healthy male characters can impart to fiction.

For men, either directly or through the children they father, are a vital part of love; and it is love, as the soap operatic title of *In Love & Trouble* suggests,[6] which is most operative in that early volume. It assumes various forms. It may be the love between a parent and child, surely the most consistently positive type of love in Walker's fiction. It is her love for her dying baby which impels Rannie Toomer to chase a urinating mare in a rainstorm so as to collect "Strong Horse Tea," a folk medicine. It is her love for her daughter Dee that enables Mama to call her "Wangero Leewanika Kemanjo" in acknowledgment of her new Afro identity, but her equally strong love for her other child, the passive Maggie, which enables her to resist Dee/Wangero's demand for old quilts (Maggie's wedding present) to decorate her apartment ("Everyday Use"). Then again, the love of *In Love & Trouble* may be between a woman and God ("The Welcome Table"); and it may even have an erotic dimension, as with the sexually-repressed black nun of "The Diary of an African Nun" who yearns for her "pale lover," Christ. And granted, the love of *In Love & Trouble* is often distorted, even perverse: a father lops off his daughter's breasts in part because he confuses her with his dead sister, whom he both loved and loathed ("The Child Who Favored Daughter"); a young black girl and her middle-aged French teacher, the guilt-ridden survivor of the holocaust, fantasize about each other but never interact ("We Drink the Wine in France"); a dumpy hairdresser stabs and burns her husband's Black Power pamphlets as if they were his mistress: "'Trash!' she cried over and over . . . 'I kill you! I kill you!'" ("Her Sweet Jerome"). But in one form or another, love is the single most palpable force in *In Love & Trouble*. This is not the case in *You Can't Keep*, and the volume suffers accordingly.

What happened to love in the later collection? Consider the case of "Laurel." What does that supposedly "together" black radical narrator see in wimpy Laurel? Easy answer: his "frazzled but beautifully fitting jeans": "It occurred to me that I could not look at Laurel without wanting to make love with him." As the black radical and her mousy lover engage in "acrobatics of a sexual sort" on Atlanta's public benches, it is clear that "love" is not an issue in this story: these characters have simply fallen in lust. And as a result, the reader finds it impossible to be concerned about the ostensible theme of the story: the ways in which segregation thwarts human relationships. Who cares that segregation "was keeping us from strolling off to a clean, cheap hotel" when all they wanted was a roll in the sack? Likewise, the husband and wife of "Coming Apart," who speak almost ad nauseum on the subjects of pornography and sadomasochism, seem to feel nothing for each other: they are simply spokespersons for particular attitudes regarding contemporary sexual mores, and ample justification for Mootry-Ikerionwu's observation that characterization is definitely not Alice Walker's strong suit.[7] Without love, without warmth, this ostensible Everywife and Everyhusband connect literally only when they are copulating; and as a result Walker's statements regarding the sexual exploitation of women, far from being enriched by the personal touch of seeing how it affects one typical marriage, collapses into a dry lecture punctuated by clumsy plugs for consciousness-raising essays by Audre Lorde, Luisah Teish, and Tracy A. Gardner. Similarly, its title notwithstanding, "The Lover" has nothing to do with love. The story's liberated heroine, having left her husband and child for a summer at an artists' colony in New England, decides—just like that—to have an affair with the lupine Ellis: "when she had first seen him she had thought . . . 'my lover,' and had liked, deep down inside, the illicit sound of it. She had never had a lover; he would be her first. Afterwards, she would be truly a woman of her time." Apparently this story was meant to be a study of how one woman—educated, intelligent, creative—uses her newly-liberated sensuality to explore her sense of womanhood, her marriage, her career as a jazz poet. But the one-night-stand quality of her relationship with Ellis, not to mention the inappropriateness of him as a "lover"—he likes to become sexually involved each summer "with talkative women who wrote for *Esquire* and the *New York Times*" because they "made it possible for him to be included in the proper tennis sets and swimming parties at the Colony"—makes the story's heroine seem like a fool. And that points to a major problem with *You Can't Keep a Good Woman Down:* whereas the stories of *In Love & Trouble* move the reader to tears, to shock, to thought, those of the latter volume too often move him to guffaws. Too bad they weren't meant to be humorous.

One would think that a writer of Alice Walker's stature and experience would be aware that, since time began, the reduction of love to fornication has been the basis of jokes, from the ridiculous to the sublime. And whether they come across as comic caricatures (*vide* Laurel and Ellis), examples of bathroom humor, or zany parodies, the characters, subject matter, and writing style of most of the stories in *You Can't Keep a Good Woman Down* leave the reader with a she's-gotta-be-kidding attitude that effectively undercuts its very serious intentions. Consider the subject matter. In stories like "Porn," "A Letter of the Times," and "Coming Apart," Walker *attacks* pornography, sado-masochism, and violence against women by *discussing* them: it's a technique that many writers have used, but it can backfire by (1) appealing to the prurient interests of some readers, (2) imparting excitement to the forbidden topic, or (3) discussing the controversial subject matter so much that it becomes noncontroversial, unshocking; and without the "edge" of controversy, these serious topics often seem to be treated satirically—even when that is not the case. This is what happens in many stories in *You Can't Keep*, and the problem is compounded by the weak characters. The story "Coming Apart" is a good example: the husband dashes home from his bourgeois desk job to sit in the john and masturbate while drooling over the "Jivemates" in *Jiveboy* magazine. None of this shocks: we see so many references to genitalia and elimination in *You Can't Keep* that they seem as mundane as mailing a letter. Worse, the husband himself (called "he" to emphasize his role as Typical Male) comes across as a rather dense, naughty adolescent boy. He is so clearly suffering from a terminal case of the Peter Pan syndrome that it's impossible to believe that he'd respond with "That girl's onto something" when his equally-vapid wife (called "she") reads him yet another anti-pornography essay from her library of black feminist sociological tracts. Walker's-gotta-be-kidding, but she isn't. Likewise, the story "Fame" has a streak of crudity that leaves the reader wondering how to respond. For the most part, "Fame" consists of the ruminations of one Andrea Clement White (Walker always uses all three names), a wildly successful and universally admired writer who returns to her old college to receive her one-hundred-and-eleventh major award. She doesn't much like her former (Caucasian) colleagues or the banquet they are giving her, as her thoughts on the imminent award speech testifies:

> "This little lady has done . . ." Would he have said "This little man . . ."? But of course not. No man wanted to be called little. He thought it referred to his penis. But to say "little lady" made men think of virgins. Tight, tiny pussies, and moments of rape. (Walker's ellipses)

*   *   *

As Andrea Clement White degenerates from Famous Author to a character type from farce—the salty-tongued granny, the sweet old lady with the dirty mind—everything Walker was trying to say about identity, success, black pride has dissipated. We keep waiting for Walker to wink, to say that "Fame" is a satire; but it isn't.

The reader's uncertainty about how to respond to *You Can't Keep a Good Woman Down* is not dispelled by the writing style of many of the stories. Funny thing about lust: when you confuse it with love and try to write about it passionately, the result sounds curiously like parody. The following passage from "Porn" reads like a Harlequin romance:

> She was aflame with desire for him.
>
> On those evenings when all the children [from the respective previous marriages] were with their other parents, he would arrive at the apartment at seven. They would walk hand in hand to a Chinese restaurant a mile away. They would laugh and drink and eat and touch hands and knees over and under the table. They would come home. Smoke a joint. He would put music on. She would run water in the tub with lots of bubbles. In the bath they would lick and suck each other, in blissful delight. They woud admire the rich candle glow on their wet, delectably earth-toned skins. Sniff the incense—the odor of sandal and redwood. He would carry her in to bed.
> *Music. Emotion. Sensation. Presence.*
> *Satisfaction like rivers*
> *flowing and silver.*

Except for the use of controlled substances and the licking and sucking, this is pure Barbara Cartland. Likewise, the narrator's passion for Laurel (in the story of the same name) makes one blush—over the writing: "I thought of his musical speech and his scent of apples and May wine with varying degrees of regret and tenderness"; their "week of passion" had been "magical, memorable, but far too brief."

One might be inclined to excuse these examples on the grounds that love (or lust, or whatever) tends naturally towards purple prose. Unfortunately, however, similar excesses undermine *You Can't Keep* even when the characters' hormones are in check. Here is Andrea Clement White once again, musing on her professional achievements while awaiting the award at her banquet:

> If she was famous, she wondered fretfully . . . , why didn't she *feel* famous? She had made money . . . Lots of money. Thousands upon thousands of dollars. She had seen her work accepted around the world, welcomed even, which was more than she'd ever dreamed possible for it. And yet—there remained an emptiness, no, an ache, which told her she had not achieved what she had set out to achieve.

The theme is stale; worse, the writing itself is trite, clichéd; and frankly one wonders how anyone with so unoriginal a mind could be receiving her one hundred and eleventh major award. The same triteness mars "A Sudden Trip Home in the Spring," in which Sarah Davis, a black scholarship student at northern Cresselton College, is "immersed in Camusian philosophy, versed in many languages" and the close personal friend of the small-eyed, milky-legged, dirty-necked blonde daughter of "one of the richest men in the world." Sarah is BWOC at Cresselton: "She was popular"; "Her friends beamed love and envy upon her"; her white tennis partners think that she walks "'Like a gazelle'." There is a momentary suggestion that Sarah takes her situation and her classmates with a grain of salt ("She was interesting, 'beautiful,' only because they had no idea what made her, charming only because they had no idea from where she came"), but this theme and tone are quickly abandoned as the tale lapses into a curiously un-black reworking of the you-can't-go-home-again concept. If irony is what Walker has in mind, it certainly doesn't come through; and the over-all impression one gets from "A Sudden Trip" is that, like her 1973 biography of Langston Hughes, this is an earnest story intended for adolescent readers who appreciate simplistic themes, characters, and writing styles.

The mature reader's uncertainty over how to respond to "A Sudden Trip" takes on a new wrinkle when one considers that Sarah Davis's prototype was another black scholarship student from rural Georgia attending an exclusive northern college: Alice Walker.[8] The least effective, most seemingly comic heroines in Walker's short fiction were inspired by Walker herself. These predominate in *You Can't Keep a Good Woman Down.*

Walker has never denied that there are some autobiographical dimensions to her stories. When "Advancing Luna—and Ida B. Wells" was first published in *Ms.* magazine, Walker included a disclaimer that "Luna and Freddie Pye are composite characters, and their names are made up. This is a fictionalized account suggested by a number of real events"; and John O'Brien's 1973 interview with Walker offers further details.[9] Similarly, Walker in a 1981 interview with Kristin Brewer discusses the autobiographical basis of her earliest story, 1967's "To Hell with Dying" *(IL&T).*[10] Anyone familiar with Walker's personal life will see the significance of the references to Sarah Lawrence, the doorless first apartment in New York, and the job at the Welfare Department in "Advancing Luna" *(YCK);* or the stay at a New England artists' colony in "The Lover" *(YCK);* or the marriage to a New York Jew, the baby girl, the novel, and the house in the segregated South in "Laurel" *(YCK).* There is nothing inherently wrong with using oneself as the prototype for a story's character; the problem is that the writer tends, of course, to present his fictionalized self in the most flattering—even fantastic—light possible; and too readily that self assumes a larger role in the story than may be warranted by the exigencies of plot and characterization. Consider "Advancing Luna," in which the speaker—who is "difficult to distinguish from Walker herself"[11]—takes over the story like kudzu. We really don't need to hear all about her ex-boyfriends, her getting "high on wine and grass" with a Gene Autry lookalike who paints teeth on fruit, or her adventures in glamorous Africa ("I was taken on rides down the Nile as a matter of course"). Her palpable self-absorption and self-congratulation draw the story's focus away from its titular heroine, poor Luna—the selfless victim of interracial rape who ostensibly is an adoring friend and confidante of the narrator. The reader's immediate response (after confusion) is that the story is really quite funny—and with that response, all of Walker's serious commentary on rape, miscegenation, and segregation have dissipated. We see the same inadvertently comic, Walker-inspired heroine in "Laurel" and "The Lover." In the latter, the jazz poet "had reached the point of being generally pleased with herself," and no wonder. What with her "carefully selected tall sandals and her naturally tall hair, which stood in an elegant black afro with exactly seven strands of silver hair," and her "creamy brown" thighs and "curvaceous and strong legs," she is able to stop meals the way other women stop traffic: "If she came late to the dining room and stood in the doorway a moment longer than necessary—looking about for a place to sit after she had her tray—for that moment the noise from the cutlery already in use was still." (Really, who could blame Ellis for wanting her so?) If only there were an element of self-mockery in "The Lover"; if only Walker were being ironic in "A Sudden Trip"; if only she were lampooning the shopworn notion of the successful but unsatisfied celebrity in "Fame"; if only she were parodying romantic writing styles (and there by puncturing those "love affairs" undertaken purely to prove one's "sexual liberation") in stories like "Porn," "Laurel," and "The Lover." But there is absolutely nothing in Alice Walker's interviews, nothing in her many personal essays, nothing in her friends' and colleagues' reviews of her books, nothing anywhere to suggest that she is being anything but dead serious in *You Can't Keep a Good Woman Down.*

What is especially unfortunate about the unintentional humor of *You Can't Keep* is that Walker is quite capable of handling her material very effectively; in several stories, for example, she excels at narrative technique. Consider "How Did I Get Away with Killing One of the Biggest Lawyers in the State? It Was Easy" *(YCK)*. At first glance, the narrative voice seems untenable: how is it that a poor little black girl from Poultry Street writes such perfect English? (Placed entirely in quotation marks, the story is "written" by her.) We learn the answer at the end of the story: having murdered Bubba, the white lawyer who became her lover after raping her, the narrator/confessor stole all the money from his office safe and used it to finance her college education. Hence her flawless English, and the irony of her "confession": there is no repentance here, and no reader can blame her. The point of view also is consistent and effective. The same cannot be said of the long and rambling "Source," which unfortunately occupies the second most prominent position in *You Can't Keep*—the very end. It has no identifiable point of view, and suffers accordingly. "Source" would have been far more effective had Walker utilized what has been identified as her "ruminative style": "a meandering yet disciplined meditation."[12] It is seen in those stories (first-person or otherwise) which essentially record one character's impressions or thoughts, such as "Fame" *(YCK)*, "Roselily" *(IL&T)*, and "The Diary of an African Nun" *(IL&T)*. The sometimes staccato, sometimes discursive third-person narration of "Roselily"—"She feels old. Yoked."—is reminiscent of E. A. Robinson's account of another dubious love affair, "Eros Turannos" ("She fears him, and will always ask / What fated her to choose him"). Likewise, the barely-restrained first-person narration of "The Diary of an African Nun" is very evocative of Li Po's "The River-Merchant's Wife: A Letter," and it comes as no surprise that Walker attributes her fondness for short literary forms to the Oriental poetry she has loved since college.[13] Also effective is the shifting point of view: the black father's and black daughter's disparate attitudes towards her affair with a married white man is conveyed by the alternating perspectives of "The Child Who Favored Daughter" *(IL&T)*. This rhythmic technique is usually identified as cinematic, but it also owes much to the blues, as Walker herself is well aware.[14]

This blues quality in the narrative points to the bases of several of her best stories: the oral tradition. Whereas stories based on Walker's own experiences tend, as noted, to be over-written and hence inadvertently comic, her most memorable tales are often inspired by incident which were told to her—be they actual accounts (e.g., "The Revenge of Hannah Kemhuff" [*IL&T*] depicts her mother's rebuff by a white woman while trying to obtain government food during the Depression) or black folk tales (e.g., "Strong Horse Tea").[15] A particularly striking example is "The Welcome Table" *(IL&T):* having been ejected bodily from an all-white church, an old black lady meets Christ on a local road, walks and talks with him, and then is found frozen to death, with eyewitnesses left wondering why she had been walking down that cold road all alone, talking to herself. It could be right out of Stith Thompson. The importance of the oral tradition in Walker's stories is further evident in direct addresses to the reader ("'you know how sick [my husband] makes me now when he grins'" ["Really, *Doesn't* Crime Pay?," *IL&T*]) and parenthetical asides ("I scrooched down as small as I could at the corner of Tante Rosie's table, smiling at her so she wouldn't feel embarrassed or afraid" ["The Revenge of Hannah Kemhuff," *IL&T*]). The oral quality of Walker's stories is as old as folk tales, ballads, and slave narratives, and as new as Joan Didion, who shares with Walker a flair for using insane or criminal female narrators: compare Maria in *Play It as It Lays* with the would-be chain saw murderess in "Really, *Doesn't* Crime Pay?" *(IL&T)* or the coolly-detached killer of "How Did I Get Away with Killing . . ." *(YCK)*.[16] Curiously, when the teller of the tale is an emotionally-stable omniscient narrator, the oral tale techniques tends to backfire.

For example, the narrator's remark at the opening of "Elethia" *(YCK)*— "A certain perverse experience shaped Elethia's life, and made it possible for it to be true that she carried with her at all times a small apothecary jar of ashes"—sounds regrettably like a voice-over by John-Boy Walton.

Clearly the oral tradition is a mixed blessing for Walker's fiction; but it is a particualr liability when, as in so many folk tales and ballads, there is a paucity of exposition. Consider "Entertaining God" *(IL&T)*, in which a little boy worships a gorilla he has stolen from the Bronx Zoo. The story would make no sense to a reader unfamiliar with Flannery O'Connor's *Wise Blood*,[17] and where a lack of preliminary information tends to draw the reader into O'Connor's novel, it alienates him in "Entertaining God": the story comes across as a disjointed, fragmentary, aborted novella. Another *Wise Blood*-inspired story, "Elethia" (in which a character with a habit of lurking about museums steals a mummy which proves to be a stuffed black man), does not fare much better. Similarly, as Chester J. Fontenot points out, "The Diary of an African Nun" *(IL&T)*, although "only six pages in length, . . . contains material for a novella."[18] Expanded to that length, "The Diary" could take an honorable place alongside another first-person account by a disenchanted nun, *The Nun's Story*—assuming, of course, that Walker did not turn it into a series of socioeconomic lectures disguised as chatty personal letters as she did with African missionary Nettie's letters in *The Color Purple*. Lack of exposition can be extreme in Walker's short stories. Consider this extract from "Porn" *(YCK):* "They met. Liked each other. Wrote five or six letters over the next seven years. Married other people. Had children. Lived in different cities. Divorced. Met again to discover they now shared a city and lived barely three miles apart." How is the reader to respond to this? Is Walker making a statement about the predictability, the lamentable sameness of the lives lived in the ostensibly individuality-minded 1970s? Or is she just disinclined to write out the details? The more one reads *You Can't Keep*, the more one tends (albeit reluctantly) towards the latter.

Walker's disinclination for exposition, and the concomitant impression that many of her stories are outlines or fragments of longer works, is particularly evident in a technique which mars even her strongest efforts: a marked preference for "telling" over "showing." This often takes the form of summaries littered with adjectives. In "Advancing Luna" *(YCK)*, for example, the narrator waxes nostalgic over her life with Luna in New York: "our relationship, always marked by mutual respect, evolved into a warm and comfortable friendship which provided a stability and comfort we both needed at that time." But since, as noted earlier, the narrator comes across as vapid and self-absorbed, and since the only impressions she provides of Luna are rife with contempt for this greasy-haired, Clearasil-daubed, poor-little-rich-white-girl from Cleveland, the narrator's paean to their mutual warmth and friendship sounds ridiculous. No wonder critic Katha Pollitt stated outright that she "never believed for a minute" that the narrator and Luna were close friends.[19] Even more unfortunate is Walker's habit of telling the reader what the story is about, of making sure that he doesn't overlook a single theme. For example, in "The Abortion" (YCK), the heroine Imani, who is just getting over a traumatic abortion, attends the memorial service of a local girl, Holly Monroe, who had been shot to death while returning home from her high school graduation. Lest we miss the point, Walker spells it out for us: "every black girl of a certain vulnerable age was Holly Monroe. And an even deeper truth was that Holly Monroe was herself [i.e., Imani]. Herself shot down, aborted on the eve of becoming herself." Similarly transparent, here is one of the last remarks in the story "Source" (YCK). It is spoken by Irene, the former teacher in a federally-funded adult education program, to her ex-hippie friend, Anastasia/Tranquility: "'I was looking toward "government" for help; you were looking to Source [a California guru]. In both cases, it was the wrong direction—any direction that is away from ourselves is the wrong direction.'" The irony of their parallel situations is quite clear without having Irene articulate her epiphany in an Anchorage bar. Even at the level of charactonyms, Walker "tells" things to her reader. We've already noted the overused "he"/"she" device for underscoring sex roles, but even personal names are pressed into service. For example, any reasonably perceptive reader of the vignette "The Flowers" (IL&T) will quickly understand the story's theme: that one first experiences reality in all its harshness while far from home, physically and/or experientially; one's immediate surroundings are comparatively "innocent." The reader would pick up on the innocence of nearsightedness even if the main character, ten-year-old Myop, hadn't been named after myopia. Likewise, "The Child Who Favored Daughter" is actually marred by having the father kill his daughter because he confuses her with his dead sister named "Daughter." The hints of incest,[20] the unclear cross-generational identities, and the murky Freudian undercurrents are sufficiently obvious without the daughter/Daughter element: it begins to smack of Abbott and Costello's "Who's on First?" routine after just a few pages. Alice Walker's preference for telling over showing suggests a mistrust of her readers, or her texts, or both.

One might reasonably ask how a professional writer with twenty years' experience could seem so unsure about her materials and/or her audience, could have such uneven judgment regarding fictional technique, could seem so strained or defensive in her short stories. Part of the answer may be that she is a cross-generic writer. Leslie Stephen felt that newspaper writing was lethal for a fiction writer, and perhaps the same may be said for journalistic writing—especially when the magazine's target readership is a special interest group. Whatever the case, as a short story writer Alice Walker seems to alternate between (1) presenting editorials as fiction, (2) experimenting with the short story as a recognized literary form, and (3) rather self-consciously writing "conventional" short stories. At best, the results are mixed.

The magazine editorials which masquerade as short stories are among Walker's least successful efforts. The classic example of this is "Coming Apart" *(YCK)*. It began as the introduction to a chapter on violence against third world women in *Take Back the Night;* then, with the title of "A Fable," it ended up in *Ms.* magazine, for which Walker happened to be a contributing editor; and now, unrevised, it is being marketed as a short story in *You Can't Keep a Good Woman Down.*[21] The volume contains several stories which occupy this No Man's Land between journalism and fiction: "Advancing Luna," "Porn," "A Letter of the Times"— and, somewhat less transparently, "Elethia, "Petunias," and "Source"— all exist so that Walker (or a mouthpiece character) can make some statement about pornography, racism, politics, sado-masochism, the Search for Self, whatever. Perhaps these "stories" have some impact when read in isolation, months apart, in a magazine such as *Ms.*; but when packaged as a collection of short stories they are predictable and pedantic. The omniscient narrators and mouthpiece characters rarely get off their soapboxes; too often they resort to lecturing other characters or the reader. Consider this appraisal of the husband in "Coming Apart": "What he has refused to see . . . is that where white women are depicted in pornography as 'objects,' black women are depicted as animals. Where white women are depicted at least as human beings, black women are depicted as shit." The insistence upon the points Walker is trying to make would be appropriate for editorials or magazine essays, but it doesn't wash in a short story.

Those stories in which Walker attempts to experiment with what is commonly held to be "the short story" are a bit stronger, although they often have that fragmentary, unpolished quality alluded to earlier. Frequently the experimental pieces are very short: "Petunias" *(YCK)* is a one-page diary entry by a woman blown up by her Vietnam veteran son; it is entirely in italics, as are "The Flowers" *(IL&T)* and "Elethia" *(YCK)*. As Mel Watkins notes in the *New York Times Book Review,* Alice Walker's shorter pieces tend to be "thin as fiction," and he is probably correct to classify them as that short story offshoot, "prose poems."[22] Longer pieces also can be experimental. For example, "Roselily" *(IL&T)* utilizes a point/counterpoint format, alternating fragments of the wedding ceremony with the thoughts of the bride: the phrase "to join this man and this woman" triggers "She thinks of ropes, chains, handcuffs, his religion." The irony is as heavy-handed as the imagery, but the device does work in this story. Experimentation with structure just as often fails, however. "Entertaining God" *(IL&T)* offers three discrete cinematic scenes—one of the boy and the gorilla, another (evidently a flashback) of his father, and a third of his mother, a librarian turned radical poet; but the scenes never really connect. Perhaps it was meant to be what Walker has termed (in reference to *Meridian*) a "crazy quilt story,"[23] but if so the quilting pieces never do form a pattern. The same quality of uncertainty and incompletion is evident in "Advancing Luna," which offers four—count 'em, four—separate endings with such pretentious titles as "Afterwords, Afterwards, Second Thoughts," "Discarded Notes," and "Imaginary Knowledge." Apparently meant to be thought-provoking, instead they suggest that Walker is indecisive about why she even wrote the story—or, what is worse, is resorting to experimentation as an end in itself.

In light of all this, one might expect Walker's more "conventional" stories to be uniformly stronger than the essay/story hybrids or the experimental efforts, but such is not always the case. All too often, conventionality brings out the banal, the sentimental, and the contrived in Alice Walker. Not surprisingly, two of her earliest stories—"To Hell with Dying" *(IL&T)* and "A Sudden Trip Home in the Spring" *(YCK)*—are very conventional in terms of structure, characterization, and action. In each, a young woman returns to her rural Southern home from college up North at the death of an elderly loved one. Old Mr. Sweet in "To Hell with Dying" is a sort of dipsomaniac Uncle Remus, wrinkled and white-haired, with the obligatory whiskers, a nightshirt redolent of liniment, and a fondness for singing "Sweet Georgia Brown" to the narrator, who helps to "revive" him during his periodic fake deathbed scenes. In short, he is very much the sentimentalized "old darky" character that Walker challenged so vigorously in "Elethia," that O'Connoresque tale of the grinning, stuffed Uncle Albert in the white man's restaurant window. Sarah Davis, the heroine of the equally sentimental "A Sudden Trip," summarizes what she learned by attending her estranged father's funeral: "'sometimes you can want something a whole lot, only to find out later that it wasn't what you *needed* at all.'" Is it any wonder that black writer Ishmael Reed has called Walker "the colored Norman Rockwell'"?[24]

Her sentimental streak has been noted by many of her commentators (Jerry H. Bryant admits to a lump in his throat), and Walker herself acknowledges she is "nostalgic for the solidarity and sharing a modest existence can sometimes bring."[25] Perhaps it does have a place in some of the stories from early in her career. But it seems frankly incongruous in the work of a woman who prides herself on being a hard-hitting realist, and it poses particular problems in her handling of the stories' endings. The potentially incisive "Fame" is all but ruined when the tough-as nails Andrea Clement White melts at hearing a little black girl sing a slave song. Likewise, "The Lover" *(YCK)* ends with the jazz poet heroine in a reverie: she "lay in bed next day dreaming of all the faraway countries, daring adventures, passionate lovers still to be found." Perhaps in part to avoid these final lapses into sentimentality, Walker sometimes doesn't "end" her stories: she leaves them "open." It can be a very effective technique in stories such as "Strong Horse Tea" *(IL&T)* or "The Child Who Favored Daughter" *(IL&T)*, where the pain is underscored by the lack—indeed, the impossibility—or resolution in the character's situations. Probably Walker's strongest non-sentimental endings belong to three of the most conventional stories: "The Revenge of Hannah Kemhuff" *(IL&T)*, "Nineteen Fifty-Five" *(YCK)*, and "Source" *(YCK)*. In "The Revenge," Mrs. Sarah Marie Sadler Holley, fearing that a black rootworker will be able to use them in spells against her, stores her feces "in barrels and plastic bags in the upstairs closets" rather than trust "the earthen secrecy of the water mains." Her psychotic behavior turns her husband against her, and she lets herself die in a chilling dénouement that would do Miss Emily Grangerford proud. Walker has used the psychology of guilt and fear in lieu of the Jesus-fixed-her-but-good attitude held by Hannah's prototype, Walker's mother, and the refusal to sentimentalize enhances the story. Likewise, "Nineteen Fifty-Five," a strong story with which to open *You Can't Keep* but atypical of the volume, is a sort of docudrama tracing the career of Elvis Presley (Traynor) through the eyes of blues great Big Mama Thornton (Gracie Mae Still). Still never does understand this sleepy-eyed white man or his alien world, and her reaction to seeing his funeral on television—"One day this is going to be a pitiful country, I thought"—is the perfect conclusion to the story. No sentiment, no commentary. Finally, "Source" offers a surprisingly nonsentimental ending to an insistently nostalgia-soaked story. Whether they are grooving in a Marin County commune with Peace, Calm, and Bliss (didn't nostalgia for the '60s end with *Easy Rider*?) or getting it together in the '70s in an Anchorage bar (sort of *"The Big Chill* Goes Alaskan"), the story of Irene and Anastasia/Tranquility has little for anyone. But the ending of the story—that is, after the now-reconciled heroines have hugged "knee against knee, thigh against thigh, breast against breast, neck nestled against neck"—is quite provocative: a group of tourists, peering through the mists, believe they are seeing Mt. McKinley: "They were not. It was yet another, nearer, mountain's very large feet, its massive ankles wreathed in clouds, that they took such pleasure in." Suggestive without being saccharine, and ironic without that "tinge of cynicism"[26] which undercuts so many of Walker's endings, it is an ideal fade-out conclusion to a collection that, with varying degrees of success, seeks to pose questions, to raise issues, to offer no pat answers.

The strengths and weaknesses of *In Love & Trouble* and *You Can't Keep a Good Woman Down* offer little clue as to the direction Alice Walker will take as a writer of short fiction in years to come. Surely she will continue to write short stories: Walker personally believes that women are best suited to fiction of limited scope—David Bradley points out that this is "the kind of sexist comment a male critic would be pilloried for making"[27]—and she feels further that, as her career progresses, her writing has been "always moving toward more and more clarity and directness."[28] The often fragmentary and rambling tales of *You Can't Keep,* published eight years after the moving and tightly constructed *In Love & Trouble,* would suggest that this is not the case. At this point in her career as a short story writer, one wishes that Walker would acknowledge the validity of Katha Pollitt's appraisal of *You Can't Keep:* "Only the most coolly abstract and rigorously intellectual writer" can achieve what Walker attempts in this recent volume, but unfortunately that is not what she is like: "As a storyteller she is impassioned, sprawling, emotional, lushly evocative, steeped in place, in memory, in the compelling power of narrative itself. A lavishly gifted writer, in other words—but not of this sort of book."[29] What Alice Walker needs is to take a step backward: to return to the folk tale formats, the painful exploration of interpersonal relationships, the naturally graceful style that made her earlier collection of short stories, the durable *In Love & Trouble,* so very fine. Touch base, lady.

Notes

1. Alice Walker, *In Love & Trouble: Stories of Black Women* (New York: Harcourt Brace Jovanovich, n.d.), [i].
2. Barbara Christian discusses the significance of the agwu and its Western counterpart, "contrariness," in "A Study of *In Love and [sic] Trouble:* The Contrary Women of Alice Walker," *Black Scholar* 12 (March–April, 1981), 21–30, 70–71.
3. Alice Walker, *You Can't Keep a Good Woman Down* (New York: Harcourt Brace Jovanovich, 1981), [i].
4. Barbara Christian, "Alice Walker: The Black Woman Artist as Wayward," in Mari Evans, ed., *Black Women Writers (1950–1980): A Critical Evaluation* (Garden City, New York: Anchor Press/Doubleday, 1984), p. 468.
5. Trudier Harris, "From Victimization to Free Enterprise: Alice Walker's *The Color Purple,*" *Studies in American Fiction* 14 (Spring, 1986), 5.
6. In her review of *In Love & Trouble,* June Goodwin notes that "The title may hover on 'The Edge of Night,' but none of the rest of 'In Love and Trouble' has an inch of the soap opera about it" (*Christian Science Monitor* 65 [September 19, 1973], 11).
7. Maria K. Mootry-Ikerionwu, ["Review of *The Color Purple*"], *College Language Association Journal* 27 (March, 1984), 348.
8. The connection between Sarah Davis and Alice Walker is made by Martha J. McGowan, "Atonement and Release in Alice Walker's *Meridian,*" *Critique* 23 (1981), 36; and Jacqueline Trescott, "A Child of the South, a Writer of the Heart," *The Washington Post* (August 8, 1976), G3.
9. "Advancing Luna—and Ida B. Wells," *Ms.* 6 (July, 1977), 75; John O'Brien,

"Alice Walker," in *Interviews With Black Writers* (New York: Liveright, 1973), p. 196.

10. Kristin Brewer, "Writing to Survive: An Interview with Alice Walker," *Southern Exposure* 9 (Summer, 1981), 13.

11. McGowan [see note 8], 33.

12. Peter Erickson, "'Cast Out Alone/To Heal/and Re-Create Ourselves': Family-Based Identity in The Work of Alice Walker," *College Language Association Journal* 23 (September, 1979), 91.

13. "I have been influenced—especially in the poems in *Once*—by Zen epigrams and by Japanese haiku. I think my respect for short forms comes from this" (O'Brien [see note 9], pp. 193–94).

14. Barbara Christian points out the "almost cinematic rhythm" of the alternating points of view in "The Contrary Women" [see note 2], 26. The blues connection has been remarked by Mel Watkins in the *New York Times Book Review* (March 17, 1974), 41; John F. Callahan, "The Higher Ground of Alice Walker," *New Republic* 171 (September 14, 1974), 22; and Walker herself: "'I am trying to arrive at that place where black music already is; to arrive at that unselfconscious sense of collective oneness; that naturalness, that (even when anguished) grace" (O'Brien, p. 204).

15. Walker discusses the genesis of "The Revenge of Hannah Kemhuff" in Mary Helen Washington, "An Essay on Alice Walker" in Roseann P. Bell, Bettye, J. Parker, and Beverly Guy-Sheftall, eds., *Sturdy Black Bridges: Visions of Black Women in Literature* (Garden City, New York: Anchor Press/Doubleday, 1979), p. 136; and Claudia Tate, "Alice Walker," in *Black Women Writers at Work* (New York: Continuum, 1985), p. 186.

16. In the Winter, 1970–1971 issue of *American Scholar*, Mark Schorer reviewed both Didion's *Play It As It Lays* and Walker's *The Third Life of Grange Copeland*. Schorer argued that "One page of Didion's novel is enough to show us that she is the complete master of precisely those technical qualities in which Alice Walker is still deficient. One [may] read literally dozens of novels without encountering the kind of novelistic authority that she wields so coolly." Perhaps Walker, taking her cue from Schorer, has been emulating Didion's example. Certainly this might help account for the Didionesque quality in so much of Walker's fiction.

17. Walker asserts that O'Conner "'is the best of the white southern writers, including Faulkner,'" and that she has been an important influence on her work (O'Brien, p. 200). See also Alice Walker's essay "Beyond the Peacock: The Reconstruction of Flannery O'Connor," *Ms.* 4 (December, 1975), 77–79, 102–06.

18. Chester J. Rontenot, "Alice Walker: 'The Diary of an African Nun' and Du-Bois' Double Consciousness," in Bell, et al., eds., *Sturdy Black Bridges*, p. 151.

19. Katha Pollitt, "Stretching the Short Story," *The New York Times Book Review*, (May 24, 1981), 9.

20. For a full discussion of the incest theme in this story, see Trudier Harris, "Tiptoeing through Taboo: Incest in 'The Child Who Favored Daughter,'" *Modern Fiction Studies* 28 (Autumn, 1982), 495–505.

21. Walker explains the publishing history of "Coming Apart" in a disclaimer at the beginning of the story (*YCK*, pp. 41–42).

22. Watkins [see note 14], 41.

23. "'A crazy-quilt story is one that can jump back and forth in time, work on many different levels, and one that can include myth. It is generally much more evocative of metaphor and symbolism than a novel that is chronological

in structure, or one devoted, more or less, to rigorous realism . . .'" (quoted in Tate [see note 15], p. 176).

24. Quoted in Trescott [see note 8], G3.
25. Jerry H. Bryant, ["Review of *In Love & Trouble*"], *Nation*, 217 (November 12, 1973), 502; Alice Walker, "The Black Writer and the Southern Experience," *New South* 25 (Fall, 1970), 24.
26. Carolyn Fowler, "Solid at the Core," *Freedomways* 14 (First Quarter, 1974), 59.
27. David Bradley, "Telling the Black Woman's Story: Novelist Alice Walker," *New York Times Magazine* (January 8, 1984), 36.
28. Quoted in Brewer [see note 10], 15.
29. Pollitt, 15.

◆◆◆◆◆◆◆◆◆◆◆◆◆◆

Race, Gender, and Nation in *The Color Purple*

LAUREN BERLANT

The passion with which native intellectuals defend the existence of their national culture may be a source of amazement; but those who condemn this
exaggerated passion are strangely apt to forget that their own psyche and
their own selves are conveniently sheltered behind a French or German culture which has given full proof of its existence and which is uncontested.
                    —FRANTZ FANON, "On National Culture"

Ask anyone up Harlem way
who that guy Bojangles is.
They may not know who's President
But they'll tell you who Bojangles is.
                    —"Bojangles of Harlem," *Swing Time*

"**D**ear God, I am fourteen years old. I am I have always been a good
girl. Maybe you can give me a sign letting me know what is happening
to me."[1] *The Color Purple* begins with the striking out—but not the
erasure—of "I am." Celie's crisis of subjectivity has both textual and
historical implications: her status as a subject is clarified, in the course
of the novel, by her emergence from the enforced privacy of a prayer-
letter to God sometime in her fourteenth year, to public speaking, of a
sort, during a community celebration on the Fourth of July, during the
1940s. The appearance of the Fourth of July in the novel's final moments
appears to be a ratification of Celie's own personal liberation at the nation's mythicopolitical origin, the birth of the American "people." But
what Independence Day resolves for the identity of Anglo-Americans it
has raised as a question for Afro-Americans:[2] along with narrating Celie's history, *The Color Purple* stages, in its journey to this final day, an
instance of black America's struggle to clarify its own national identity[3]
from the point of view of American populism.[4]

The Color Purple problematizes tradition-bound origin myths and
political discourse in the hope of creating and addressing an Afro-American nation constituted by a rich, complex, and ambiguous culture. But
rather than using patriarchal languages and logics of power to describe
the emergence of a postpatriarchal Afro-American national consciousness, Celie's narrative radically resituates the subject's national identity
within a mode of aesthetic, not political, representation. These discursive
modes are not "naturally" separate, but *The Color Purple* deliberately
fashions such a separation in its attempt to represent a national culture
that operates according to "womanist" values rather than patriarchal

forms.[5] While political language is laden with the historical values and associations of patriarchal power, aesthetic discourse here carries with it a utopian force that comes to be associated with the spirit of everyday life relations among women.

Alice Walker has said that her intent with *The Color Purple* was to supplant the typically patriarchal concerns of the historical novel—"the taking of lands, or the births, battles, and deaths of Great Men"—with the scene of "one woman asking another for her underwear."[6] Walker manipulates the horizon of expectations of the historical novel[7] by situating the text within the traditionally confessional, local, privatized concerns of the autobiographical epistolary novel and, from this point of view, expanding to include the broader institutional affiliations and experiences of Afro-American women.[8] This is why the reemergence of nationalism at the end of the novel is puzzling: Celie's New World aesthetic and the celebration of the American revolution seems a contradictory alliance in the postpatriarchal culture set up by the novel.

Unlike *The Color Purple*, Walker's early novel *Meridian* explicitly addresses the *paradoxes* of Afro-American identity. Suffering a "hybrid"[9] affiliation to both sides of the hyphen, the Afro-American citizen learns not of the inalienable rights but of the a priori inferiority and cultural marginality of Afro-Americans—as if the "Afro" in the complex term were a syntactical negation of "American." Meridian, the woman whose political biography is told in the novel, learns of her contested relation to the rights of full American citizens as Celie and many Americans do: in public school, where the ideology of American identity is transmitted as if a part of the very air students inhale. On one important occasion, Meridian participates in an oratorical competition at her high school,

> reciting a speech that extolled the virtues of the Constitution and praised the superiority of The American Way of Life. The audience cared little for what she was saying, and of course they didn't believe any of it, but they were rapt, listening to her speak so passionately and with such sad valor in her eyes.[10]

Suddenly the meaning of what she says pierces Meridian's awareness; she almost faints, simultaneously gaining and losing "consciousness" on comprehending the horrible joke American national ideology has played on her, reproducing itself in her mind like a kind of vague dream or baby talk. On awakening to the hypocrisy behind the discourse of "inalienable rights," Meridian opposes the American assertion that it is a privilege just to be able to utter these phonemes unconsciously. To Meridian, black nationalism must dedicate itself to constructing a political and cultural context in which one might, indeed, enjoy a positive relation to national identity, rather than a negative relation to a race always already marked by its status as a social "problem."

> For she understood, finally, that the respect she owed her life was to continue
> . . . to live it. . . . And that this existence extended beyond herself to those
> around her because, in fact, the years in America had created them One
> Life.[11]

The movement in these phrases from the solipsism of everyday life to
the symbolic unity of "One Life" takes place under the symbolic and
political force of "years in America." Despite its crucially oppressive role
in the historical formation of racial consciousness, America in this novel
remains the sign and utopian paradigm of national identity. Meridian's
new selflessness, born of an American-inspired melding of individual self-
interest with populist social concerns, serves as a model for the future
nation Afro-Americans can construct, founded on a transformation of
their atomized historical experience into a mass of resources and a spirit
of courage and survival.

Meridian is Walker's most explicitly and narrowly "political" novel.[12]
It exposes the gap between the official claims of American democracy and
the state's exploitative and repressive practices, and views "personal"
relationships as symptoms of the strained political situation. The novel
is critical of the sexism within the civil rights movement, for example.
Nonetheless *Meridian* subordinates the struggle within gender to the
"larger" questions raised by the imminent exhaustion or depletion of the
movement itself. Meridian's theory of "One Life" dissolves the barriers
of class and education between herself and the black community at large
and effectively depoliticizes the struggle with the movement's patriarchal values and practices by locating the "personal" problems of sexism
within the nationalist project.

In contrast, *The Color Purple* problematizes nationalism itself, in
both its Anglo- and Afro-American incarnations. Most strikingly, the
Anglo-American brand of national pride is lampooned. Like Meridian,
Celie and Nettie first encounter the concept and the myth of American
national identity as a fundamental element of basic literacy disseminated
by public schools. But unlike Meridian, Celie is never fooled or impressed
by the nation's self-mythification. She reports:

> The way you know who discover America, Nettie say, is think bout cucum-
> bers. That what Columbus sound like. I learned all about Columbus in first
> grade, but look like he the first thing I forgot. She say Columbus come here
> in boats call the Neater, the Peter, and the Santomareater. Indians so nice to
> him he force a bunch of 'em back home with him to wait on the queen.

The Color Purple opens its discourse on the problematics of Afro-American national-historical identity by revealing the manifest irrelevancy of
the classic American myth to Celie. Her comic reduction of the American
origin tale to a matter of garden-variety phonetics not only indicates the
vital importance of oral and folk transmission to less literate communities
like the one in which Celie lives, but also suggests the crucial role oral
transmission plays in the reproduction of the nation itself, from genera-

tion to generation. Elsewhere, for instance, Shug and Celie's rambling discussion of the world during World War II—which ranges among subjects such as the war, U.S. Government theft of land from an "Indian tribe," Hollywood, national and local scandals—represents the haphazard, ad hoc fashion with which the nation disseminates and perpetuates itself among its citizens, even in everyday life.[13]

To maintain power among the people—indeed, to maintain "the people"—America must maintain a presence as accessible and intimate as the familial name and tradition.[14] Celie must gain agency within her immediate, "subjective" environment before she can come to terms with her "impersonal" or institutional relations.

The Color Purple opens with Celie falling through the cracks of a language she can barely use. Her own limited understanding, her technical insecurity, and her plain sense of powerlessness are constructed in contrast to the powerful discourses that share the space with her stuttered utterances. The epigraph of *The Color Purple*, for example, is Stevie Wonder's imperious exhortation, *"Show me how to do like you/ Show me how to do it."* Clearly this quotation is a direction as well as a request to the muses, contemporary and historical: *imitatio* is the graphic mode of this novel. Showing me something that is an action you *do* is not only intimately pedagogical, teaching me how to repeat the component gestures of the "doing" that is uniquely like "you"; the epigraph can also be read as the novel's most explicit political directive, deployed to turn individuals into self-conscious and literate users/readers of a cultural semiotic.[15]

For example, Shug is the novel's professor of desire and self-fulfillment, and as such her "example" is not only symbolic but technical, practical. Her first gift of knowledge to Celie is transmitted through a picture Celie and her stepmother see that has fallen out of Mr. _____'s wallet. The answer to Celie's question "What it is?" is: "The most beautiful woman I ever saw. . . . I see her there in furs. Her face rouge. Her hair like somethin tail. She grinning. . . ." On the very next page Celie dresses exactly like Shug to keep her father from raping Nettie. Even before Celie possesses technical language about sex, pregnancy, and her body, she "learns" from what Shug "does" in the picture about the standard connection between male sexual desire and the desire to degrade women: "He beat me for dressing trampy but he do it to me anyway." In this regime there is no such thing as "mere" or passive reading: reading is an act of cultural self-assertion, an engagement in the mimesis of social relations.

The crucial intertwining of private and public acts and consciousness signified by the ambiguity of the epigraph's "you" is answered by another ambiguously placed line, hovering above the text proper, also in italics: *"You better not never tell nobody but God. It'd kill your mammy."* This unsigned, double-negative message marks the contested ground on which Celie's negative relation to discourse is established. The disembodied voice pronounces a death threat against Celie's mother, and holds Celie hostage; it is never directly attributed to "Pa," but we learn through linguistic repetition that it must be his. By the end of the third paragraph of Celie's first letter, he repeats the advisory locution "You better" with a similar but different message: "shut up and git used to it."

Lost in a wilderness of unnamed effects, Celie is nonetheless able to resist her silencing by embodying for God's (and the reader's) benefit the generic scene of female humiliation. "Sister Celie" is raised to the level of female exemplum when every woman who sees her tells her, in effect, "You got to fight." Stripped of any right to the privacy of her body, and sentenced to vocal exile, she manages to "speak" in public by becoming a talking book, taking on her body the rape, incest, slave labor, and beating that would otherwise be addressed to other women, her "sisters." Celie's response to these incursions into her autonomy is to enter history for the first time—not really by "asking another woman for her underwear," but by crossing out "I am" and situating herself squarely on the ground of negation.

Celie's particular negation arises not only from the (f)act of rape, effecting her bifurcation into a subject and a subject-made-object-to-itself. Rape here only intensifies the negation that grows from the ongoing patriarchal subjugation of women. Her oppression, as represented early in the novel, circulates around the vulnerabilities that grow from her gender, as constructed within the social space which her "Pa" respectably occupies.

But gender oppression is neither the only nor the main factor operating in the oppressive paternal ideology: behind the story Celie thinks she knows, in which the father's control of the family's "private" resources effectively gives him license to violate "his" women, is a story that reveals not the family's private or internal structure but its social and historical placement. Behind "Pa"'s story, as Celie discovers, is the story of her biological father's lynching and murder.

The Color Purple telegraphs the traumatic transformation of Celie's family history by emphasizing Nettie's generic departure from standard epistolary form to the fairy tale. Nettie writes her, "Once upon a time, there was a well-to-do farmer who owned his own property near town. Our town, Celie." Celie's biological father, who, like her mother, is never named in the book (not even by a _____), has been lynched. We receive no eyewitness reports of this event, and no spot or discursive mark verifies the father's life or death. "And so, one night, the man's store was burned down, his smithy destroyed, and the man and his two brothers dragged out of their homes in the middle of the night and hanged." Unlike Celie after her rape, the lynched father cannot speak, act, desire for himself. Moreover, as "Pa" tells Celie, "Lynched people don't git no marker." How does this lynching, and its resistance to representation, transform the cultural politics of this novel, no longer confined to witnessing violence deployed on women by men?

The surprising emergence of racial violence, the murder of three black men by an indeterminate group Nettie calls "the white merchants," induces Celie's second semiotic collapse. The first collapse, which opens the novel, emerges from Celie's confusion about what is "happening" to her in the present tense. Celie's second collapse under the weight of painful knowledge is unconnected to the facts of her contemporary situation: rather, its effects reach back to her origin, and in so doing completely destabilize her identity. This crisis is evident in Celie's almost catatonic announcement—in which, uncharacteristically, all her verbs are disrupted—"My daddy lynch. My mama crazy. All my little half-brothers and sisters no kin to me. My children not my sister and brother. Pa not pa."

In this revised autobiographical tale, racism succeeds sexism as the cause of social violence in the narrative. The switch from a sexual to a racial code, each of which provides a distinct language and a distinct logic of social relations, releases into the text different kinds of questions about Celie's identity: the new information challenges what Celie (and her readers) mistakenly thought they already knew about the horrific systematic sexual violence that seemed to be the distinguishing mark of family life for women.

For Celie and Nettie's biological father, race functions much as gender functions for the sisters: not as a site of positive identification for the victim, but as an excuse for the oppressor's intricate *style* of cultural persecution. Lynching, in his narrative, has a structural equivalence to Celie's rape, in its violent reduction of the victim to a "biological" sign, an exemplum of subhumanity. This mode of vigilante white justice was a common threat to Southern blacks through the 1930s: Angela Davis, and Frederick Douglass long before her, record the reign of terror propagated by white men ostensibly on behalf of white women's vulnerability to the constant danger of being raped—by black men.[16]

In the narrative of *The Color Purple* the first violation, rape, is succeeded by the second and prior act, lynching: a "logic of equivalence"[17] is installed in the narrative that in effect makes race a synonym for scandalous, transgressive Afro-American sexuality.[18] Both in the conventional link between racial and sexual violence, and in the novel, gender difference takes on the pressure of justifying and representing racial oppression. The (unrepresented) act of lynching effects a transfer at the moment of brutal contact from one (the racial) system of oppression to another (the sexual)—precisely the scandalous code that terrorizes Celie at the beginning of the novel.

This complex substitution of paternal tales effectively frees Celie to reclassify her early experience of sexual violence as a *misunderstanding*.

Incest, the collapse of structural taboos that ensure the sexual and economic dissemination of the family, is also a figure for the primal illiteracy with which she has been afflicted. The perversion that marked Celie's entry into consciousness had circumscribed her understanding of the world: fundamentally negated by father and husband, in the church and in the marketplace she would also stay as invisible as possible to avoid provoking further violation. Thus it is understandable that the new tale of paternal origins empowers Celie—because Pa is not pa. Having eliminated the perversion from her memory of being raped by her stepfather, the rapes themselves seem to disappear. Celie then recovers from the guilt and shame that had stood in the way of her "right" to control her body and her pleasure.

But this paternal plot twist also short-circuits whatever legitimate understanding of power's institutional operations Celie might have gained from knowing the complicated motives behind these familial events. If one effect of the second origin tale is to revise Celie's comprehension of the paternal conditions of her production, another simultaneous effect is to repress the scene of history insofar as the extrafamilial elements of social relations are concerned. She understands that people hurt people; but she has no curiosity about the larger, situational motives of what appears to be personal behavior.

For instance, the new origin tale reveals yet a third factor driving the transformation of social life and of signification: it reveals the white men's *economic* aim to liquidate the father and his two brothers.

> And as [the father] did so well farming and everything he turned his hand to prospered, he decided to open a store, and try his luck selling dry goods as well. Well, his store did so well that he talked his two brothers into helping him run it. . . . Then the white merchants began to get together and complain that this store was taking all the black business away from them. . . . This would not do."

The store the black men owned took business away from the white men, who then interfered with the free market by lynching their black competitors. Thus class relations, in this instance, are shown to motivate lynching. Lynching was the act of violence white men performed to *racialize*—to invoke the context of black inferiority and subhumanity—the victim; the aura of sexual transgression is also always produced around the lynched by the lynchers, white men guarding the turf of their racial and sexual hegemony.

But Celie never understands it this way, for a number of different reasons. First, the language of Nettie's fairy tale encourages the substitution of family discourse for the language of capital relations. Rather than naming names—her own father's, her mother's, her stepfather's—Nettie emphasizes abstract kinship terms like "the man and his two brothers," "the wife," "the widow," "the stranger" to describe their positions in the tale. Because the importance of the story to Celie lies in its transmission of new information about her family history, the tale brackets class issues within the context of family relations, as if the capitalist economy is generated by the operations of family ideology.

Second, Nettie's fairy tale reflects—without really reflecting on—the historical proximity of racial and sexual oppression to the class struggle that marks Afro-American experience.[19] Yet because her fairy-tale rhetoric emphasizes the personal over the institutional or political components of social relations, the nonbiologized abstraction of class relations virtually disappears from the text.

Third, Celie's disregard of the class issues available in this narrative also serves Walker's desire to effect a shift within the historical novel. The fairy-tale paradigm Nettie provides replaces the "realist" *mise en scène* that had previously governed the novel's representations of intimate familial violence; in so diminishing the centrality of Alfonso's/the stepfather's rapes of Celie, the text abandons its demystification of male behavior in the family to focus on a reconstruction of the "family"—this time under the care of women. This suggests that Celie and Nettie's feminist fairy tale (the "womanist" historical novel) absorbs and transforms the traditional functions of patrifocal-realist mimesis; and that this transformation makes possible the movement of *The Color Purple* into its communal model of utopian representation, in which a partnership of capitalism and sisterhood plays a central role.

In *The Color Purple*, then, the identity crisis that grows from the violence within the family during Celie's childhood is "explained," traced to its origin, in two significantly different ways. The first narrative installs the greed of patriarchal sexual practice in the unflattering mirror of the "private" family; the injustices manifested in the world outside that central core—for example, in Mr. _____'s sadistic treatment of Harpo—appear from the initial point of view to extend, in a vast synchronicity, from the father's private example.

In contrast, the second family fairy tale represents Celie's crisis of self-comprehension—now an inheritance from her mother—as an effect not of sexual abuse but of a relatively noncoagulated set of practices that have escaped full representation within the mainstream culture: class relations filtered through racial animosity, sexual relations resulting from economic domination. Whereas the first representation of family life located evil forces in the most personal of bodies and intentions, the second tale reveals a more general dispersion of responsibility among unnamed and alien subjects and institutions. Still, reflected in the realm of social theatrics that includes but is not contained within the family scene, sexism and racism provide privatizing images for class struggle, making the lynching appear to Celie a personal and "natural"—but not political—event that takes place on "the father's" so-called private body. This set of textual associations, in which class relations become absorbed by personal histories, forms a paradigm in *The Color Purple: capitalism* becomes the sign of "political" history's repression, both in the everyday life consciousness of the subject and in the narrative at large.

Finally, the very *unreality* to the sisters of the new originary fairy tale extends in part from their alienation from the political and historical context within which these acts took place. Neither woman has ever lived outside of the family in the public sphere of American racism. The story of Celie's original parentage marks the first time in her represented life that specifically racist practices come close to hurting her. In *The Color Purple* the burden of operating within a racist social context, which includes working through the oppressive collaboration of racism and sexism, is generally deflected from Celie's tale onto events in the economic and cultural marketplace.

The trial of thinking and making it through the "racial problem" in *The Color Purple* falls mainly to Sofia Butler, the "amazon" who enters Mr. _____'s extended family as Harpo's first wife. The voice of sexual and racial *ressentiment*—for instance, she twice expresses a desire to "kill" her sexual and racial oppressors—Sofia is the first woman Celie knows who refuses to accede to both the patriarchal and the racist demand that the black woman demonstrate her abjection to her oppressors. But the mythic test of Sofia's strength takes place in her refusal to enter the servitude of double discourse demanded of blacks by white culture. She says "Hell no" to the mayor's wife's "complimentary" suggestion that Sofia come to work as her maid; next Sofia answers the mayor's scolding slap of her face with her own powerful punch. For her effort to stay honest in the face of the white demand for black hypocrisy, Sofia gains incarceration in a set of penal institutions that work by a logic similar to that of lynching: to racialize the scene of class struggle in the public sphere and to deploy prejudice against "woman" once behind the walls of the prison and the household. As Sofia tells Celie about her stay in prison: "Every time they ast me to do something, Miss Celie, I act like I'm you. I jump up and do just what they say."

The social coercion of Afro-Americans to participate in a discourse that proclaims their unworthiness is resisted by Sofia, and then performed on Sofia's behalf by Squeak. Squeak's telltale name, in its expression of her distorted, subvocalized voice, describes her original purpose in this text: she enters the narrative as Harpo's dutiful replacement for Sofia, who had refused to allow Harpo to dominate and to beat her.

Squeak knows well how to be properly submissive. But faced with Sofia's crisis Squeak subversively uses her expertise in "proper" feminine self-negating hypocrisy in her supplication for special treatment to the warden of Sofia's prison. The warden is conventionally known as her "cousin," since he is the "illegitimate" father of three of Squeak's siblings. This sloppy familial euphemism leads to a comedy of double- and quadruple-talk that includes Squeak asking for (and getting) the *opposite* of what the warden incorrectly *thinks* she wants. (She wants Sofia released from the prison to serve the rest of her sentence as the mayor's maid; she tells the warden that Sofia is not suffering enough in prison, and that to Sofia the most exquisite torture would be being a white woman's maid; he "fornicates" with Squeak and releases Sofia to the mayor's household.)

The warden's "liberties" with Squeak, so different in representational mode than the young Celie's rapes, also serve as the diacritical mark that organizes Squeak's insertion into the "womanist" order. Having exposed herself to sexual, racial, and political abuse in the name of communal solidarity, Squeak assumes the right to her given name, Mary Agnes. She also earns the right to "sing." She wins these privileges by learning to lie and to produce wordplay while seeming to be an unconscious speaker of the enslaved tongue: Squeak attains social mastery in learning to ironize the already-doubled double-talk that marks the discursive situation of the female Afro-American subject in the white patriarchal public sphere.

The degree of discursive self-alienation expressed in the multiple inversions of language that become the violated ground of both rape and humor in *The Color Purple* in part reflects W. E. B. Du Bois' classic observation, in *The Souls of Black Folk*, that his "people" is marked by a "double consciousness."[20] For American blacks, according to Du Bois, irony takes on an almost allegorical charge as the split or "colonized" subject shuttles between subjectivity and his or her cultural, "racial" status as Object. Henry Louis Gates, Jr. has further elaborated on the cultural machinery of Afro-American "double consciousness" by employing Mikhail Bakhtin's reading of class discourses. Gates suggests that colonized discourse is twisted simultaneously in opposite directions: toward an internal polemic and an external irony.[21] Crucially, each of these discursive modes requires the subject's internalized awareness of a hostile audience. This is the context of a priori negation that results in the inevitable production of double consciousness for socially marginalized citizens.[22]

Frantz Fanon complicates the claissic model of colonized double consciousness by characterizing the body that houses the different modes of self-alienation he feels (Blackness and Objectness) as yet another unsutured site of identity. Rather than reading his fragmentation as the fragmentation of a whole, Fanon observes that the inscription of the white parody of black culture—"I was battered down by tom-toms, cannibalism, intellectual deficiency, fetishism, racial defects, slave-ships, and above all else, above all: 'Sho' good eatin'"—on the colonized black body creates a metonymic paradox. On his body the parts do not stand in for a whole; nor do they add up to a whole. "What else could it be for me but an amputation, an excision, a hemorrhage, that spattered my whole body with black blood? But I did not want this revision, this thematization. All I wanted was to be a man among other men."[23] Body parts erupting blood—not red human blood but the black blood of a race and the indelible ink of cultural textuality—constitute him a priori as a mass of part-objects with no relation to a whole.

Fanon here uses the sensation of dismemberment as an allegory for the effects of racist discourse: the fractured body stands in for the fragmented relation to identity suffered by subjects of a culture who have learned the message of their negation before they had a chance to imagine otherwise. This process of part-identification is different from that of the subject described by post-structuralism, who shuttles between the ruse of self-presence and its dissolution.[24] By definition, the colonized subject is unable to produce even the mirage of his or her own totality. Fanon's catalogue of the society's names for him identifies the surplus naming of the marginalized subject as the crucial incision of history into the subject's selfconsciousness.

Fanon speaks within the racist discursive context *already reproducing* the white parody of black culture: this is surely the spirit in which Walker represents Harpo, the black parody of a white man (Harpo Marx) who compensates for his voicelessness with music, whose character is expressed in his "feminine" pathos as well as his pathetic aping of masculine pretensions. The tragic aphonia of Celie's mother and the witty, ironic repartee about "uncle Tomming" by Shug, Squeak, and Sofia reveal the even more complex negotiation required of women who aspire to legitimacy in the face of both sexism and racism. Celie's youthful masquerade as Shug in order to deflect her father's sexual greed can also be read as a complex and contradictory message growing out of this kind of negating context. So what looks like simply irony or sarcasm already contains the negating effects of cultural delegitimation. Blackness does not signify except from inside the negative space prepared for it by the history of white culture's relation to black; the same general idea operates in gender relations as well for the Afro-American woman making her way in the context of a double erasure.

The only relief from such torturous negotiating exists in conversation among women. Speaking as a "woman" among women in *The Color Purple* also involves countering the delegitimating pressure of specifically female marginality by finding expression and refuge in wordplay, in the masterful and courageous deployment of language in irony, in rage, in fun, in lies, in song, and in deadly silences. In the racially and sexually fractured situation, back talk resulted in punishment; among women in a man's world, the back talk produces pleasure.

The singers Shug and Mary Agnes articulate professionally the fact and the privileges (current and imminent) of female speech in the liberatory distinction between words and music in, for example, "Miss Celie's Blues." As Celie says, "It all about some no count man doing her wrong, again. But I don't listen to that part. I look at her [Shug] and I hum along a little with the tune." All the speaking women in the novel learn to turn a phrase in acts of defiance and self-expression.[25] They "fight" for the right to take an *attitude:* style itself, apart from content and reference, becomes the first pure note of female signifying.

Celie first displays the pleasure of speech within a female context in her complex response to Corinne, whom Celie sees in town carrying her stolen child, Olivia. Celie invites Corinne to escape the racist glares of the white men in the marketplace by sitting in her wagon; Corinne expresses her gratitude to Celie with a pun on the word "hospitality." Celie demonstrates the power of the joke: "*Horse*pitality, she say. And I git it and laugh. It feel like to split my face." When Mr. _____ comes out, he realizes immediately that this shared joke, such as it is, threatens his control over the discursive space in which Celie lives. "What you setting here laughing like a fool fer?" he says. Her split face all too graphically refers to the scars she bears, the mask of dumbness she hides behind, and also refers to an object posed, but not yet constituted, the split face that produces plurivocal discourse, not a muted utterance from a victimized shadow.

The implicit context of a priori negation for Afro-Americans that obtains in American culture undergoes a dramatic shift when Nettie's African letters are read into the record. Nettie's letters from Africa at first seem to provide an indigenous alternative history for black consciousness that reverses its traditional invisibility or debasement in the racist American context. To the missionaries, the mission to convert the Africans to Christianity seems specially authorized by a providential and historical allegiance of all "Africans." Aware of a potential problem arising from cultural differences between missionaries and the objects of their attention, Samuel articulates the special privilege he, Corinne, and Nettie will enjoy in Africa:

> Samuel . . . reminded us that there is one big advantage we have. We are not white. We are not Europeans. We are black like the Africans themselves. And that we and the Africans will be working for a common goal: the uplift of black people everywhere.

Nettie records with awe how different the world looks to her from the point of view of African/racial dominance: "Something struck in me, in my soul, Celie, like a large bell, and I just vibrated." With amazement she witnesses Americans in Harlem who worship Africa, not America. She reports with pride about an Afro-American church in which God is black. And there's the great text of racial *ressentiment:* in the Olinka origin narrative, while men are secondary productions of African culture expelled into the nakedness and vulnerability of Otherness. The pure pleasure Nettie derives from reading Blackness from a proper and sanctified point of view is the affective origin of the specifically nationalist politics previously repressed in *The Color Purple:* what hope and uplift can Africans all over the world take from their common field of history?

The missionaries' attempt to forge a response to this question produces ambiguous answers. Their version of pan-African consciousness forges a strong sense of world-historical identity within the Afro-American community that in part derives from the greatness of African culture in the centuries before European imperialism. The Afro-American church also sees the spiritual power of the African other-world inhabiting its own driving spirit to convert and to empower the masses of Africans, now disenfranchised from power and progress, economic, cultural, and spiritual.

The white, Western-identified missionaries who sponsor Samuel's particular mission tend, on the other hand, to keep the contemporaneous tribal cultures at arm's length: a white female missionary, for example, "says an African daisy and an English daisy are both flowers, but totally different kinds. The man at the Society says she is successful because she doesn't 'coddle' her charges." The values that lead the missionary society to think it has a progressive message to deliver to the heathen brethren are shown to be well-intentioned, patronizing, misguided, and culturally destructive. While Samuel clearly identifies his destiny with that of the African people, he also unintentionally aims to reproduce the normative social relations of Western culture in the midst of his attempt to reform their spirit.

The primary site of cultural contact between the missionaries and the Africans is pedagogical: the connection between cultural literacy and power established early in the novel is reiterated in the missionaries' retraining of the tribal peoples in the "superior" and Christian practices and materials of Western culture. The issue that brings to the surface the contradictions inherent in the missionaries' creation of a pan-African consciousness is in the sphere of gender relations. Samuel feels compelled to lecture the Olinka women on the virtues of monogamy over polygamy, even though the alliances made among the wives of individual men render the polygamous women far more powerful than Corinne, for example, feels in her ambiguous relation to Nettie. Nettie, in turn, smugly offers to reveal to the Olinka women the movement among women in civilized nations toward liberation from patriarchal oppression in the public and private spheres. But there too the Olinka women see the limitations of Nettie's apparent freedom of movement and knowledge: she is "the missionary's drudge," an "object of pity and contempt." In short, as Samuel later painfully realizes, what passed for racial identification across borders and historical differences was really a system of cultural hegemony disguised as support and uplift.

The event that clarifies how politically useful the missions are to the European imperialists, standing as agents or prophets of spiritual progress, is the coming of the big road. Generous in their estimation of human nature, the Olinka refuse to understand that the theory of property and propriety under which they live is irrelevant to the Western juridical code. Most natives assume (as American white people always do, notes Nettie) that the superpower force that cuts through the jungle builds a road to the tribe, for the tribe; they admire Western technology, viewing it as they view roofleaf, something nature makes in abundance for the well-being of its devoted people.

But Samuel, Corinne, and Nettie are no more sophisticated in their understanding of the ways of "civilized" culture than are the "natives": this is one instance where the pan-national racial identification between American and African blacks proves sadly accurate. Too late, the missionaries realize that the road threatens their mission; desperately, they exhaust their resources trying to protect the tribe. The only survivors are the tribal citizens who can read well enough to see their death sentence in Western culture and join the *mbeles*, the underground group of radicalized Olinka.

Samuel could have foreseen the failure of his mission. His life story, the only male autobiographical narrative in *The Color Purple* privileged to replace (temporarily) the reigning female subjectivity, reveals the shallowness with which he understood his own cultural privilege. He tells Nettie of the time in his youth that he encountered W. E. B. Du Bois, whose impatience with the pretensions of missionary culture could have taught Samuel that Pan-Africanism requires material transformation of the techniques of power before a new spirit would have any place to grasp:

> Madame, he said, when Aunt Theodosia finished her story and flashed her famous medal around the room, do you realize King Leopold cut the hands off workers who, in the opinion of his plantation overseers, did not fulfill their rubber quota? Rather than cherish that medal, Madame, you should regard it as a symbol of your unwitting complicity with this despot who worked to death and brutalized and eventually exterminated thousands and thousands of African peoples.

Like the lynched body, the black hand here not only serves as a figure of racial "justice" for whites, but also becomes a kind of rebus for the metonymic "hand" of capitalism, in which the worker is an economic appendage reduced to the (dis)embodiment of his or her alienation.[26] This kind of symbolism was on Du Bois' mind in the period after World War I, when "lying treaties, rivers of rum, murder, assassination, mutilation, rape, and torture have marked the progress of Englishman, German, Frenchman, and Belgian on the Dark Continent." The Pan-African movement, organized by Du Bois to counter the European exploitation of Africa's plentiful resources, took up the question of Belgium in 1919 and 1921 much as these hands "take up" the question of slavery.[27] Du Bois saw in the capitalist infiltration of Africa the origins of world racism against blacks: "'Color' became in the world's thought synonymous with inferiority, 'Negro' lost its capitalization, and Africa was another name for bestiality and barbarism."

The ramifications of the peculiar kind of racism produced by capitalism led Du Bois to try to organize all of the African nations of the world: to create a "people" that would fight for its right to national self-determination, for the (he would say, inevitable) democratization of capital, and for the eradication of the racist representations that have masked the capitalist pilfering of Pan-African resources. But Samuel does not go as far as Du Bois did in attacking the origin of contemporary racism in Western relations of capital, even though Nettie's letters register the information that local traditions of land and cultural ownership are completely subsumed to the absentee ownership of the non-African nations feeding off the continent's wealth. Instead, Samuel sees his failure to understand his unwitting complicity with colonialist practices as a flaw in his theory of spirit. The mission's total powerlessness to prevent the destruction of the culture they had come to "save" provokes Samuel and Nettie to redefine what it means to serve God.

> God is different to us now, after all these years in Africa. More spirit than ever before, and more internal. Most people think he has to look like something or someone—a roofleaf or Christ—but we don't. And not being tied to what God looks like, frees us.

The link between the theory and practices of "capitalism" and of "religion" or spirit is the key to the novel's reformulation of mainstream Afro-American nationalist politics and consciousness. Having spent the first part of the novel tracing the pernicious effects of the national-patriarchal-capitalist domination of personal and natural resources, Walker opens the second part with Nettie's moving tributes to the fabulous richness of African culture, read as a pan-national phenomenon. Nettie unconsciously quotes "America, the Beautiful" in her report of it: "And we kneeled down right on deck and gave thanks to God for letting us see the land for which our mothers and fathers cried—and lived and died— to see again."

The missionaries' disillusioned removal to the United States signals a transformation of their relation to both African and American nationalism. By viewing America as the place of the new redeemed church shorn of idols, Samuel and Nettie repeat seventeenth-century Puritan religious and civil representations of America as the only site where a sanctified and defetishized church might have a chance for survival. In so embracing the theory of an idol-free America, the missionaries refute their initial intention to enrich their historical affiliation with Africa—Africa seen as a body of land with a distinctive history—and with the problem of Afro-American political disenfranchisement to which Pan-Africanism had been a response. And to replace the cultural and political solution Pan-African nationalism had offered to the missionaries, a religion free from boundaries and margins emerges based on unmediated relations of Being to Being.

The last half of the novel, after Nettie's letters are discovered, traces how the characters' departure from formal alliances—based on race, organized religion, politics—takes the form of a nationalist aesthetic that places essences (human and inhuman) in their proper social relation regardless of apparent material conditions and contradictions. Capitalism, as we shall see, is no longer a hegemonic and mystified mode of exploitation; rather, it becomes an extension of the subject's spiritual *choices*. And the hybrid, fractured status of Afro-American signification re-emerges in its earliest form: instead of infusing the African side of the compound term with the positive historical identification usually denied in the American context, the last half of the novel returns "Africa" to the space of disappointment and insufficiency, finally overwhelmed by the power of "America" to give form to the utopian impulse.

Every transformation of belief that marks Samuel and Nettie's return "home" to America has a correlate in a change of Celie's worldview—sexual, social, and spiritual. For Celie, like Nettie, sexual awakening not only transforms her relation to her body and to pleasure in general, but also leads to a major shift in her understanding and mastery of power in the world. It is Shug Avery who saves Celie from being paralyzed by rage at Mr. _____'s concealment of Nettie's letters; Shug also channels Celie's confusion at the collapse of her original way of understanding the world into a radical revision of that understanding—starting with God, the prime Author and Audience of her tortured inner life.

This shift in Celie's mode of belief reveals to her a world saturated by a sensual beauty that signifies God's work. "Admiration" is Shug's word for worship: Celie's religion, like Nettie's, is transformed from a social, institutional enterprise to an aestheticized and surprisingly solitary sexual practice. Admiring the color purple is equated with what Celie calls "making love to God," an act she performs with the aid of a reefer.

Celie adopts a mode of sensual pleasure and power beyond the body that effectively displaces the injustices that have marked her tenure in the quotidian. She heralds her glorious transformation into self-presence by shedding her scarred historical body as she leaves Mr. _____ : "I'm pore, I'm black, I may be ugly and can't cook, *a voice say to everything listening*. But I'm here" (my emphasis). This pure and disembodied voice speaks of its liberation from the disfigured body and enacts, through disembodiment, the utopian scene of self-expression from Celie's point of view. In this scene, the negated, poor, black, female body—created for Mr. _____'s pleasure, profit, and scorn—is replaced by a voice that voids the vulnerability of the bodied historical subject. To Mr. _____'s prophecy that Celie will fail in the world because she has neither talent, beauty, nor courage "to open your mouth to people," Celie performs her triumphant Being—"I'm here"—and asserts the supremacy of speech over the physical, material despotism characteristic of patriarchy. Her new mode of counteropposition also deploys the supernatural power of language, turning Mr. _____'s negativity back on himself: "Until you do right by me, I say, everything you even dream about will fail." The authority of this curse comes from nature: "I give it to him straight, just like it come to me. And it seem to come to me from the trees." Speech here becomes the primary arena of action: the natural world lends not its material resources but a spiritual vitality that can always assert itself while the body is threatened and battered. And writing, as the fact of the letters suggests, is the place where the voice is held in trust for the absent subject who might be seeking a way of countering the patriarchal and racist practices of the social world.

This revision of Celie's point of view frees her from her imprisonment in stoic passivity. But if Celie's body has taken a beating, it also carries the traces of her violently inscribed history: multiple rape, incest, disenfranchisement through a marriage trade made between two men (in which Celie and her cow have equivalent status), as well as through her stepfather's repression of her mother's will, and, finally, sexual, economic, and psychological exploitation and abuse by Mr. _____ and his family. Celie's ascension to speech, a new realm of "bodiless" happiness, does not include coming to terms with these events as she leaves them behind: she is completely reborn, without bearing witness to the scars left in knowledge and memory.

Indeed, in her new domestic regime Celie first occupies her "old" social powerlessness like a natural skin. According to Shug, Celie would have been happy to devote her life to being Shug's maid; but Shug insists that Celie find meaningful work for herself. And the rest, as they say, is history: the letter Celie writes to Nettie describing Shug's capitalization of her production of "perfect pants" is signed "Your Sister, Celie/Folkpants, Unlimited./Sugar Avery Drive/Memphis, Tennessee." Through Shug, both a sexual and economic provider, Celie gains the *nom du père* of capitalism: a trademark, which becomes a part of Celie's new signature, itself a reflection of Shug's own nominal dissemination on the road map of her culture.

Celie's Folkpants provides such a service for the woman or man who purchases them as well. The simple message Folkpants advertises is that the pants truly are for "the people," marketed for all genders. The unisexuality of the pants deemphasizes the importance of fashion in the social context in which the pants are worn: following the ethical and aesthetic shift from worshipping the white male God to appreciating the presence of spirit and color, Celie emphasizes fabric, print, and color in their conception and distribution.

A mode of ontological mimesis governs the specifications of each pair of pants, tailoring each to embody the essential person but not his or her physical body: one size, one cut fits all. Each pair of Folkpants is shown to release the wearer into authentic self-expression. At the book's end this semiotic democracy, based on the authenticity of all speaking subjects, reflected in and enacted by their commodity relations, replaces the sexism and racism of "natural" languages of the body and consciousness.

In addition, when grammar enters the realm of manifest struggle, the essence of the expression reigns over its historical or conventional usage. Darlene, who works in Celie's factory, tries to teach Celie "proper" English.

> You say US where most folks say WE, she say, and peoples think you dumb.
> Colored peoples think you a hick and white folks be amuse.
> What I care? I ast. I'm happy.

Shug settles the argument by asserting that Celie can "talk in sign language for all I care": in Shug's revisionary semiotic, the medium of transmission is proclaimed as transparent while "the message" is everything. She embraces an aesthetic of live performance: a mode of discourse that can only be activated in the performance of a speech act between a living speaker and a co-present receiver. As a result, all speech acts become intersubjective and are therefore authentic within the speech context created by the confluence of subjectivities. Shug here produces the "theory" of the everyday life language practiced by Celie: the populist elements of such an ethic are vital to the formation of the Folkpants industry.

The vestments of "the people" quickly become the ligaments of a new family as the workshop where the Folkpants are made moves from Shug's house to the house of Celie's birth. Celie's return to this house, however, is not represented as a confrontation with long-buried memories of sexual violation or personal danger. On this go-round, the house comes with yet a third new prehistoric origin myth, in which the Mother has protected her daughters from the deadliest penetration of patriarchy by preserving her property for the girls. The wicked stepfather, trespassing on their property as he has on Celie's body, had wrested it from the sisters; his death sets them free from their exile and they return, one at a time.

This move does more than to bring them back to the Mother: it also provides closure to the narrative genealogy of racism and class struggle inscribed in Celie's family history. Celie now situates herself firmly in her family's entrepreneurial tradition; she runs her business from the store tragically occupied by her stepfather, and her father before him. Where her father and uncles were lynched for presuming the rights of full American citizens to participate in a free market, and where her stepfather survived by doing business exclusively for and with whites,

Celie's business is as perfectly biracial as it is unisexual, employing both Sofia and a white worker to sell her goods so that *everyone* will be well served.

Thus it would seem that capitalism, figured as a small (but infinitely expandable) family-style business, provides for the socially marginalized characters in *The Color Purple* the motivating drive for forging a positive relation to social life. The family-as-business has the power and the resources to absorb adversity while providing the ground for social relations based on cooperation rather than on coercion. Not socialist-style cooperation, of course—Shug, Celie's financial backer, specifically orders her to hire "women . . . to cut and sew, while you sit back and design."

To join the closely knit family of female capitalists, one must simply identify with the "female world of love and ritual" that includes the everyday working relations among women that center on the home.[28] A woman can assert her allegiance to other women simply by joining the business: for men who admit a childhood/natural desire to engage in the housekeeping practices of their mothers (Harpo; Mr. _____), the franchise is conferred.

United around these activities, Celie's new family emerges from the gender and racial fractures that had threatened to destroy it. Yet it is finally not family discourse that organizes the life of the redeemed community: the last event of the novel, after Nettie and the children's return to Celie, not only fulfills the familial model of utopian capitalism that dominates the last third of the narrative, but also reinstates nationalist discourse as the proper context for Celie's autobiography.

"Dear God. Dear stars, dear trees, dear sky, dear peoples. Dear Everything. Dear God." With this lyric, the end of *The Color Purple* proclaims the ascendancy of a new mode of national and personal identity. In a letter Celie addresses not to the God who is everything but to the everything that incorporates godly spirit, she writes of the fulfillment of the womanist promise, as the community turns toward the future in expectation of more profit, pleasure, and satisfaction from their labor and from each other. Shug speaks of retiring. "Albert"/Mr. _____ prattles about the new shirt he's made. Celie speaks about "how things doing generally" while she compulsively stitches "up a bunch of scraps, try to see what [she] can make." As in the rest of the novel, the idiom of Celie's victory is deliberately apolitical: while she might have used the new formation of the utopian community as an opportunity for metacommentary about the revolutionary conditions of its production, Celie continues to favor the materials of the common language in the construction of the new social space.

And yet it is precisely at this protonationalist moment, when the changes sought within the family have been realized in the woman-identified community and extended to the outside world through the garment business, that *The Color Purple* turns back toward the kinds of explications of social life that Celie has previously rejected. In the novel's final pages, conventional mythopoetic political discourse about American culture, about "the births, battles, and deaths of Great Men" previously exiled from the text's concerns and representations, surfaces for adoption. In so doing, this radically revised and "womanized" historical novel calls into question its own carefully established social and textual metamorphosis.

Celie's rapprochement with Mr. _____ , for example, is significantly sealed when he personally places a letter in her hand—not from Nettie, but from America: the Department of Defense telegram notifying Celie of Nettie's apparent death. But this gesture comments more on the symbolic relations of patriarchal to state forms than it does on changes in the experiences or consciousness of the characters. The redemption of America is linked with the redemption of Mr. _____ , forecasting the novel's imminent refranchising of patriarchal modes of analysis and representation.

On this occasion we also witness Celie's startling use of the narrowly "political" language which, I have argued, has been absent from her practice throughout the rest of the novel. Celie's fear of Nettie's death suggests to her that, in this time of crisis, America confers on American blacks the cultural status of lynched subjects like Celie's father: "Plus," she says, "colored don't count to those people." There is nothing contradictory or insidious in this particular observation of Celie's, but it too heralds the revalorization of a mode of heretofore exiled cultural analysis.

The final day of the narrative telegraphs the novel's turn to American nationalism at its most blatant and filiopietistic: it is July 4, Independence Day. It is the first and only day narrated in the novel that takes place after Nettie's return to the fold. It is uniquely positioned to provide textual commentary about the relation between its limited set of "characters" and the operation of dominant and contested cultures that has marked Afro-American experience.

The dialogue that constitutes explicit comment on the subject of the holiday ranges from personal "complaint" to epic recognition:

> Why us always have family reunion on July 4th, say Henrietta, mouth poke out, full of complaint. It so hot.
> White people busy celebrating independence from England July 4th, say Harpo, so most black folks don't have to work. Us can spend the day celebrating each other.
> Ah, Harpo, say Mary Agnes, . . . I didn't know you knowed history.

We didn't know that Harpo knew history either: he never seemed to need to know it. With the single, special exception of Sofia's fifteen minutes of freedom on Christmas while indentured to the mayor's wife, at no other time in the novel has work on the farm or anywhere else within the black community depended on or referred to the demands of white American hegemonic culture for its work timetable or its mode of leisure. Mary Agnes' surprise at Harpo is appropriate, for this consciousness of "history" is imported specially for the novel's closing moments.

But what does the rearticulation of Celie's family within a specifically American scene do to the politics of history in *The Color Purple*? In this late moment, Celie's early assertion of her autonomy from American national identity is silently answered by the next generation's commentary: Harpo's "history" suggests instead that Afro-American culture exists confidently in the interstices of Anglo-American historical time. He characterizes the relation between Anglo- and Afro-American culture as structured around an opposition and a hierarchy that discriminates racially, and yet implies that blacks have all the room they need for full cultural self-articulation.

Possibly this shift represents a historical change—a change in the modes of cultural reproduction. Whereas the home life Celie experienced as a child and a young woman mainly involved the black community, the life she leads with Shug overlaps the circulation of blues culture throughout both black and white urban communities. Perhaps, as a result of her wider experience, a traditionally national language was the only discourse available to describe this variegated cultural landscape. If this multiracial cultural articulation, commonly known as the American "melting pot," is the main motive behind the resurgence of American consciousness, then the final images of *The Color Purple* might be said to abandon the project of specifically representing an Afro-American national culture for a less racially delimited, more pluralistic model.

But if the image of the reconstituted family in the text's final letter suggests the American melting pot, it also represents the clearly Jeffersonian cast of Celie's family. Rural, abstracted from the mainly urban scene of consumption, this "matrician" homestead remains the symbolic and actual seat of the production of Folkpants. Folkpants, in turn (no doubt soon to be joined by a line of Folkshirts designed by Mr. _____) , retain their capacity to express the consumer's unique and unmarked soul, along with embodying the ideal conditions of social relations.

From this point of view, the novel's resuscitation of American national discourse can be explained by the way Celie's "family," in the final instance, can be said to mark its own separate, specifically Afro-American recolonization of American time, American property, and mythic American self-help ideology by casually ironizing it. Harpo's droll analysis of the reason behind their July Fourth gathering minimizes the melting-pot aspect of American Independence Day, reducing the holiday to a racial and not a national celebration. Mary Agnes' uncontested depiction of Harpo's statement as history might suggest that this final event is meant to illuminate the real poverty of a politically established Anglo-

American national identity when set next to that of the Afro-American community that has fought on all grounds for the right to have everything—life, dignity, love, family, nation.

But to enter, as the novel does, into a mode of political analysis that employs the ideological myths of hegemonic culture to define Afro-American cultures raises questions about the oppositional status of the novel. Such an alliance severely problematizes the critique of conventional historical "memory" and cultural self-transmission that Walker intended to make in this "historical novel." It implicitly represents American racism as a condition of Afro-American self-celebration.

The novel's apparent amnesia about the conditions of its own production is symbolized in the denial or reversal of age heralded in the novel's and Celie's closing sentence: "Matter of fact, I think this the youngest us ever felt." As if deliberately replacing her very first utterance, "I am fourteen years old," with an assertion of victorious subjectivity and a control over the context in which she speaks, Celie commits herself to the production of a new age but ascribes no value to the influence of the past on the subject or on the culture.

Such a model for the reformulation of Afro-American national identity threatens to lose certain historical events in the rush to create the perfect relations of a perfect moment. That the text might use the repression of certain kinds of memory as a strategy for representing its new, utopian mode of production was signaled in the narrative repression of the class element in Celie's father's lynching. The profit motive killed her father and, indirectly, her mother; it made Celie vulnerable to her stepfather's sexual imperialism and almost resulted in her disenfranchisement from her property. But the novel's progressive saturation with capitalism and its fruits, along with its insistence on the significance of the product in the consumer's self-knowledge and self-expression, marks the relative cleansing of violence from its class and capital relations. The Afro-American nationalism imaged in the new familial system can be said to use the American tradition of autonomy through property to imagine the new social epoch.

The Color Purple's strategy of inversion, represented in its elevation of female experience over great patriarchal events, had indeed aimed to critique the unjust practices of racism and sexism that violate the subject's complexity, reducing her to a generic biological sign. But the model of personal and national identity with which the novel leaves us uses fairytale explanations of social relations to represent itself: this fairy tale embraces America for providing the Afro-American nation with the right and the opportunity to own land, to participate in the free market, and to profit from it. In the novel's own terms, American capitalism thus has contradictory effects. On one hand, capitalism veils its operations by employing racism, using the pseudonatural discourse of race to reduce the economic competitor to a subhuman object. In Celie's parental history, *The Color Purple* portrays the system of representation character-istic of capital relations that *creates* the situation of nationlessness for Afro-Americans.

But the novel also represents the mythic spirit of American capitalism as the vehicle for the production of an Afro-American utopia. Folkpants, Unlimited is an industry dedicated to the reproduction and consumption of a certain system of representation central to the version of Afro-American "cultural nationalism" enacted by *The Color Purple*. But Folk-pants, Unlimited also participates in the profit motive: the image of the commodity as the subject's most perfect self-expression is the classic fantasy bribe of capitalism.[29] The illogic of a textual system in which the very force that disenfranchises Afro-Americans provides the material for their national reconstruction is neither "solved" by the novel nor raised as a paradox. The system simply stands suspended in the heat of the family reunion on Independence Day.

What saves Celie and Nettie from disenfranchisement is their lifelong determination to learn, to become literate: Nettie's sense that knowledge was the only route to freedom from the repressive family scene gave her the confidence to escape, to seek "employment" with Samuel's family, to record the alternative and positive truth of Pan-African identity, to face the truth about her own history, to write it down, and to send it to Celie, against all odds. Writing was not only the repository of personal and national hope; it became a record of lies and violences that ultimately produced truth.

The Color Purple nonetheless ultimately rejects writing for an ethic of voice—from Shug's advocacy of self-present, performative discourse to Walker's own postscriptural description of herself as the books' "me-dium." The fantasy of the novel is that these voices might be preserved as pure "text," cleansed of the residues of historical oppression. Celie herself embraces a mode of cultural nationalism unable to transmit objec-tive knowledge—knowledge that does not derive from experience and intimacy—about the way institutional forms of power devolve on "pri-vate" individuals, alone and in their various social relations. Such an emphasis on individual essence, in a false opposition to institutional his-tory, seems inadequate to the construction of any national consciousness, especially one developing in a hostile, negating context. Mythic American political discourse is precisely unable to account for the uneven develop-ment of legitimacy on citizens obfuscated within the nation's rhetoric of identity. And if *The Color Purple* clearly represents anything, it is the unreliability of "text" under the historical pressure to interpret, to pre-dict, and to determine the cultural politics of the colonized signifier.

Notes

1. Alice Walker, *The Color Purple* (New York, 1982), p. 11.
2. The Fourth of July has been a politically charged holiday for Afro-Americans as well as for other marginalized groups. See Philip S. Foner, ed., *We, the Other People: Alternative Declarations of Independence by Labor Groups, Farmers, Woman's Rights Advocates, Socialists, and Blacks, 1829–1975* (Urbana, Ill., 1976), pp. 14–15.

> As long as slavery existed, most blacks refused to participate in celebrations on the Fourth of July, setting aside July 5 for that purpose. In his July 5, 1832, speech in the African Church, New Haven, Connecticut, Peter Osborne declared: "Fellow-Citizens: On account of the misfortune of our color, our fourth of July comes on the fifth; but I hope and trust that when the Declaration of Independence is fully executed, which declares that all men, without respect to person, were born free and equal, we may then have our fourth of July on the fourth." Frederick Douglass, the ex-slave and black abolitionist, summed it up succinctly in his great speech, "The Meaning of July Fourth for the American Negro," delivered in Rochester, New York, on July 5, 1852: "I am not included within the pale of this glorious anniversary! . . . This Fourth of July is *yours*, not mine. You may rejoice, but I must mourn. . . ."

3. Afro-American nationalism has generated too many important primary and secondary works to be documented in one contextualizing footnote. The anthology *Black Nationalism in America*, ed. John H. Bracey, Jr., August Meier, and Elliott Rudwick (Indianapolis and New York, 1970) contains many of these primary polemical documents. For the purposes of this essay, the most important work on the growth of and struggles within the black nationalist movement have been the complete works of W. E. B. Du Bois (his fiction, his autobiography, his book-length essays, and his journalism), now available in the Library of America collection *W. E. B. Du Bois: Writings*, ed. Nathan Huggins (New York, 1986); Frantz Fanon, *The Wretched of the Earth*, trans. Constance Farrington (New York, 1963); Fanon, *Black Skin, White Masks*, trans. Charles Lam Markmann (New York, 1967); Fanon, *Toward the African Revolution: Political Essays*, trans. Haakon Chevalier (New York, 1967); Houston A. Baker, Jr., *The Journey Back: Issues in Black Literature and Criticism* (Chicago, 1980); and Manning Marable, "The Third Reconstruction: Black Nationalism and Race in a Revolutionary America," *Social Text* (Fall 1981): 3–27.
4. The historically unique characteristics of American populist movements require the critic to take nothing for granted in evaluating the "franchising" of membership in the American national community. This is the lesson of Michel de Certeau in "The Politics of Silence: The Long March of the Indians," *Heterologies: Discourse on the Other*, Theory and History of Literature, vol. 17, trans. Brian Massumi (Minneapolis, 1986), pp. 225–33. Important work on the politics of "indigenous" or populist movements has been done by Ernesto Laclau and Chantal Mouffe in *Hegemony and Socialist Strategy: Towards a Radical Democratic Politics*, trans. Winston Moore and Paul Cammack (London, 1985), as well as in Laclau's earlier genealogy of the category "populism" in "Towards a Theory of Populism," *Politics and Ideology in Marxist Theory: Capitalism—Fascism—Populism* (London, 1977), pp. 143–98.
5. Walker, *In Search of Our Mothers' Gardens* (San Diego, 1983), p. xi. "Womanist" is a neologism of Walker's invention. Much more than an idiosyncratic translation of "feminist" into a black/third-world female tradition, the

term describes the "woman" in a range of personal and social identities: "Usually referring to outrageous, audacious, courageous or *willful* behavior. Wanting to know more and in greater depth than is considered 'good' for one. . . . *Also:* A woman who loves other women, sexually and/or nonsexually. . . . Sometimes loves individual men, sexually and/or nonsexually. . . . Traditionally universalist, as in . . . 'the colored race is just like a flower garden, with every color flower represented.'" In calling the new nationalist epistemology imaged and advocated in *The Color Purple* an "aesthetic/symbolic" logic, I mean to honor the careful historical and categorical distinctions that operate in the novel and in Walker's critical work around it. Central to her practice is a delegitimation of traditionally patriarchal-racist political practices, institutions, and language.

6. Walker, "Writing *The Color Purple*," *In Search of Our Mothers' Gardens*, p. 356.

7. The *locus classicus* of discussion about the political uses of the historical novel is Georg Lukács, *The Historical Novel*, trans. Hannah and Stanley Mitchell (London, 1962). My description of Walker's method of refunctioning the historical novel departs very little from Lukács' own valorization of Walter Scott's method in *The Heart of Midlothian*, especially the use of woman to reconstitute the national spirit. Walker's real departure from the conventions of the historical novel is located in her refusal to reinvest the "revised" national consciousness in the legitimation of patriarchal forms of authority. After Lukács, the most significant theorist of the national implications of the historical novel is Benedict Anderson, *Imagined Communities: Reflections on the Origin and Spread of Nationalism* (London, 1983).

8. *The Color Purple* repeats in practice Meridian's revelation that "One Life" always contains multiple voices (see below). Celie's autobiography is firmly in the Afro-American tradition of cultural self-exemplification epitomized in and theorized by Du Bois in *The Souls of Black Folk* (1903) and *Dusk of Dawn: An Essay Toward an Autobiography of a Race Concept* (1940). See also William L. Andrews, *To Tell a Free Story: The First Century of Afro-American Autobiography, 1760–1865* (Urbana, Ill. 1986).

9. Homi K. Bhabha, "Signs Taken for Wonders: Questions of Ambivalence and Authority under a Tree Outside Delhi, May 1817," *Critical Inquiry* 12 (Autumn 1985): 156.

10. Walker, *Meridian* (New York, 1976), p. 121.

11. Ibid., p. 200.

12. Walker has written much fiction and many essays addressing black nationalism in its recent embodiment in the civil rights movement, and contrasting it to other liberated nationalisms, notably Cuban, in *In Search of Our Mothers' Gardens*. *Meridian* addresses directly the need for national identity among Afro-Americans. Short stories from Walker's *In Love and Trouble* (San Diego, 1973), such as "Her Sweet Jerome" and "Everyday Use," see black nationalism not as an expression of Afro-American historical and political solidarity but as a way for "cultured" blacks to oppress noneducated or unsophisticated blacks. *The Color Purple* retains the positivity of *Meridian* toward national identity but also reproduces the negative, antipatriarchal, and antielitist tone of the stories by rejecting, or so it seems, a specifically political (in the narrow sense: discourse that takes place about power) articulation of Afro-American identity for an aesthetic or symbolic construction of the new national subject. In stories written between *In Love and Trouble* and *The Color Purple*, Walker also addresses the *problem* of representing the complex of racial, sexual, and national issues also at the forefront of *The Color Purple*. See especially the remarkable "Advancing Luna—and Ida

B. Wells" in *You Can't Keep a Good Woman Down* (New York, 1981), pp. 85–104.

13. It is perhaps to show with clarity the erasing or negating effects of American racism on a contested subculture that *The Color Purple* contains a number of brief narratives about the fate of native Americans. These tales exhibit the American ability to absorb symbolically a set of cultural differences it claims to honor; they also provide a stunning warning about what happens to cultures that neglect to witness their history. The result, in Samuel's simple words, is that "it became harder to think about Indians because there were none around."

    Unconscious of the history of racial displacements that distinguishes the colonization of America means, at least in *The Color Purple*, that the subculture in question has lost its ability to ready its own history, registered in the genetic traces of its dispersal among the American and Afro-American population. Nettie translates Samuel's narration of Corinne's life story:

    > Sixty years or so before the founding of the school [Spelman], the Cherokee Indians who lived in Georgia were forced to leave their homes and walk, through the snow, to resettlement camps in Oklahoma. A third of them died on the way. But many of them refused to leave Georgia. They hid out as colored people and eventually blended with us. Many of these mixed-race people were at Spelman. Some remembered who they actually were, but most did not. If they thought about it at all . . . they thought they were yellow or reddish brown and wavy haired because of white ancestors, not Indian.

    Even in a community of blood-related readers, the bodily text of the native American descendant seems more like the blank sheet of a stucco wall than it does like the crucial petroglyphs of a fading culture. This means that the cultural framework that would have made these signs legible to a "people" has vanished, and that this people is culturally illiterate—with respect to itself. Even memories passed down orally, through the family or within a community, are not strong enough to keep the meaning of national signs alive.

    Furthermore, in place of the positive identity that native American culture might have maintained had it constructed ways to protect and preserve itself, American Indians are represented here as having developed a way of life that takes its cultural negation as a given. Shug's son, working on an Indian reservation in Arizona, not only experiences racist treatment by the Indians but witnesses with sadness the Indians' reproduction of their cultural disempowerment: "But even if he [Shug's son] try to tell them how he feel [about their racism], they don't seem to care. They so far gone nothing strangers say mean nothing. Everybody not an Indian they got no use for" (p. 235).

14. Benedict Anderson writes eloquently of the way the citizen's "political love" of country partakes of the affect and the libidinal charge traditionally invested in other institutional relations of love—especially through the family. But while the family has conventionally been a signifier of disinterested, uncorrupted love (love "no matter what"), the feminist/"womanist" critique of the family aims to unveil the modes of coercion and exploitation behind the apparently objective and dispassionate quality of the Fathers' love and guidance. See Anderson, *Imagined Communities*, p. 131.

15. Houston Baker describes this mode of mass address as characteristic of the Afro-American text:

    > The text, transmitted as performance, is a public occasion . . . rather than a private act of literacy. It is a ritual statement of the solidarity and continuity of a culture; it takes its place among other transmissions and elaborations of culture

such as weddings, festivals, funerals, and so on. As such, it has a register different from the ones traditionally specified for literary texts.

See Baker, *The Journey Back*, p. 128. Robert B. Stepto has also addressed the political and aesthetic motivations of the reader reading "as" an Afro-American. See Stepto, "Distrust of the Reader in Afro-American Narratives," in *Reconstructing American Literary History*, ed. Sacvan Bercovitch, Harvard English Studies 13 (Cambridge, Mass. 1986), pp. 300–322.

16. Angela Y. Davis, "Rape, Racism and the Myth of the Black Rapist," *Women, Race and Class* (New York, 1981), pp. 172–201; Frederick Douglass, "Why Is the Negro Lynched?" *The Life and Writings of Frederick Douglass*, ed. Foner, 5 vols. (New York, 1950–75), 4:491–523.

17. The notion of the "logic of equivalence" is important to Laclau and Mouffe's arguments about the discursive texture of social relations. See Laclau and Mouffe, *Hegemony and Socialist Strategy*, p. 129.

18. Eve Sedgwick has identified a similar strategy of displacement in *Gone With the Wind*, although she sees the transference among discourses as operating more symmetrically than I see it working here. See Eve Kosofsky Sedgwick, *Between Men: English Literature and Male Homosocial Desire* (New York, 1985), p. 9.

19. Anderson points out that class struggle is often the hidden interface of racist practices. See Anderson, *Imagined Communities*, p. 137; see also Marable, "The Third Reconstruction."

20. "The Negro is a sort of seventh son, born with a veil, and gifted with second-sight in this American world,—a world which yields him no true self-consciousness, but only lets him see himself through the revelation of the other world. It is a peculiar sensation, this double-consciousness, this sense of always looking at one's self through the eyes of others, of measuring one's soul by the tape of a world that looks on in amused contempt and pity. One ever feels his twoness,—an American, a Negro; two souls, two thoughts, two unreconciled strivings; two warring ideals in one dark body, whose dogged strength alone keeps it from being torn asunder" (Du Bois, *The Souls of Black Folk*, reprinted in *Three Negro Classics* [New York, 1965], pp. 214–15).

21. Henry Louis Gates, Jr., "The Blackness of Blackness: A Critique of the Sign and the Signifying Monkey," in *Black Literature and Literary Theory*, ed. Gates (New York and London, 1984), pp. 285–321.

22. For a more extended discussion of the effects of political oppression on the construction of public discourse and of the subject's consciousness, see Lauren Berlant, "The Female Complaint," forthcoming in *Social Text*.

23. Fanon, *Black Skin, White Masks*, p. 112.

24. See Gates, "The Blackness of Blackness," pp. 297–305.

25. Nettie is an exception to this; but she has full control over the space of writing and thus from the beginning is able to use the letter as the utopian, liberated site of expression.

26. See, for example, Du Bois, "The African Roots of War," in *W. E. B. Du Bois: A Reader*, ed. Meyer Weinberg (New York, 1970), pp. 362–63.

> Thus, the world began to invest in color prejudice. The "color line" began to pay dividends. For, indeed, while the exploration of the valley of the Congo was the occasion of the scramble for Africa, the cause lay deeper. [England, France, Germany, Portugal, Italy, and Turkey, among others, all spent the last quarter of the nineteenth and the early twentieth centuries in a "scramble" for Africa.] . . .
> Why was this? What was the new call for dominion? . . .
> The answer to this riddle we shall find in the economic changes in Europe. Remember what the nineteenth and twentieth centuries have meant to organized

industry in European civilization. Slowly the divine right of the few to determine economic income and distribute the goods and services of the world has been questioned and curtailed. We called the process Revolution in the eighteenth century, advancing Democracy in the nineteenth, and Socialization of Wealth in the twentieth. But whatever we call it, the movement is the same: the dipping of more and grimier hands into the wealth-bag of the nation, until today only the ultrastubborn fail to see that democracy, in determining income, is the next inevitable step to Democracy in political power.

27. See George Pradmore, "The Pan-African Movement," in *W. E. B. Du Bois Speaks: Speeches and Addresses 1920–1963*, ed. Foner (New York, 1970), pp. 161–78.
28. Carroll Smith-Rosenberg's essay "The Female World of Love and Ritual," first published in 1975, has not only provided crucial images of American gynocentric community for historically minded readers but has also provided the proof that women were in their ordinary relations affectively vital to other women, despite having found neither articulation nor legitimation in public discourse or social institutions. See Smith-Rosenberg, "The Female World of Love and Ritual: Relations Between Women in Nineteenth-Century America," *Disorderly Conduct: Visions of Gender in Victorian America* (New York, 1985), pp. 53–76.
29. Frederic Jameson, "Reification and Utopia in Mass Culture," *Social Text* 1 (Winter 1979): 144.

◆◆◆◆◆◆◆◆◆◆◆◆◆

Color Me Zora

HENRY LOUIS GATES, JR.

O, write my name, O write ny name:
  O write my name . . .
Write my name when-a you get home . . .
Yes, write my name in the book of life . . .
The Angels in the heav'n going-to write my name.
Spiritual Underground Railroad

My spirit leans in joyousness tow'rd thine,
My gifted sister, as with gladdened heart
My vision flies along thy "speaking pages."
Ada, "A Young Woman of Color," 1836

I am only a pen in His hand
Rebecca Cox Jackson

I'm just a link in a chain.
Aretha Franklin, "Chain of Fools"

For just over two hundred years, the concern to depict the quest of the black speaking subject to find his or her voice has been a repeated topos of the black tradition, and perhaps has been its most central trope. As theme, as revised trope, as a double-voiced narrative strategy, the representation of characters and texts finding a voice has functioned as a sign both of the formal unity of the Afro-American literary tradition and of the integrity of the black subjects depicted in this literature.

Esu's double voice and the language of Signifyin(g) have served throughout this book as unifying metaphors, indigenous to the tradition, both for patterns of revision from text to text and for modes of figuration at work within the text. The Anglo-African narrators published between 1770 and 1815 placed themselves in a line of descent through the successive revision of one trope, of a scared text that refuses to speak to its would-be black auditor. In *Their Eyes Were Watching God*, Zora Neale Hurston depicts her protagonist's ultimate moment of self-awareness in her ability to name her own divided consciousness. As an element of theme and as a highly accomplished rhetorical strategy that depends for its effect on the bivocality of free indirect discourse, this voicing of a divided consciousness (another topos of the tradition) has been transformed in Ishmael Reed's *Mumbo Jumbo* into a remarkable self-reflexive representation of the ironies of writing a text in which two foregrounded voices compete with each other for control of narration itself. Whereas the development of the tradition to the publication of *There Eyes Were Watching God* seems to have been preoccupied with the mimetic possibilities of the speaking voice, black fiction after *Their Eyes* would seem even more concerned to explore the implications of doubled voices upon strategies of writing.

Strategies as effective as Hurston's innovative use of free indirect discourse and Reed's bifurcated narrative voice lead one to wonder how a rhetorical strategy could possibly extend, or Signify upon, the notions of voice at play in these major texts of the black tradition. How could a text possibly trope the extended strategies of voicing which we have seen to be in evidence in *Their Eyes* and in *Mumbo Jumbo?* To Signify upon both Hurston's and Reed's strategies of narration would seem to demand a form of the novel that, at once, breaks with tradition yet revises the most salient features through which I have been defining the formal unity of this tradition.

Just as Hurston's and Reed's texts present seemingly immovable obstacles to an equally telling revision of the tradition's trope of voicing, so too does *Invisible Man,* the tradition's text of blackness and, in my opinion, its most profound achievement in the novel. The first-person narration of *Invisible Man,* the valorization of oral narration in *Their Eyes*, and the italicized interface of showing and telling in *Mumbo Jumbo,* taken together, would seem to leave rather little space in which narrative innovation could even possibly be attempted. Alice Walker's revisions of *Their Eyes Were Watching God* and of Rebecca Cox Jackson's *Gifts of Power,* however, have defined an entirely new mode of representation of the black quest to make the text speak.

To begin to account for the signifyin(g) revisions at work in Walker's *The Color Purple,* it is useful to recall the dream of literacy figured in John Jea's autobiography. In Chapter 4, I maintained that Jea's odd revision of the scene of the Talking Book served to erase the figurative potential of this trope for the slave narrators who followed him. After Jea, slave narrators refigured a repeated scene of instruction in terms of reading and writing rather than in terms of making the text speak. While these two tropes are obviously related, it seems equally obvious that the latter represents a key reworking of the former, in terms more conducive to the directly polemical role in which the slave narratives were engaged in an antebellum America seemingly preoccupied with the future of human slavery.

While the trope of the Talking Book disappeared from the male slave narratives after Jea literalized it it is refigured in the mystical writings of Rebecca Cox Jackson, an Afro-American visionary and Shaker eldress who was a contemporary of Jea's. Jackson was a free black woman who lived between 1795 and 1871. She was a fascinating religious leader and feminist, who founded a Shaker sisterhood in Philadelphia in 1857, after a difficult struggle with her family, with her initial religious denomination, and even with the Shakers. Her extensive autobiographical writings (1830–1864) were collected and edited by Jean McMahon Humez, published in 1981, and reviewed by Alice Walker in that same year.[1] The reconstitution of Jackson's texts is one of the major scholarly achievements in Afro-American literature, both because of the richness of her texts and because the writings of black women in antebellum America are painfully scarce, especially when compared to the large body of writings by black men.

Jackson, like her contemporary black ex-slave writers, gives a prominent place in her texts to her own literacy training. Hers is a divinely inspired literacy training even more remarkable than Jea's. Writing between 1830 and 1832, just fifteen-odd years after Jea, Jackson—with or without Jea's text in mind—refigures Jea's divine scene of instruction. Jackson's refiguration of this supernatural event, however, is cast within a sexual opposition between male and female. Whereas her antecedents used the trope to define the initial sense of difference between slave and free, African and European, Jackson's revision charts the liberation of a (black) woman from a (black) man over the letter of the text. I bracket *black* because, as we shall see, Jackson freed herself of her brother's domination of her literacy and her ability to interpret, but supplanted him with a mythical white male interpreter.

Jackson, recalling Jea, writes, "After I received the blessing of God, I had a great desire to read the Bible." Lamenting the fact that "I am the only child of my mother that had not learning," she seeks out her brother to "give me one hour's lesson at night after supper or before we went to bed."[2] Her brother, a prominent clergyman in the Bethel African Methodist Episcopal Church, was often "so tired when he would come home that he had not [the] power to do so," a situation, Jackson tells us, which would "grieve" her. But the situation that grieved Jackson even more was her brother's penchant to "rewrite" her words, to revise her dictation, one supposes, to make them more "presentable." Jackson takes great care to describe her frustration in the fight with her brother to control her flow of words:

> So I went to get my brother to write my letters and to read them. . . . I told him what to put in. Then I asked him to read. He did. I said, "Thee has put in more than I told thee." This he done several times. I then said, "I don't want thee to *word* my letter. In only want thee to *write* it." Then he said, "Sister, thee is the hardest one I ever wrote for!" These words, together with the manner that he had wrote my letter, pierced my soul like a sword. . . . I could not keep from crying.[3]

* * *

This scene is an uncanny prefigurement of the battle over her public speaking voice that Janie wages with Joe Starks in *Their Eyes Were Watching God*, as we have seen in Chapter 5. Jackson's brother, "tired" from his arduous work for the Lord, cannot be relied on to train his sister to read. When she compromises by asking him to serve as her amanuensis, he "words" her letters, as Jackson puts it, rather than simply translating her words (in their correct order, as narrated) from spoken to written form. This contest over her wording is not merely the anxiety the author experiences when edited or rewritten; rather, we eventually learn that Rebecca's rather individual mode of belief not only comes to threaten the minister-brother but also leads ultimately to a severance of the kinship bond. The brother-sister conflict over the "word" of the letter, then, prefigures an even more profound conflict over the word and letter of God's will.

God, however, takes sides. He comforts the grieving Rebecca with a divine message: "And these words were spoken in my heart, 'Be faithful, and the time shall come when you can write.' These words were spoken in my heart as though a tender father spoke them. My tears were gone in a moment."[4] God was as good as his promise. Just as he had done for his servant, John Jea, the Lord taught Jackson how to read:

> One day I was sitting finishing a dress in haste and in prayer. (Jackson sustained herself by dressmaking.] This word was spoken in my mind, "Who learned the first man on earth?" "Why, God." "He is unchangeable, and if He learned the first man to read, He can learn you." I laid down my dress, picked up my Bible, ran upstairs, opened it, and kneeled down with it pressed by my breast, prayed earnestly to Almighty God if it was consisting to His holy will, to learn me to read His holy word. And when I looked on the word, I began to read. And when I found I was reading, I was frightened—then I could not read one word. I closed my eyes again in prayer and then opened my eyes, began to read. So I done, until I read the chapter. . . . So I tried, took my Bible daily and praying and read until I could read anywhere. The first chapter that I read I never could know it after that day. I only knowed it was in James, but what chapter I can never tell.[5]

When confronted with the news, Jackson's incredulous husband challenged her claim: "Woman, you are agoing crazy!" Jackson, undaunted, read to him. "Down I sat and read through. And it was in James. So Samuel praised the Lord with me." Similarly, her brother accused her merely of memorizing passages overheard being read by his children: "Once thee has heard the children read, till thee has got it by heart." Once convinced by Jackson's husband, Jackson tells us with an air of triumph, "He sat down very sorrowful."

When challenged by her doubting brother, Jackson tells us, "I did not speak," allowing her husband, Samuel, to speak in her defense. At the end of her long description of this miracle of literacy, this "gift of power," she summarizes the event as "this unspeakable gift of Almighty God to me." It is this double representation of unspeakability which connects Jackson's miracle of literacy to Alice Walker's strategies of narration in *The Color Purple*.

Despite the parallel in Jackson's mini-narrative of her fight to control her words and Janie's fight to control hers (resolved, for Jackson, by the divine discourse of God, and for Janie by the black vernacular discourse of Signifyin(g), we know that Hurston did not have access to Jackson's texts. Walker, however, makes much of this scene in her essay on Jackson, underscoring the fact that "Jackson *was* taught to read and write by the spirit within her."[6] When Walker dedicates *The Color Purple* "To the Spirit," it is to this spirit which taught Rebecca Jackson to read. It is the representation of the unfolding of this gift of the "spirit within her," an "unspeakable gift," through which Walker represents the thoroughly dynamic development of her protagonist's consciousness, within the "unspeakable" medium of an epistolary novel comprised of letters written but never said, indeed written but never read. Celie's only reader, and Rebecca's only literacy teacher, is God.

Rather than representing the name of God as unspeakable, Walker represents Celie's words, her letters addressed to "God," as unspeakable. God is Celie's silent auditor, the addressee of most of her letters, written but never sent. This device, as Robert Stepto has suggested to me, is an echo of the first line of W. E. B. Du Bois's well-known "After-Thought" to *The Souls of Black Folk:* "Hear my cry, O God the Reader." But more important to our analysis of Walker's revisions of *Their Eyes Were Watching God*, Celie's written voice to God, her reader, tropes the written yet never uttered voice of free indirect discourse which is the predominant vehicle of narrative commentary in Hurston's novel.

As I have attempted to show in Chapter 5, Hurston draws upon free indirect discourse as a written voice masked as a speakerly voice, as an "oral hieroglyphic," as Hurston put it. Celie's voice in *The Color Purple*, on the other hand, is a spoken or mimetic one. If mimesis is a showing of the fact of telling, then Celie's letters are visual representations that attempt to tell the fact of showing. Whereas Hurston represents Janie's discovery of her voice as the enunciation of her own doubled self through a free indirect "narrative of division," Walker represents Celie's growth of self-consciousness as an act of writing. Janie and her narrator speak themselves into being; Celie, in her letters, writes herself into being. Walker Signifies upon Hurston by troping the concept of voice that unfolds in *Their Eyes Were Watching God*. Whereas Janie's movement from object to subject begins with her failure to recognize an image of her colored self in a photograph, precisely at a point in her childhood when she is known merely as "Alphabet" (a figure for all names and none), Celie's ultimate movement of self-negation is her self-description in her first letter to God: "~~I am.~~" Celie, like Janie, is an absence, an erased presence, an empty set. Celie, moreover, writes in "Janie's voice," in a level of diction and within an idiom similar to that which Janie speaks. Celie, on the other hand, never speaks; rather, she writes her speaking voice, and that of everyone who speaks to her.

This remarkably self-conscious Signifyin(g) strategy places *The Color Purple* in a direct line of descent from *Their Eyes Were Watching God*, in an act of literary bonding quite unlike anything that has ever happened within the Afro-American tradition. Walker, we well know, has written at length about her relationship to Zora Neale Hurston. I have always found it difficult to identify this bond textually, by which I mean that I have not found Hurston's presence in Walker's texts. In *The Color Purple*, however, Walker rewrites Hurston's narrative strategy, in an act of ancestral bonding that is especially rare in black letters, since, as we saw in Chapter 3, black writers have tended to trace their origins to white male parents.[7]

Walker in effect, has written a letter of love to her authority figure, Hurston. While I am not aware of another epistolary novel in the Afro-American tradition, there is ample precedent in the tradition for the publication of letters. Ignatius Sancho's *Letters* were published at London in 1782. As we saw in Chapter 3, Phillis Wheatley's letters to Arbour Tanner were so well known by 1830 that they could be parodied in a broadside. Even the device of locating Celie's sister in Africa, writing letters home to her troubled sister, has a precedent in the tradition of Amanda Berry Smith's diarylike entries about her African missionary work, published in her *Autobiography* (1893).[8] But we do not have, before *The Color Purple*, an example of the epistolary novel in the black tradition of which I am aware.

Why does Walker turn to the novel of letters to revise *Their Eyes Were Watching God?* As a way of concluding this study of voices in texts, and texts that somehow talk to other texts, I would like to discuss some of the implications of Walker's Signification upon Hurston's text by examining, if only briefly, a few of the more startling aspects of the rhetorical strategies at work in *The Color Purple* and its use of the epistolary form of narration.[9]

The Color Purple is comprised of letters written by two sisters, Celie and Nettie. Celie addresses her letters first to God and then to Nettie, while Nettie, off in the wilds of Africa as a missionary, writes her letters to Celie—letters intercepted by Celie's husband, stashed away in a trunk, and finally read by Celie and Shug Avery, her friend, companion, and lover. Nettie's unreceived letters to Celie appear, suddenly, almost at the center of the text and continue in what we might think of as the text's middle passage with interruptions of three letters of Celie's addressed to God. Then Celie's addressee is Nettie, until she writes her final letter, which is addressed to God (twice) and to the stars, trees, the sky, to "peoples," and to "Everything." While I do not wish to diminish the importance of the novel's plot or its several echoes of moments in Hurston's novel, I am more interested here in suggesting the formal relationship that obtains between the strategies of narration of *Their Eyes* and of *The Color Purple*. Like Janie, Celie is married to a man who would imprison her, indeed brutalize her. Unlike Janie, however, Celie is liberated by her love for Shug Avery, the "bodaciously" strong singer with whom she shares the love that Janie shared with Tea Cake. It is Shug Avery, I shall argue, who stands in this text as Walker's figure for Hurston herself. Perhaps it will suffice to note that this is Celie's text, a text of becoming as is *Their Eyes*, but a becoming with a signal difference.

The most obvious difference between the two texts is that Celie writes herself into being, before our very eyes. Whereas Janie's moment of consciousness is figured as a ritual speech act, for Celie it is the written voice which is her vehicle for self-expression and self-revelation. We read the letters of the text, as it were, over Celie's shoulder, just as we overhear Janie telling her story to Phoeby as they sit on Janie's back porch. Whereas Janie and the narrator do most of Janie's speaking (in an idiomatic free indirect discourse), in *The Color Purple* two of the novel's three principal characters do all of the writing. Celie is her own author, in a manner that Janie could not possibly be, given the third-person form of narration of *Their Eyes*. To remind the reader that we are rereading letters, the lower border of each page of *The Color Purple* is demarcated by a solid black line, an imitation of how the border of a photoduplicated letter might look if bound in hardcover.

What is the text's motivation for the writing of letters? Nettie writes to Celie because she is far away in Africa. Celie writes to God for reasons that Nettie recapitulates in one of her letters:

> I remember one time you said your life made you feel so ashamed you couldn't even talk about it to God, you had to write it, bad as you thought your writing was. Well, now I know what you meant. And whether God will read letters or no, I know you will go on writing them; which is guidance enough for me. Anyway, when I don't write to you I feel as bad as I do when I don't pray, locked up in myself and choking on my own heart. I am so *lonely, Celie*.

The italicized command that opens the novel—"*You better not never tell nobody but God. It'd kill your mammy.*"—which we assume has been uttered by Celie's stepfather, is responded to literally by Celie. Celie writes to God for the same reason that Nettie writes to Celie, so that each may read the text of her life, almost exactly or simultaneously as events unfold.

This is the text's justification of its own representation of writing. But what are Walker's motivations? As I suggested above, Celie writes herself into being as a text, a text we are privileged to read over her shoulder. Whereas we are free to wonder aloud about the ironies of self-presentation in a double-voiced free indirect discourse, the epistolary strategy eliminates this aspect of reader response from the start. Celie writes her own story, and writes everyone else's tale in the text except Nettie's. Celie writes her text, and is a text, standing in discrete and episodic letters, which we, like voyeurs, hurriedly read before the addressees (God and Nettie) interrupt our stolen pleasures. Celie is a text in the same way in which Langston Hughes wrote (in *The Big Sea*) that Hurston was a book—"a perfect book of entertainment in herself."[10] We read Celie reading her world and writing it into being, in one subtle discursive act. There is no battle of voices here, as we saw in *Their Eyes*, between a disembodied narrator and a protagonist; Celie speaks—or writes—for Celie and, of course, to survive for Nettie, then for Shug, and finally for Celie.

Ironically, one of the well-known effects of the epistolary narrative is to underscore the illusion of the real, but also of the spontaneous.[11] The form allows for a maximum of identification with a character, precisely because the devices of empathy and distance, standard in third-person narration, no longer obtain. There is no apparent proprietary consciousness in the epistle, so readers must supply any coherence of interpretation of the text themselves. Samuel Richardson understood this well:

> It is impossible that readers the most attentive, can always enter into the views of the writer of a piece, written, as hoped, to Nature and the moment. A species of writing, too, that may be called new; and every one putting him and herself into the character they read, and judging of it by their own sensations.[12]

Celie recounts events, seemingly as they unfold; her readers decide their meaning. Her readers piece together a text from the fragmented letters which Celie never mails and which Celie, almost all at once, receives. But Walker escapes the lack of control over how we read Celie precisely by calling before us a writing style of such innocence with which only the most hardened would not initially sympathize, then eventually *empathize*. By showing Celie as the most utterly dynamic of characters, who comes to know her world and to trust her readings of her world, and by enabling Celie to compel from us compassion for the brutalities she is forced to suffer, followed triumphantly by Celie's assertion of control (experiential control that we learn of through her ever-increasing written control of her letters), Walker manipulates our responses to Celie without even once revealing a voice in the text that Celie or Nettie does not narrate or repeat or edit.

How is this different from first-person narration in a fluid, or linear, narrative? Again, a remarkably self-conscious Richardson tells us in *Clarissa:*

> Such a sweetness of temper, so much patience and resignation, as she seems
> to be mistress of; yet writing of and in the midst of *present* distresses! How
> *much more* lively and affecting, for that reason, must her style be; her mind
> tortured by the pangs of uncertainty (the events then hidden in the womb of
> fate) *than* the dry, narrative, unanimated style of persons, relating difficulties
> and dangers surmounted; the relator perfectly at ease; and if himself unmoved
> by his own story, not likely greatly to affect the reader![13]

Unlike the framed tales of Janie in *Their Eyes* or of the nameless protagonist of *Invisible Man*, the reader of a novel of letters does not, indeed
cannot, know the outcome of Celie's tale until its writing ceases. The
two voices that narrate Ishmael Reed's "anti-detective" novel, for instance, are troped in *The Color Purple* almost by a pun that turns upon
this fact: whereas a topos of *Mumbo Junmbo* is a supraforce searching
for its text, for its "writing," as Reed puts it, Celie emerges as a force,
as a presence, by writing all-too-short letters which, taken together, her
readers weave or stitch together as both the text of *The Color Purple*
and the autobiographical text of Celie's life and times, her bondage and
her freedom. Celie charts her growth of consciousness day to day, or
letter to letter. By the end of the novel, we know that Celie, like Reed's
silent character, "jes' grew." Celie, moreover, "jes' grew" by writing her
text of herself. Whereas Reed's Jes Grew disappears, at the end of *The
Color Purple* we are holding Celie's text of herself in our hands. It is we
who complete or close the circle or chain of Jes Grew Carriers, in an act
of closure that Jes Grew's enemies disrupt in *Mumbo Jumbo*. When
Nettie inevitably gets around to asking Celie how she managed to change
so much, Celie quite probably could respond, "I jes grew, I 'spose,"
precisely because the tyranny of the narrative present can only be overthrown by a linear reading of her letters, from first to last. Celie does
not recapitulate her growth, as does Ellison's narrator or Hurston's Janie; only her readers have the leisure to reread Celie's text of development, the text of her becoming. Celie exists letter to letter; her readers
supply the coherence necessary to speak of a precisely chartable growth,
one measured by comparing or compiling all of the fragments of experience and feeling that Celie has selected to write.

Let us consider this matter of what I have called the tyranny of the
narrative present. Celie, as narrator or author, presents herself to us,
letter to letter, in a continuous written present. The time of writing is
Celie's narrative present. We see this even more clearly when Celie
introduces Nettie's first letter, the first letter that Celie and Shug recover from the attic trunk:

Dear God,

This the letter I been holding in my hand.

The text of Nettie's letter follows, as an embedded narrative. This narrative present is comprised of (indeed, *can* be comprised of) only one event:

the process of writing itself. All other events in *The Color Purple* are in the narrative past: no matter how near to the event Celie's account might be, the event is past, and it is this past about which Celie is writing.

We can see this clearly in Celie's first letter. The letter's first paragraph both underscores the moment of writing and provides a frame for the past events that Celie is about to share with her addressee, God:

> Dear God,
> I am fourteen years old. ~~I am~~ I have always been a good girl.

Celie places her present self ("I am") under erasure, a device that reminds us that she is writing, and searching for her voice by selecting, then rejecting, word choice or word order, but also that there is some reason why Celie was once "a good girl" but no longer feels that she can make this claim before God. Because "a good girl" connotes the avoidance of sex, especially at the age of fourteen, we expect her fall from grace to be a fall of sensual pleasure. Celie tells us that we were right in this suspicion, but also wrong: there has been no pleasure involved in her "fall." Her account of the recent past explains:

> Last spring after little Lucious come I heard them fussing. He was pulling on her arm. She say It too soon, Fonso, I ain't well. Finally he leave her alone. A week go by, he pulling on her arm again. She says Naw, I ain't gonna. Can't you see I'm already half dead, an all of these chilren.
> She went to visit her sister doctor over Macon. Left me to see after the others. He never had a kine word to say to me. Just say You gonna do what your mammy wouldn't. First he put his thing up gainst my hip and sort of wiggle it around. Then he grab hold my titties. Then he push his thing inside my pussy. When that hurt, I cry. He start to choke me, saying You better shut up and git used to it.
> But I don't never git used to it. And now I feels sick every time I be the one to cook. My mama she fuss at me an look at me. She happy, cause he good to her *now*. But too sick to last long. (emphasis added)

Celie has been raped by the man she knows as her father. Her tale of woe has begun. Celie's first letter commences in a narrative present, shifts to a narrative past, then, in the letter's penultimate sentence, returns to a narrative present signified by "now." Prophetically, she even predicts the future, her mother's imminent death. In the narrative past, Celie develops, in fact controls, the representation of character and event. In the narrative present, Celie reveals to us that hers is the proprietary consciousness that we encounter in third-person narration, rendered in an epistle in a first-person narrative present. Celie, as author of her letters to God, might not be able to know what course events shall take, but the past belongs to her, salient detail by salient detail. We only know of Celie's life and times by her recounting of their significance and meaning, rendered in Celie's own word order. In this epistolary novel, the narrator of Celie's tale is identical with the author of Celie's letters.

Because there is no gap here, as we saw in *Their Eyes* between the text's narrator and Janie, there would seem to be no need to bridge this gap through free indirect discourse.

This, however, is not the case in *The Color Purple*. While the gap between past and present is not obliterated, the gap between who sees and who speaks *is* obliterated by Celie's curious method of reporting discourse. The epistolary form's necessary shift between the narrative present and the narrative past creates the very space in which free indirect discourse dwells in Celie's narrative. It is in her representation of free indirect discourse that Walker undertakes her most remarkable revision of *Their Eyes Were Watching God*.

The Color Purple is replete with free indirect discourse. The double-voiced discourse of *Their Eyes* returns in the text of Celie's letters. Celie, as I have said, is the narrator and author of her letters. The narrator's voice, accordingly, is the voice of the protagonist. This protagonist, moreover, is divided into two parts: Celie, the character whose past actions we see represented in letters (an active but initially dominated and undereducated adolescent), and that other Celie, who—despite her use of written dialect—we soon understand is a remarkably reflective and sensitive teller, or writer, of a tale, or her own tale. Because of the curious interplay of the narrative past (in which Celie is a character) and a narrative present (in which Celie is the author), Celie emerges as both the subject and the object of narration. The subject-object split, or reconciliation, which we have seen in Hurston's use of free indirect discourse, in *The Color Purple* appears as the central rhetorical device by which Celie's self-consciousness is represented, in her own capacity to write a progressively better-structured story of herself.

Whereas Hurston represents Janie's emergent self in the shifting level of diction in the narrator's commentary and in the black-speech-informed indirect discourse, Walker represents Celie's dynamism in her ability to control her own narrative voice (that is, her own style of writing) but also in her remarkable ability to control all other voices spoken to Celie, which we encounter only in Celie's representation of them. Celie represents these voices, this spoken discourse, through the rhetorical device of free indirect discourse. It is Celie's voice that is always a presence whenever anyone in her world is represented as having spoken. We can, therefore, never be certain whether a would-be report, or mimesis, of dialogue is Celie's or the character's whose words we are overhearing or, more precisely, reading over Celie's shoulder.

Let me be clear: no one speaks in this novel. Rather, two sisters correspond with each other, through letters which one never receives (Celie's) and which the other receives almost all at once (Nettie's). There is no true mimesis, then, in *The Color Purple*, only diegesis. But, through Celie's mode of apparently reporting speech, underscored dramatically by her written dialect voice of narration, we logically assume that we are being shown discourse, when all along we never actually are. Celie only tells us what people have said to her. She never shows us their words in direct quotation. Precisely because her written dialect voice is identical in diction and idiom to the supposedly spoken words that pepper her letters, we believe that we are overhearing people speak, just as Celie did when the words were in fact uttered. We are not, however; indeed, we can never be certain whether or not Celie is showing us a telling or telling us a showing, as awkward as this sounds. In the speeches of her characters, Celie's voice and a character's merge into one, almost exactly as we saw happen in *Their Eyes* when Janie and her narrator speak in the merged voice of free indirect discourse. In these passages from *The Color Purple*, the distinction between mimesis and diegesis is apparently obliterated: the opposition between them has collapsed.

This innovation, it seems to me, is Walker's most brilliant stroke, her most telling Signifyin(g) move on Hurston's text. Let us examine just a few of scores of examples. The first is Celie's account of Mr. _____'s sisters, named Carrie and Kate, as one of Walker's Signifyin(g) gestures toward Jean Toomer's *Cane*, where Carrie Kate appears as a central character in "Kabnis."[14] (Walker, incidentally, loves *Cane* almost as much as she does *Their Eyes*, as she writes in "Zora Neale Hurston: A Cautionary Tale and a Partisan View."[15]) Celie's depiction of Carrie and Kate's discourse follows:

> Well that's no excuse, say the first one, Her name Carrie, other one name Kate. When a woman marry she spose to keep a decent house and a clean family. Why, wasn't nothing to come here in the winter time and all these children have colds, they have flue, they have direar, they have newmonya, they have worms, they have the chill and fever. They hungry. They hair ain't comb. They too nasty to touch.

Who is speaking in these passages: Carrie and Kate, or Celie, or all three? All three are speaking, or, more properly, no one is speaking, because Celie has merged whatever was actually said with her own voice and has written it out for us in a narrative form that aspires to the spoken but never represents or reports anyone else's speech but Celie's on one hand, and Celie-cum-characters' on the other. Celie is in control of her narration, even to the point of controlling everyone else's speech, which her readers cannot encounter without hearing their words merged with Celie's.

We can see Celie's free indirect discourse in another example, which reveals how sophisticated an editor Celie becomes, precisely as she grows in self-awareness.[16] Celie is introducing, or framing, one of Nettie's letters, in a narrative present:

> It's hot, here, Celie, she write. Hotter than July. Hotter than August *and*
> July. Hot like cooking dinner on a big stove in a little kitchen in August and
> July. Hot.

Who said, or wrote, these words, words which echo both the Southern
expression "a cold day in August" and Stevie Wonder's album *Hotter
Than July?* Stevie Wonder? Nettie? Celie? All three, and no one. These
are Celie's words, merged with Nettie's, in a written imitation of the
merged voices of free indirect discourse, an exceptionally rare form in
that here even the illusion of mimesis is dispelled.

I could cite several more examples, but one more shall suffice. This
moving scene appears just as Celie and Shug are beginning to cement
their bond, a bond that bespeaks a sisterly, and later a sexual, bonding:

> Shug saying Celie. Miss Celie. And I look up where she at.
> She say my name again. She say this song I'm bout to sing is call Miss
> Celie's song. Cause she scratched it out of my head when I was sick. . . .
> First time somebody made something and name it after me.

Once again, Celie's voice and Shug's are merged together into one, one
we think is Shug's but which can only be Celie's-and-Shug's, simultaneous, inseparable, bonded.

What are we to make of Walker's remarkable innovation in Hurston's
free indirect discourse? We can assume safely that one of Hurston's purposes in the narrative strategies at play in *Their Eyes* was to show James
Weldon Johnson and Countee Cullen, and just about everyone else in the
New Negro Renaissance that dialect not only was not limited to two
stops—humor and pathos—but was fully capable of being used as a literary language even to write a novel. Dialect, black English vernacular
and its idiom, as a literary device was not merely a figure of spoken
speech; rather, for Hurston, it was a storehouse of figures. As if in a
coda to the writing of *Their Eyes*, Hurston even published a short story
entirely in the vernacular, entitled "Story in Harlem Slang" (1942), complete with a "Glossary."[17] Yet, just as Johnson had edited or interpreted
the language of the black vernacular in his rendition of the "Seven Sermons in Verse" that comprise *God's Trombones* (1927), so too had Hurston merged dialect and standard English in the idiom of the free indirect
discourse that gradually overtakes the narrative commentary in *Their
Eyes*. Hurston showed the tradition just how dialect could blend with
standard English to create a new voice, a voice exactly as black as it is
white. (Johnson, of course, had "translated" from the vernacular into
standard English.) Walker's Signifyin(g) riff on Hurston was to seize
upon the device of free indirect discourse as practiced in *Their Eyes* but
to avoid standard English almost totally in Celie's narration. The initial
impression that we have of Celie's naiveté slowly reveals how one can
write an entire novel in dialect. This, we must realize, is as important a

troping of *Their Eyes* as is the page-by-page representation of Celie's writing of her own tale. If Hurston's writing aspired to the speakerly, then Walker's apparently speaking characters turn out to have been written.

There are other parallels between the two texts which provide evidence of their Signifyin(g) relationship. Whereas Janie's sign of self-awareness is represented as her ability to tell Phoeby her own version of events, Walker matches this gesture by having Celie first write her own texts, discover her sister's purloined letters, arrange them with Shug in "some kind of order," as Shug says to Celie, then read them so that a second narrative unfolds which both completes and implicitly comments on Celie's narrative which has preceded it. This newly recovered narrative is a parallel text. This initial cache of unreceived letters functions as a framed tale within Celie's tale, as do Nettie's subsequently received letters, recapitulating events and providing key details absent from Celie's story. Nettie's letters are written in standard English, not only to contrast her character to Celie's but also to provide some relief from Celie's language. But even this narrative Celie controls, by ordering their reading but especially by introducing them, within her letters, with her own commentary. Nettie's letters function as a second narrative of the past, echoing the shift from present to past that we see within the time shifts of Celie's letters. But Nettie's discovered letters are *The Color Purple*'s structural revision of Janie's bracketed tale. We recognize a new Celie once Nettie's letters have been read. Celie's last letter to God reads:

> Dear God,
>
> That's it, say Shug. Pack your stuff. You coming back to Tennessee with me.
> But I feels daze.
> My daddy lynch. My mama crazy. All my little half-brothers and sisters no kin to me. My children not my sister and brother. Pa not pa.
> You must be sleep.

Order has been restored, the incest taboo has not been violated, Celie is confused but free and moving.

Janie's Signifyin(g) declaration of independence read in the starkest of terms to her husband, Joe, in *Their Eyes* is repeated in *The Color Purple*. As Celie is about to leave with Shug, this exchange occurs between her and her husband:

> Celie is coming with us, say Shug.
> Mr. _____'s head swivel back straight. Say what? he ast.
> Celie is coming to Memphis with me.
> Over my dead body, Mr. _____ say,
> . . . what wrong now?

> You a lowdown dog is what's wrong, I say. It's time to leave you and enter into the Creation. And your dead body just the welcome mat I need.
>
> Say what? he ast. Shock.
>
> All round the table folkses mouths be dropping open. . . .
>
> Mr. _____ start to sputter. ButButButButBut. Sound like some kind of motor.

This marvelous exchange refigures that between Janie and Joe. Celie's newly found voice makes "folkses mouths" drop open, and Mr. _____'s voice inarticulate and dehumanized, "like some kind of motor." A bit later, Celie continues, in triumph, to curse her oppressor:

> Any more letters come? I ast.
>
> He say, What?
>
> You heard me, I say. Any more letters from Nettie come?
>
> If they did, he say, I wouldn't give 'em to you. You two of a kind, he say. A man try to be nice to you, you fly in his face.
>
> I curse you, I say.
>
> What that mean? he say.
>
> I say, Until you do right by me, everything you touch will crumble.

This quasi-Hoodoo curse reads like one of Hurston's recipes for revenge that she published in her classic work on Vaudou, entitled *Tell My Horse* (1938). Significantly, these exchanges—Celie's first open defiance of her husband, Albert—are repeated or written in Celie's first two letters addressed to Nettie rather than to God. Celie's husband's desperate response follows:

> He laugh. Who you think you is? he say. You can't curse nobody. Look at you. You black, you pore, you ugly, you a woman. Goddam, he say, you nothing at all.

But Albert no longer has the power of the word over Celie, just as in Hurston Joe cannot recoup from Janie's Signifyin(g) on his manhood in public. This exchange continues:

> Until you do right by me, I say, everything you even dream about will fail. I give it to him straight, just like it come to me. And it seem to come to me from the trees,.
>
> Whoever heard of such a thing, say Mr. _____. I probably didn't whup your ass enough.
>
> Every lick you hit me you will suffer twice, I say. Then I say, You better stop talking because all I'm telling you ain't coming just from me. Look like when I open my mouth the air rush in and shape words.
>
> Shit. he say. I should have lock you up. Just let you out to work.
>
> The jail you plan for me is the one in which you will rot, I say. . . .
>
> I'll fix her wagon! say Mr. _____, and spring toward me.
>
> A dust devil flew up on the porch between us, fill my mouth with dirt. The dirt say, Anything you do to me, already done to you.
>
> Then I feel Shug shake me. Celie, she say. And I come to myself.
>
> I'm pore, I'm black, I may be ugly and can't cook, a voice say to everything listening. But I'm here.
>
> Amen, say Shug. Amen, amen.

* * *

Celie has at last issued her liberating (and liberated) call, while her friend Shug, like any black audience, provides the proper ritual response to a masterful performance: "Amen, say Shug. Amen, amen." Celie speaks herself free, as did Janie, but in a speaking we know only by its writing, in a letter to Nettie. Celie has conquered her foe, Albert, and the silences in her self, by representing an act of speech in the written word, in which she turns Albert's harsh curses back on him, masterfully.

Just as this scene of instruction echoes Janie's, so too is *The Color Purple* full of other thematic echoes of *Their Eyes Were Watching God*. Houses confine in *The Color Purple* just as they do in *Their Eyes*, but Celie, Nettie, Shug, and Janie all find a form of freedom in houses in which there are no men: Nettie's hut in Africa, Shug's mansion in Tennessee, and Janie's empty home in Eatonville. The home that Nettie and Celie inherit will include men, but men respectful of the inherent strength and equality of women. Celie and Nettie own this home, and the possession of property seems to preclude the domination of men.

Shug would seem to be a refugee from *Their Eyes*. It is Shug who teaches Celie that God is not an "old white man," that God is nature and love and even sex, that God is a sublime feeling:

> Here's the thing, say Shug. The thing I believe. God is inside you and inside everybody else. You come into the world with God. But only them that search for it inside find it. And sometimes it just manifest itself even if you not looking, or don't know what you looking for. Trouble do it for most folks, I think. Sorrow, lord. Feeling like shit.
>
> It? I ast.
>
> Yeah, It. God ain't a he or a she, but a It.
>
> But what do it look like? I ast.
>
> Don't look like nothing, she say. It ain't a picture show. It ain't something you can look at apart from anything else, including yourself. I believe God is everything, say Shug. Everything that is or ever was or ever will be. And when you can feel that, and be happy to feel that, you've found It.

But it is also Shug who teaches Celie about Janie's lyrical language of the trees, a language of nature in which God speaks in the same metaphors in which he spoke to Janie, a divine utterance which led Janie to enjoy her first orgasm, an experience that Shug tells Celie is God's ultimate sign of presence:

> She say, My first step from the old white man was trees. Then air. Then birds. Then other people. But one day when I was sitting quiet and feeling like a motherless child, which I was, it come to me: that feeling of being part of everything, not separate at all. I knew that if I cut a tree, my arm would bleed. And I laughed and I cried and I run all round the house. I knew just what it was. In fact, when it happen, you can't miss it. It sort of like you know what, she say, grinning and rubbing high up on my thigh.
>
> *Shug!* I say.
>
> Oh, she say. God love all them feelings. That's some of the best stuff God

did. And when you know God loves 'em you enjoys 'em a lot more. You can just relax, go with everything that's going, and praise God by liking what you like.

God don't think it dirty? I ast.

God don't think it dirty? I ast. And if we miss Shug's connection with Janie, Walker first describes Shug in terms in which she has described Hurston:

She do more then that. She git a picture. The first one of a real person I ever seen. She say Mr. _____ was taking something out of his billfold to show Pa an it fell out an slid under the table. Shug Avery was a woman. The most beautiful woman I ever saw. She more pretty then my mama. She bout ten thousand times more prettier then me. I see her there in furs. Her face rouge. Her hair like some thin tail. She grinning with her foot up on somebody motorcar. Her eyes serious tho. Sad some.

Compare that description with Walker's description of Hurston:

[She] loved to wear hats, tilted over one eye, and pants and boots. (I have a photograph of [Hurston] in pants, boots, and broadbrim that was given to me by her brother, Everette. She has her foot up on the running board of a car—presumably hers, and bright red—and looks racy.)[18]

There are several other echoes, to which I shall allude only briefly. Celie's voice, when she first speaks out against the will of Mr. _____, "seem to come to me from the trees" just as Janie's inner voice manifests itself under the pear tree. Celie, like Janie, describes herself as a "motherless child." Key metaphors repeat: Hurston's figure of nature mirroring Janie's emotions—"the rose of the world was breathing out smell" (*Their Eyes*)—becomes Shug and Celie's scene in which Shug teaches Celie to masturbate, using a mirror to watch herself:

I stand there with the mirror.

She say, What, too shame even to go off and look at yourself? And you look so cute too, she say, laughing. All dressed up for Harpo's, smelling good and everything, but scared to look at your own pussy. . . .

I lie back on the bed and haul up my dress. Yank down my bloomers. Stick the looking glass tween my legs. Ugh. All that hair. Then my pussy lips be black. Then inside look like a wet rose.

It a lot prettier than you thought, ain't it? she say from the door.

Later, in her first letter to Nettie, Celie uses the figure of the rose again in a simile: "Shug a beautiful something, let me tell you. She frown a little, look out cross the yard, lean back in her chair, look like a big rose."

In the same way that Walker's extends to the literal Hurston's figure of the rose of the world breathing out smell, she also erases the figurative aspect of Janie's metaphor for her narration to Phoeby ("mah tongue is in mah friend's mouf") by making Shug and Celie literal "kissin-friends," or lovers. That which is implicit in Hurston's figures Walker makes explicit. Walker, in addition, often reverses Hurston's tropes: whereas

Their Eyes accounts for the orgasm Janie experiences under the pear tree by saying, in free indirect discourse, "So this was a marriage!", Celie writes that when Mr. _____ beats her, she turns herself into a tree:

> He beat me like he beat the children. Cept he don't never hardly beat them. He say, Celie, git the belt. The children be outside the room peeking through the cracks. It all I can do not to cry. I make myself wood. I say to myself, Celie, you a tree. That's how come I know trees fear man.

Their Eyes' circular narration, in which the end is the beginning and the beginning the end, *The Color Purple* tropes with a linear narration. There are several other examples of these Signifyin(g) riffs.

Walker has Signified upon Hurston in what must stand to be the most loving revision, and claim to title, that we have seen in the tradition. Walker has turned to a black antecedent text to claim literary ancestry, or motherhood, not only for content but for structure. Walker's turn to Hurston for form (and to, of all things, the topoi of medieval romance known as "The Incestuous Father" and "The Exchanged Letter" for plot structure),[19] openly disrupts the patterns of revision (white form, black content) that we have discussed in Chapter 3. Even Walker's representation of Celie's writing in dialect echoes Hurston's definition of an "oral hieroglyphic," and her ironic use of speakerly language which no person can ever speak, because it exists only in a written text. This, too, Walker tropes, by a trick of figuration, one so clever that only Esu's female principle could have inspired it: people who speak dialect *think* that they are saying standard English words; when they write the words that they speak as "dis" or "dat," therefore, they spell "this" and "that." Walker, like Hurston, masters the illusion of the black vernacular by its writing, in a masterful exemplification of the black trope of Stylin' out.

Walker's revision of Hurston stands at the end of a chain of narration. Walker's text, like those by Toni Morrison, James Baldwin, Ann Petry, Paule Marshall, Leon Forrest, Ernest Gaines, John Wideman, and others, afford subsequent writers tropes and topoi to be revised. Endings, then, imply beginnings. Increasingly, however, after Walker and Reed, black authors could even more explicitly turn to black antecedent texts for both form and content. The tradition of Afro-American literature, a tradition of grounded repetition and difference, is characterized by its urge to start over, to begin again, but always to begin on a well-structured foundation. Our narrators, our Signifiers, are links in an extended ebony chain of discourse, which we, as critics, protect and explicate. As Martin Buber puts the relation in *The Legend of Baal-Shem:*

> I have told it anew as one who was born later. I bear in me the blood and spirit of those who created it, and out of my blood and spirit it has become new. I stand in the chain of narrators, a link between links; I tell once again the old stories, and if they sound new it is because the new already lay dormant in them when they were told for the first time.

While the principal silent second text is *Their Eyes Were Watching God*, Walker's critique of Celie's initial conception of God, and especially its anthropomorphism, revises a key figure in Rebecca Cox Jackson's narrative and perhaps surfaces as a parable for the so-called noncanonical critic.

Just after Celie and Shug have discovered, arranged, and read Nettie's purloined letters, Celie writes this to Nettie:

Dear Nettie,
    I don't write to God no more, I write to you.
    What happen to God, ast Shug.
    Who that? I say.
    . . . what God do for me? I ast.
    She say, Celie! Like she shock. He gave you life, good health, and a good woman that love you to death.
    Yeah, I say, and he give me a lynched daddy, a crazy mama, a lowdown dog of a step pa and a sister I probably won't ever see again. Anyhow, I say, the God I been praying and writing to is a man. And act just like all the other mens I know. Trifling, forgitful, and lowdown.

A few pages lager, Shug describes to Celie the necessity of escaping the boundaries caused by the anthropomorphism of God and calls this concept that of "the old white man." This, Celie confesses, is difficult: "Well, us talk and talk about God, but I'm still adrift. Trying to chase that old white man out of my head." Shug responds that the problem is not only "the old white man," but all men:

Still, it is like Shug say, You have got to git man off your eyeball, before you can see anything a'tall.
    Man corrup everything, say Shug. He on your box of grits, in your hand, and all over the road. He try to make you think he everywhere. Soon as you think he everywhere, you think he God. But he ain't. Whenever you trying to pray, and man plop himself on the other end of it, tell him to git lost, say Shug. Conjure up flowers, wind, water, a big rock.

This passage, most certainly, constitutes an important feminist critique of the complex fiction of male domination. But it also recalls a curious scene in Rebecca Cox Jackson's text. Indeed, Walker's text Signifies upon it. Earlier, I discussed Jackson's supernatural mastery of literacy. Jackson was careful to show that God's gracious act of instruction freed her from the domination and determination of her words (their order, their meaning) by her minister-brother, who be rearranging her words sought to control their sense. Jackson indeed became free, and freely interprets the Word of God in her own, often idiosyncratic way. But is Jackson's a truly liberating gesture, a fundamental gesture of a nascent feminism?

Jackson substitutes a mystical "white man," the image of whom Shug and Celie seek to dispel, for the interpretive role of the male, the relation of truth to understanding, of sound and sense. Jackson's account is strikingly vivid:

A white man took me by my right hand and led me on the north side of the
room, where sat a square table. On it lay a book open, and he said to me,
"Thou shalt be instructed in this book, from Genesis to Revelations." And
then he took me on the west side, where stood a table. And it looked like the
first. And said, "Yea, thou shall be instructed from the beginning of creation
to the end of time." And then he took me on the east side of the room also,
where stood a table and book like the two first, and said, "I will instruct
thee—yea, thou shall be instructed from the beginning of all things to the
end of all things. Yea, thou shall be well instructed. I will instruct."

When Samuel handed me to this man at my own back door, he turned
away. I never saw him any more. When this man took me by the hand, his
hand was soft like down. He was dressed all in light drab. He was bareheaded.
His countenance was serene and solemn and divine. There was a father and
a brother's countenance to be seen in his face.

And then I awoke, and I saw him as plain as I did in my dream. And after
that he taught me daily. And when I would be reading and come to a hard
word, I would see him standing by my side and he would teach me the word
right. And often, when I would be in meditation and looking into things which
was hard to understand, I would find him by me, teaching and giving me
understanding. And oh, his labor and care which he had with me often caused
me to weep bitterly, when I would see my great ignorance and the great
trouble he had to make me understand eternal things. For I was so buried in
the depth of the tradition of my forefathers, that it did seem as if I never
could be dug up.[20]

Jackson opposes the "white man" who would "teach me the word right,"
he who would stand "by me, teaching and giving me understanding,"
with the delineation of understanding imposed by her brother and, curiously enough, by "the depth of the tradition of my forefathers." So oppressive was the latter that, she admits, "it did seem as if I never could
be dug up."

Shug and Celie's conception of God Signifies upon these passages from
Jackson. Jackson's "white man" and Celie's, the speaking interpreter and
the silent reader, are identical until Celie, with Shug's help, manages to
"git man off your eyeball." Whereas Jackson suffocates under the burden
of tradition, "buried in the depth" as she puts it, Walker's text points to
a bold new model for a self-defined, or internally defined, notion of tradition, one black and female. The first step toward such an end, she tells
us, was to eliminate the "white man" to whom we turn for "teaching"
and the "giving [of] understanding." This parable of interpretation is
Walker's boldest claim about the nature and function of the black tradition and its interpretation. To turn away from, to step outside the white
hermeneutical circle and into the black is the challenge issued by
Walker's critique of Jackson's vision.

Notes

1. Rebecca Cox Jackson, *Gifts of Power: The Writings of Rebecca Jackson, Black Visionary, Shaker Eldress*, ed. by Jean McMahon Humez (Amherst: University of Massachusetts Press, 1981). See Alice Walker, "Gifts of Power: The Writings of Rebecca Jackson," in *In Search of Our Mothers' Gardens: Womanist Prose by Alice Walker* (New York: Harcourt Brace Jovanovich, 1983), pp. 71–82. The review first appeared in the November–December 1981 issue of *Black Scholar*. In a letter, Walker has informed me that Jackson's book "was the first book I read (I read almost nothing while writing *The Color Purple*) and reviewed *after* I finished. I took it as a sign that I was on the right track." The uncanny resemblances between key figures in Jackson's and Walker's texts suggest that forms of tradition and patterns of revision can be remarkably complex, indeed cultural.

2. Jackson, *Gifts of Power*, p. 107.

3. Ibid.

4. Ibid., pp. 107–8.

5. Ibid., p. 108.

6. Walker, "Gifts of Power," p. 73.

7. For Walker's explicit comments on Hurston, see *In Search of Our Mothers' Gardens*, pp. 83–116.

8. Amanda Smith, *An Autobiography: The Story of the Lord's Dealings with Mrs. Amanda Smith, the Colored Evangelist; Containing an Account of her Life Work of Faith and Her Travels in America, England, Ireland, Scotland, India and Africa, as an Independent Missionary* (1893; Chicago: Christian Witness Co., 1921). I wish to thank Mary Helen Washington for pointing this out to me.

9. Alice Walker, *The Color Purple* (New York: Harcourt Brace Jovanovich, 1982).

10. Quoted in Walker, *In Search of Our Mothers' Gardens*, p. 100.

11. Terry Eagleton discusses these aspects of epistolary fiction in *The Rape of Clarissa: Writing, Sexuality and Class Struggle in Samuel Richardson* (Minneapolis: University of Minnesota Press, 1982), p. 25.

12. Cited in ibid., p. 25.

13. Ibid., p. 26.

14. Jean Toomer, *Cane*, p. 204. Walker informs me that "All names in *Purple* are *family* or Eatonton, Georgia, community names. Kate was my father's mother. In real life she was the model for Annie Julia (in the novel), my grandfather's 'illegitimate' daughter (who in the novel is the wife, but who in real life was the granddaughter of Albert who in the novel is her father). It was *she*, Kate, my grandmother, who was murdered by her lover (he shot her) when my dad was eleven. Carrie was an aunt. But your version is nice, too, and my version is so confusing. For instance, the germ for Celie is Rachel, my step-grandmother: she of the poem 'Burial' in *Revolutionary Petunias*."

15. Walker writes, "*There is no book more important to me than this one* (including Toomer's *Cane*, which comes close, but from what I recognize is a more perilous direction)." *In Search of Our Mothers' Gardens*, p. 86. See also "The Divided Life of Jean Toomer," pp. 60–65.

16. Kate Nickerson points this out in an unpublished essay, "'From Listening to the Rest': On Literary Discourse Between Zora Neale Hurston and Alice Walker," p. 57.

17. Zora Neale Hurston, "Story in Harlem Slang," *The American Mercury* 45 (July 1942): 84–96.
18. Walker, "Zora Neale Hurston," p. 88.
19. See Margaret Schlauch, *Chaucer's Constance and Accused Queens* (New York: New York University Press, 1927), pp. 63–69. I am deeply appreciative of Dr. Elizabeth Archibald for pointing this out to me.
20. Jackson, *Gifts of Power*, pp. 146–47.

◆◆◆◆◆◆◆◆◆◆◆◆◆◆◆

Lettered Bodies and Corporeal Texts

WENDY WALL

In *Gyn/Ecology*, Mary Daly describes how one ideological group establishes power by imprinting its traces on the bodies of other people. Imprinting, she explains, often involves invading, cutting, impressing, and fragmenting.[1] In its depiction of rape, wife-beating, genital mutilation, and facial scarification, *The Color Purple* abounds with instances in which authority is inscribed on the human body. In the text, a patriarchy maintains power by rewriting the female body into powerlessness, thus denying the woman's ability to authorize herself. During the course of the novel, however, Celie learns to authorize herself through her letters; she acquires a means of re-inscribing the imprints and the contours of her body in such a way as to allow self-expression. Initially, she writes to heal the rift that has ensued from her sexual violation, to create an identity from fragmentation. Her writing takes a form, however, that yokes together unity and disparity, in that the epistolary style necessarily divides as it unifies; it consists of a series of discrete entries that form a whole. Likewise the "self" that emerges from Celie's development is a decentered one, precariously poised against and rift with a sense of Otherness. The novel, then, presents a strange conflation of text and body; both the novel's form and the main character's corporeal existence are disjunct entities with malleable, tenuous boundaries. When Mr. _____ sees Sophia giving Harpo orders, he predicts, "she going to switch the traces on you"[2]; Celie's development in the novel allows her to "switch the traces" imprinted on her, traces that limit and define her by circumscribing her within a fixed frame.

Celie's texts are born when she is raped and silenced; the epigraph to Celie's letters proclaims a threat: "You better not tell nobody but God. It'd kill your mammy." This external silencing forces a second mode of expression to unfold—Celie's diary-letters to God. She writes to understand the violation that has threatened her identity. "I am" are words under erasure in the first page, thus revealing the instability of her existence and the threat of "I am not" that plagues her. She crosses out the present tense of the verb, replacing it with the past: "I have always been a good girl." Her texts seek to recover that "goodness" that would allow her to state her existence without the mark of erasure; she wants to receive a reciprocal sign that will order her life and thus rewrite her as whole.

Although Celie's letters provoke no reciprocal communication, her lettered plea creates a means for her to enter a world of signification and rewrite herself. "Letter language" in *The Color Purple* is not merely, as Ian Watt suggests of the form, "the nearest record of consciousness in ordinary life"[3]; it is more than a window into the mental processes of the fictionalized individual (although Nettie's claim that writing allows her to release "bottled up" emotions suggests that this function is implicit as well). Celie's naiveté and brutal honesty in self-presentation also deny a critique of her letters as a series of concealments, erasures, or lies. Her writing is neither a pure channel of communication nor a duplicitous self-misrepresentation, but a complex means of restructuring herself, an active process in which she moves toward a self-realization through the mediation of language. In her letters, she may not merely convey, but reshape (by articulating in a form) her private internal experiences that remain hidden from her life of labouring acquiescence. The letters act as a second memory, a projected body that holds this hidden self.

Letters are the culmination of a series of anti-selves that Celie creates to mediate between herself and her oppressive environment. When she describes to Harpo how she copes with Mr. _____'s abuse, she reveals her strategy for relocating and thus preserving a "self." "It all I can do not to cry," she states, "I make myself wood. I say to myself, Celie, you a tree." She resists the impulse to rebel by becoming inanimate, a state which infects her entire world; for in ministering to Harpo, she realizes that she has lost all sentience: "Patting Harpo back not even like patting a dog. It more like patting another piece of wood. Not a living tree. . . ." Celie's attempt to negate her pain by desensitizing herself creates within her hollow spaces. In one instance, she attempts to overcome this numbness by placing a static image between herself and her world. While making love to her husband, she imagines the picture she has of Shug Avery "whirling and laughing" so that she can respond. "I know what he doing to me he done to Shug Avery and maybe she like it," Celie thinks, "I put my arm around him." Art becomes the second mediation which tries to counteract this first desensitizing barrier. Celie's letters create this mediation implicitly throughout the text, as she attempts both to preserve herself from and rewrite herself into sentience.

Letters become the surrogate body for Celie, an inanimate form that serves a dual purpose; it fends off pain by siphoning off her feelings of degradation, as well as allowing her to express and thus feel the intensity of her emotions. Her self-division is imposed upon her by her external circumstances; yet by displacing a part of herself onto this second body, she keeps intact that division. She compartmentalizes a suppressed "self" through her letters. The letters become the tenuous skin of her body, framing her internal thoughts in a realm separate from her outward actions. They demarcate inside/outside for Celie, persistently uncovering her inexpressible (and thus contained) thoughts. When Mr. _____ returns from hearing Shug sing, Celie has a thousand questions running through her mind; yet she merely works silently in the fields, displacing these queries onto her diary. In this way, writing perpetuates that initial fragmentation, and the letter form becomes a separate bodily frame.

Paradoxically, it is through writing that she attempts to keep intact a self, to unify the rift that has been inflicted upon her, to re-member her violated body through language. These letters, then, are poised against self-destruction; they are an attempt to preserve a "real" self by burying it within a diary. Celie's reason for not actively resisting the brutalities inflicted upon her is a strong sense of survival; she can survive these abuses only by recording them in a diary which acts as her second memory. She displaces her voice onto this silent, uncommunicated text. The letters become an attempt to keep her from being swallowed in anonymity; she knows that her mother's death was caused by her mother's attempt to align herself with her external life, specifically with her husband—"trying to believe his story kilt her" Celie writes. Celie's "nonbelief" is registered in her letters, thus preventing her from a rebellion that would cause her to be beaten, like Sophia, into submission. Nettie tells of meeting Sophia: "She suddenly sort of erased herself. It was the strangest thing, Celie! One minute I was saying howdy to a living woman. The next minute nothing living was there. Only a shape." When Celie contemplates herself in a mirror, she sees a being riddled with negation: "Nothing special here for nobody to love. No honey-colored hair, no cuteness. Nothing young and fresh." Yet, it is her act of contemplating herself in the mirror that invigorates her (gives her "blooming blood"), just as her contemplation of herself in her letters transforms and creates her anew.

The text of the novel, then, functions both to contain and fragment Celie. This process is accentuated by the epistolary form which, by definition, divides the text into tiny contained "packets" of language, recorded years apart, surrounded by space and gaps. Each letter is a separate entity with a recognizable border. When collected together, these letters create a form which divides, as Janet Altman explains, one marked by "hiatuses of all sorts: time lags between event and recording, between message transmission and reception; spatial separation between writer and addressee."[4] These gaps act as barriers between the writer and the outside world. Letters, Christina Gillis notes, imprison the self in words, safely locking the person between salutation and signature, and thus shutting out dialogue.[5] The autobiographical and non-retrospective stance "cloisters" the fictional writer temporally as well as spatially; because Celie cannot reflect on her actions from a later privileged viewpoint, but instead records them *as* she lives, she becomes framed in time, sealed in, what H. Porter Abbot calls, the true "hermetic fiction."[6] The notion of identity is problematized by this form. "To maintain existence through epistolary communication is a risky endeavor," Gillis remarks.

"Despite assertions of authenticity we are struck with the fragility of letters."[7] Celie is thus seen as a serial being, struggling to unite herself in a form that necessarily fractures (and makes tenuous) an identity.

Recent critical theory persistently reminds us that writing always fragments the self as it strives for an imposed unity; yet the epistolary style, with its emphasis on discrete entries and its limitation to a first person narration emphasizes these inherent disjunctive qualities of language. It is a continually interrupted text, "a paradox of patterned disorder: spatial design against temporal,"[8] and one which continually straddles the gulf between presence and absence. Within this disorder, Gillis states, "the whole cannot be examined without regard for the individual parts."[9] This commonplace is reinvested with meaning when discussing the epistolary form; for it exists only as a collection of fragments, piece-meal sections stitched together into a whole that coheres while revealing its seams. It is difficult to talk about Alice Walker's work without invoking the metaphor of the quilt, since it is her primary means of describing her art, and her characters' means of artistic expression.[10] The appropriateness of this folk craft in describing the epistolary style is obvious in that both are wholes that show the process of their construction.

The very form of *The Color Purple*, then, produces an analogue to the female body within the text, as both are continually fragmented and re-membered. Mr. _____ conceals Nettie's letters because she refuses to be seduced by him; he rapes her language because he is denied her body. The location of these letters also reveals a link with the body; they are hidden in a trunk along with Shug's underwear and pornographic pictures. Mr. _____'s abduction of Nettie's letters not only reveals the tenuousness of their communication, evidenced by the continual interruptions inherent in the epistolary form, but also exposes him as a voyeur to female communication. In *The Rape of Clarissa*, Terry Eagleton notes that letters are illicit intercourse; "The letter comes to signify female sexuality," he suggests, "that folded, secret place which is always open to violent intrusion."[11] Mr. _____'s erotic desires are displaced onto letters as well as pornography. "The male's desire to view the female's letter is namelessly voyeuristic," Eagleton states.[12] Both the female body and its texts become subject to violation by the male, who retains the power to encroach upon these private spheres.

Mr. _____'s trunk frames together the stolen letters and the fetishized female body, connecting the disrupted linguistic text and the dismembered body. African genital mutilation labeled in the text as "female initiation rites" (and "a bit of bloody cutting") similarly divides the body. A clitoridectomy desensitizes the female to erotic pleasure, thus binding her as an object for male exchange, silencing the language of her body. This bodily dismemberment creates a gap within the female, making her a "cipher" or a blank, like the spaces between Celie's entries that create narrative fissures in the text.

In some African cultures, the clitoridectomy is an attempt to strip away what is masculine in the female genitalia, to deny her phallic power by removing this protrusion.[13] Likewise, circumcision is considered a defeminization of the male. Genital mutilation is, thus, an attempt to recodify gender distinctions, to write sexual differentiation on the body through ritual. While the violence of these rituals seems to police the power structures of the society in a quite inhumane way, these rites also contain the radical notion that gender can be inscribed. Throughout *The Color Purple*, inherent biological gender characteristics are questioned; gender becomes an imposed categorization. Harpo tries to beat Sophia into being a submissive wife but eventually learns to enjoy his domestic role as housekeeper and let her play the "masculine" role in the marriage. Shug usurps masculine power when she speaks her mind: "Shug act more manly than most men . . . she bound to live her life and be herself no matter what," Mr. _____ comments. When he realizes that "Sophie and Shug are not like men . . . but they not like women either," we see that the codes attached to the body have been deconstructed. Celie is then free to alter a socially "gendered" role; she may engage in a lesbian relationship with Shug, one that replaces her role as wife, and she also may undertake what is considered a masculine position in establishing a business, albeit one that markets a female craft, sewing. Phallic power becomes a transferable quality which may be acquired and abandoned at will; like letters, these traces of power can be redirected.

The second aspect of the female initiation rite involves facial scarification, wounds which emblemize a submission to the traditions of the dominant power within the culture. The Olinka villagers force the young people to undergo this rite, "carving their identification as a people into their children's faces." This serves as the text's most obvious presentation of the authorization of the body; the inscription of a heritage on the body limits that person to a set culture and a set gender. Adam's decision to undergo this rite of initiation, however, subverts the aim of the ritual; as an American and a man, the marks on his body mis-identify. His outward signs misrepresent and thus scramble the means of gender and race identification.

Throughout the novel, Celie learns that the socially circumscribed body can be dissembled and reconstructed by re-imagining the self and projecting that image onto the world through language. Her shift in focus away from the physical body onto a dispersed self follows a pattern in the text of denying the "imagized" body. Nettie hangs Olinka art in her cabin, "platters, mats and pieces of tribal cloth" rather than her pictures of Christ, the Apostles, Mary, the Crucifixion, or other missionaries; these physical portraits make her feel "small." She feels engulfed by these representations that surround and limit her. Similarly, Nettie explains that Biblical illustrations are misleading; they depict bodies that are images of the power structure, rather than drawing them to correspond to historical evidence. The skin of the Ethiopians is "whitened" in the English Bible. "It is the pictures in the bible that fool you," Nettie states, "The pictures that illustrate the words. All of the people are white and so you just think all the people from the bible were white too. . . ." She severs the text into word and the picture that attempts to gloss it, a division that allows the picture to be erased and redrawn.

Shug also realizes that imagining God's body reduces him to a limited entity; the only body that is powerful enough to provide a form for the divine is a white man, since he inhabits the dominant position of power within her world. This is, of course, problematic since that position is infiltrated with corruption and tyranny. Shug ridicules Celie's image of God as a man "big and old and tall and graybearded and white" who wears "white robes and goes barefooted" and has "bluish gray" eyes. She tells Celie that her conception of God stems from a white ideological structure which is projected onto the Bible through the church. "When I found out God was white and a man, I lost interest," Shug says. Both Shug and Nettie attest to the falsity of the image of God, the depiction that "fixes" the words of scripture within a political system; from them, Celie learns to free "fixed" words for her imagination to recreate, to re-authorized God by deconstructing his body.

Shug's conception of God both relocates and regenders him. She argues that "God ain't a her or a she, but a It." Gender disappears when the body is elided, and God becomes internal; she tells Celie:

> God is inside you and inside everybody else . . . Don't look like nothing . . .
> It ain't a picture show. It ain't something you can look at apart from anything
> else, including yourself. I believe God is everything.

Celie's text of private letters to God, which have been directed toward the task of creating an internal self, are then quite appropriately addressed to this interior being. Once God is freed from his bodily limitations, he can pervade all of nature; Shug finds him by dissociating herself from his image:

> My first step from the old white man was trees. Then air, Then birds, Then
> other people. But one day when I was sitting quiet and feeling like a mother-
> less child, which I was, it come to me: that feeling of being part of everything,
> not separate at all, I knew that if I cut a tree, my arm would bleed . . .

Formerly, Celie reimagined herself as a tree in order to desensitize herself to pain and abuse; she is now encouraged to recuperate that tree-state in order to feel. The mediation between herself and the world is re-valued positively.

The attempt to dispel God's body, however, is a difficult task for Celie, who has bound up herself and her world in imagined, fixed states.

She realizes that Shug's advice ("You have to git man off your eyeball, before you can see anything a'tall") will allow her to believe once again in a spiritual being, but her old image of the "white-haired man" stubbornly resists erasure. "Whenever you trying to pray," Shug tells Celie, "and man plop himself on the other end of it, tell him to get lost . . . Conjure up flowers, wind, water, a big rock." But Celie, who has conjured up many anti-selves as mediators, can only see these substitute bodies as weapons; "every time I conjure up a rock, I throw it," she states. Celie's fear of rebellion reappears here; she wants to conserve the fixed image and can only dislodge it by violence. The move toward creating a porous, interchangeable body is one riddled with conflict.

Nettie writes Celie that she has undergone this same shift in perception toward internalizing God:

> God is different to us now, after all these years in Africa. More spirit than ever before and more internal. Most people think he has to look like something or someone—a roofleaf or Christ—but we don't. And not being tied to what God look like frees us.

Celie can, then, in her last letter write to "Dear God, dear stars, dear trees, dear sky, dear peoples. Dear everything. Dear God." This listing reveals that the form that God inhabits has become plural and interchangeable; he is identified in conjunction with this series of natural phenomena. She can give God a new form, shaped to her own contours; this allows her and God to "make love just fine." The sexual rift that had spawned her letters is retranslated into sexual harmony with this new understanding of a deity. Yet, this sexual dialogue between Celie and God then replaces her letters. Once more, letter and body become functional counterparts.

The deconstruction of the actual body of God is accompanied by a reinterpretation of racial traces on the body in the creation myth in Genesis. The Olinka people displace the Christian myth of origin through their belief that Adam was merely the first white man; he was an aberration, an albino, that was cast out from the African society because of his bodily disfigurement. Thus Genesis' original parents become mere societal defects within this culture, and white skin color is devalued. The Olinkas believe that snake means "parent"; within the myth, then, white culture attempts to crush their parents (the black people) for casting them out, rather than the devil for causing their fall. Instead of the creation myth explaining the fall, the Olinkas read it as an explanation of white prejudice. Differences in language subvert the missionaries' myth of creation; "naked" means "white." Thus Adam and Even cannot get rid of their nakedness, the trace of their race. The fall becomes cyclical as the bodies change in time; the outcast body recreates this societal exclusion. The Olinkas' revision of Genesis opens up the Eden story, implicating the body within a structure of interpretation; traces on the skin can be rewritten through myth.[14]

When Celie learns to reinscribe traces of race and gender on the body of God and to revisualize the biblical stories, she may then shift her perceptions of her own gendered role. Both Celie's letters and her notion of the body are unravelled and reconstructed. One scene is unwittingly telling in revealing this shift. After discovering that her husband has suppressed Nettie's letters, she decides to go to Memphis with Shug. "Over my dead body, Mr. _____ say"; Celie replies, "It's time to leave you and enter into the Creation. And your dead body just the welcome mat I need." Her flippant threat to dismember her husband to free herself ironically notes a serious shift in her thinking; for she is liberated only through bodily experience, through refragmenting herself in her letters and through her lesbian relationship with Shug. The function of her writing changes, as her conception of her own body is changed. Celie gradually begins to assert herself, airing her covert thoughts and resisting her position as slave to her husband. After she has established her independence in the scene I have described above, she still is hesitant to speak these thoughts that have previously been relegated to writing. When Shug informs her of her new affair, she is too hurt to reply; instead she writes her response. The conversation continues with Celie writing sarcastic remarks and Shug attempting verbally to persuade Celie of her love. This scene suggests an intermediary stage in Celie's development, as she dissolves this second "textual" body, her letters, and absorbs that "self" into herself once again.

The body acts as the ground which allows her to change. For she initially had been fragmented by an external force, by rape; but when she takes control of that fragmentation—solidifying the rupture by displacing part of herself into her letters—she is able to reunify herself. As she shifts her conception of her body (from ugliness to beauty, from stability to malleability), she similarly learns that she can reinscribe the confinements that had silenced her. Because Celie no longer writes what she cannot say but *records* her active self-authorization, her letters cease to act as an "other" confined self. The differences between inside and outside lessen as she no longer has to compartmentalize in letters a radically different internal self; instead she can release this self to interact with the external world. She can refuse to act as slave to her family, she can demand personal satisfaction in her relationships, she can realize her significance. The body is released into the form of her "lettered" text: an identity that is porous and disjunct. The division of internal/external that had been erected and affirmed by her letters is transmuted as more nebulous and elastic boundaries are constructed. She no longer contains herself completely. Celie rewrites the traces imprinted on her that had defined her, switching their signification and thus authorizing herself.

Alice Walker addresses her book "To the spirit: Without whose assistance Neither this book Nor I would have been written"; this dedication yokes together bodies and texts as written forms. When Walker signs the book "A.W., author and medium," she defines herself as a vessel in which the spirit may flow; this outer force reshapes the contours of her body so as to allow it to become a medium for writing. In her essay, "Writing *The Color Purple*," she describes her characters as autonomous entities which she merely coordinates and situates in an environment: "They . . . didn't like seeing buses, cars, or other people whenever they attempted to look out," Walker says of her new characters, "'Us don't want to be seeing none of this,' they said. 'It make us can't think.'"[15] She then proceeds to relocate in California in a climate that these characters can enjoy. This displacement of authorial responsibility, though not a unique literary device, calls attention to the notion of authorship as a mediating channel between internal imaginative characters and an outside world; with this connection, the author is linked to her main character. Like Celie's, Walker's body is equated with the text; both are written by this Other form. The textual apparatus reveals a clear link between the body and the linguistic text, implicating both within fields of interpretation and inscription.

The novel ends with an attempt to celebrate a unity that totalizes and recuperates all loose strands created through the plot. The family which had been rent by incest in the opening pages is now reconstructed, the stray sister returned. Celie's biological origins are rewritten and recovered through Nettie's letters. Anonymity is thwarted, as Mr. _____ loses his elided name and becomes Albert; similarly Mary Agnes regains her voice and name, and Celie is able to give her letters a signature. Time is stayed as Celie realizes that she is growing younger in her happiness, a state founded on the communion that exists because she and her family are safely enjoined. The traditional image of the harmonious banquet is rewritten into the barbeque. This form of banquet, Tashi notes, links the characters with the African community across the sea. The text thus works to coalesce into a formal supreme order. Bound up in Walker's metaphor of quilting is the notion of a final product as a pieced-together collage of assembled but disparate beings; this metaphor highlights the struggle for coherence and integrity evident in the conclusion of the text.

The unity that exists in the closure of the book, however, is a qualified one. Harpo reminds us that this closely-knit tie between the black family occurs only because there is a common enemy; they band together on the fourth of July, separate from the white people who celebrate a different history. Earlier in the text, the family similarity consolidated when Sophia was imprisoned. It is quite striking that Squeak, Harpo's lover, is willing to be raped by the white deputy, so that Harpo's wife can be released from prison, a gesture even more unusual because the family *expects* this sacrifice. The book traces out how these internal differences are repressed so that this greater chasm can be addressed; the individual's identity and the social harmony are unities that conceal difference and disruption beneath their surface. This thematic juxtaposition of unity and disunity corresponds to the epistolary structure, where parts remain disparate even as they are drawn together into a whole.

The text addresses the current rift between Anglo-American feminism and French feminist theories concerning the notion of bodily fragmentation and gender construction. Mainstream American feminists, like Mary Daly who I have quoted above, concentrate on the powerlessness of the fragmented woman—how she is silenced within the culture by forces that deny her coherence. French feminists, however, see disjunction and disunity as a desired state. Woman's marginal position creates her as internally divisive and "partitioned"; as one feminist notes, "this division-in-herself marks woman's specificity,"[16] and thus makes her capable of disrupting fixities within the culture.

In *The Color Purple*, Walker walks a thin line between these two notions, positioning herself between the two. She does not fail to point out the horrors of Celie's violent division by rape, yet she indicates that Celie's control of this division serves as a tool for reworking her position. Violation can be revised so as to become an empowering experience. At the conclusion of the novel, Celie's merging of consciousness, however, merely points to another existing division; the focus of the book shifts from the split within black culture along gender lines to the split between an oppressive white power structure and this unified black culture. Although Celie can resolve her double-consciousness, she still will have to suppress her desires within the culture at large; for when Eleanor Jane's baby grows up, Sophie makes it clear that he will subject her people to internal division: "I got my own troubles . . . and when Reynolds Stanley grow up, he's gon be one of them." When Eleanor Jane argues that her son will be different ("I won't let him be mean to colored"), Sophie cries, "You and whose army?" With this dialogue, the reader is left knowing that Celie, like the others, will once again silently acquiesce externally while revolting internally.

In noting this process of unity/disunity, Walker furthers W. E. B. Du Bois' famous remark on the Afro-American's double-consciousness; for she locates this division within the black community as well as in its relationship with a more powerful ruling class. The issue of sexism is problematized because its roots are within the African culture. For this reason, her book is quite controversial, playing off two critical camps. And it has been decried by both feminists and black literary theorists as a result. Its attempt to explore the gap between these two polemical ideologies makes the book an unsettling force.

The qualified unity at the conclusion of the book also calls attention to Alice Walker's attempt to situate her text within a dialogue created by postmodernist inquiry. The strange nature of communication in the text—signaled by the criss-crossed letters, letters written to an absence, letters received from the dead, and hidden and confiscated letters—undercuts the stability of a community formed through mutual understanding and calls attention to the inherent problems within the processes of reading, writing, and interpretation. Her use of the epistolary style introduces the reader to hermeneutical issues; "Diary fiction, by its very nature," Abbot states, "keeps the subject of verbal representation in focus."[17] It is a form which "explicitly articulates the problematics involved in the creation, transmission, and reception of literary texts."[18] In epistolary synecdoche, text stands for writer; we see no distanced description of the writer, but the world solely as a construction of language, with tremendous emphasis on the act of writing. Specifically, in *The Color Purple*, the fact that no letters are ever exchanged (so that a running dialogue can occur) indicates a very contemporary solipsistic view of the absence within communication, or rather, the model of sender/receiver broken down completely. The fragmentation of the text and its connections to the body are issues currently addressed by such theorists as Peter Brooks and Roland Barthes, who both use an erotic model to explain textual interpretation.[19]

It would be negligent to argue, then, that *The Color Purple*, in its attempt to conserve and preserve a material grounding for artifice, is a throwback to a simpler, naive type of writing. For the work acknowledges and revises the changed relationship between a text and its reader. The epistolary form complicates the notion of audience, making the reader a voyeur (like Albert) to a private and intimate confession. This is an unsettling position; reading is portrayed as an act of intrusion, of violation. The writer must also become unsettled within a form that accentuates what Derrida terms a "crise de la destination"; it constantly asks "for whom and to whom does the writer write?" Walter Ong notes that the form disrupts the notion of the writer:

> The audience of the diarist is . . . encased in fictions. First of all, we do not normally talk to ourselves—certainly not in long, involved sentences and paragraphs. Second, the diarist pretending to be talking to himself has also, since he is writing, to pretend he is somehow not there. And to what self is she talking? To the self he imagines he is? Or would like to be?[20]

Celie's diary fiction is complicated further by her salutations both to God and to her sister, entities whose existence are called into question. The dislocation of the addressee and thus the audience indicates a text aware of its readers; this awareness perhaps prompts such texts as John Barth's *Letters* and Saul Bellows' *Herzog*, which, like *The Color Purple*, use the epistolary form within a postmodernist discourse.[21]

Walker's grounding of her text within a historical framework and a defined feminist polemic implicates her within a current investigation into the future of fiction. John Barth's famous essay, "The Literature of Exhaustion," predicted that the novel form could only be saved by a program of self-conscious play.[22] "In the future," Raymond Federman echoes in *Surfiction*, "the primary purpose of fiction will be to unmask its own fictionality, to expose the metaphor of its own fraudulence."[23]

Critics, tired of this novelistic *ecriture* in postmodernism, have variously seen this self-exposure as evasive, unethical, or narrowly focused. Ihab Hassan notes of recent fiction:

> Whatever is truly new in it evades the social, historical and aesthetic criteria that gave an identity to the avant-garde in other periods. The force of evasion or absence in the new literature is radical indeed; it strikes at the roots and induces, metaphorically, a great silence.[24]

Walker's text attempts to re-energize the novel by appropriating a new history and a feminist perspective that refuses social evasion and thus explodes this imminent silence.

In recreating a literary form that unsettles critical communities and by utilizing what I have presented as a "dialectical unity," Walker has attempted to write a space for her novel within the postmodernist program. She echoes Borges' argument against the novel's exhaustion: "Literature is not exhaustible for the simple and sufficient reason that no single book is. A book is not an isolated entity; it is a relationship, an axis of innumerable relationships.[25] *The Color Purple* seeks to foreground the plurality of these "innumerable relationships" through the epistolary form as well as through the novel's emphasis on revisionary history. Walker exploits an elusive, elliptical writing style, informed with the play between presence and absence. She attempts to reinscribe the novel, placing it in a liberating but precarious position—one that reveals the text's self-awareness of the subversive, fragmenting nature of language, and yet absorbs that dialectical play within a new postmodern container, a new elastic form. This form attempts to work within a grounded polemic, thus responding to the challenge of social and political problems, to the frighteningly real pressures that threaten the human body. What can the novel do once it admits its own fictional process of construction? *The Color Purple* answers by "switching the traces" that threaten to silence literary forms and by positing a qualified affirmation by "fragmented unity"; it is a quilt that exposes its seams and yet still may function to accommodate the human body: simultaneously rewriting coldness into warmth, disparate interpretative axes into a mosaic and dialogic voice, oppression into self-authorization.

Notes

1. Mary Daly, *Gyn/Ecology: A Metaethics of Radical Feminism* (Boston: Beacon Press, 1978), see p. 110 and pp. 155–178.
2. Alice Walker, *The Color Purple* (New York: Washington Square Press, 1982), p. 41.

3. Ian Watt, *The Rise of the Novel* (Berkeley: University of California Press, 1957), p. 193.

4. Janet Altman, *Epistolarity: Approaches to a Form* (Columbus: Ohio State University, 1982), p. 140.

5. Christina Gillis, *The Paradox of Privacy* (Gainesville, Fla.: Univ. of Florida Press, 1984), p. 5. On pages 1–13, Gillis discusses *Clarissa*'s epistolary style in terms of a spatial correspondence: the rendering of internal space through architecture, while I discuss this private space as the human body itself.

6. H. Porter Abbot, "Letters to the Self: the Cloistered Writer in Nonretrospective Fiction," *PMLA* 95 (1980), p. 23.

7. Gillis, cited above, p. 9.

8. Ibid., cited above, p. 5.

9. Ibid.

10. See, for example, her essay, "Writing *The Color Purple*," in which she describes her simultaneous quilting and writing, and *In Search of Our Mothers' Gardens*, a collection of essays that invoke this metaphor throughout.

11. Terry Eagleton, *The Rape of Clarissa* (Minneapolis: University of Minnesota Press, 1982), p. 54.

12. Ibid.

13. See Mary Daly's discussion of clitoridectomies in *Gyn/Ecology*, cited above.

14. It is also strange that this reinterpretation of the myth is not included in Nettie's letters, thus revealing that either some letters are suppressed, or this revision is Celie's own; in either case, Celie alone authorizes this new interpretation within the text—her new conception of the malleable body written into history.

15. Alice Walker, "Writing *The Color Purple*," in *Black Women Writers (1950–1980)*, ed. Mari Evans (Garden City, N.Y.: Doubleday, 1983), p. 454.

16. Alice Jardine, in "Gynesis," states this in discussing Eugenie Leomoiine-Luccioni's ideas in particular. *Diacritics* 12 (1982), p. 62.

17. H. Porter Abbot, *Diary Fiction: Writing as Action* (Ithaca: Cornell University Press, 1984), p. 39.

18. Altman, cited above, p. 212.

19. Peter Brooks' *Reading for the Plot* discusses the reader's drive to work through and thus "plot" a text in terms of the "desire" for satiation. Roland Barthes' *The Pleasure of the Text*, directly links the body and the text; he describes the reader's surrender to the jouisance of reading, the play of contradictions and immersion into a world of sensation. His *S/Z* also discusses the fragmentation of the female body by fracturing Balzac's *Sarrasine* into a series of codes; text and body are linked implicitly.

20. Walter Ong, "The Writer's Audience Is Always a Fiction," *PMLA* 90 (1975), p. 20.

21. Perhaps my argument resonates with the strategy used by Borges's Pierre Menard, whose exact reconstruction of *Don Quixote* is interpreted differently in light of his historical era; for Alice Walker merely appropriates the epistolary form, rather than subverting it in any significant fashion. Yet, she cannot have used a mode of communication specifically associated with the female innocently. This form signals that certain issues will be at stake within the text; Altman notes that "the choice of the epistle as a narrative instrument can foster certain patterns of thematic emphasis, narrative action. . . ." Thus Walker's appropriation of this form *at this time* reveals a self-conscious attempt to address current issues of gender hermeneutics, issues which would not have existed in the same critical climate as when, for example, *Clarissa* was written. And Walker does modify and relocate this

female discourse, situating it within an Afro-American tradition, thus reinscribing this female form.

22. John Barth, "The Literature of Exhaustion," in *Surfiction*, ed. Raymond Federman (Chicago: Swallow Press, 1975), p. 33.

23. Raymond Federman, in his introduction to *Surfiction* (Chicago: Swallow Press, 1975), p. 8.

24. Ihab Hassan, *The Literature of Silence* (New York: Alfred A. Knopf, 1967), p. 41.

25. Jorge L. Borges, "A Note on (Toward) B. Shaw," as quoted by Robert Alter, cited above.

◆◆◆◆◆◆◆◆◆◆◆◆◆◆

Poetry as Preface to Fiction

THADIOUS DAVIS

The recent popularity of fiction by African-American women authors has almost obscured the remarkable work in poetry since the 1960s. Throughout the 1970s and 1980s, poets, such as June Jordan, Sonia Sanchez, Jayne Cortez, and Audre Lorde, have engendered a distinctly female world while empowering a distinctly African-American vision of life. Several of these women writers are multi-talented, working in poetry and in fiction. For example, Sherley Anne Williams has created the *Peacock Poems* and *Dessa Rose*, a feminist historical novel, and Rita Dove has produced award-winning poetry and short fiction. The best known of those who have moved easily between literary genres and creative forms is Alice Walker, the premiere African-American and Southern author of her generation. The fiction which she has produced since 1970 accelerated in acclaim with the publication of *The Color Purple* in 1983; however, her poetry, first published in 1968, has yet to attract a critical audience. Perhaps that is because Walker, a "womanist," is more engaging as a fictionist into whose works those outside of her referential realm as a Southern-born woman of color can enter safely with recognizable gendered signposts for attenuating their own experiences. Perhaps it is because her poetry is less accessible in its muted explorations of gendered pain and racial deprivation. Perhaps it is because few readers choose these days to curl up with a book of poems after a long day or week of multiple assaults to the senses. Or perhaps, as a cynic might think, it is simply bad poetry.

Walker's four books of poetry have appeared almost evenly spaced in her career: *Once* in 1968; *Revolutionary Petunias* in 1973; *Goodnight, Willie Lee, I'll See You in the Morning* in 1979; and *Horses Make a Landscape Look More Beautiful* in 1984. (It is more than likely now time for another volume to appear, given the spacing of the first four.) This near regularity in publication prompted my rereading Walker's poems, at first individually, then contextually, and finally intertextually with her novels and essays. The result is this meditation on the function of poetry in the career and canon of a fiction writer.

While not the most powerful of African-American poetic voices, Walker's is most instructive about the artist's resources and resonance.

> The writing of my poetry is never consciously planned, although I become aware that there are certain emotions I would like to explore. Perhaps my unconscious begins working on poems from these emotions long before I am aware of it. I have learned to wait patiently (sometimes refusing good lines, images, when they come to me, for fear they are not lasting), until a poem is

ready to present itself—*all* of itself, if possible. I sometimes feel the urge to write poems way in advance of ever sitting down to write. There is a definite restlessness, a kind of feverish excitement that is tinged with dread. The dread is because after writing each batch of poems I am always convinced that I will never write poems again. I become aware that I am controlled by them, not the other way around. I put off writing as long as I can. Then I lock myself in my study, write lines and lines and lines, then put them away, underneath other papers, without looking at them for a long time. I am afraid that if I read them too soon they will turn into trash; or worse, something so topical and transient as to have no meaning—not even to me—after a few weeks. . . . I realize that while I am writing poetry, I am so high as to feel invisible, and in that condition it is possible to write anything.[1]

Ten years after these words first appeared in John O'Brien's 1973 *Interviews with Black Writers*, Alice Walker collected them with few emendations into *In Search of Our Mothers' Gardens: Womanist Prose*. Her disclosures, rhetorically typical of poets' descriptions of process and practice, situate poetry at one necessary emotional center of her creative life; moreover, they offer an experiential reference symbolically locating her poetry in relation to her fiction: "Then I lock myself in my study, write lines and lines and lines, then put them away, underneath other papers, without looking at them for a long time." In context, her reference is to obscuring the lines from immediate sight, away from any possibility of rereading or revising or rethinking or restructuring, but taken within the grain of her canon, the reference may be read as a sign of a conscious relocation of the poetry as subtext underneath texts, those other papers, and read as a signal of transference taking place from the poetry to fiction, her other writings.

Walker's canon is much more organic and holistic than reading the fiction alone or the fiction and the essays might lead one to infer. It flows from the often dark interior, an internality which once refracted takes shape in the literal, the externality of physical places, people, voices, and institutions, all reflections of the visions conjured out of the night of a soul's deep struggle to actualize its existence concretely in discrete moments. Those moments transmuted become the action and events, the mythologies of multiple selves so prominent in her fictions.

Once, her first book of poems, originated from a traumatic pregnancy in Walker's senior year at Sarah Lawrence. During the winter of 1965, she contemplated suicide, practicing how to slash her wrists with a razor blade she kept under her pillow. Fortunately, the act proved unnecessary because a college friend located an abortionist. The experience of waiting suspended between life and death, and of finding sudden release spilled out in one week of nonstop writing of the poems in *Once*, published three years later. Her discovery in the experience was, she has said, "how alone woman is, because of her body." Aloneness of the female body, including mind and matter, is the authorizing moment for her poetry and also the premise for much of her fiction. She has recalled about *Once:*

"the book itself did not seem to me important; only the writing of the poems, which clarified for me how very much I loved being alive. It was this feeling of gladness that carried over into my first published short story, 'To Hell with Dying.'"

Not only that first published story, but all those in her first book of short stories, *In Love & Trouble: Stories of Black Women* (1973), which ends with "To Hell with Dying," reconfigure the emotional nexus of *Once*. The thematic divisions of the two books are identical in exploring the immediate past and the unimagined future: Africa, love, civil rights, suicide, though the ordering is not. The ironical story "The Diary of an African Nun" reconstitutes the emotionally ambivalent tone of "Karamojans," a sequence of short poems set in an East Africa rife with cultural clashes and the incongruities between European and African ideology. The African name chosen for Dee, the ambiguously figured daughter in the story "Everyday Use," is "Wangero Leewanika Kemanjo," comparable to "Wangari," the Kikuyu name given to the "I" narrator, a young African-American college student in "African Images: Glimpses from a Tiger's Back," the poetic sequence opening *Once* and questioning how to reclaim an alien heritage. The explosive dynamics of interracial love affairs and patriarchal approval links "The Child Who Favored Daughter" back to "Ballad of the Brown Girl": "the next morning/her slender/neck broken/ her note short/and of cryptic/collegiate make—/just 'Question—./did ever brown/daughter to black/father a white/baby/take—?'"[2] Intergenerational attraction and sexual desire between black female students and their white male teachers connect "We Drink the Wine in France" from *In Love & Trouble* and "So We've Come At Last To Freud" from *Once*. Marilyn of "Chic Freedom's Reflection" defines Ann Marion, the comfort-conscious revolutionary in *Meridian* (1976); "Compulsory Chapel" resurfaces in the unflattering representation of Saxon College also in *Meridian*. Though seemingly superficial in a truncated sketch, such parallels abound as do numerable others between *Once* and the later fictional texts. A positioning of parallels does, however, suggest a surface function of Walker's poetry in relationship to her fiction. *Once*, and the poems that follow it, charts an emotive-responsive chronicle of autobiographical incidents and an emotionally ciphered exploration of formative ideas that are developed thematically in subsequent fictional texts, both short stories and novels.

Walker has said that since the writing of that first book of poems "it seems to me that all of my poems—and I write groups of poems rather than singles—are written when I have successfully pulled myself out of a completely numbing despair, and stand again in the sunlight. Writing poems is my way of celebrating with the world that I have not committed suicide the evening before." A function of her poetry, then, is a psychological exploration of self, a mediating of the consciousness of one's very existence and an attending to the emotional determinants of that existence, which is subsequently reformulated and inscribed in her fiction. For Walker, poetry is the experience of emotional purging, a release of emotion in expressions usually brief, but occasionally extended over several moods encapsulating one dominant idea, the development of which takes place in the longer fictional pieces. In "How Poems are Made/A Discredited View," she writes:

> Letting go
> in order to hold on
> I gradually understand how poems are made.
>
> There is a place the fear must go.
> There is a place the choice must go.
> There is a place the loss must go.
> The leftover love.
> The love that spills out
> of the too full cup
> and runs and hides
> its too full self
> in shame.
>
> . . . .
>
> I understand how poems are made.
> They are the tears
> that season the smile.[3]

One of the dominant discourses in Walker's poetry is the idea of "the too full self," the spilling over into a reconciliation of self, the healing of the fractured physical body or mind, beautifying it to reflect the reality of an inner beauty or essence, the "soul" in both a black linguistic sense and a philosophical sense. As an erasure of a fractured and wounded self, reconciliation comes out of pain and despair, dark nights of the soul struggling with epistemological and existential questions. "Sometimes I feel so bad/I ask myself/Who in the world/Have I murdered?" This question posed in "Family Of" from *Horses Make a Landscape Look More Beautiful* is not unlike the one Meridian's mother asks, "Have you stolen anything?" "Would you kill for freedom" is another of the questions in *Revolutionary Petunias;* it is the same question that culminates in Meridian Hill's ideological split with her radical friends. To release oneself from the physical prison that the body maimed by cultural conditional and social constructs can become requires self-examination, but also self-confrontation. In the title poem of *Revolutionary Petunias*, "Sammy Lou of Rue/sent to his reward/the exact creature who/murdered her husband,/using a cultivator's hoe/with verve and skill;/and laughed fit to kill/in disbelief/at the angry, militant pictures of herself."[4] On her way to the electric chair, Sammy Lou's last words are "'Always respect the word of God,'" and "'Don't yall forget to *water*/my purple petunias.'" She prefigures Sofia in *The Color Purple*, and the short sketch "Petunias" from *You Can't Keep a Good Woman Down* (1981) and the unnamed narrator of "How Did I Get Away with Killing One of the Biggest Lawyers in the State? It Was Easy" from the same collection of short stories. A racially defined avenger, Sammy Lou refuses the images projected onto her. Having taken the life of a destroyer, she goes to her own death preserving both beauty and life.

The cumulative effect of much of Walker's poetry is strangely unsettling because death and what Sweet Honey in the Rock calls "The Other Side" are not mysterious or frightening, but rather comforting, a resort area for refurbishing the worn body, a respite for the tired mind, a relief for the bruised and abused ego, sight for the blinded eye. In the poems of *Revolutionary Petunias*, the Civil Rights movement becomes an agent for freeing individuals from a spiritually deadening lethargy that functioned as an escape from the racism circumscribing their lives. Freedom, however, burdens with isolation and loneliness and death. "[W]e, cast out alone/to heal/and re-create ourselves," Meridian writes of "catharsis, redemption and hope," individual transcendence over suffering and confusion.[5]

In her poetry, Walker situates a self within familial and social constructs, just as she does in her prose. Though there is an active social consciousness, its manifestations are in a passive, reflexive unconsciousness tapped primarily in moments of poetic experiences, that might loosely be termed out of body to evoke the spirituality embedded in the transforming or transformed self. The title poem ending the collection *Goodnight, Willie Lee, I'll See You in the Morning* (1979) argues resurrection and reunion both in the here and now and in the hereafter where promised renewals and beginnings can occur:

> Looking down into my father's
> dead face
> for the last time
> my mother said without
> tears, without smiles
> without regrets
> but with *civility*
> 'Good night, Willie Lee, I'll see you
> in the morning.'
> And it was then I knew that the healing
> of all our wounds
> is forgiveness
> that permits a promise
> of our return
> at the end.[6]

* * *

This tone, the civility of the mother's voice and the compassion of the daughter's thought, anticipates the conclusion of *The Color Purple*, published four years later, with a reformulated premise that healing, forgiveness, and return, literally from the dead in the novel, are the balm of familial misery and personal pain.

The metaphysical concerns prefaced in the poetry coalesce in the transformations of *The Temple of My Familiar* (1989), though Walker's first novel, *The Third Life of Grange Copeland* (1970), and those thereafter also privilege the necessary seed of transformative power, of control over the ideality of self and the reality of self reflected in the physical world. Meridian's spiritual essence, for instance, is part of the spirituality prefaced by the concentration of vision, sight, renewal and return of beauty. The trope prevalent throughout is the eye, blinded by a brother's BB gun and a family's racially determined poverty in the rural South. The healthy sighted eye is torn and shattered, bloodied and scarred, into unseeing and a sickness of self unseen. "Did I change after the accident?" is the persistent question Walker asks after confronting her memories of never looking up and retreating into herself after being wounded in the eye. (See "Beauty: When the Other Dancer is the Self," which ends *In Search of Our Mothers' Gardens*.)

Hierarchies of power oppress the powerless until by miracle or verbal design, the powerless transform self by accessing, without naming, the resources that might otherwise be labeled liabilities. Walker's expressed particularities encompass Southern segregation, American racism, family violence, macho expressionism, female reproduction, and more. In "Remember?" the poem functioning as invocation in *Horses*, she asks:

> Remember me?
> I am the girl
> with the dark skin
> whose shoes are thin
> I am the girl
> with rotten teeth
> I am the dark
> rotten-toothed girl
> with the wounded eye
> and the melted ear.

The autobiographical references in this inscription of self convey a meaning that all the particles of a fully alive being are not aspects of health and happiness; sickness and despair also make up the litanies of the poet intoning worlds different from her archetypal American South, worlds in which the dark wounded girl becomes the woman "with the healing eye/the ear that hears" and "offering two flowers/whose roots are twin/ Justice and Hope." Written before *The Color Purple*, the poem evokes not only associations with Walker herself, but with her daughter Celie and the ideology sustaining her within her self and world.

Walker's strongest poems may be those in which her history, heritage, and hope in the South collide, implode, and reverberate with pain and longing and desire for changing the landscape of oppression delimiting her youth. "What is the point/of being artists/if we cannot save our life?" Walker asks in "Songless" from *Horses:*

> That is the cry
> that wakes us
> in our sleep.
> Being happy is not the only
> happiness.

Midway in the poem, she turns to a new archetype of difference for the songless:

> They say in Nicaragua
> the whole
> government
> writes,
> makes music,
> and paints, saving their own
> and helping the people save
> their own lives.

The landscape of oppression and the potential of the artist to change it shift imperceptibly from the American South to Latin America, a shift most evident in *The Temple of My Familiar.* It confirms that the world Walker sees in an unlimited sightedness is that same large encompassing one observable by Rebecca Grant Walker, who, as a toddler, stared into her mother's bluish scarred eye and saw a world there, the world shaped as she believed it shaped after seeing it repeatedly on the television show *The Blue Marble.* The "I" consciousness, narrated voice as opposed to the eye, the seeing and sightless orb, the sense and the senseless must be supplanted by vision (inner) and visionary spirituality.

Impinging upon the ideology of Walker's canon is a positive discourse on reproduction; a metaphor driving the rebirth, transformation imagery. Access to region and to gender is through adversity, the South of poverty and segregation, the body of pregnancy and abortion or birth, both adversities that can become something other only after reconciliation and healing, and sometimes death, have been completed. Groups of poems in *Once* and *Revolutionary Petunias* prefigure these concerns structured into *The Third Life of Grange Copeland*, particularly in the character Mem, who is brutalized because she is a reproducing female, and in *Meridian*, but most graphically in *The Color Purple* in Celie's life, latently in Shug's and Sofia's. Like the poems, all of these fictional texts incorporate the gender-based adversities of reproduction and loss, and amend the physical and emotional impact of racial discrimination and regional poverty.

In the long poem "In These Days" from *Horses*, Walker writes:

> Gloria made me aware of how much we lose by denying,
> exiling or repressing parts of ourselves
> So that other parts,
> grotesque and finally lethal
> may creep into that light.
> 'Women must seize the sources of reproduction,' she says
> knowing her Marx and her Sanger too.

Yet it is not modern philosophy, politics, or science, that most of her poems infuse into her fictional texts. It is an old-fashioned religion, long since rejected by Walker herself, but nonetheless troubling the life waters of the contemporary writer, the educated daughter away from family and folk, legend and lore, while still revealing meaningful constructs she can ascribe to those others. As in "Burial" from *Revolutionary Petunias*, an autobiographical poem in which she returns with her daughter to the South for the funeral of her grandmother Rachel Walker and meditates on that life:

> As a young woman, who had known her? Tripping
> eagerly, 'loving wife,' to my grandfather's
> bed. Not pretty, but serviceable. A hard
> worker, with rough, moist hands. Her own babies dead
> before she came.
> *Came to seven children,*
> *To aprons and sweat,*
> *Came to quiltmaking.*
> *Came to canning and vegetable gardens*
> *big as fields.*
> *Came to fields to plow.*
> *Cotton to chop.*
> *Potatoes to dig.*
> *Came to multiple measles, chickenpox,*
> *and croup.*
> *Came to water from springs.*
> *Came to leaning houses one story high.*
> *Came to rivalries. Saturday night battles.*
> *Came to straightened hair, Noxzema, and*
> *feet washing at the Hardshell Baptist church.*
> *Came to zinnias around the woodpile.*
> *Came to grandchildren not of her blood*
> *whom she taught to dip snuff without sneezing.*
> *Came to death blank, forgetful of it all.*

Rachel Walker's life is the stuff that Celie's is made of. That old time religion at Ward's Chapel A.M.E. cannot comfort when this life is remembered, but it can foreground the reality or the necessity of a faith beyond the self, whether that faith be in a daughter's touch or voice, in feminism or womanism, in civil right or activism, in artistic freedom or determination, all figured somehow on the edge of eye, as Walker reflects at the end of "Burial": "Not for the dead, but for the memories. None of/them sad. But seen from the angle of her/death." Seeing and insisting on that internality's right to external meaning and being is what Walker does best in her poems, just sitting at a fire, watching a garden, planting a tree, observing the beauty of being alive, and this is the quiet notion of life celebration that she reconstitutes in her fiction. Walker concludes "On Stripping the Bark from Myself," from *Goodnight, Willie Lee*, with the stanza:

> My struggle was always against
> an inner darkness: I carry within myself
> the only known keys
> to my death—to unlock life, or close it shut
> forever. A woman who loves woodgrains, the color
> yellow
> and the sun, I am happy to fight
> all outside
> murderers
> as I see I must.

Resurgence and resurrection, the simplicity of a soul raised from the dead in a repetitious rite of rebirth, renewal, reproduction, this is the self-mission of Walker's poetry that is the subtext in her novels and stories. That poetic mission is Alice Walker's preface to fiction and to life.

Notes

1. Alice Walker, *In Search of Our Mothers' Gardens: Womanist Prose* (San Diego: Harcourt Brace Jovanovich, 1983), p. 250.
2. *Once* (New York: Harcourt Brace Jovanovich, 1968), p. 73.
3. *Horses Make a Landscape Look More Beautiful* (San Diego: Harcourt Brace Jovanovich, 1984), p. 17.
4. *Revolutionary Petunias & Other Poems* (New York: Harcourt Brace Jovanovich, 1973), p. 29.
5. *Meridian* (New York: Harcourt Brace Jovanovich, 1976), p. 219.
6. *Good Night, Willie Lee, I'll See You in the Morning* (New York: Dial Press, 1979), p. 53.

◆◆◆◆◆◆◆◆◆◆◆◆◆◆

Reading and Resistance: *The Color Purple*

BELL HOOKS

The Color Purple broadens the scope of literary discourse, asserting its primacy in the realm of academic thought while simultaneously stirring the reflective consciousness of a mass audience. Unlike most novels by any writer it is read across race, class, gender, and cultural boundaries. It is truly a popular work—a book of the people—a work that has many different meanings for many different readers. Often the meanings are not interesting, contained as they are within a critical discourse that does not resist the urge to simplify, to overshadow, to make this work by a contemporary African-American writer mere sociological treatise on black life or radical feminist tract. To say even as some critics do that it is a modern day "slave narrative" or to simply place the work within the literary tradition of epistolary sentimental novels is also a way to contain, restrict, control. Categorizing in this way implies that the text neither demands nor challenges, rather that it can be adequately and fully discussed within an accepted critical discourse, one that remains firmly within the boundaries of conservative academic aesthetic intentionality. While such discourse may illuminate aspects of the novel it also obscures, suppresses, silences. Michel Foucault's comments on discourse in *The History of Sexuality* serve as a useful reminder that critical vision need not be fixed or static, that, ". . . discourse can be both an instrument and an effect of power, but also a hindrance, a stumbling block, a point of resistance and a starting point for an opposing strategy."

To critically approach *The Color Purple* from an oppositional perspective, it is useful to identify gaps—spaces between the text and conventional critical points of departure. That the novel's form is epistolary is most obvious, so apparent even that it is possible to overlook the fact that it begins not with a letter but an opening statement, a threatening command—speaker unidentified. "You better not never tell nobody but God. It'd kill your mammy." Straightaway Celie's letter writing to God is placed in a context of domination; she is obeying orders. Her very first letter reveals that the secret that can be told to no one but god has to do with sexuality, with sexual morality, with a male parent's sexual abuse of a female child. In form and content the declared subject carries traces of the sentimental novel with its focus on female characters and most importantly the female as potential victim of exploitative male sexual desire but this serves only as a background for deviation, for subversion.

Significantly, *The Color Purple* is a narrative of "sexual confession." Statements like: "First he put his thing up against my hip and sort of wiggle it around. Then he grabs hold my titties. Then he put his thing inside my pussy." refer solely to sexual encounters. Throughout *The Color Purple* sexuality is graphically and explicitly discussed. Though a key narrative pattern in the novel it is usually ignored. As readers approaching this novel in the context of a white supremacist patriarchal society wherein black women have been and continue to be stereotyped as sexually loose, a black woman writer imagining a black female character who writes about sexuality in letters to God, using graphic and explicit language, may not seem unusual or even interesting, particularly since graphic descriptions of sexual encounters conforms to a current trend in women's writing, but this is most unlikely. As it is the culture's fascination with sexual autobiography that has led to a burgeoning of fiction and true life stories focusing on sexual encounters. This trend is especially evident in popular woman-centered novels. Attracting mass audiences in similar ways as their nineteenth century predecessors, these new works captivate readers not by covert reference to sexual matters but by explicit exposure and revelation. They completely invert the values of the Victorian novel. While the nineteenth century female protagonist as innocent had no language with which to speak sexual desire, the contemporary heroine in the woman-centered novel is not only the speaking sex, the desiring sex; she is talking sex.

Celie's life is presented in reference to her sexual history. Rosaline Coward's witty essay, "The True Story Of How I Became My Own Person," in her collection *Female Desires*, warns against the reproduction of an ideology where female identity is constructed solely in relationship to sexuality, where sexual experience becomes the way in which a woman learns self-knowledge.

> There's a danger that such structures reproduce the Victorian ideology that sexuality is somehow outside social relationships. The idea that a woman could become her own person just through sexual experiences and the discovery of sexual needs and dislikes again establishes sexual relations as somehow separate from social structures.

Walker reproduces this ideology in *The Color Purple*. Patriarchy is exposed and denounced as a social structure supporting and condoning male domination of women, specifically represented as black male domination of black females, yet it does not influence and control sexual desire and sexual expression. While Mr. Albert, dominating male authority figure, can become enraged at the possibility that his wife will be present at a jukejoint, he has no difficulty accepting her sexual desire for another female. Homophobia does not exist in the novel. Celie's sexual desire for women and her sexual encounter with Shug is never a controversial issue even though it is the catalyst for her resistance to male domination, for her coming to power. Walker makes the powerful suggestion that sexual desire can disrupt and subvert oppressive social structure because it does not necessarily conform to social prescription, yet this realization is undermined by the refusal to acknowledge it as threatening, dangerous.

Sexual desire, initially evoked in the novel as a subversive transformative force, one that enables folk to radically break with convention
(Mr. Albert's passion for Shug transcends marriage vows; Celie's acceptance and fulfillment of her desire for a female leads her to reject heterosexuality; Shug's free floating lust shared with many partners, each
different from the other, challenges the notion of monogamous coupling)
is suppressed and finally absent—a means to an end but not an end in
itself. Celie may realize she desires women, express that longing in a
passionate encounter with Shug, but just as the signifier lesbian does
exist to name and affirm her experience, no social reality exists so that
she can express that desire in ongoing sexual practice. She is seduced
and betrayed. Seduced by the promise of an erotic vocation wherein
sexual fulfillment is deemed essential to self-recovery and self-realization, she must deny the primacy of this sexual awakening and the pain
of sexual rejection.

Ironically, Shug's rejection serves as a catalyst enabling Celie and
Albert to renew and transform their heterosexual bonding. Walker upholds the promise of an intact heterosexual bond with a relational sce-
nario where the point of intimate connection between coupled male and
female is not the acting out of mutual sexual desire for one another but
the displacement of that desire onto a shared object—in this case Shug.
Given such a revised framework for the establishment of heterosexual
bonds, sex between Shug and Celie does not threaten male-female bonding or affirm the possibility that women can be fulfilled in a life that
does not include intimate relationships with men. As Mariana Valverde
emphasized in Sex, Power, and Pleasure: "Lesbianism is thus robbed of
its radical potential because it is portrayed as compatible with heterosexuality, or rather as part of heterosexuality itself. The contradiction that
our society creates between hetero- and homosexuality are wished away
and social oppression is ignored." Wedded by their mutual desire for
Shug, their shared rejection, Celie and Albert are joined in a sustained
committed relationship. Reunited, they stand together, "two old fools
left over from love, keeping each other company under the stars."

Shug, whose very name suggests that she has the power to generate
excitement without the ability to provide substantive nourishment, must
also give up sexual pleasure. Betrayed by the sexual desire that has been
the source of her power, Shug's lust for a young man is not depicted as
an expression of sexual liberation, of longing for a new and different
sexual pleasure. Instead, it is a disempowering force, one that exposes
her vulnerability and weakness. Placed within a stereotypical heterosexist framework wherein woman is denied access to ongoing sexual
pleasure which she seeks and initiates, as the novel progresses Shug is
depicted as an aging female seducer who fears the loss of her ability to
use sex as a means to attract and control men, as a way to power. Until
this turning point, sex has been for Shug a necessary and vital source of

pleasure. As object of intense sexual desire, she has had power to shape and influence the actions of others but always in the direction of a higher good.

Ultimately, Walker constructs an ideal world of true love and commitment where there is no erotic tension—where there is no sexual desire or sexual pleasure. Just as the reader's perception of Shug is dramatically altered towards the end of the novel, the way we see and understand Celie's sexual history, her sexual confession changes when it is revealed that she has not been raped by her real father. The tragedy and trauma of incest, so graphically and poignantly portrayed, both in terms of the incest-rape and Celie's sexual healing which begins when she tells Shug what happened, is trivialized as the novel progresses. Presented in retrospect as though it was all an absurd drama, the horror of Celie's early sexual experience and the pleasure of her sexual awakening assume the quality of spectacle, of exaggerated show. A curious talk told in part as a strategy to engage and excite the reader's imagination before attention is diverted towards more important revelations. Given the fascination in this culture with sex and violence, with race and sex, with sexual deviance, a fascination which is recognized and represented most often in pornography, Walker's subject has immediate appeal. Readers are placed in the position of voyeurs who witness Celie's torment as victim of incest-rape, as victim of sexual violence in a sadistic master-slave relationship; who watch her sexual exploration of her body and experience vicarious pleasure at her sexual awakening as she experiences her first sexual encounter with Shug. Ironically, pornographic fiction consumed by a mass audience is a genre which has always included narratives describing women engaged in sexual acts with one another, observed by powerful others usually men. Walker subverts this pattern. As readers we represent the powerful other. Her intent is not to sexually titillate but to arouse disgust, outrage, and anger at male sexual exploitation of females to encourage appreciate and acceptance of same-sex female sexual pleasure.

To achieve this end, which is fundamentally anti-male domination, Walker relies on similar narrative strategies and preoccupations as those utilized in the pornographic narrative. Annette Kuhn's essay on representation and sexuality which focuses on pornography's "Lawless seeing" points to the connection between pornographic fiction and other simple narratives:

> . . . in pornographic stories, literary as well as visual, characters are never very strongly developed or psychologically rounded human beings. They perform function, they take on roles already fixed within the commonplace fantasies that porn constructs—the sexually active woman, the Peeping Tom, the plumber out on his rounds. In porn, characters are what they do, and given a minimal amount of familiarity with the genre, the reader needs little by way of explanation in order to understand what is going on. Pornography has a good deal in common with other simple forms of narrative, stories in which

characters are no more than what they do and the reader has some general idea, as soon as the story begins, of who is going to do what to whom, and with what outcome. . . In many respects, pornographic stories work like fairy tales.

Characters are very much what they do in *The Color Purple*. Mr. _____ is brute, Lucious the rapist, Harpo the buffoon, Celie the sexual victim, Shug the sexual temptress. Many of the characters perform roles that correspond with racial stereotypes. The image of "the black male rapist" resonates in both racial and sexual stereotypes, Walker's characterization cannot be viewed in a vacuum as though it does not participate in these discourses which have been primarily used to reinforce domination, both racial and sexual.

Pornography participates in and promotes a discourse that exploits and aesthesizes domination. Kuhn asserts that pornography insists on sexual difference, that sexual violence in master-slave scenarios reduces this difference to relations of power. Feminists who focus almost exclusively on male violence against women as the central signifier of male domination also view sexual difference as solely a relation of power. Within pornography Kuhn states, there is

> . . . an obsession with the otherness of femininity, which in common with many forms of otherness seems to contain a threat to the onlooker. Curiosity turns to terror, investigation to torture, the final affirmation of the objecthood of the other. The feminine here represents a threat to the masculine, a threat which demands containment. Sexual violent pornography of this kind concretises this wish for containment in representations which address the spectator as masculine and place the masculine on the side of container of the threat. It insists that sexuality and power are inseparable.

Walker inverts this paradigm. Presuming a female spectator, (women and specifically white women from privileged classes are the primary audience for women centered novels), she constructs a fiction in which it is the masculine threat, represented by black masculinity; that must be contained, controlled, and ultimately transformed. Her most radical re-visioning of the oppressive patriarchal social order is her insistence on the transformation of Mr. Albert. He moves from male oppressor to enlightened being, willingly surrendering his attachment to the phallocentric social order reinforced by the sexual oppression of women. His transformation begins when Celie threatens his existence, when her curse disempowers him. Since sexuality and power are so closely linked to politics of domination, Mr. Albert must be completely desexualized as part of the transformative process.

Unable to reconcile sexuality and power, Walker replaces the longing for sexual pleasure with an erotic metaphysic animated by a vision of the unity of all things, by the convergence of erotic and mystical experience. Ritually enacted as Shug initiates Celie into a spiritual awakening wherein belief in God as white male authority figure, who gives orders and punishes, is supplanted by the vision of a loving God who wants believers to celebrate life, to experience pleasure, a God who is annoyed, "if you walk by the color purple in a field somewhere but don't notice it." In *The Color Purple* Christianity and patriarchy are oppressive social structures which promote anhedonia. Celie and Albert, as oppressed and oppressor, must as part of their personal transformation learn to feel pleasure and develop a capacity to experience happiness. Concurrently, Nettie and Samuel, laboring as missionaries in Africa, develop a critical consciousness that allows them to see the connections between Western cultural imperialism and Christianity; this enables them to see God in a new way. Nettie writes to Celie, "God is different to us now, after all these years in Africa, more spirit than ever before, and more internal." Though critical or religious beliefs which reinforce sexist and racist domination, Shug insists on the primacy of a spiritual life, constructing a vision of spirituality which echoes the teachings of religious mystics who speak of healing alienation through recognition of the unity of all life.

Spiritual quest is connected with the effort of characters in *The Color Purple* to be more fully self-realized. This effort merges in an unproblematic way with a materialist ethic which links acquisition of goods with the capacity to experience emotional well-being. Traditionally mystical experience is informed by radical critique and renunciation of materialism. Walker positively links the two. Even though her pronounced critique of patriarchy includes an implicit indictment of perverse individualism which encourages exploitation, (Albert is transformed in part by his rejection of isolation and self-sufficiency for connection and interdependency), Celie's shift from underclass victim to capitalist entrepreneur has only positive signification. Albert, in his role as oppressor, forces Celie and Harpo to work in the fields, exploiting their labor for his gain. Their exploitation as workers must cease before domination ends and transformation begins. Yet Celie's progression from exploited black woman, as woman, as sexual victim, is aided by her entrance into the economy as property owner, manager of a small business, storekeeper—in short capitalist entrepreneur. No attention is accorded aspects of this enterprise that might reinforce domination, attention is focused on how useful Celie's pants are for family and friends; on the way Sophia as worker in her store will treat black customers with respect and consideration. Embedded in the construction of sexual difference as it is characterized in *The Color Purple* is the implicit assumption that women are innately less inclined to oppress and dominate than men; that women are not easily corrupted.

Rewarded with economic prosperity for her patient endurance of suffering, Celie never fully develops capacities for sustained self-assertion. Placed on a moral pedestal which allows no one to see her as a threat, she is always potential victim. By contrast Sophia's self-affirmation, her refusal to see herself as victim, is not rewarded. She is consistently punished. Sadly, as readers witness Celie's triumph, her successful effort to resist male domination which takes place solely in a private familial context, we bear witness to Sophia's tragic fate, as she resists sexist and racist oppression in private and public spheres. Unlike Celie or Shug, she is regarded as a serious threat to the social order and is violently attacked, brutalized, and subdued. Always a revolutionary, Sophia has never been victimized or complicit in her own oppression. Tortured and persecuted by the State, treated as though she is a political prisoner, Sophia's spirit is systematically crushed. Unlike Celie she cannot easily escape and there is no love strong enough to engender her self-recovery. Her suffering cannot be easily mitigated as it would require radical transformation of society. Given all the spectacular changes in *The Color Purple* it is not without grave and serious import that the character who most radically challenges sexism and racism is a tragic figure, who is only partially rescued—restored to only a semblance of sanity. Like the lobotomized Native American Indian in *One Flew Over The Cuckoo's Nest*, Sophia's courageous spirit evokes affirmation, even as her fate strikes fear and trepidation in the hearts and minds of those who would actively resist oppression.

Described as a large woman with a powerful presence, Sophia's vacant position in the kinship network is assumed by Squeak, a thin petite woman, who gains presence only when she acts to free Sophia, passively enduring rape to fulfill her mission. This rape of a black woman by a white man does not have grievous traumatic negative consequences even though it acts to reinforce sexist domination of females and racist exploitation. Instead, it is a catalyst for positive change—Sophia's release, Squeak asserting her identity as Mary Agnes. Such a benevolent portrayal of the consequences of rape contrasts sharply with the images of black male rapists, images which highlight the violence and brutality of their acts. That the text graphically emphasized the horror and pain of black male sexist exploitation of black females while de-emphasizing the horror and pain of racist exploitation of black women by white men that involves sexual violence is an unresolved contradiction if Walker's intent is to expose the evils of sexist domination. These contrasting depictions of rape dangerously risk reinforcing racist stereotypes that perpetuate the notion that black men are more capable of brutal sexist domination than other groups of men.

Throughout *The Color Purple* exposure of the evils of patriarchal domination are undercut by the suggestion that this form of domination is not necessarily linked to race and class exploitation. Celie and Albert are able to eradicate sexism in their relationship. The threat of masculine domination ceases when Albert forgoes phallic privilege and serves as a helpmate to Celie, assuming a "feminine" presence. However the phallocentric social order which exists outside the domain of private relationships remains intact. As symbolic representation of masculine otherness, the phallus continues to assert a powerful presence via the making of pants, that both women and men will wear. This is not a radical re-visioning of gender. It is a vision of inclusion that enables women to access power via symbolic phallic representation. And as French feminist Antoinette Fougue reminds us: "Inversion does not facilitate the passage to another kind of structure. The difference between the sexes is not whether or not one does or doesn't have a penis, it is whether or not one is an integral part of a phallic masculine economy." Within *The Color Purple* the economy Celie enters as entrepreneur and land owner is almost completely divorced from structures of domination. Immersed in the ethics of a narcissistic new age spiritualism wherein economic pros-perity indicates that one is chosen—blessed, Celie never reflects criti-cally on the changes in her status. She writes to Nettie, "I am so happy. I go love. I got work. I got money, friends and time."

Indeed the magic of *The Color Purple* is that it is so much a book of our times, imaginatively evoking the promise of a world in which one can have it all; a world in which sexual exploitation can be easily overcome; a world of unlimited access to material well being; a world where the evils of racism are tempered by the positive gestures of concerned and caring white folks; a world where sexual boundaries can be transgressed at will without negative consequences; a world where spiritual salvation is the lot of the elect. This illusory magic is sustained by Walker's literary technique, the skillful combining of social realism and fantasy, the fairy tale and the fictionalized autobiographical narrative.

As the fictive autobiography of an oppressed black woman's journey from sexual slavery to freedom, *The Color Purple* parodies those pri-mary texts of autobiographical writing which have shaped and influenced the direction of African-American fiction—"the slave narrative." With the publication of slave autobiographies oppressed African-American slaves moved from object to subject, from silence into creating a revolu-tionary literature—one that changed the nature and direction of African-American history; that laid the groundwork for the development of a distinct African-American literary tradition. Slave autobiographies worked to convey as accurately as possible the true story of slavery as experienced and interpreted by slaves without apology or exaggeration. The emphasis on truth had a twofold purpose, the presentation of reliable sources, and most importantly, the creation of a radical discourse on slavery that served as a corrective and a challenge to the dominant culture's hegemonic perspective. Although Walker conceived of *The Color Purple* as a historical novel, her emphasis is less on historical accuracy and more on an insistence that history has more to do with the interpersonal details of everyday life at a given historical moment than with significant dates, events, or important persons. Relying on histori-cal referents only in so far as they lend an aura of credibility to that which is improbable and even fantastic, Walker mocks the notion of historical truth, suggesting that it is subordinate to myth, that the mythic has far more impact on consciousness. This is most evident in the letters from Africa. Historical documents, letters, journals, articles, provide autobiographical testimony of the experience and attitudes of nineteenth century black missionaries in Africa, yet Walker is not concerned with a correspondence between the basic historical fact that black missionaries did travel to Africa and providing the reader with a fictive account of those travels that is plausible. Walker uses the basic historical fact as a frame to enhance the social realism of her text while super-imposing a decidedly contemporary perspective. Historical accuracy is altered to serve didactic purposes—to teach the reader history not as it was but as it should have been.

A revolutionary literature has as its central goal the education for critical consciousness, creating awareness of the forces that oppress and recognition of the way those forces might be transformed. One important aspect of the slave narrative as revolutionary text was the insistence that the plight of the individual narrator be linked to the oppressed plight of all black people so as to arouse support for organized political effort for social changes. Walker appropriates this form to legitimize and render authentic Celie's quest without reflecting this radical agenda. Celie's plight is not representative; it is not linked to collective effort to effect radical social change. While she is a victim of male domination, Shug is not. While she has allowed patriarchal ideology to inform her sense of self, Sophia has not. By de-emphasizing the collective plight of black people, or even black women, and focusing on the individual's quest for freedom as separate and distinct, Walker makes a crucial break with that revolutionary African-American literary tradition which informs her earlier work, placing this novel outside that framework. Parodying the slave narrative's focus on facial oppression, Walker's emphasis on sexual oppression, acts to delegitimize the historical specificity and power of this form. Appropriating the slave narrative in this way she now invalidates both the historical context and the racial agenda. Furthermore, by linking this form to the sentimental novel as though they served similar functions, Walker strips the slave narrative of its revolutionary ideological intent and content connecting it to Eurocentric bourgeois literary traditions in such a way as to suggest it was merely derivative and in no way distinct.

Slave narratives are a powerful record of the particular unique struggle of African-American people to write history—to make literature—to be a self-defining people. Unlike Celie, the slave who recorded her or his story was not following the oppressors' orders, was not working within a context of domination. Fundamentally, this writing was a challenge, a resistance affirming that the movement of the oppressed from silence into speech is a liberatory gesture. Literacy is upheld in the slave narrative as essential to the practice of freedom. Celie writes not as a gesture of affirmation or liberation but as a gesture of shame. Nettie recalls, "I remember one time you said your life made you feel so ashamed you couldn't even talk about it to God. You had to write it." Writing then is not a process which enables Celie to make herself subject, it allows distance, objectification. She does not understand writing as an act of power, or self-legitimation. She is empowered not by the written word but by the spoken word—by telling her story to Shug. Later, after she has made the shift from object to subject she ceases to write to God and addresses Nettie which is an act of self-affirmation.

Taken at face value Celie's letter writing appears to be a simple matter-of-fact gesture when it is really one of the most fantastical happenings in *The Color Purple*. Oppressed, exploited as laborer in the field, as worker in the domestic household, as sexual servant, Celie finds time to write—this is truly incredible. There is no description of Celie with pen in hand, no discussion of where and when she writes. She must remain invisible so as not to expose this essential contradiction—that as dehumanized object she projects a self in the act of writing even as she records her inability to be self-defining. Celie as writer is a fiction. Walker, as writing subject, oversees her creation, constructing a narrative that purports to be a space where the voice of an oppressed black female can be heard even though the valorization of writing and the use of the epistolary form, suppress and silence that voice.

Writing in a manner that reads as though she is speaking, talking in the voice of a black folk idiom, Celie as poor and exploited black female, appears to enter a discourse from which she has been excluded—the act of writing, the production of story as commodity. In actuality, her voice remains that of appropriated other—interpreted—translated—represented as authentic unspoiled innocent. Walker provides Celie a writing self, one that serves as a perfect foil for her creator. Continually asserting her authorial presence in *The Color Purple*, she speaks through characters sharing her thoughts and values. Masquerading as just plain folks, Celie, Nettie, Shug, and Albert are the mediums for the presentation of her didactic voice. Through fictive recognition and acknowledgement, Walker pays tribute to the impact of black folk experience as a force that channels and shapes her imaginative work, yet her insistent authorial presence detracts from this representation.

Traces of traditional African-American folk expression as manifest in language and modes of story-telling are evident in Celie's letters, though they cannot be fully voiced and expressed in the epistolary form. There they are contained and subsumed. Commenting on the use of the epistolary form in *Seduction and Betrayal: Women and Literature*, Elizabeth Hardwick suggests, "A letter is not a dialogue or even an omniscient exposition. It is a fabric of surfaces, a mask, a form as well suited to affectations as to the affection. The letter is, by its natural shape, self-justifying; it is one's own evidence, deposition, a self-serving testimony.

In a letter the writer holds all the cards, controls everything. . ." That Celie and Nettie's letters are basically self-serving, is evident when it is revealed that there has never been a true correspondence. And if readers are to assume that Celie is barely able to read and write as her letters suggest, she would not have been able to comprehend Nettie's words. Not only is the inner life of the characters modified by the use of the epistolary form, the absence of correspondence restricts information, enables the letters to serve both the interest of the writers, and the interests of an embedded didactic narrative. Functioning as a screen, the letters keep the reader at a distance, creating the illusion of intimacy where there is none. The reader is always voyeur, outsider looking in, passively awaiting the latest news.

Celie and Nettie's letters testify, we as readers bear witness. They are ontological—an explanation of being—which asserts that understanding the self is the pre-condition for transformation, for radical change. Narrating aspects of their personal history, they engage in a ongoing process of demythologizing that makes new awareness and change possible. They recollect to recover and restore. They seek to affirm and sustain the initial bond of care and connection experienced with one another in their oppressive male-dominated family. Since the mother is bonded with the father, supporting and protecting his interests, mothers and daughters within this fictive patriarchy suffer a wound of separation and abandonment; they have no context for unity. Mothers prove their allegiance to fathers by betraying daughters; it is only a vision of sisterhood that makes woman bonding possible. By eschewing the identity of Mother, black women in *The Color Purple*, like Shug and Sophia, rebelliously place themselves outside the context of patriarchal family norms, revisioning mothering so that it becomes a task any willing female can perform, irrespective of whether or not she has given birth. Displacing motherhood as central signifier for female being, and emphasizing sisterhood, Walker posits a relational basis for self-definition that valorizes and affirms woman bonding. It is the recognition of self in the other, of unity, and not self in relationship to the production of children that enables women to connect with one another.

The values expressed in woman bonding—mutuality, respect, shared power, and unconditional love—become guiding principles shaping the new community in *The Color Purple* which includes everyone, women and men, family and kin. Reconstructed black males, Harpo and Albert are active participants expanding the circle of care. Together this extended kin network affirms the primacy of a revitalized spirituality, in which everything that exists is informed by godliness, in which love as a force that affirms connection and intersubjective communion makes an erotic metaphysic possible. Forgiveness and compassion enable individuals who were estranged and alienated to nurture one another's growth. The message conveyed in the novel that relationships no matter how seriously impaired can be restored is compelling. Distinct from the promise of a happy ending, it allows for the recognition of conflict and pain, for the possibility of reconciliation.

Radical didactic messages add depth and complexity to *The Color Purple* without resolving the contradictions between radicalism—the vision of revolutionary transformation and conservation—the perpetuation of bourgeois ideology. When the novel concludes Celie has everything her oppressor has wanted and more—relationships with chosen loved ones; land ownership; material wealth; control over the labor of others. She is happy. In a *Newsweek* interview, Walker makes the revealing statement, "I liberated Celie from her own history. I wanted her to be happy." Happiness is not subject to re-vision, radicalization. The terms are familiar, absence of conflict, pain, and struggle; a fantasy of every desire fulfilled. Given these terms, Walker creates a fiction wherein an oppressed black woman can experience self-recovery without a dialectical process; without collective political effort; without radical change in society. To make Celie happy she creates a fiction where struggle—the arduous and painful process by which the oppressed work for liberation has no place. This fantasy of change without effort is a dangerous one for both oppressed and oppressor. It is a brand of false consciousness that keeps everyone in place and oppressive structures intact. It is just this distortion of reality that Walker warns against in her essay "If the Present Looks Like the Past:"

> In any case, the duty of the writer is not to be tricked, seduced, or goaded into verifying by imitation or even rebuttal other people's fantasies. In an oppressive society it may well be that all fantasies indulged in by the oppressor are destructive to the oppressed. To become involved in them in any way at all is, at the very least, to lose time defining yourself.

For oppressed and oppressor the process of liberation, individual self-realization and revolutionary transformation of society, requires confrontation with reality, the letting go of fantasy. Speaking of his loathing for fantasy Gabriel Garcia Marquez explains:

> . . . I believe the imagination is just an instrument for producing reality and that the source of creation is always, in the last instance, reality. Fantasy, in the sense of pure and simple Walt Disney-style invention without any basis in reality is the most loathsome thing of all. . . . children don't like fantasy either. What they do like is imagination. The difference between the one and the other is the same as between a human being and a ventriloquist's dummy.

The tragedy embedded in the various happy endings in *The Color Purple* can be located at that point where fantasy triumphs over imagination, where creative power is suppressed. Still there are crucial moments in the novel where the imagination works to liberate, to challenge, to make the new real and possible. These moments affirm the integrity of artistic vision, restore and renew.

◆◆◆◆◆◆◆◆◆◆◆◆◆

Rewriting the Heroine's Story
in *The Color Purple*

LINDA ABBANDONATO

Alice Walker's novel *The Color Purple* begins with a paternal injunction of silence:

> You better not never tell nobody but God. It'd kill your mammy.

Celie's story is told within the context of this threat: the narrative is about breaking silences, and, appropriately, its formal structure creates the illusion that it is filled with unmediated "voices." Trapped in a gridlock of racist, sexist, and heterosexist oppressions, Celie struggles toward linguistic self-definition. She is an "invisible woman," a character traditionally silenced and effaced in fiction; and by centering on her, Walker replots the heroine's text. I want to show how Celie's story—the story of that most marginalized of heroines the black lesbian—challenges patriarchal constructions of female subjectivity and sexuality and thus makes representation itself a compelling issue for all women, regardless of their ethnicity or sexual orientation.[1] I begin by exploring the question of representation and considering *The Color Purple* in relation to feminist theoretical discourses on femininity. I then argue that by exposing and opposing a powerful ideological constraint, institutionalized or "compulsory" heterosexuality, the novel appropriates the woman's narrative for herself, in effect reinscribing "herstory."[2]

To substantiate my claim that *The Color Purple* is a conscious rewriting of canonical male texts, I propose a literary connection that is at once obvious and unlikely: the novel's epistolary form invites us to trace its ancestry all the way to *Clarissa*. Both novels represent a woman's struggle toward linguistic self-definition in a world of disrupted signs: Celie, like Clarissa, is imprisoned, alienated, sexually abused, and driven into semiotic collapse (see Castle's excellent analysis of Clarissa's collapse). *The Color Purple*, however, stands in a parodic or at least an irreverent relation to the monolithic *Clarissa*. The comparison between two fictions so radically separate historically and culturally is appropriate, I think, because *Clarissa* fully endorses the bourgeois morality that *The Color Purple* attacks and because Samuel Richardson himself (at least as constructed in our literary histories) perfectly symbolizes white patriarchy: the founding father of the novel (by convention, if not in fact), he tells the woman's story, authorizing her on his terms, eroticizing her suffering, representing her masochism as virtue and her dying as the emblem of womanly purity. *Clarissa*, even if largely unread now, occupies a dominant place in literature: its myths and values are recirculated in many fictions, especially in the ideology of romances, with which women are most fully engaged as readers and as writers.

Buried beneath the monumental edifice of works like *Clarissa*, male-authored volumes that tell the woman's story "as an Exemplar to her sex," lie a mass of texts by women. The history of publishing is a record of female silencing; as many feminist critics have pointed out, women traditionally experienced educational and economic disadvantages and other cultural constraints that prohibited them from writing.[3] When they overcame oppressive technologies of gender and took up the forbidden pen, the technologies of print could always be deployed against them. This may seem an overrehearsed, even an outdated argument, but the problems are still acute for women of color. Feminist attempts to revise the canon and address sexism in discourse are frequently marred by their failure to recognize heterosexism and racism; the counternarratives of femininity that emerge continue to erase women who are not white or heterosexual. Sojourner Truth's lament, "Ain't I a woman?" is insistently echoed in the contemporary writings of lesbians and women of color.[4]

Alice Walker too, in her nonfictional prose, protests the exclusion of black women writers from feminist revisions of literary histories; and in *The Color Purple*, she shows her heroine trapped in the whole range of possible oppressions. Celie's struggle to create a self through language, to break free from the network of class, racial, sexual, and gender ideologies to which she is subjected, represents the woman's story in an innovative way. Can a book like *The Color Purple* make any real difference to the hegemony of patriarchal discourses? Placed beside *Clarissa* on my bookshelf, *The Color Purple* symbolically suggests in its physical size the position and power of the "womanist" text within the canon: dominated by the weight, prolixity, and authority of masculine accounts of female subjectivity, it may nonetheless challenge and displace those "masternarratives."[5]

Walker gives several definitions for the term *womanist*, which is, of course, her coinage: "A black feminist or feminist of color. . . . Usually referring to outrageous, audacious, courageous or *willful* behavior. . . . A woman who loves other women, sexually and/or nonsexually." I choose the phrase *womanist text* in preference to *woman's text* (i.e., a book written by a woman) to stress that the problem of representation cannot be resolved simply by the inclusion of more women writers in a male-dominated canon. While it is important for women to tell their stories, to gain a voice in literary and theoretical discourses and thereby achieve a certain empowerment, the ideological constraints on representation must also be considered. Put bluntly, how can a woman define herself differently, disengage her self from the cultural scripts of sexuality and gender that produce her as feminine subject? In *Alice Doesn't*, Teresa de Lauretis distinguishes between "woman" as an ideological construct and "women" as historical subjects and argues that women experience a double consciousness in relation to their representation in film: seduced into identification with woman, they are yet aware of their exclusion, of their nonrepresentation in that construct. If women are always constituted as objects (of desire, of the gaze) or as other, if "female" is always the negative of the positive value "male," women find themselves situated in a negative space, neither participating in patriarchal discourses nor able to escape from them. When Lauren Berlant describes Celie as "falling through the cracks of a language she can barely use . . . crossing out 'I am' and situating herself squarely on the ground of negation," she attributes Celie's situation to saintly self-renunciation; but I propose a different explanation. Celie's burden in building a self on a site of negation is shared by any woman who attempts to establish an identity outside patriarchal definition. If women are constituted as subjects in a man-made language, then it is only through the cracks in language, and in the places where ideology fails to cohere, that they can begin to reconstruct themselves. Luce Irigaray points out that "if [women] keep on speaking the same language together, [they're] going to reproduce the same history. Begin the same stories all over again." She urges women to "come out of [men's] language." But it is no easy task for women to authorize themselves as women, to disengage their feminine identity from the ideological masternarratives that inscribe it. Feminist discourse itself is inevitably corrupt, deeply implicated in the sexism of language and in patriarchal constructions of gender. As de Lauretis argues, women's theories of reading, writing, sexuality, and ideology are based "on male narratives of gender . . . bound by the heterosexual contract; narratives which persistently tend to reproduce themselves in feminist theories." The challenge facing feminists is no less than to "rewrite cultural narratives, and to define the terms of another perspective—a view from 'elsewhere.'"

I suggest that *The Color Purple* offers that "view from 'elsewhere.'" It succeeds partly because Celie's sexual orientation provides an alternative to the heterosexual paradigm of the conventional marriage plot: her choice of lesbianism is politically charged, a notion I develop later. For the moment I want only to point out that the novel is also lesbian in the much broader sense implied by Adrienne Rich's concept of the "lesbian continuum," which spans the whole spectrum of women's friendships and sisterly solidarity. Walker's own term *womanist* is clearly influenced by Rich; and in this womanist text, the eroticism of women's love for women is at once centralized and incorporated into a more diffuse model of woman-identifying women.

Another way in which *The Color Purple* offers a view from elsewhere is through its displacement of standard English. Aware that *"the master's tools can never dismantle the master's house,"* Alice Walker has confronted the challenge of constructing an alternative language. The significance of her achievement here has been overlooked, partly because critics often insist on confining the novel to the genre of realism and thus evaluate the Southern black vernacular solely for its authenticity. Indeed, Walker herself disingenuously describes her role as that of a medium, communicating on behalf of the spirits who possessed her. She seems to intend this myth of creative inspiration literally, and it is attractive because we certainly experience the novel as filled with voices that address us directly. With Celie we undergo a metamorphosis of experience, aligning ourselves fully with her vision of the world since she insists on being taken on her own terms. Her language is indeed so compelling that we actually begin to *think* as Miss Celie—like Shug, we have her song scratched out of our heads—because by participating in her linguistic processes, we collaborate in her struggle to construct a self. For various reasons, then, we are distracted from the extreme skill with which Walker exploits her formal and linguistic resources, and thus we underestimate the degree to which the text is language as performance. There is a clue, however, in what is commonly perceived as a flaw in the novel—the sequence of letters from Nettie, which invariably disappoint readers. If signifying is "a form of meta-communication, where the surface expression and the intrinsic position diverge," we can regard *The Color Purple* as an elaborate act of signifying, since the apparently impoverished and inarticulate language of the illiterati turns out to be deceptively resonant and dazzlingly rich. By incorporating Nettie's letters into Celie's text, Walker illuminates the contrast between Celie's spare suggestiveness and Nettie's stilted verbosity. Thus the expressive flexibility of the black vernacular, a supposedly inferior speech, is measured against the repressed and rigid linguistic codes to which Nettie has conformed; the position of standard (white) English is challenged, and Celie's vitality is privileged over Nettie's dreary correctness. Nettie has been imaginatively stunted, her language bleached white and her ethnicity virtually erased. Always the Other Woman, one who lacks an identity of her own, she is cast in the preposterous role of a black missionary who attempts to impose the ideology of her oppressors onto a culturally self-sufficient people. Nettie's story perfectly illustrates the way society construes women as subjects (or as subject-objects, in de Lauretis's phrase): neither represented within the white mainstream nor able to construct a selfhood outside it, Nettie is internally divided, experiencing her subjectivity as otherness.

Celie, by contrast, refuses to enter the linguistic structures (and strictures) of white patriarchy, commenting that "only a fool would want you to talk in a way that feel peculiar to your mind," and so retains a discourse that is potentially subversive. We might compare Walker's technique with Irigaray's linguistic playfulness, fragmented phrases, and poetic cadences, which are similar in purpose, though not in style, to the suppleness, the sharp wit, and the compression of the black vernacular: each mode of expression represents both resistance to the hegemonic discourse and the deliberate use of linguistic nonconformity to position the self outside the dominant system. In *The Color Purple* the dialect is both naturalistic and symbolic, and if we try to confine the work to realism, we may easily miss the complexity of Walker's womanist aims. Her purposeful transgression of generic boundaries has also been perceived as a lack of artistic control, although it is entirely consistent with current feminist practice; and some of the criticisms directed at Walker imply a covert form of racism—an assumption that black novelists should (or can) write only in the realistic vein established by Richard Wright.[6]

By adopting the crazy quilt, the craft of her foremothers, as the structuring principle of her fiction, Alice Walker places herself within a tradition of black female creativity. This differently crafted, quilted novel, is also differently sexual: its formal structure allows many playful variations on a sexual theme. Some designs emerge clearly, but the overall pattern is extremely complicated; themes and relationships are introduced and inverted or turned, like a piece of fabric, inside out, so that the pattern can be traced a new way. Triadic combinations proliferate: characters are constantly realigned in an intricate network of configurations, apparently in a continual state of metamorphosis until the final utopian vision, the brave new world of the ending.[7]

The novel moves freely through time and space, juxtaposing the African motifs with the African American, thus supplying a dialectical commentary on the two cultures. Comic reversals of expectation are part of the scheme: for example, the Christian missionaries, striving to impose monogamy on the Olinkas, inadvertently reinforce [polygymy] because the Olinkas believe (quite rightly, as it turns out) that Samuel is married to both Corinne and Nettie. The treatment of incest is particularly interesting: although in one part of her design Walker reveals the full horror of father-daughter rape, she weaves in complications, twisting her narrative thread in ways that challenge the taboo. And if the incest taboo is subverted in this novel, so too is that other taboo homosexuality. I suggest that the great twentieth-century cultural narratives of sexuality and socialization, Freud's oedipal theory and Lévi-Strauss's theory of kinship systems and the exchange of women, are played out in the drama of Celie's life. The two theories center on the incest taboo and mesh together precisely. Both also explain, and have been used to reinforce, our system of "compulsory heterosexuality." As I have suggested, Celie's lesbianism is politically significant, subverting masculine cultural narratives of femininity and desire and rewriting them from a feminist point of view.

Let us consider briefly how those narratives explain and reinforce heterosexuality, both in the construction of societies through kinship systems and in the enculturation of individuals within those societies.

Lévi-Strauss describes the exchange of women as "the system of binding *men* together" (emphasis added), thus defining marriage as a social contract between men and viewing the kinship system as a means of reinforcing male power through the circulation of women. Lévi-Strauss concludes that the incest taboo is "the supreme rule of the gift," designed to ensure exogamy. Compulsory heterosexuality thus becomes the basis on which society operates and the exchange of women the condition whereby the patriarchy flourishes. Women are prevented from becoming subjects in an economy where they are exchanged as objects, and homosexual desire becomes taboo, like incest, because it disrupts the terms of the social contract. Naturally, this system can only operate smoothly so long as sexual nonconformity is kept invisible. An important project of feminism, then, is to make the invisible visible: to topple the dominant ideology by placing the unorthodox and the marginalized at the center of the discursive and cultural stage. Thus feminist theory constructs homosexuality as a powerfully subversive threat to the social order: Eve Sedgwick, for example, takes up René Girard's notion of "triangular desire"—which in turn develops Lévi-Strauss's theory of the exchange of women as a form of bonding between men—and argues that homophobia functions to suppress recognition of the homosociality on which patriarchal domination depends. Irigaray's coining of the word *hom(m)osexualité* plays on a pun to suggest a similar concept of society as founded on a masculine economy of sameness, so that homosexual relations must be forbidden: "*Because they openly interpret the law according to which society operates, they threaten in fact to shift the horizon of that law.*"

Psychoanalytic accounts of enculturation also rest on the prohibition of incest, as enforced through the castration complex; in the oedipal plot, the phallus becomes the coveted marker of sexual difference and desire. Lacan's famous diagram of the identical doors labeled "Ladies" and "Gentlemen" suggests the different ideological worlds that the subject enters according to gender; although gender, like the signs on the doors, is no more than an arbitrary and fictional construct, subjects who wish to function within the symbolic order must pass through one of those doors. The successful inscription of subjects as masculine or feminine, as "ladies" or "gentlemen," depends on acquiescence to the Law of the Father and on suppression of the polymorphously perverse drives of infancy; in the process, heterosexuality is reinforced as a cultural institution. An important objection to the oedipal scheme is that it predicates female sexuality on a masculine paradigm, thus effacing the very subject of femininity it claims to investigate. Women are effectively excluded from being desiring subjects or from having their sexuality theorized except through a distorting masculine lens. Consequently the lesbian remains outside the framework of representation, becoming, in effect, unrepresentable. Feminist critiques of the oedipal theory have challenged its masculine economy of desire and exposed its inadequacy as an account of female sexuality. Adrienne Rich, for example, wonders why the female child should redirect her libidinal activity from the original object of desire, the mother, to the father and concludes that heterosexuality is a political institution into which women are conscripted ideologically, by force and through the censorship of alternative models of sexuality.[8]

But what happens when the taboo is broken and women refuse to be co-opted into a system of compulsory heterosexuality, refuse in effect to become objects of exchange between men? Or, in Irigaray's words, "[W]hat if these 'commodities' refused to go to 'market'?"

This is, of course, the question posed by *The Color Purple*, which reduces the system of compulsory heterosexuality to its basic level, making it abstract. The representations of male tyranny are in one sense reductive or crude and in another sense emblematic, their implications far-reaching. The specific systems of oppression that operate in Celie's life symbolize the more or less subtle operations of patriarchal power in the lives of women everywhere.

Compulsory heterosexuality enforces Celie's subjugation and erases her subjectivity. Celie graphically represents this situation when she begins her story by placing "I am" *sous rature*. Trapped from the start into complicity in the shameful secret of incest, Celie makes a timid plea to God: "Maybe you can give me a sign letting me know what is happening to me." But how can Celie be given a sign when she *is* a sign, a mere object of exchange between men? The God she conceptualizes is a cruel father whose identity merges ominously with Pa's; when asked whose baby she is carrying, Celie tells the lie that is the truth: "I say God's. I don't know no other man or what else to say."

When Celie marries Mr. _____, this man with no name becomes part of the system of male oppression, joining God the Patriarch and Pa in an unholy trinity of power that displaces her identity. The marriage negotiations take place entirely between the stepfather and the husband: Celie is handed over like a beast of burden, identified with the cow that accompanies her. Physically and psychologically abused by stepfather and husband alike, Celie is denied a status as subject. Her sexuality and reproductive organs are controlled by men, her children are taken from her, and her submission is enforced through violence. In her terrified acquiescence to such blatant male brutality, Celie symbolically mirrors Everywoman. Fear of rape, for example, is so habitual that it has become naturalized and conditions women automatically; when it circumscribes their movements, we call it Common Sense, and our judicial system holds women who lack it accountable for male violence. Celie bleakly represents the plight of her more privileged sisters, who are victimized by social tyrannies like antiabortion legislation, the kidnapping of children, and state intervention in the family and in individuals' sexual orientation.

Celie's vernacular is used to poignant effect in the double negative of

"I don't have nothing." Her connection with her sex is severed; doubly silenced, by father and by husband, Celie sends dead letters to an absentee God, and the only "sign" she eventually gets—the discovery that her real father was lynched—shatters an already eroded identity and precipitates her semiotic collapse. Her attempt to make sense of her new family history breaks down into the negative tautology of "Pa not Pa" (as Berlant has also argued).

This is a puzzling moment in the text. Why does Walker set up incest at the beginning and then reinscribe family relations halfway through? And what is the effect on the reader of discovering that "Pa not Pa"? At one level, I would argue, the revelation makes no difference at all: Celie was still raped, and by a man who was in every respect socially, if not biologically, her father. But suggestions of incest recur too insistently for the question to be dismissed so easily. What, for example, do we make of the marriage of "Sister Nettie" and "Brother Samuel" or of his claim that "we behave as brother and sister to each other"? Shug and Celie, sisters in spirit, become lovers in the flesh. Albert complains that Shug loves him like a brother—but Celie responds, "What so bad about that?" Shug has an affair with a boy who subsequently becomes "like a son. Maybe a grandson." Time and again, the incest taboo is symbolically dissolved as the different categories of social relations, family and sexual, are intertwined.

Perhaps this focus on incest is an honest and courageous attempt to situate sexuality where it belongs: in the heart of the family. If the family is the site of sexual repression and taboo, it is also the place where sexuality is engendered, in the fullest sense.[9] Yet, the Pa-Celie sexual relation, though initially presented as an actual violation of a primary taboo, turns out to be not literal incest but a social and symbolic equivalent. The novel seems to delve into the oedipal drama to unravel and then reweave the complexities, and the discovery that "Pa not Pa" confronts Celie with another contradiction. The Pa who is not Pa is yet—irrevocably—Pa. Her history has been shattered, and she cannot connect with the revised version sent by sister Nettie.

It is her love for Shug that enables Celie to bury her sad double narrative of paternal origins and construct a new identity within a feminine domain. In an earlier scene in the novel, Celie tells her story to Shug, breaking the father's injunction of silence and discovering a sister-lover, compassion and passion combined. Significantly, that first erotic encounter involves both women in a reciprocal mother-infant exchange: "Then I feels something real sort and wet on my breast, feel like one of my little lost babies mouth. . . . Way after while I act like a little lost baby too." The anaclitic satisfaction represented here suggests a symbolic return to the preoedipal stage, an idealized state of innocent eroticism; it is, in Foucault's words, about "bodies and pleasure."[10]

Subsequently, when disconnected from her *nom-du-père* by the discovery that her paternity is indeed a legal fiction, Celie is rescued from an identity crisis by Shug, who tells her, "Us each other's people now"; the two women have mothered each other and now elect to be woman-identified women. Implicit here is an escape from patriarchal law. In breaking the taboo against homosexuality, Celie symbolically exits the masternarrative of female sexuality and abandons the position ascribed to her within the symbolic order. Instead, she chooses a mode of sexuality that Freud describes as "infantile"; but perhaps the value of that term should be reassessed. Shug, for example, is enviably infantile: as poly-morphously perverse as a child, she pursues her pleasures without guilt or repression. Her sexual pluralism reminds us that sexuality is the site not only of regulation but of subversion; as Carole Vance argues, sexual-ity remains, in the end, "flexible, anarchic, ambiguous, layered with mul-tiple meanings, offering doors that open to unexpected experience. The connection of both sexual behavior and fantasy to infancy, the irrational, the unconscious, is a source of both surprise and pleasure." It is this highly disruptive potential—sexuality's ability to resist the ideological laws that operate through its very terrain, to survive and flourish in "aberrant" forms despite the cultural imposition of a norm—that Shug's erotic behavior suggests; she embodies and embraces the notion of jouis-sance as a liberating power.

Celie's initiation into eroticism is linked with her growing sense of self and her capacity to see wonder in the world. Taught by Shug, whose religious practice is to "admire," Celie metamorphoses into a Miranda, taking childlike delight in the brave new world to which her latent sen-sory responses have been awakened. If homosexuality involves narcis-sism, as Freud believes, we see its positive and empowering effect on Celie. In loving Shug, Celie becomes a desiring subject, and in being loved by Shug, she is made visible to herself as an object of desire. In contrast to the repression that Celie has experienced in accepting her social position as a "mature" woman in a phallocentric culture, her "infan-tile regression" is an act of radical rebellion. By choosing "deviancy," "immaturity," and the "sickness" that lesbianism signifies in a system of compulsory heterosexuality, Celie enacts a critique not of the oedipal theory itself but of the sexist socialization that it insightfully yet uncriti-cally represents.

In a hostile review of the novel, Trudier Harris describes Celie as "a bale of cotton with a vagina" and dismisses Celie and Shug's love affair as a "schoolgirl fairytale," thereby missing the radical political implica-tions of the shift from vagina to clitoris that the lesbian relationship involves. In Freud's theory the clitoral orgasm is notoriously immature; and within the culture, I would suggest, the notion of the mature vaginal orgasm still predominates, since it is a necessary myth within our com-pulsorily heterosexual society. For a long time Celie's clitoris remained "undiscovered"; and while real women in heterosexual relationships undoubtedly have lovers more skillful and sensitive than Mr. _____ (even if his being signified in this way does mischievously imply that he is the archetypal male), the ideological construct woman still seems to be experiencing orgasm without reference to her clitoris. Think of representations of sexuality in popular films, for example. In the typical love scene, the camera show a couple commencing missionary-position sex and, eight seconds later, moves in to a close up of the woman's face to reveal that, miraculously, she is in the throes of orgasm, her mouth wide open, perhaps to suggest that place where the camera is forbidden to go. At this climactic point, the scene dissolves from the screen in an act of self-censorship, and we are left with the dominant image of the desirable woman in our culture: passive, available, and obligingly able to reach instant vaginal orgasm. If film directors know about the clitoris, or about active female desire, film censors are surely involved in the conspiracy to keep such knowledge inadmissible.

What this practice suggests is that the ideology of popular culture subjects women to a mild form of psychological clitoridectomy, and perhaps for the same reason that real clitoridectomies are performed: as Kathleen Barry argues, they ensure that women will not form erotic attachments to one another. I would suggest that the erotic zone of the clitoris *has* to be censored in social constructions of sexuality, since its mapping on the female body would allow women to "just say no" to the coveted male organ.

So, for Celie, the discovery of the clitoris (and of the possibility of sexual fulfillment with a woman) is accompanied by a whole range of other discoveries that relegate man to the margins of a world he has always dominated. The most significant of these is a reconceptualization of God the Patriarch. Describing her feminist redefinition of God, Shug makes an explicit connection between spiritual and sexual jouissance.

> My first step from the old white man was trees. . . . Then birds. Then other people. But one day . . . it come to me: that feeling of being part of everything, not separate at all. . . . In fact, when it happen, you can't miss it. It sort of like you know what, she say, grinning and rubbing high up on my thigh.

In answer to Celie's shocked protest, Shug maintains, "God love all them feelings. That's some of the best stuff God did." And shortly afterward she echoes the title of the novel by observing, "I think it pisses God off if you walk by the color purple in a field somewhere and don't notice it." This is a moment of epiphany for Celie, and we might notice her appropriately detumescent metaphor when, in severing the connection between "man" and "God," she observes that "[n]ext to any little scrub of a bush in my yard, Mr. _____'s evil sort of shrink." Phallocentrism has collapsed: the transformation of God from the "old white man" to a new form of otherness, the ungendered creator of the color purple, is one of the major metamorphoses of the novel.

Finally, what is meant by that richly allusive symbol, the color purple? Clearly, in part, it represents the wonder of the natural world, to which Celie's eyes have been newly awakened: "I been so busy thinking about him I never truly notice nothing God make. Not a blade of corn (how it do that?) not the color purple (where it come from?)."

The color purple is encoded within the novel as a sign of indomitable female spirit. For example, Celie makes red-and-purple pants for Sofia (who has survived a brutal beating by the police that leaves her "the color of eggplant"): "I dream Sofia wearing these pants, one day she was jumping over the moon." Consider also Walker's definitions of *womanist*, which are represented by the color purple. One of those definitions, quoted in part earlier, is embodied by Shug: "A woman who loves other women, sexually and/or nonsexually. . . . Sometimes loves individual men, sexually or nonsexually." Another definition refers to female joie de vivre, or exuberance; and in her fourth and final definition, Walker states suggestively, "Womanist is to feminist as purple to lavender."

But most daringly significant is the use of the color purple to encode the specifically feminine jouissance experienced by Celie. Associated with Easter and resurrection, and thus with spiritual regeneration, purple may also evoke the female genitalia; indeed, Walker makes the color connection explicit in "One Child of One's Own" by provocatively describing a black woman's vagina as "the color of raspberries and blackberries—or scuppernongs and muscadines." In that essay Walker complains that white women feminists "cannot imagine that black women have vaginas. Or if they can, where imagination leads them is too far to go."

What I want to suggest is that in *The Color Purple*, in her representation of the unrepresentable, Walker dares us to arrive at the place where "imagination . . . is too far to go."

Notes

1. In *The Heroine's Text*, Nancy Miller defines the "euphoric text" as built on a "trajectory of ascent" and ending with the heroine's integration into society. Miller confines her study to eighteenth-century novels, but her model provides a useful contrast to *The Color Purple*, demonstrating how Walker's novel subverts the conventional plot by rewriting the story of seduction within a lesbian framework.

   In emphasizing the relevance of Celie's story for all women, I do not mean to deny the specificity of her oppression as a black lesbian. Indeed, any blanket reference to women as a category is in any case controversial; my paper does suggest briefly that in feminist discourse this usage tends to reinforce the marginalization of "minority" groups, but I should also note that some feminists would like to abandon the term altogether. Kristeva claims that "to believe that one 'is a woman' is almost as absurd and obscurantist as to believe that one 'is a man'" ("La femme, ce n'est jamais ça," *Tel quel* 59 [1974]: 19–24; qtd, in Moi 163); Monique Wittig provocatively declares, "Lesbians are not women" (110).

2. The term *compulsory heterosexuality* originated with Gayle Rubin: her influential essay "The Traffic in Women" synthesizes readings of Freud, Lacan, Marx, and Lévi-Strauss to account for our enculturation into the sex-gender system. See also Adrienne Rich. The term *herstory* comes from Alice Walker's feminist prose (see esp. *Search*).

3. Classic feminist texts that deal with the problem of silencing include Virginia Woolf's *Room of One's Own*, Tillie Olsen's *Silences*, Patricia Meyer Spacks's *Female Imagination*, Elaine Showalter's *Literature of Their Own*, and Sandra M. Gilbert and Susan Gubar's *Madwoman in the Attic*.

4. See, e.g, Gloria T. Hull, Patricia Bell Scott, and Barbara Smith's anthology *Some of Us Are Brave* and Cherrie Moraga and Gloria Anzaldua's *This Bridge Called My Back*. Several essays collected in Showalter's *New Feminist Criticism* also focus on writing by black women and lesbians: Barbara Smith's "Towards a Black Feminist Criticism," Deborah E. McDowell's "New Directions for Black Feminist Criticism," and Bonnie Zimmerman's "What Has Never Been: An Overview of Lesbian Feminist Literary Criticism."

Printing presses geared toward "minority" groups have been set up recently: for example, the Kitchen Table: Women of Color Press. But in *The Sexual Mountain and Black Women Writers: Adventures in Sex, Literature, and Real Life*—a title so provocative that it invites speculation about men's place in black feminism—Calvin Hernton describes the male speaker's misogyny at a meeting set up to establish a new African American publishing company: "[The speaker] went into a tirade against black women writers . . . claiming that they had 'taken over' the publishing world in a conspiracy against black male writers" (xv). Note also Trudier Harris's allegation that Alice Walker became a media favorite by "waiting in the wings of the feminist movement and the power it had generated long enough for her curtain call to come" (155). Guilty of success, Toni Morrison and Alice Walker bear the brunt of such animosity; compare the personal and critical hostility directed at the flamboyant Zora Neale Hurston, who eventually "disappeared" under its pressure.

5. "Masternarratives" is, of course, Fredric Jameson's term, though he uses it more generally to denote the hegemonic discourse of the ruling class and intends no specific reference to gender.

6. I refer to the conventional assessment of Wright as a realistic writer, though it seems to me that this, too, is misplaced, that his works are, rather, surrealistic. Molly Hite discusses the critical blindness that has resulted from applying conventions of classic realism to *The Color Purple*.

The feminist tradition of transgressing generic boundaries can be traced at least to Woolf's *Room of One's Own*, which inscribes its feminist social and cultural criticisms within an incisively ironic narrative framework. The strategy is most notably continued in the work of the French feminists, particularly Luce Irigaray, Hélène Cixous, and Catherine Clément; the issue here is a renegotiation of the relation between the personal and the impersonal, or the alleged objectivity of academic discourse. Disrupting generic boundaries is connected with disrupting gender boundaries: feminist writers use subversive narrative strategies to infiltrate and reshape ideological fictions of femininity.

7. For discussions of quilting in Walker's work, see Barbara Christian; Lindsey Tucker; Houston A. Baker, Jr., and Charlotte Pierce-Baker. See Showalter's "Piecing and Writing" for a critique of the revival of feminine crafts as tropes in feminist fictions and theory.

8. For an opposing view, see Cora Kaplan, who objects to Rich's concept of "intellectual" lesbianism as a political solution, arguing that it has produced among feminists a new source of sexual shame and guilt: "Any pleasure that accrues to women who take part in heterosexual acts is therefore necessarily tainted; at the extreme end of this position, women who 'go with men' are considered collaborators . . ." (52). Note also Paula Webster's argument that by privileging lesbianism, feminist discourse has constructed an alternative sexual hierarchy that creates new prohibitions and reduces women's "relationships with eroticism to issues of preference and purity . . ." (387).

9. Michel Foucault argues that "the family is the most active site of sexuality" and that incest is "constantly being solicited and refused . . . a thing that is continuously demanded in order for the family to be a hotbed of constant sexual incitement" (109).

10. One could argue that if Celie symbolically returns to a preoedipal state, her subversive language, with its poetic pulsions and absences, can be connected with Kristeva's concept of the semiotic chora.

◆◆◆◆◆◆◆◆◆◆◆◆◆◆

Patches: Quilts and Community in Alice Walker's "Everyday Use"

HOUSTON A. BAKER, JR., AND CHARLOTTE PIERCE-BAKER

During the Depression and really hard time, people often paid their debts with quilts, and sometimes their tithe to the church too.

—*The Quilters*

A patch is a fragment. It is a vestige of wholeness that stands as a sign of loss and a challenge to creative design. As a remainder or remnant, the patch may symbolize rupture and impoverishment; it may be defined by the faded glory of the already gone. But as a fragment, it is also rife with explosive potential of the yet-to-be-discovered. Like woman, it is a liminal element between wholes.

Weaving, shaping, sculpting, or quilting in order to create a kaleidoscopic and momentary array is tantamount to providing an improvisational response to chaos. Such activity represents a nonce response to ceaseless scattering; it constitutes survival strategy and motion in the face of dispersal. A patchwork quilt, laboriously and affectionately crafted from bits of worn overalls, shredded uniforms, tattered petticoats, and outgrown dresses stands as a signal instance of a patterned wholeness in the African diaspora.

Traditional African cultures were scattered by the European slave trade throughout the commercial time and space of the New World. The transmutation of quilting, a European, feminine tradition, into a black women's folk art, represents an innovative fusion of African cloth manufacture, piecing, and appliqué with awesome New World experiences— and expediencies. The product that resulted was, in many ways, a double patch. The hands that pieced the master's rigidly patterned quilts by day were often the hands that crafted a more functional design in slave cabins by night. The quilts of Afro-America offer a *sui generis* context (a weaving together) of experiences and a storied, vernacular representation of lives conducted in the margins, ever beyond an easy and acceptable wholeness. In many ways, the quilts of Afro-America resemble the work of all those dismembered gods who transmute fragments and remainders into the light and breath of a new creation. And the sorority of quiltmakers, fragment weavers, holy patchers, possesses a sacred wisdom that it hands down from generation to generation of those who refuse the center for the ludic and unconfined spaces of the margins.

Those positioned outside the sorority and enamored of wholeness often fail to comprehend the dignity inherent in the quiltmakers' employment of remnants and conversion of fragments into items of everyday use. Just as the mysteries of, say, the blues remain hidden from those in happy circumstances, so the semantic intricacies of quiltmaking remain incomprehensible to the individualistic sensibility invested in myths of a postindustrial society. All of the dark, southern energy that manifests itself in the conversion of a sagging cabin—a shack really—into a "happy home" by stringing a broom wire between two nails in the wall and making the joint jump, or that shows itself in the "crazy quilt" patched from crumbs and remainders, seems but a vestige of outmoded and best-forgotten customs.

To relinquish such energy, however, is to lose an enduring resource-fulness that has ensured a distinctive aesthetic tradition and a unique code of everyday, improvisational use in America. The tradition-bearers of the type of Afro-American energy we have in mind have always in-cluded ample numbers of southern, black women who have transmuted fragments of New World displacement into a quilted eloquence scarcely appreciated by traditional spokespersons for wholeness. To wit: even the perspicacious and vigilant lion of abolitionism Frederick Douglass responded to Monroe A. Major's request for inclusions in his book *Noted Negro Women:*

> We have many estimable women of our variety but not many famous ones. It is not well to claim too much for ourselves before the public. Such extrava-gance invites contempt rather than approval. I have thus far seen no book of importance written by a negro woman and I know of no one among us who can appropriately be called famous.

Southern black women have not only produced quilts of stunning beauty, they have also crafted books of monumental significance, works that have made them appropriately famous. In fact, it has been precisely the appropriation of energy drawn from sagging cabins and stitched re-mainders that has constituted the world of the quiltmakers' sorority. The energy has flowed through such women as Harriet Brent Jacobs, Zora Neale Hurston, and Margaret Walker, enabling them to continue an an-cestral line elegantly shared by Alice Walker.

In a brilliant essay entitled "Alice Walker: The Black Woman Artist as Wayward," Professor Barbara Christian writes: "Walker is drawn to the integral and economical process of quilt making as a model for her own craft. For through it, one can create out of seemingly disparate everyday materials patterns of clarity, imagination, and beauty." Profes-sor Christian goes on to discuss Walker's frequently cited "In Search of Our Mothers' Gardens" and her short story "Everyday Use." She convincingly argues that Walker employs quilts as signs of functional beauty and spiritual heritage that provide exemplars of challenging con-vention and radical individuality, or "artistic waywardness."

The patchwork quilt as a trope for understanding black women's crea-tivity in the United States, however, presents an array of interpretive possibilities that is not exhausted by Professor Christian's adept criticism of Walker. For example, if one takes a different tack and suggests that the quilt as metaphor presents not a stubborn contrariness, a wayward individuality, but a communal bonding that confounds traditional definitions of art and of the artist, then one plays on possibilities in the quilting trope rather different from those explored by Christian. What we want to suggest in our own adaptation of the trope is that it opens a fascinating interpretive window on vernacular dimensions of lived, creative experience in the United States. Quilts, in their patched and many-colored glory offer not a counter to tradition, but, in fact, an instance of the only legitimate tradition of "the people" that exists. They are representations of the stories of the vernacular natives who make up the ninety-nine percent of the American population unendowed with money and control. The class distinction suggested by "vernacular" should not overshadow the gender specificity of quilts as products of a universal woman's creativity—what Pattie Chase in *The Contemporary Quilt* calls "an ancient affinity between women and cloth." They are the testimony of "mute and inglorious" generations of women gone before. The quilt as interpretive sign opens up a world of *difference*, a nonscripted territory whose creativity with fragments is less a matter of "artistic" choice than of economic and functional necessity. "So much in the habit of sewing something," says Walker's protagonist in the remarkable novel *The Color Purple*, "[that] I stitch up a bunch of scraps, try to see what I can make."

The Johnson women, who populate the generations represented in Walker's short story "Everyday Use," are inhabitants of southern cabins who have always worked with "scraps" and seen what they could make of them. The result of their labor has been a succession of mothers and daughters surviving the ignominies of Jim Crow life and passing on ancestral blessings to descendants. The guardians of the Johnson homestead when the story commences are the mother—"a large, big-boned woman with rough, man-working hands"—and her daughter Maggie, who has remained with her "chin on chest, eyes on ground, feet in shuffle, ever since the fire that burned the other house to the ground" ten or twelve years ago. The mood at the story's beginning is one of ritualistic "waiting": "I will wait for her in the yard that Maggie and I made so clean and wavy yesterday afternoon." The subject awaited is the other daughter, Dee. Not only has the yard (as ritual ground) been prepared for the arrival of a goddess, but the sensibilities and costumes of Maggie and her mother have been appropriately attuned for the occasion. The mother daydreams of television shows where parents and children are suddenly—and pleasantly—reunited, banal shows where chatty hosts oversee tearful reunions. In her fantasy, she weighs a hundred pounds less, is several shades brighter in complexion, and possesses a devastatingly quick tongue. She returns abruptly to real life meditation, reflecting on her own heroic, agrarian accomplishments in slaughtering hogs and cattle and preparing their meat for winter nourishment. She is a robust provider who has gone to the people of her church and raised money to send her light-complexioned, lithe-figured, and ever-dissatisfied daughter Dee to college. Today, as she waits in the purified yard, she notes the stark differences between Maggie and Dee and recalls how the "last dingy gray board of the house [fell] in toward the red-hot brick chimney" when her former domicile burned. Maggie was scarred horribly by the fire, but Dee, who had hated the house with an intense fury, stood "off under the sweet gum tree . . . a look of concentration on her face." A scarred and dull Maggie, who has been kept at home and confined to everyday offices, has but one reaction to the fiery and vivacious arrival of her sister: "I hear Maggie suck in her breath. 'Uhnnnh,' is what it sounds like. Like when you see the wriggling end of a snake just in front of your foot on the road. 'Uhnnnh'."

Indeed, the question raised by Dee's energetic arrival is whether there are words adequate to her flair, her brightness, her intense colorfulness of style which veritably blocks the sun. She wears "a dress so loud it hurts my eyes. There are yellows and oranges enough to throw back the light of the sun. I feel my whole face warming from the heat waves it throws out." Dee is both serpent and fire introduced with bursting esprit into the calm pasture that contains the Johnsons' tin-roofed, three-room, windowless shack and grazing cows. She has joined the radical, black nationalists of the 1960s and 1970s, changing her name from Dee to Wangero and cultivating a suddenly fashionable, or stylish, interest in what she passionately describes as her "heritage." If there is one quality that Dee (Wangero) possesses in abundance, it is "style": "At sixteen she had a style of her own: and knew what style was."

But in her stylishness, Dee is not an example of the indigenous rapping and styling out of Afro-America. Rather, she is manipulated by the style-makers, the fashion designers whose semiotics the French writer Roland Barthes has so aptly characterized. "Style" for Dee is the latest vogue—the most recent fantasy perpetuated by American media. When she left for college, her mother had tried to give her a quilt whose making began with her grandmother Dee, but the bright daughter felt such patched coverings were "old-fashioned and out of style." She has returned at the commencement of "Everyday Use," however, as one who now purports to know the value of the work of black women as holy patchers.

The dramatic conflict of the story surrounds the definition of holiness. The ritual purification of earth and expectant atmosphere akin to that of Beckett's famous drama ("I will wait for her in the yard that Maggie and I made so clean and wavy yesterday afternoon.") prepare us for the narrator's epiphanic experience at the story's conclusion.

Near the end of "Everyday Use," the mother (who is the tale's narrator) realizes that Dee (a.k.a, Wangero) is a *fantasy* child, a perpetrator and victim of: "words, lies, other folks's habits." The energetic daughter is as frivolously careless of other peoples' lives as the fiery conflagration that she had watched ten years previously. Assured by the makers of American fashion that "black" is currently "beautiful," she has conformed her own "style" to that notion. Hers is a trendy "blackness" cultivated as "art" and costume. She wears "a dress down to the ground . . . bracelets dangling and making noises when she moves her arm up to shake the folds of the dress out of her armpits." And she says of quilts she has removed from a trunk at the foot of her mother's bed: "Maggie can't appreciate these quilts! She'd probably be backward enough to put them to everyday use." "Art" is, thus, juxtaposed with "everyday use" in Walker's short story, and the fire goddess Dee, who has achieved literacy only to burn "us with a lot of knowledge we didn't necessarily need to know," is revealed as a perpetuator of institutional theories of aesthetics. (Such theories hold that "art" is, in fact, defined by social institutions such as museums, book reviews, and art dealers.) Of the two quilts that she has extracted from the trunk, she exclaims: "But they're 'priceless.'" And so the quilts are by "fashionable" standards of artistic value, standards that motivate the answer that Dee provides to her mother's question: "'Well,' I said, stumped. 'What would *you* do with them?'" Dee's answer: "Hang them." The stylish daughter's entire life has been one of "framed" experience; she has always sought a fashionably "aesthetic" distance from southern expediencies. (And how unlike quilt frames that signal social activity and a coming to completeness are her *frames.*) Her concentrated detachment from the fire, which so nearly symbolizes her role vis-à-vis the Afro-American community (her black friends "worshipped . . . the scalding humor that erupted like bubbles in lye") is characteristic of her attitude. Her goals include the appropriation of exactly what *she* needs to remain fashionable in the eyes of a world of pretended wholeness, a world of banal television shows, framed and institutionalized art, and polaroid cameras—devices that instantly process and record experience as "framed" photograph. Ultimately, the framed polaroid photograph represents the limits of Dee's vision.

Strikingly, the quilts whose *tops* have been stitched by her grandmother from fragments of outgrown family garments and quilted after the grandmother's death by Aunt Dee and her sister (the mother who narrates the story) are perceived in Dee's polaroid sensibility as merely "priceless" works of an institutionally, or stylishly, defined "art world." In a reversal of perception tantamount to the acquisition of sacred knowledge by initiates in a rite of passage, the mother/narrator realizes that she has always worshipped at the altars of a "false" goddess. As her alter ego, Dee has always expressed that longing for the "other" that characterizes inhabitants of oppressed, "minority" cultures. Situated in an indisputably black and big-boned skin, the mother has secretly admired the "good hair," full figure, and well-turned (i.e., "whitely trim") ankle of Dee (Wangero). Sacrifices and sanctity have seemed in order. But in her epiphanic moment of recognition, she perceives the fire-scarred Maggie—the stay-at-home victim of southern scarifications—in a revised light. When Dee grows belligerent about possessing the quilts, Maggie emerges from the kitchen and says with a contemptuous gesture of dismissal: "She can have them, Mama. . . . I can 'member Grandma Dee without quilts." The mother's response to what she wrongly inter-prets as Maggie's hang-dog resignation before Dee is a radical awakening to godhead:

> When I looked at her . . . something hit me in the top of my head and ran down to the soles of my feet. Just like when I'm in church and the spirit of God touches me and I get happy and shout. I did something I never had done before: hugged Maggie to me, then dragged her into the room, snatched the quilts out of Miss Wangero's hands and dumped them into Maggie's lap.

Maggie is the arisen goddess of Walker's story; she is the sacred figure who bears the scarifications of experience and knows how to con-vert patches into robustly patterned and beautifully quilted wholes. As an earth-rooted and quotidian goddess, she stands in dramatic contrast to the stylishly fiery and other-oriented Wangero. The mother says in response to Dee's earlier cited accusation that Maggie would reduce quilts to rags by putting them to everyday use: "'She can always make some more,' I said. 'Maggie knows how to quilt.'" And, indeed, Maggie, the emergent goddess of New World improvisation and long ancestral memory, does know how to quilt. Her mind and imagination are capable of preserving the wisdom of grandmothers and aunts without material prompts: "I can 'member . . . without the quilts," she says. The secret to employing beautiful quilts as items of everyday use is the secret of crafty dues.

In order to comprehend the transient nature of all wholes, one must first become accustomed to living and working with fragments. Maggie has learned the craft of fragment weaving from her women ancestors: "It was Grandma Dee and Big Dee who taught her how to quilt herself." The conjunction of "quilt" and "self" in Walker's syntax may be simply a serendipitous accident of style. Nonetheless, the conjunction works magnificently to capture the force of black woman's quilting in "Every-day Use." Finally, it is the "self," or a version of humanness that one calls the Afro-American self, that must, in fact, be crafted from fragments on the basis of wisdom gained from preceding generations.

What is at stake in the world of Walker's short story, then, is not the prerogatives of Afro-American women as "wayward artists." Individual-ism and a flouting of convention in order to achieve "artistic" success constitute acts of treachery in "Everyday Use." For Dee, if she is any-thing, *is* a fashionable denizen of America's art/fantasy world. She is removed from the "everyday uses" of a black community that she scorns, misunderstands, burns. Certainly, she is "unconventionally" black. As such, however, she is an object of holy contempt from the archetypal weaver of black wholeness from tattered fragments. Maggie's "Uhnnnh" and her mother's designation "Miss Wangero" are gestures of utter contempt. Dee's sellout to fashion and fantasy in a television-manipulated world of "artistic" frames is a representation of the *complicity of the clerks*. Not "art," then, but use or function is the signal in Walker's fiction of sacred creation.

Quilts designed for everyday use, pieced wholes defying symmetry and pattern, are signs of the scarred generations of women who have always been alien to a world of literate words and stylish fantasies. The crafted fabric of Walker's story is the very weave of blues and jazz traditions in the Afro-American community, daringly improvisational modes that confront breaks in the continuity of melody (or theme) by riffing. The asymmetrical quilts of southern black women are like the off-centered stomping of the jazz solo or the innovative musical showmanship of the blues interlude. They speak a world in which the deceptively shuffling Maggie is capable of a quick change into goddess, an unlikely holy figure whose dues are paid in full. Dee's anger at her mother is occasioned principally by the mother's insistence that paid dues make Maggie a more likely bearer of sacredness, tradition, and true value than the "brighter" sister. "You just don't understand," she says to her mother. Her assessment is surely correct where institutional theories and systems of "art" are concerned. The mother's cognition contains no categories for framed art. The mother works according to an entirely different scale of use and value, finally assigning proper weight to the virtues of Maggie and to the ancestral importance of the pieced quilts that she has kept out of use for so many years. Smarting, perhaps, from Dee's designation of the quilts as "old-fashioned," the mother has buried the covers away in a trunk. At the end of Walker's story, however, she has become aware of her own mistaken value judgments, and she pays homage that is due to Maggie. The unlikely daughter is a *griot* of the vernacular who remembers actors and events in a distinctively black "historical" drama.

Before Dee departs, she "put on some sunglasses that hid everything above the tip of her nose and her chin." Maggie smiles at the crude symbolism implicit in this act, for she has always known that her sister saw "through a glass darkly." But it is the mother's conferral of an ancestral blessing (signaled by her deposit of the quilts in Maggie's lap) that constitutes the occasion for the daughter's first "real smile." Maggie knows that it is only communal recognition by elders of the tribe that confers ancestral privileges on succeeding generations. The mother's holy recognition of the scarred daughter's sacred status as quilter is the best gift of a hard-pressed womankind to the fragmented goddess of the present.

At the conclusion of "Everyday Use," which is surely a fitting precursor to *The Color Purple*, with its sewing protagonist and its scenes of sisterly quilting, Maggie and her mother relax in the ritual yard after the dust of Dee's departing car has settled. They dip snuff in the manner of African confreres sharing cola nuts. The moment is past when a putatively "new" generation has confronted scenes of black, everyday life. A change has taken place, but it is a change best described by Amiri Baraka's designation for Afro-American music's various styles and discontinuities. The change in Walker's story is the "changing same." What has been reaffirmed at the story's conclusion is the value of the quiltmaker's motion and strategy in the precincts of a continuously undemocratic South.

But the larger appeal of "Everyday Use" is its privileging of a distinctively woman's craft as *the* signal mode of confronting chaos through a skillful blending of patches. In *The Color Purple*, Celie's skill as a fabric worker completely transmutes the order of Afro-American existence. Not only do her talents with a needle enable her to wear the pants in the family, they also allow her to become the maker of pants par excellence. Hence, she becomes a kind of unifying goddess of patch and stitch, an instructress of mankind who bestows the gift of consolidating fragments. Her abusive husband Albert says: "When I was growing up . . . I use to try to sew along with mama cause that's what she was always doing. But everybody laughed at me. But you know, I liked it." "Well," says Celie, "nobody gon laugh at you now. . . . Here, help me stitch in these pockets."

A formerly "patched" separateness of woman is transformed through fabric craft into a new unity. Quilting, sewing, stitching are bonding activities that begin with the godlike authority and daring of women, but that are given (as a gift toward community) to men. The old disparities are transmuted into a vision best captured by the scene that Shug suggests to Celie: "But, Celie, try to imagine a city full of these shining, blueblack people wearing brilliant blue robes with designs like fancy quilt patterns." The heavenly city of quilted design is a form of unity wrested by the sheer force of the woman quiltmaker's will from chaos. As a community, it stands as both a sign of the potential effects of black women's creativity in America, and as an emblem of the effectiveness of women's skillful confrontation of patches. Walker's achievement as a southern, black, woman novelist is her own successful application of the holy patching that was a staple of her grandmother's and great-grandmother's hours of everyday ritual. "Everyday Use" is, not surprisingly, dedicated to "your grandmama": to those who began the line of converting patches into works of southern genius.

INTERVIEWS

◆◆◆◆◆◆◆◆◆◆◆◆◆

A Conversation with Alice Walker

SHARON WILSON

[**E**ditor's Note: Alice Walker is the author of *The Color Purple*, for which she won both a Pulitzer Prize and an American Book Award for Fiction in 1983. She has also written two earlier novels, two short story collections, many books of poetry, and a collection of "womanist prose," *In Search of Our Mothers' Gardens*. Her forthcoming book of poems is titled *Horses Make a Landscape Look More Beautiful*. Ms. Walker was born in Eatonton, Georgia, and now makes her home in San Francisco with her daughter Rebecca and her partner Robert Allen. The following interview with *Kalliope*'s Sharon Wilson was conducted as a television program with studio audience participation. Ms. Walker appeared on the "Worth Quoting" series in February when she was in Jacksonville, Florida for a reading sponsored by *Kalliope* and the Women's center of Florida Junior College at Jacksonville.]

KALLIOPE: The first time I heard of you, I was a great fan of Zora Neale Hurston. You wrote, in *Ms.* a piece about Zora and looking for her grave, and your feelings about her. I wrote you a letter about your piece because it moved me so much, and you wrote me a wonderful letter back. Since then you've been instrumental in bringing Zora back into print, and I've been lucky enough to find out about all your other writing, and have grown to care about it very much.

WALKER: Thank you.

KALLIOPE: When I first read that piece, one of the things that struck me most was the point where you're out in the overgrown weeds in the graveyard. You're trying to call Zora to ask her, "Where are you?" You wanted her to answer you. In *The Color Purple* also, you're calling on some people to come to you, and they do. Is Zora any place in your book? Is some of her spirit in Shug?

WALKER: Oh, I think so. Yes. How could that not be? But Shug is also partly my aunts who worked as domestics up North and who would come to visit us in the South. I couldn't believe they cleaned anybody else's house, because they looked like they needed somebody to clean theirs. They had wonderful nails, and were all beautifully dressed—just fantastically vibrant women with great perfumes. It still astonishes me that my aunts worked every day for other people and yet retained such a magical life of their own, which we saw during the summer and sometimes on very brief weekend visits.

KALLIOPE: Like Zora's book *Their Eyes Were Watching God*, *The Color Purple* is written in folk dialect.

319

WALKER: Black folk English.

KALLIOPE: I've read a lot of white critics who seem to find something innovative in this. Do white critics tend to praise you for innovation when really what you're doing is more like jazz—a brilliant improvisation on traditional themes?

WALKER: Well, actually, I'm not doing anything but writing the way my parents speak. We all have a right to do that, and I don't think there's anything especially innovative. This was the way my grandparents spoke, this is the way my mother speaks today, and I want to capture that. Especially for my daughter, who has a very different kind of upbringing and who doesn't get to Georgia very often. I want her to know when she grows up what her grandparents, her great-grandparents, sounded like, because the sound is so amazingly alive. The language is so beautiful, and one of its beauties is its brevity. People said what they had to say. They did not beat around the bush, they did not take all day—they didn't *have* all day. They'd say this, that, and the other thing, and be done with it. I like that very much, and that's partly why the novel is written so succinctly. I wanted to underscore that kind of directness.

KALLIOPE: The novel begins directly with heartbreak and goes on from there, with Celie having her babies taken away from her. It reminds me of the scene in *The Third Life of Grange Copeland*—she took her poisoned baby out to the fields.

Critics are talking now about your three novels as a kind of trilogy in terms of the growth of men and women understanding each other—at least to a certain degree—at the end. Do you ever think of the books as a trilogy?

WALKER: No, no.

KALLIOPE: . . . or just that there are three of them, and you'll write a fourth and fifth and sixth.

WALKER: No, no. I don't think like critics, actually. I'm always trying to give voice to specific people in the hope that if I do that, then that specific kind of person will be better understood, really brought into the common fund of people that we have knowledge of and therefore we share with, and are in community with. Criticism is something that I don't fully approve of, because I think for the critic it must be very painful to always look at things in a critical way. I think you miss so much. And you have to sort of shape everything you see to the way you're prepared to see it.

KALLIOPE: You have to always be analyzing, "Now why did I cry on page 76?"

WALKER: Yes, instead of just having a good cry. Tears are great for you. I don't mean that we should just wallow in suffering, but actually what happens when you don't cry is that you accumulate toxins in your body. It's a physiological fact that you need to cry.

KALLIOPE: I know you feel somewhat uncomfortable that now you're sort of a media darling, and you've never sought that. It's all happened to you in a way, by accident, after writing seriously for more than twenty years. A few years ago Toni Morrison was the media darling. Do you think the publishing business picks one writer—one female writer or one black writer—that they are going to pay attention to and neglects the rest?

WALKER: I don't think so. First of all, I don't really think of myself as a media darling. I do very little of this. Very, very little.

KALLIOPE: But they do it to you even when you don't want them to.

WALKER: Well, it's hard for them to do it to me if I stay at home, if I stay in my garden and in the country. But it's true that even when you narrow it down, there's still a good bit of media intrusion. I think that what happened with *The Color Purple* was the surprise of its being chosen as a Pulitzer Prize winner. I think that made a lot of people notice it who wouldn't have. The media wouldn't have noticed it particularly had it not won the prize. And to tell you the truth, I'm still rather astonished that it did. It's not the kind of book that I would have thought anyone in this country—except a very, very few people—would have given a prize to.

KALLIOPE: Theodore Roethke once said that he thought that one of the crimes of writing was to waste technical skill on a trivial theme. That sounds good on the surface, but that kind of thing always terrifies me, because I always want to know who is going to decide if a theme is trivial. I think that traditionally the white male publishing world has decided that black themes are trivial and that women's interests are trivial. Do you think that's changing any, and if so, how have we accomplished it?

WALKER: Well, I no longer really think very much about what white males are thinking. The exceptions often think somewhat the way we do, but the sort of run-of-the-mill white males—who knows what they're thinking? On the other hand, women have, over the last twenty years, really forged a community of readers, writers, and activists. That is what we're seeing. We're seeing that feminists and womanists have actually come of age, so that we are able to talk to each other. And we have done it largely by not using the white male literary establishment or the white male political establishment.

KALLIOPE: As managing editor of *Kalliope*, I still get a lot of letters from women whose work I have accepted, saying, "I'm so happy to have a place for my work. It's been turned down by this person and that person who said, 'We're not interested in what happens in the kitchen, what happens in the bedroom, what happens with your children.'" I think those areas of interest are still not taken seriously in other ways, and I think it's important that we're trying to do this.

WALKER: Well, we take them seriously. That's where we always have to start. If we don't take them seriously, why should anybody else? But if we do take them seriously, we can do whatever we like with them. We can share, we can write, we can read, we can grow. The main thing is for us to be serious.

KALLIOPE: In *In Search of Our Mothers' Gardens*, at one point you say history isn't everything. I think you mean by that, just because everything has happened this way in the past doesn't mean we have to let it go on happening—that we do have the power to change.

WALKER: Well, some people don't like optimism. And for those, what can I do? I write. The people who insist on being pessimistic will just be that way. It's too bad, because it's more fun being an optimist, I've discovered. I used to be extremely pessimistic. But unless we have hope, unless we can grow together and really feel that we can endure, survive, and overcome—what is there? We can just sit and wait for the bombs to fall on us and crawl into little holes that won't save us either. When I write I don't really worry too much about the people who are not going to understand. I know that many people won't. There are many things that other people do that *I* don't understand. And I always feel that they have a right not to understand, just as I have a right to present my vision of reality.

KALLIOPE: The poet, Marilyn Hacker, who's a feminist editor as well, once wrote in a poem addressed to another writer, ". . . but you know about words. You have had time to figure out that hardly anyone comes back to bed because of a poem." And yet it seems to me that the main purpose of our art is to make people change. Like Rilke's "Apollo"—"you must change your life."

WALKER: Oh, yes.

KALLIOPE: And it seems to be obvious, especially from *Our Mothers' Gardens*, that real changes have happened. You said at one point that your brothers had acknowledged children they hadn't acknowledged before. A lot of lives changing out of that.

WALKER: Oh, yes. I'm not just saying in my personal life, or my brothers' lives, but I think that we live in change. It's absolutely necessary, and art is supposed to do that. I think we were given art to heal ourselves, and by extension, to help other people heal themselves. Otherwise, what is it for? If it's just to hang on the wall or to be a decoration, it's useless. It's an object that has no function. Though I don't underestimate the power of decoration, either.

KALLIOPE: Is there a connection between this and other traditions of African art that are still somewhat utilitarian in a sense of healing, of being part of our everyday work, of being more in the fabric of our lives . . . as compared to the way Western art has become more purely decorative today?

WALKER: Well, I think so. In Native American culture, when someone is hurt very deeply, either physically or spiritually, the way you tell they are recovering is this: if it's a woman and she makes baskets, she will start making a basket even more beautiful, more intricate than before, because out of her suffering, she has managed to instill more into it. By the time she finishes the basket, she is well.

KALLIOPE: Speaking about healing—you and I both have daughters that are mixed-race. I still worry about the tradition I see in fiction of the tragic mulatto, and that this is the role model my daughter has. Do you see any changes in this in the future? Are there writers I'm not familiar with who are dealing with this issue in a more positive way?

WALKER: I think so. I think in *The Color Purple* what happens with Mary Agnes is that she just becomes a part of this family, becomes what she always has been. I think one of the things we do recognize in black culture is that black people come in all colors. I think we have to keep emphasizing that, and seeing it as the positive thing that it is.

KALLIOPE: And not divisive.

WALKER: And not divisive, no. For white people who have been very keen on staying white—if that's the way they want it, then that's fine. But it means then they come in one color and are just one segment that has separated itself from the rest of humankind, and are very isolated in the world because they are a minority.

KALLIOPE: We have a studio audience with us today, and we would like to take some questions from the studio audience as well.

GUEST 1: Alice, you grew up in a big family. Did you feel that you were different when you were growing up?

WALKER: Oh, yes. I felt I was quite different. I was quieter and I needed more space, I needed more time on my own. And it was O.K.— they were quite happy for me to be different and I continue to be so. But I sometimes think I'm not as different as I thought from, for instance, my father. I thought he was just totally different from me, but in fact, deep down, I am very much like him. We like the same things. He likes to cook, he likes to feed people, he likes the out-of-doors. He was a totally natural kind of person, and those are the things I value too. So I see myself in him, even though I always thought—my God, who is this man?

KALLIOPE: I think as we have children, too, all of a sudden we find our parents' voices coming out of our throats, and we go, "Aaah! Where did *that* come from?"

WALKER: Yes, where did that come from? It came from Mama, yes it did.

GUEST 2: I got to know you as Sharon did, through your search of information and materials on Zora Neale Hurston, which I appreciate very much. I would like to know how you felt upon the completion of your book and the works that you found.

WALKER: I felt great. Well, no, I felt sad to find her where I found her, in the cemetery without a marker and very overrun with weeds. It was one of the times when I felt badly for us as a human species. I felt—

we can do better than that. But on the other hand, I felt really happy to have been able to go there and to search and to find what I have found and to have all of her words, to help them get back into the world. I loved doing *I Love Myself.* It was a great boost for my own spirit. It was like having one of my aunts come back.

GUEST 3: I would be interested in knowing if you have trouble with your public differentiating between the experience of your protagonist and your own personal experience?

WALKER: I don't think so. I feel so often that we are all so much the same in many ways. I was just reading an article by Doris Lessing who believes the human species is really a single organism with the same brain. She says that sometimes she will have a thought or an idea, and at the same time from a totally different part of the world, that same thought will emerge at the same time. And that this is constantly happening. She never says, "I have an idea." She says, "There's an idea around." And Howard Thurman, a great theologian, talked about how if you go deeply enough in yourself, it is inevitable that you will come up in someone else.

GUEST 4: As a child, I met Zora Neale Hurston because she was the guest of my mother's sorority in Tallahassee at Florida A & M University. She was a very fantastic person but I didn't know—and I don't guess she knew, either—that she would be someone we would all be talking about today. I read in one of the reviews that you visited Eatonville and disguised yourself as her niece?

WALKER: It wasn't hard.

GUEST 4: Were you able to find anyone who remembered her well enough to give you what you were looking for? Also, I wonder if you would compare your manner of writing with that of Zora Neale Hurston?

WALKER: I met one of the people who appeared in one of her books, Mrs. Mosley. Mrs. Mosley had just gotten out of the hospital and she wasn't too happy to see us. We were a great intrusion, and I was sorry. But I did want very much, before all of these people died out, to try to have some sense of what Zora's life had been when she was in Eatonville. And I met an elderly doctor who had been Zora's friend and doctor, and we had a good talk about her. I don't think I really needed the disguise, but I was short of funds, and this was the only chance I would have of actually finding out anything. And so I really did that, but I don't know if I would do that the same way today. About the writing—I think Zora's writing throughout is much lighter-hearted than mine. I had to grow into being an optimist. I think she was always an optimist, and I think that's the major difference in our work.

GUEST 5: The letters in *The Color Purple* were such a marvelous device for getting the story across—it emerges and flows so beautifully from them. Did you originally visualize the book that way, or was it just fortuitous inspiration that you struggled to reach?

WALKER: Writing *The Color Purple* was not so much struggle—the struggle was really in trying to get out of New York and move to California so I could have space and time to write. But it was more of a letting go, of just trying to clear my channels enough so that the characters could get through. The letter method seemed best on a number of levels, including the historical. We were talking earlier about Sojourner Truth and about having her children sold from her—how when she cried out a mother's grief, none but God heard her. That, in a way, is the precursor of a letter to God. I can imagine Sojourner Truth saying, "God, what can I do—they've sold my children." Celie is able to write, "Dear God, this has happened to me and I have to tell somebody and so I write to you."

GUEST 6: *Meridian* was my favorite book by you. I would like to know whether Meridian was a real person. I could think of a person who could fit that description almost exactly.

WALKER: That's great because that means she is real. But she's not necessarily a real person that I knew. She is more a composite and her function is to help us relate in a personal way to a period of history very important to the development of our country, the Civil Rights era.

GUEST 6: Could you give an explanation of the end of *Meridian* where the man takes over Meridian's place?

WALKER: Yes, she passes on her role to him. It means that we are all struggling to change and to grow. You know, in the church when you're coming up for communion and the preacher says, "As these depart, others come forth . . ." Remember that? Well, it's sort of like that. As you grow beyond something, you move on to the next thing. But someone else is coming to where you were, and they go through then what you went through, and then they go on.

KALLIOPE: You have a lot of people who love you very much, who are sending you letters. You have people who want you to make appearances. How do you handle this—how do you keep enough time for your own life and your own work?

WALKER: Well, I say no an awful lot. But it's necessary. Otherwise, I wouldn't be able to work. And I really do. I know what my work is and it really comes first.

KALLIOPE: Do you have a new project you're getting ready for?

WALKER: Well, I just finished a new book, a collection of poems. It's called *Horses Make A Landscape Look More Beautiful*. The title is a quote from a Native American holy person whose name is Lame Dear. I'm also working on the script for *The Color Purple* movie which gives me many moments of worry and concern. And hope.

◆◆◆◆◆◆◆◆◆◆◆◆◆

Alice Walker: An Interview

JOHN O'BRIEN

Alice Walker's first collection of poems, *Once*, was published when she was only twenty-four. Her first novel, *The Third Life of Grange Copeland*, appeared two years later. Her second collection of poems, *Revolutionary Petunias*, is due in 1973, and a collection of short stories will be published either in late 1973 or early 1974. All of this suggests how productive Alice Walker has been in so short a time. Along the way she has also managed to publish essays, teach, and raise a family. Yet the most amazing thing is less the ambition she has demonstrated than the maturity she has achieved so early.

The thematic scope of her poetry is the past, both personal and historical. *Once* catalogues her experiences in the civil rights demonstrations of the 1960s and her travels in Africa. The poems are highly personal, recounting first loves and early disappointments. *Revolutionary Petunias* indicates that since her first collection, Walker learned more about both her craft and her subjects. Her poems are less marked by abstract observations than by a dependance upon brief anecdotes and precise memories. The language is sharper; the forms, more disciplined. And there is a simplicity of style and imagery which, as Yeats knew, is arrived at only after much labor, but appears spontaneous. More so than the first volume, *Revolutionary Petunias* focuses on specific memories that belong to her family, her small Southern town, and herself.

Walker's most notable accomplishment, however, has been in fiction. *The Third Life of Grange Copeland* traces the life of its hero from his early boyhood through his reckless youth, and finally to his old age. It is a novel of education, in which Walker demonstrates a remarkable ability to show the change and transformation of a character without violating either her characters or human nature. For her subject she chooses a character who is uneducated, oftentimes inarticulate, deprived, abused by his family, and usually trapped by circumstances which he seems unable to control. In other words, she picks an unlikely character in whom to explore the possibility of growth and change. Most impressive about her fiction is Walker's power as a storyteller. She does not indulge in awkward asides in which characters have revelations, or in extended dialogues where they work out the themes of the novel. Walker depends upon her capacity to render theme in terms of action.

The interview was arranged through the help of Miss Walker's editor, Hiram Haydn. Because of a complicated set of circumstances we were forced to conduct the interview through the mail. I sent a long list of questions which she reshaped and worked together, so that—rather than answering specific questions—she most frequently developed brief essays. Her responses are expansive, illuminating, and painstakingly phrased. Miss Walker lives in Jackson, Mississippi, where she is at work on another novel.

INTERVIEWER: Could you describe your early life and what led you to begin writing?

WALKER: I have always been a solitary person, and since I was eight years old (and the recipient of a disfiguring scar, since corrected, somewhat), I have daydreamed—not of fairytales—but of falling on swords, of putting guns to my heart or head, and of slashing my wrists with a razor. For a long time I thought I was very ugly and disfigured. This made me shy and timid, and I often reacted to insults and slights that were not intended. I discovered the cruelty (legendary) of children, and of relatives, and could not recognize it as the curiosity it was.

I believe, though, that it was from this period—from my solitary, lonely position, the position of an outcast—that I began to really see people and things, to really notice relationships and to learn to be patient enough to care about how they turned out. I no longer felt like the little girl I was. I felt old, and because I felt I was unpleasant to look at, filled with shame, I retreated into solitude, and read stories and began to write poems.

But it was not until my last year in college that I realized, dearly, the consequences of my daydreams. That year I made myself acquainted with every philosopher's position on suicide, because by that time it did not seem frightening or even odd—but only inevitable. Nietzsche and Camus made the most sense, and were neither maudlin nor pious. God's displeasure didn't seem to matter much to them, and I had reached the same conclusion. But in addition to finding such dispassionate commentary from them—although both hinted at the cowardice involved, and that bothered me—I had been to Africa during the summer, and returned to school healthy and brown, and loaded down with sculptures and orange fabric—and pregnant.

I felt at the mercy of everything, including my own body, which I had learned to accept as a kind of casing, over what I considered my real self. As long as it functioned properly, I addressed it, pampered it, led it into acceptable arms, and forgot about it. But now it refused to function properly. I was so sick I could not even bear the smell of fresh air. And I had no money, and I was, essentially—as I had been since grade school—alone. I felt there was no way out, and I was not romantic enough to believe in maternal instincts alone as a means of survival; in any case, I did not seem to possess those instincts. But I knew no one who knew about the secret, scary thing abortion was. And so, when all my efforts at finding an abortionist failed, I planned to kill myself, or— as I thought of it then—to "give myself a little rest." I stopped going down the hill to meals because I vomited incessantly, even when nothing came up but yellow, bitter, bile. I lay on my bed in a cold sweat, my head spinning.

While I was lying there, I thought of my mother, to whom abortion is a sin; her face appeared framed in the window across from me, her head wreathed in sunflowers and giant elephant-ears (my mother's flowers love her; they grow as tall as she wants); I thought of my father, that suspecting, once-fat slowly shrinking man, who had not helped me at all since I was twelve years old, when he bought me a pair of ugly saddle-oxfords I refused to wear. I thought of my sisters, who had their own problems (when approached with the problem I had; one sister never replied, the other told me—in forty-five minutes of long-distance carefully enunciated language—that I was a slut). I thought of the people at my high-school graduation who had managed to collect seventy-five dollars, to send me to college. I thought of my sister's check for a hundred dollars that she gave me for finishing high school at the head of my class: a check I never cashed, because I knew it would bounce.

I think it was at this point that I allowed myself exactly two self-pitying tears; I had wasted so much, how dared I? But I hated myself for crying, so I stopped, comforted by knowing I would not have to cry— or see anyone else cry—again.

I did not eat or sleep for three days. My mind refused, at times, to think about my problem at all—it jumped ahead to the solution. I prayed to—but I don't know Who or What I prayed to, or even if I did. Perhaps I prayed to God awhile, and then to the Great Void awhile. When I thought of my family, and when—on the third day—I began to see their faces around the walls, realized they would be shocked and hurt to learn of my death, but I felt they would not care deeply at all, when they discovered I was pregnant. Essentially, they would believe I was evil. They would be ashamed of me.

For three days I lay on the bed with a razorblade under my pillow. My secret was known to three friends only—all inexperienced (except verbally), and helpless. They came often to cheer me up, to bring me up-to-date on things as frivolous as classes. I was touched by their kindness, and loved them. But each time they left, I took out my razorblade and pressed it deep into my arm. I practiced a slicing motion. So that when there was no longer any hope, I would be able to cut my wrists quickly, and I hoped) painlessly.

In those three days, I said good-bye to the world (this seemed a high-flown sentiment, even then, but everything was beginning to be unreal); I realized how much I loved it, and how hard it would be not to see the sunrise every morning, the snow, the sky, the trees, the rocks, the faces of people, all so different and it was during this period that all things began to flow together; the face of one of my friends revealed itself to be the friendly, gentle face of a lion, and I asked her one day if I could touch her face and stroke her mane. I felt her face and hair, and she really was a lion; I began to feel the possibility of someone as worthless as myself attaining wisdom). But I found, as I had found on the porch of that building in Liberty County, Georgia—when rocks and bottles bounced off me as I sat looking up at the stars—that I was not afraid of death. In a way, I began looking forward to it. I felt tired. Most of the poems on suicide in *Once* come from my feelings during this period of waiting.

On the last day for miracles, one of my friends telephoned to say someone had given her a telephone number. I called from the school, hoping for nothing, and made an appointment. I went to see the doctor and he put me to sleep. When I woke up, my friend was standing over me holding a red rose. She was a blonde, gray-eyed girl, who loved horses and tennis, and she said nothing as she handed me back my life. That moment is engraved in my mind—her smile, sad and pained and frightfully young—as she tried so hard to stand by me and be my friend. She drove me back to the school and tucked me in. My other friend, brown, a wisp of blue and scarlet, with hair like thunder, brought me food.

That week I wrote without stopping (except to eat and go to the toilet) almost all of the poems in *Once*—with the exception of one or two, perhaps, and these I no longer remember.

I wrote them all in a tiny blue notebook that I can no longer find— the African ones first, because the vitality and color and friendships in Africa rushed over me in dreams the first night I slept. I had not thought about Africa (except to talk about it) since I returned. All the sculptures and weavings I had given away, because they seemed to emit an odor that made me more nauseous than the smell of fresh air. Then I wrote the suicide poems, because I felt I understood the part played in suicide by circumstances and fatigue. I also began to understand how alone woman is, because of her body. Then I wrote the love poems (love real and love imagined), and tried to reconcile myself to all things human. "Johann" is the most extreme example of this need to love even the most unfamiliar, the most fearful. For, actually when I traveled in Germany I was in a constant state of terror and no amount of flattery from handsome young German men could shake it. Then I wrote the poems of struggle in the South. The picketing, the marching, all the things that had been buried, because when I thought about them the pain was a paralysis of intellectual and moral confusion. The anger and humiliation I had suffered was alwys in conflict with the elation, the exaltation, the *joy* I felt when I could leave each vicious encounter or confrontation whole, and not—like the people before me—spewing obscenities, or throwing bricks. For, during those encounters, I had begun to comprehend what it means to be lost.

Each morning, the poems finished during the night were stuffed under Muriel Rukeyser's door—her classroom was an old gardener's cottage in the middle of the campus. Then I would hurry back to my room to write some more. I didn't care what she did with the poems. I only knew I wanted someone to read them as if they were new leaves sprouting from an old tree. The same energy that impelled me to write them carried them to her door.

This was the winter of 1965, and my last three months in college. I was twenty-one years old, although *Once* was not published till three years later, when I was twenty-four; (Muriel Rukeyser gave the poems to her agent, who gave them to Hiram Haydn—who is still my editor at Harcourt, Brace—who said right away that he wanted them; so I cannot claim to have had a hard time publishing, yet). By the time *Once* was published, it no longer seemed important—I was surprised when it went, almost immediately, into a second printing—that is, the book itself did not seem to me important; only the writing of the poems, which clarified for me how very much I love being alive. It was this feeling of gladness that carried over into my first published short story, "To Hell With Dying," about an old man saved from death countless times by the love of his neighbor's children. I was the children, and the old man.

I had gone into this memory because I think it might be important for other women to share. I don't enjoy contemplating it; I wish it had never happened. But if it had not, I firmly believe I would never have survived to be a writer. I know I would not have survived at all.

Since that time, it seems to me that all of my poems—and I write groups of poems rather than singles—are written when I have successfully pulled myself out of a completely numbing despair, and stand again in the sunlight. Writing poems is my way of celebrating with the world that I have not committed suicide the evening before.

Langston Hughes wrote in his autobiography that when he was sad, he wrote his best poems. When he was happy, he didn't write anything. This is true of me, where poems are concerned. When I am happy (or neither happy nor sad), I write essays, short stories, and novels. Poems—even happy ones—emerge from an accumulation of sadness.

INTERVIEWER: Can you describe the process of writing a poem? How do you know, for instance, when you have captured what you wanted to?

WALKER: The writing of my poetry is never consciously planned; although I become aware that there are certain emotions I would like to explore. Perhaps my unconscious begins working on poems from these emotions long before I am aware of it. I have learned to wait patiently (sometimes refusing good lines, images, when they come to me, for fear they are not lasting), until a poem is ready to present itself—*all* of itself, if possible. I sometimes feel the urge to write poems way in advance of ever sitting down to write. There is a definite restlessness, a kind of feverish excitement that is tinged with dread. The dread is because after writing each batch of poems I am always convinced that I will never write poems again. I become aware that I am controlled by them, not the other way around. I put off writing as long as I can. Then I lock myself in my study, write lines and lines and lines, then put them away, underneath other papers, without looking at them for a long time. I am afraid that if I read them too soon they will turn into trash; or worse, something so topical and transient as to have no meaning—not even to me—after a few weeks. (This is how my later poetry-writing differs from the way I wrote *Once*). I also attempt, in this way, to guard against the human tendency to try to make poetry carry the weight of half-truths, of cleverness. I realize that while I am writing poetry, I am so high as to feel invisible, and in that condition it is possible to write anything.

INTERVIEWER: What determines your interests as a writer? Are there preoccupations you have which you are not conscious of until you begin writing?

WALKER: You ask about "preoccupations." I am preoccupied with the spiritual survival, the survival *whole* of my people. But beyond that, I am committed to exploring the oppressions, the insanities, the loyalties, and the triumphs of black women. In *The Third Life of Grange Copeland*, ostensibly about a man and his son, it is the women and how they are treated that colors everything. In my new book *In Love & Trouble: Stories of Black Women*, thirteen women—mad, raging, loving, resentful, hateful, strong, ugly, weak, pitiful, and magnificent, try to live with the loyalty to black men that characterizes all of their lives. For me, black women are the most fascinating creations in the world.

Next to them, I place the old people—male and female—who persist in their beauty in spite of everything. How do they do this, knowing what they do? Having lived what they have lived? It is a mystery, and so it lures me into their lives. My grandfather, at eighty-five, never been out of Georgia, looks at me with the glad eyes of a three-year-old. The pressures on his life have been unspeakable. How can he look at me in this way? "Your eyes are widely open flowers/ Only their centers are darkly clenched/ To conceal/ Mysteries/ That lure me to a keener blooming/ Than I know/ And promise a secret/ I must have." All of my "love poems" apply to old, young, man, woman, child, and growing things.

INTERVIEWER: Your novel, *The Third Life of Grange Copeland*, reaffirms an observation I have made about many novels: there is a pervasive optimism in these novels, an indomitable belief in the future, and in man's capacity for survival. I think that this is generally opposed to what one finds in the mainstream of American literature. One can cite Ahab, Gatsby, Jake Barnes, Young Goodman Brown. . . . You seem to be writing out of a vision which conflicts with that of the culture around you.

What I may be pointing out, is that you do not seem to see the profound evil present in much of American literature.

WALKER: It is possible that white male writers are more conscious of their own evil (which, after all, has been documented for several centuries—in words and in the ruin of the land, the earth—) than black male writers, who, along with black and white women, have seen themselves as the recipients of that evil, and therefore on the side of Christ, of the oppressed, of the innocent.

The white women writers that I admire: Chopin, the Brontës, Simone De Beauvoir, and Doris Lessing, are well aware of their own oppression and search incessantly for a kind of salvation. Their characters can always envision a solution, an evolution to higher consciousness on the part of society, even when society itself cannot. Even when society is in the process of killing them for their vision. Generally, too, they are more tolerant of mystery than is Ahab, who wishes to dominate, rather than be on equal terms with the whale.

If there is one thing African-Americans have retained of their African heritage, it is probably animism: a belief that makes it possible to view all creation as living, as being inhabited by spirit. This belief encourages knowledge perceived intuitively. It does not surprise me, personally, that scientists now are discovering that trees, plants, flowers, have feelings . . . emotions, that they shrink when yelled at; that they faint when an evil person is about who might hurt them.

One thing I try to have in my life and in my fiction is an awareness of and openness to mystery, which, to me, is deeper than any politics, race, or geographical location. In the poems I read, a sense of mystery, a deepening of it, is what I look for—for that is what I respond to. I have been influenced—especially in the poems in *Once*—by Zen epigrams and by Japanese haiku. I think my respect for short forms comes from this. I was delighted to learn that in three or four lines a poet can express mystery, evoke beauty and pleasure, paint a picture—and not dissect or analyze in any way. The insects, the fish, the birds, and the apple blossoms in haiku are still whole. They have not been turned into something else. They are allowed their own majesty, instead of being used to emphasize the majesty of people; usually the majesty of the poets writing.

INTERVIEWER: A part of your vision—which is explored in your novel—is a belief in change, both personal and political. By showing the change in Grange Copeland you suggest the possibility of change in the political and social systems within which he lives.

WALKER: Yes, I believe in change: change personal, and change in society. I have experienced a revolution (unfinished, without question, but one whose new order is everywhere on view) in the South. And I grew up—until I refused to go—in the Methodist Church, which taught me that Paul *will* sometimes change on the way to Damascus, and that

Moses—that beloved old man—went through so many changes he made God mad. So Grange Copeland was *expected* to change. He was fortunate enough to be touched by love of something beyond himself. Brownfield did not change, because he was not prepared to give his life for anything, or *to* anything. He was the kind of man who could never understand Jesus (or Ché or King or Malcolm or Medgar) except as the white man's tool. He could find nothing of value within himself and he did not have the courage to imagine a life without the existence of white people to act as a foil. To become what he hated was his inevitable destiny.

A bit more about the "Southern Revolution." When I left Eatonton, Georgia, to go off to Spelman College in Atlanta (where I stayed, uneasily, for two years), I deliberately sat in the front section of the Greyhound bus. A white woman complained to the driver. He—big and red and ugly—ordered me to move. I moved. But in those seconds of moving, everything changed. I was eager to bring an end to the South that permitted my humiliation. During my sophomore year I stood on the grass in front of Trevor-Arnett Library at Atlanta University and I listened to the young leaders of SNCC. John Lewis was there, and so was Julian Bond—thin, well starched and ironed in light-colored jeans, he looked (with his cropped hair that still tried to curl) like a poet (which he was). Everyone was beautiful, because everyone (and I think now of Ruby Doris Robinson who since died) was conquering fear by holding the hands of the persons next to them. In those days, in Atlanta, springtime turned the air green. I've never known this to happen in any other place I've been—not even in Uganda, where green, on hills, plants, trees, begins to dominate the imagination. It was as if the air turned into a kind of water—and the short walk from Spelman to Morehouse was like walking through a green sea. Then, of course, the cherry trees—cut down, now, I think—that were always blooming away while we—young and bursting with fear and determination to change our world—thought, beyond our fervid singing, of death. It is not surprising, considering the intertwined thoughts of beauty and death, that the majority of the people in and around SNCC at that time were lovers of Camus.

Random memories of that period: myself, moving like someone headed for the guillotine, with (as my marching mate) a beautiful girl who spoke French and came to Spelman from Tuskegee, Alabama ("Chic Freedom's Reflection" in *Once*), whose sense of style was unfaltering, in the worst of circumstances. She was the only really blackskinned girl at Spelman who would turn up dressed in stark white from head to toe—because she knew, instinctively, that white made an already beautiful black girl look like the answer to everybody's prayer: myself, marching about in front of a restaurant, seeing—inside—the tables set up with clean napkins and glasses of water. The owner standing in front of us barring the door. A Jewish man who went mad on the spot, and fell to the floor: myself, dressed in a pink faille dress, with my African roommate, my first real girl friends, walking up the broad white steps of a broad white church. And men (white) in blue suits and bow-ties materializing on the steps above with axe-handles in their hands (see: "The Welcome Table" in *In Love & Trouble*). We turned and left. It was a bright, sunny day. Myself, sitting on a porch in Liberty County, Georgia, at night, after picketing the jailhouse (where a local black schoolteacher was held) and holding in my arms the bleeding head of a little girl— where is she now?—maybe eight or ten years old, but small, who had been cut by a broken bottle held by one of the mob in front of us. In this memory there is a white girl I grew to respect because she never flinched and never closed her eyes, no matter what the mob—where are they now?—threw. Later, in New York, she tried to get me to experiment with LSD with her, and the only reason I never did was because on the night we planned to try it I had a bad cold. I believe the reason she never closed her eyes was because she couldn't believe what she was seeing. We tried to keep in touch—but, because I had never had very much (not even a house that didn't leak), I was always conscious of the need to be secure. Because she came from an eleven-room house in the suburbs of Philadelphia and, I assume, never had worried about material security, our deepest feelings began to miss each other. I identified her as someone who could afford to play poor for awhile (her poverty interrupted occasionally by trips abroad), and she probably identified me as one of those inflexible black women black men constantly complain about: the kind who interrupt lighthearted romance by saying, "Yes, well . . . but what are the children going to eat?"

The point is that less than ten years after all these things I walk about Georgia (and Mississippi)—eating, sleeping, loving, singing, burying the dead—the way men and women are supposed to do, in a place that is the only "home" they've ever known. There is only one "for coloreds" sign left in Eatonton, and it is on a black man's barber shop. He is merely outdated. Booster, if you read this, *change* your sign!

INTERVIEWER: I wonder how clear it was to you what you were going to do in your novel before you started? Did you know, for instance, that Grange Copeland was capable of change?

WALKER: I see the work that I have done already as a foundation. That being so, I suppose I knew when I started *The Third Life of Grange Copeland* that it would have to cover several generations, and nearly a century of growth and upheaval. It begins around 1900 and ends in the sixties. But my first draft (which was never used, not even one line, in the final version) began with Ruth as a civil-rights lawyer in Georgia going to rescue her father, Brownfield Copeland, from a drunken accident, and to have a confrontation with him. In that version she is married—also to a lawyer—and they are both committed to insuring freedom for black people in the South. In Georgia, specifically. There was lots of love-making and courage in that version. But it was too recent, too superficial—everything seemed a product of the immediate present. And I believe nothing ever is.

So, I brought in the grandfather. Because all along I wanted to explore the relationship between parents and children: specifically between daughters and their father (this is most interesting, I've always felt; for example, in "The Child Who Favored Daughter" in *In Love & Trouble*, the father cuts off the breasts of his daughter because she falls in love with a white boy; why this, unless there is sexual jealousy?), and I wanted to learn, myself, how it happens that the hatred a child can have for a parent becomes inflexible. *And* I wanted to explore the relationship between men and women, and why women are always condemned for doing what men do as an expression of their masculinity. Why are women so easily "tramps" and "traitors" when men are heroes for engaging in the same activity? Why do women stand for this?

My new novel will be about several women who came of age during the sixties and were active (or not active) in the Movement in the South. I am exploring their backgrounds, familial and sibling connections, their marriages, affairs, and political persuasions, as they grow toward a fuller realization (and recognition) of themselves.

Since I put together my course on black women writers, which was taught first at Wellesley College and later at the University of Massachusetts, I have felt the need for real critical and biographical work on these writers. As a beginning, I am writing a long personal essay on my own discovery of these writers (designed, primarily, for lectures), and I hope soon to visit the birthplace and home of Zora Neale Hurston, Eatonville, Florida. I am so involved with my own writing that I don't think there will be time for me to attempt the long, scholarly involvement that all these writers require. I am hopeful, however, that as their books are reissued and used in classrooms across the country, someone will do this. If no one does (or if no one does it to my satisfaction), I feel it is my duty (such is the fervor of love) to do it myself.

INTERVIEWER: Have women writers, then, influenced your writing more than male? Which writers do you think have had the more direct influence upon you?

WALKER: I read all of the Russian writers I could find, in my sophomore year in college. I read them as if they were a delicious cake. I couldn't get enough: Tolstoi (especially his short stories, and the novels, *The Kruetzer Sonata* and *Resurrection*—which taught me the importance of diving through politics and social forecasts to dig into the essential spirit of individual persons—because otherwise, characters, no matter what political or current social issue they stand for, will not live), and Dostoyevski, who found his truths where everyone else seemed afraid to look, and Turgenev, Gorky and Gogol—who made me think that Russia must have something floating about in the air that writers breathe from the time they are born. The only thing that began to bother me, many years later, was that I could find almost nothing written by a Russian woman writer.

Unless poetry has mystery, many meanings, and some ambiguities (necessary for mystery) I am not interested in it. Outside of Basho and Shiki and other Japanese haiku poets, I read and was impressed by the poetry of Li Po, the Chinese poet, Emily Dickinson, e.e. cummings (deeply) and Robert Graves—especially his poems in *Man Does, Woman Is;* which is surely a pure male-chauvinist title, but I did not think about that then. I liked Graves because he took it as given that passionate love between man and woman does not last forever. He enjoyed the moment, and didn't bother about the future. My poem, "The Man in the Yellow Terry," is very much influenced by Graves.

I also loved Ovid and Catullus. During the whole period of discovering haiku and the sensual poems of Ovid, the poems of e.e. cummings and William Carlos Williams, my feet did not touch the ground. I ate, I slept, I studied other things (like European history) without ever doing more than giving it serious thought. It could not change me from one moment to the next, as poetry could.

I wish I had been familiar with the poems of Gwendolyn Brooks when I was in college. I stumbled on them later. If there was ever a *born* poet, I think it is Brooks. Her natural way of looking at anything, of commenting on anything, comes out as a vision, in language that is peculiar to her. It is clear that she is a poet from the way your whole spiritual past begins to float around in your throat when you are reading, just as it is clear from the first line of *Cane* that Jean Toomer is a poet, blessed with a soul that is surprised by nothing. It is not unusual to weep when reading Brooks, just as when reading Toomer's "Song of the Sun" it is not unusual to comprehend—in a flash—what a dozen books on black people's history fail to illuminate. I have embarrassed my classes occasionally by standing in front of them in tears as Toomer's poem about "some genius from the South" flew through my body like a swarm of golden butterflies on their way toward a destructive sun. Like DuBois, Toomer was capable of comprehending the black soul. It is not "soul" that *can* become a cliché , but rather something to be illuminated rather than explained.

The poetry of Arna Bontemps has strange effects on me too. He is a great poet, even if he is not recognized as such until after his death. Or is never acknowledged. The passion and compassion in his poem, "A Black Man Talks of Reaping," shook the room I was sitting in the first time I read it. The ceiling began to revolve and a breeze—all the way from Alabama—blew through the room. A tide of spiritual good health tingled the bottom of my toes. I changed. Became someone the same, but different. I understood, at last, what the transference of energy was.

It is impossible to list all of the influences on one's work. How can you even remember the indelible impression upon you of a certain look on your mother's face? But random influences are these: music; which is the art I most envy.

Then there's travel—which really made me love the world, its vastness, and variety. How moved I was to know that there is no center of the universe. Entebbe, Uganda or Bratislava, Czechoslovakia exist no matter what we are doing here. Some writers—Camara Laye, or the man who wrote *One Hundred Years of Solitude* (Gabriel Garcia Marquez)—have illumined this fact brilliantly in their fiction, which brings me to African writers I *hope* to be influenced by: Okot p'tek has written my favorite modern poem, "Song of Lawino." I am also crazy about *The Concubine* by Elechi Ahmadi (a perfect story, I think), *The Radiance of the King*, by Camara Laye, and *Maru*, by Bessie Head. These writers do not seem afraid of fantasy, of myth and mystery. Their work deepens one's comprehension of life by going beyond the bounds of realism. They are like musicians: at one with their cultures and their historical subsconscious.

Flannery O'Connor has also influenced my work. To me, she is the best of the white southern writers, including Faulkner. For one thing, she practiced economy. She also knew that the question of race was really just the first question on a long list. This is hard for just about everybody to accept, we've been trying to answer it for so long.

I did not read *Cane* until 1967, but it has been reverbating in me to an astonishing degree. *I love it passionately;* could not possibly exist without it. *Cane* and *Their Eyes Were Watching God* are probably my favorite books by black American writers. Jean Toomer has a very feminine sensibility (or phrased another way, he is both feminine and masculine in his perceptions), unlike most black male writers. He loved women.

Like Toomer, Zora Neale Hurston was never afraid to let her characters be themselves, funny talk and all. She was incapable of being embarrassed by anything black people did, and so was able to write about everything with freedom and fluency. My feeling is that Zora Neale Hurston is probably one of the most misunderstood, least appreciated writers of this century. Which is a pity. She is great. A writer of courage, and incredible humor, with poetry in every line.

When I started teaching my course in black women writers at Wellesley (the first one, I think, ever), I was worried that Zora's use of black English of the twenties would throw some of the students off. It didn't. They loved it. They said it was like reading Thomas Hardy, only better. In that same course I taught Nella Larsen, Frances Watkins Harper (poetry and novel), Dorothy West, Ann Petry, Paule Marshall, etc. Also Kate Chopin and Virginia Woolf—not because they were black, obviously, but because they were women and wrote, as the black women did, on the condition of humankind from the perspective of women. It is interesting to read Woolf's *A Room of One's Own* while reading the poetry of Phillis Wheatley, to read Larsen's *Quicksand* along with *The Awakening.* The deep-throated voice of Sojourner Truth tends to drift across the rooom while you're reading. If you're not a feminist already, you become one.

INTERVIEWER: Why do you think that the black woman writer has been so ignored in America? Does she have even more difficulty than the black male writer, who perhaps has just begun to gain recognition?

WALKER: There are two reasons why the black woman writer is not taken as seriously as the black male writer. One is that she's a woman. Critics seem unusually ill-equipped to intelligently discuss and analyze the works of black women. Generally, they do not even make the attempt; they prefer, rather, to talk about the lives of black women writers, not about what they write. And, since black women writers are not—it would seem—very likable—until recently they were the least willing worshipers of male supremacy—comments about them tend to be cruel.

In Nathan Huggins's very readable book, *Harlem Renaissance,* he hardly refers to Zora Neale Hurston's work, except negatively. He quotes from Wallace Thurman's novel, *Infants of the Spring,* at length, giving us the words of a character, "Sweetie Mae Carr," who is alledgedly based on Zora Neale Hurston. "Sweetie Mae" is a writer noted more "for her ribald wit and personal effervescence than for any actual literary work. She was a great favorite among those whites who went in for Negro prodigies." Mr. Huggins goes on for several pages, never quoting Zora Neale Hurston herself, but rather the opinions of others about her character. He does say that she was "a master of dialect," but adds that "Her greatest weakness was carelessness or indifference to her art."

Having taught Zora Neale Hurston, and of course, having read her work myself, I am stunned. Personally, I do not care if Zora Hurston was fond of her white women friends. When she was a child in Florida, working for nickels and dimes, two white women helped her escape. Perhaps this explains it. But even if it doesn't, so what? Her work, far from being done carelessly, is done (especially in *Their Eyes Were Watching God*) almost too perfectly. She took the trouble to capture the beauty of rural black expression. She saw poetry where other writers merely saw failure to cope with English. She was so at ease with her blackness it never occurred to her that she should act one way among blacks and another among whites (as her more sophisticated black critics apparently did).

It seems to me that black writing has suffered, because even black critics have assumed that a book that deals with the relationships between members of a black family—or between a man and a woman—is less important than one that has white people as a primary antagonist. The consequences of this is that many of our books by "major" writers (always male) tell us little about the culture, history, or future, imagination, fantasies, etc. of black people, and a lot about isolated (often improbable) or limited encounters with a nonspecific white world. Where is the book, by an American black person (aside from *Cane*), that equals Elechi Amadi's *The Concubine*, for example? A book that exposes the *subconscious* of a people, because the people's dreams, imaginings, rituals, legends, etc. are known to be important, are known to contain the accumulated collective reality of the people themselves. Or, in *The Radiance of the King*, the white person is shown to be the outsider he is, because the culture he enters into in Africa *itself* [expels] him. Without malice, but as nature expells what does not suit. The white man is mysterious, a force to be reckoned with, but he is not glorified to such an extent that the Africans turn their attention away from themselves and their own imagination and culture. Which is what often happens with "protest lliterature." The superficial becomes—for a time—the deepest reality, and replaces the still waters of the collective subconscious.

When my own novel was published, a leading black monthly admitted (the editor did) that the book itself was never read; but the magazine ran an item stating that a *white* reviewer had praised the book (which was, in itself, an indication that the book was no good—such went the logic) and then hinted that the reviewer had liked my book because of my life-style. When I wrote to the editor to complain, he wrote me a small sermon on the importance of my "image," of what is "good" for others to see. Needless to say, what others "see" of me is the least of my worries, and I assumed that "others" are intelligent enough to recover from whatever shocks my presence might cause.

Women writers are supposed to be intimidated by male disapprobation. What they write is not important enough to be read. How they live, however, their "image," they owe to the race. Read the reason Zora Neale Hurston gave for giving up her writing. See what "image" the Negro press gave her, innocent as she was. I no longer read articles or reviews unless they are totally about the work. I trust that someday a generation of men and women will arise who will forgive me for such wrong as I do not agree I do, and will read my work because it is a true account of my feelings, my perception, and my imagination, and because it will reveal something to them of their own selves. They will also be free to toss it—and me—out of a high window. They can do what they like.

INTERVIEWER: Have you felt a great deal of coercion to write the kind of fiction and poetry that black wrtiers are "supposed" to write? Does this ever interfere with what you *want* to write?

WALKER: When I take the time to try to figure out what I am doing in my writing, where it is headed, and so on, I almost never can come up with anything. This is because it seems to me that my poetry is quite different from my novels (*The Third Life of Grange Copeland* and the one I am working on now); for example, *Once* is what I think of as a "happy" book, full of the spirit of an optimist who loves the world and al the sensations of caring in it; it doesn't matter that it began in sadness; *The Third Life of Grange Copeland*, though sometimes humorous and celebrative of life, is a grave book in which the characters see the world as almost entirely menacing. The optimism that closes the book makes it different from most of my short stories, and the political and personal content of my essays makes them different—again—from everything else. So I would not, as some critics have done, categorize my work as "gothic." I would not categorize it at all. Eudora Welty, in explaining why she rebels against being labeled "gothic," says that to her "gothic" conjures up the supernatural, and that she feels what she writes has "something to do with real life." I agree with her.

I like those of my short stories that show the plastic, shaping, almost painting quality of words. In "Roselily" and "The Child Who Favors Daughter" the prose is poetry, or, prose and poetry run together to add a new dimension to the language. But the most that I would say about where I am trying to go is this: I am trying to arrive at that place where black music already is; to arrive at that unselfconscious sense of collective oneness; that naturalness, that (even when anguished) grace.

The writer—like the musician or painter—must be free to explore, otherwise she or he will never discover what is needed (by everyone) to be known. This means, very often, finding oneself considered "unacceptable" by masses of people who think that the writer's obligation is not to explore or to challenge, but to second the masses' motions, whatever they are. Yet the gift of loneliness is sometimes a radical vision of society or one's people that has not previously been taken into account. Toomer was, I think, a lonely, wandering man, accustomed to being tolerated and misunderstood—a man who made choices many abhorred—and yet, *Cane* is a great reward; though Toomer himself probably never realized it.

The same is true of Zora Neale Hurston. She is probably more honest in her fieldwork and her fiction, than she is in her autobiography, because she was hesitant to reveal how different she really was. It is interesting to contemplate what would have been the result and impact on black women—since 1937—if they had read and taken to heart *Their Eyes Were Watching God*. Would they still be as dependent on material things—fine cars, furs, big houses, pots and jars of face creams—as they are today? Or would they, learning from Janie that materialism is the dragrope of the soul, become a nation of women immune (to the extent that is possible in a blatantly consumerist society like ours) to the accumulation of things, and aware, to their core, that love, fulfillment as women, peace of mind, should logically come before, not after, selling one's soul for a golden stool on which to sit. Sit and be bored.

Hurston's book, though seemingly apolitical, is in fact, one of the most radical novels (without being a tract) we have.

INTERVIEWER: Christianity is implicitly critized in your work. Is that because it has historically been both racist and antifeminist?

WALKER: Although I am constantly involved, internally, with religious questions—and I seem to have spent all of my life rebelling against the church and other peoples' interpretations of what religion is—the truth is probably that I don't believe there is a God, although I would like to believe it. Certainly I don't believe there is a God beyond nature. The world is God. Man is God. So is a leaf or a snake. . . . So, when Grange Copeland refuses to pray at the end of the book, he is refusing to be a hypocrite. All his life he has hated the Church and taken every opportunity to ridicule it. He has taught his granddaughter, Ruth, this same humorous contempt. He does, however, appreciate the humanity of man-womankind as a God worth embracing. To him, the greatest value a person can attain is full humanity, which is a state of oneness with all things, and a willingness to die (or to live) so that the best that has been produced can continue to live in someone else. He "rocked himself in his own arms to a final sleep" because he understood that man is alone—in his life as in his death—without any God but himself (and the world).

Like many, I waver in my convictions about God, from time to time. In my poetry I seem to be for; in my fiction, against.

I am intrigued by the religion of the black Muslims. By what conversion means to black women, specifically, and what the religion itself means in terms of the black American past: our history, our "race memories" our absorption of Christianity, our *changing* of Christianity to fit our needs. What will the new rituals mean? How will this new religion imprint itself on the collective consciousness of the converts? Can women be free in such a religion? Is such a religion, in fact, an anachronism? So far I have dealt with this interest in two stories, "Roselily," about a young woman who marries a young Muslim because he offers her respect and security, and "Everyday Use" a story that shows respect for the "militance" and progressive agricultural programs of the Muslims, but at the same time shows skepticism about a young man who claims attachment to the Muslims because he admires the rhetoric. It allows him to acknowledge his contempt for whites, which is all he believes the group is about.

In other stories, I am interested in Christianity as an imperialist tool used against Africa ("Diary of an African Nun") and in Voodoo used as a weapon against oppression (The Revenge of Hannah Kemhuff"). I see all of these as religious questions.

INTERVIEWER: Could you tell me about the genesis of your title poem "Revolutionary Petunias"? Why was "Sammy Lou" chosen as the heroine of the poem?

WALKER: The poem "Revolutionary Petunias" did not have a name when I sat down to write it. I wanted to create a person who engaged in a final struggle with her oppressor, and won, but who, in every other way, was "incorrect." Sammy Lou in the poem is everything she should not be: her name is Sammy Lou, for example; she is a farmer's wife; she works in the fields. She goes to church. The walls of her house contain no signs of her blackness—though that in itself reveals it; anyone walking into that empty house would know Sammy Lou is black. She is so incredibly "incorrect" that she is only amused when the various poets and folksingers rush to immortalize her heroism in verse and song. She did not think of her killing of her oppressor in that way. She thought—and I picture her as tall, lean, black, with short, badly straightened hair and crooked teeth—that killing is never heroic. Her reaction, after killing this cracker-person, would be to look up at the sky and not pray or ask forgiveness but to say—as if talking to an old friend—"Lord, you know my heart. I never wanted to have to kill nobody. But I couldn't hold out to the last, like Job. I had done took more than I could stand."

Sammy Lou is so "incorrect" she names her children after Presidents and their wives: she names one of them after the founder of the Methodist church. To her, this does not mean a limitation of her blackness, it means she feels she is so black she can absorb—and change—all things, since everybody knows that a black-skinned Jackie Kennedy still bears resemblance only to her own great aunt, Sadie Mae Johnson.

But the most "incorrect" thing about Sammy Lou is that she loves flowers. Even on her way to the electric chair she reminds her children to water them. This is crucial, for I have heard it said by one of our cultural visionaries that whenever you hear a black person talking about the beauties of nature, that person is not a black person at all, but a Negro. This is meant as a putdown, and it is. It puts down all of the black folks in Georgia, Alabama, Mississippi, Texas, Louisianna—in fact, it covers just about everybody's Mama. Sammy Lou, of course, is so "incorrect" she does not even know how ridiculous she is for loving to see flowers blooming around her unbearably ugly gray house. To be "correct" she should consider it her duty to let ugliness reign. Which is what "incorrect" people like Sammy Lou refuse to do.

Actually, the poem was to claim (as Toomer claimed the people he wrote about in *Cane* who, as you know, were all as "incorrect" as possible) the most incorrect black person I could, and to honor her as my own—on a level with, if not above the most venerated saints of the black revolution. It seems our fate to be incorrect (look where we live, for example), and in our incorrectness, stand.

Although Sammy Lou is more a rebel than a revolutionary (since you need more than one for a revolution) I named the poem "Revolutionary Petunias" because she is not—when you view her kind of person histori-cally—isolated. She is part of an ongoing revolution. Any black revolu-tion, instead of calling her "incorrect" will have to honor her single act of rebellion.

Another reason I named it "Revolutionary Petunias" is that I like petunias and like to raise them because you just put them in any kind of soil and they bloom their heads off—exactly, it seemed to me, like black people tend to do. (Look at the blues and jazz musicians, the blind singers from places like Turnip, Mississippi, the poets and writers and all-around blooming people you know, who—from all visible evidence—achieved their blooming by eating the air for bread and drinking muddy water for hope.) Then I thought too, of the petunias my mother gave me when my daughter was born, and of the story (almost a parable) she told me about them. Thirty-seven years ago, my mother and father were coming home from somewhere in their wagon—my mother was pregnant with one of my older brothers at the time—and they passed a deserted house where one lavender petunia was left, just blooming away in the yard (probably to keep itself company)—and my mother said Stop! let me go and get that petunia bush. And my father, grumbling, stopped and she got it, and they went home, and she set it out in a big stump in the yard. It never wilted, just bloomed and bloomed. Every time the family moved (say twelve times) she took her petunia—and thirty-seven years later she brought me a piece of that same petunia bush. It had never died. Each winter it lay dormant and deadlooking, but each spring it came back, more lively than before.

What underscored the importance of this story for me is this: modern petunias do not live forever. They die each winter and the next spring you have to buy new ones.

In a way, the whole book is a celebration of people who will not cram themselves into any ideological or racial mold. They are all shouting Stop! I want to go get that petunia!

Because of this they are made to suffer. They are told that they do not belong, that they are not wanted, that their art is not needed, that nobody, who is "correct," could love what they love. Their answer is resistance, without much commentary; just a steady knowing that they stand at a point where—with one slip of the character—they might be lost, and the bloom they are after wither in the winter of self-contempt. They do not measure themselves against black people or white people; if anything, they learn to walk and talk in the presence of DuBois, Hurston, Hughes, Toomer, Attaway, Wright, and others—and when they bite into their pillows at night these spirits comfort them. They are aware that the visions that created them were all toward a future where all people—

and flowers too—can bloom. They require that in the midst of the bloodiest battles or revolution this thought not be forgotten.

When I married my husband there was a law that said I could not. When we moved to Mississippi three years after the lynching of Cheney, Schwerner and Goodman, it was a punishable crime for a black person and a white person of opposite sex to inhabit the same house. But I felt then—as I do now—that in order to be able to live at all in America I must be unafraid to live anywhere in it, and I must be able to live in the fashion and with whom I choose. Otherwise, I'd just as soon leave. If society (black or white) says, Then you must be isolated, an outcast—then I will be a hermit. Friends and relatives may desert me, but the dead—Douglass, DuBois, Hansberry, Toomer, and the rest—are a captive audience. . . . These feelings went into two poems, "Be Nobody's Darling," and "While Love is Unfashionable."

INTERVIEWER: There is one poem in *Revolutionary Petunias* which particularly interests me—"For My Sister Molly Who in the Fifties." Can you tell me about what went into the structuring of this rather long poem, and perhaps something about the background of it?

WALKER: "For My Sister Molly Who in the Fifties" is a pretty real poem. It really is about one of my sisters, a brilliant, studious girl who became one of those Negro Wonders—who collected scholarships like trading stamps and wandered all over the world. (Our home town didn't even have a high school, when she came along). When she came to visit us in Georgia it was—at first—like having Christmas with us all during her vacation. She loved to read and tell stories; she taught me African songs and dances; she cooked fanciful dishes that looked like anything but plain old sharecropper food. I loved her so much it came as a great shock—and a shock I don't expect to recover from—to learn she was ashamed of us. We were so poor, so dusty and sunburnt. We talked wrong. We didn't know how to dress, or use the right eating utensils. And so, she drifted away, and I did not understand it. Only later, I realized that sometimes (perhaps), it becomes too painful to bear: seeing your home and family—shabby and seemingly without hope—through the eyes of your new friends and strangers. She had felt—for her own mental health—that the gap that separated us from the rest of the world was too wide for her to keep trying to bridge. She understood how delicate she was.

I started out writing this poem in great anger; hurt, really. I thought I could write a magnificently vicious poem. Yet, even from the first draft, it did not turn out that way. Which is one of the great things about poetry. What you really feel, underneath everything else, will present itself. Your job is not to twist that feeling. So that although being with her now is too painful with memories for either of us to be comfortable,

I still retain (as I hope she does) in memories beyond the bad ones, my picture of a sister I loved, "Who walked among the flowers and brought them inside the house, who smelled as good as they, and looked as bright."

This poem (and my sister received the first draft, which is hers alone, and the way I wish her to relate to the poem) went through fifty drafts (at least) and I worked on it, off and on, for five years. This has never happened before or since. I do not know what to say about the way it is constructed other than to say that as I wrote it the lines and words went, on the paper, to a place comparable to where they lived in my head.

I suppose, actually, that my tremendous response to the poems of W. C. Williams, cummings and Basho convinced me that poetry is more like music—in my case, improvisational jazz, where each person blows the note that she hears—than like a cathedral, with every stone in a specific, predetermined place. Whether lines are long or short depends on what the poem itself requires. Like people, some poems are fat and some are thin. Personally, I prefer the short thin ones, which are always like painting the eye in a tiger (as Muriel Rukeyser once explained it). You wait until the energy and vision are just right, then you write the poem. If you try to write it before it is ready to be written you find yourself adding stripes instead of eyes. "Too many stripes and the tiger herself disappears. You will paint a photograph (which is what is wrong with "Burial") instead of creating a new way of seeing.

The poems that fail will always haunt you. I am haunted by "Ballad of the Brown Girl" and "Johann" in *Once*, and I expect to be haunted by "Nothing is Right" in *Revolutionary Petunias*. The first two are dishonest, and the third is trite.

The poem "The Girl Who Died #2" was written after I learned of the suicide of a student at the college I attended. I learned, from the dead girl's rather guilty sounding "brothers and sisters" that she had been hounded constantly because she was so "incorrect," she thought she could be a black hippie. To top that, they tried to make her feel like a traitor because she refused to limit her interest to black men. Anyway, she was a beautiful girl. I was shown a photograph of her by one of her few black friends. She was a little brownskinned girl from Texas, away from home for the first time, trying to live a life she could live with. She tried to kill herself two or three times before, but I guess the brothers and sisters didn't think it "correct" to respond with love or attention, since everybody knows it is "incorrect" to even think of suicide if you are a black person. And, of course, black people do not commit suicide. Only colored people and Negroes commit suicide. (See "The Old Warrior Terror": Warriors, you know, always die on the battlefield). I said, when I saw the photograph, that I wished I had been there for her to talk to. When the school invited me to join their Board of Trustees, it was her face that convinced me. I know nothing about Boards and never really trusted them; but I can listen to problems pretty well. . . . I believe in listening—to a person, the sea, the wind, the trees, but especially to young black women whose rocky road I am still traveling.

Essayists

LINDA ABBANDONATO is a graduate student in English at the University of Southern California at Los Angeles.

HOUSTON A. BAKER, JR., is the Albert M. Greenfield Professor of Human Relations at the University of Pennsylvania. His many books include *Afro-American Poetics: Revisions of Harlem and the Black Aesthetic, Blues, Ideology, and Afro-American Literature, The Journey Back*, and *Workings of the Spirit: The Poetics of Afro-American Women's Writing*.

LAUREN BERLANT is an associate professor of English at the University of Chicago. She is the author of *The Anatomy of National Fantasy: Hawthorne, Utopia, and Everyday Life*.

ELLIOT BUTLER-EVANS is an associate professor of English at the University of California, Santa Barbara. He is the author of *Race, Gender, and Desire: Narrative Strategies in the Fiction of Toni Cade Bambara, Toni Morrison, and Alice Walker*.

BARBARA CHRISTIAN is a professor of African-American Studies at the University of California, Berkeley. She is the author of *Black Feminist Criticism: Perspectives on Black Women Writers* and *Black Women Novelists: The Development of a Tradition 1892–1976*.

MICHAEL COOKE was a professor of English at Yale University; his books include *The Blind Man Traces the Circle, Romantic Will*, and *Afro-American Literature in the 20th Century: The Achievement of Intimacy*.

THADIOUS DAVIS is a professor of English at Brown University. His books include *Faulkner's "Negro": Art and the Southern Context* and *Satire or Evasion?: Black Perspectives on Huckleberry Finn*.

HENRY LOUIS GATES, JR., is the W. E. B. Du Bois Professor of the Humanities at Harvard University and the chair of the Afro-American Studies Department at Harvard. His books include *Figures in Black, The Signifying Monkey*, and *Loose Canons: Notes on the Culture Wars*.

BELL HOOKS is a professor of English and Women's Studies at Oberlin University and visiting professor at the City College of New York. Her books include *Ain't*

I a Woman: Black Women and Feminism, Black Looks: Race and Representation and, with Cornel West, *Breaking Bread: Insurgent Black Intellectual Life.*

THEODORE O. MASON, JR., is an associate professor of English at Kenyon College.

DEBORAH E. MCDOWELL is an associate professor of English at the University of Virginia, Charlottesville. She is the general editor of the Beacon Press Black Women Writers Series and the coeditor, with Arnold Rampersad, of *Slavery and the Literary Imagination.*

ALAN NADEL is an associate professor of Language, Literature, and Communications at Rensselaer Polytechnic University. He is the author of *Invisible Criticism: Ralph Ellison and the American Canon.*

ALICE HALL PETRY is a professor of English at the Rhode Island School of Design. She is the author of *Understanding Anne Tyler, Fitzgerald's Craft of Short Fiction* and the editor of *Critical Essays on Anne Tayler.*

CHARLOTTE PIERCE-BAKER teaches English at the University of Pennsylvania, where she also directs the program in Innovative Study in Teaching and the Humanities.

WENDY WALL is an assistant professor of English at Northwestern University, Evanston.

MARY HELEN WASHINGTON is a professor of English at the University of Maryland, College Park. She is the editor of several books, including *Black-eyed Susans: Classic Stories by and About Black Women* and *Memory of Kin: Stories About Family by Black Writers.*

Chronology

1944	February 9: Born Alice Walker in Eatonville, Georgia, the eighth child of Willie Lee and Minnie (Grant) Walker, both sharecroppers.
1952	Shot with a BB gun and blinded in one eye.
1961–63	Attends Spelman College; becomes involved with the civil rights movement.
1964	Travels to Africa; begins writing the poems that will later appear as *Once*.
1965	Receives BA from Sarah Lawrence College.
1965–68	Deeply involved in the civil rights movement, including voter registration drives in Georgia and campaigns for welfare rights and Head Start in Mississippi. Works in welfare department in New York City.
1967	Marries Melvyn Roseman Leventhal, a white civil rights lawyer.
1968	Publishes *Once*, a book of poetry.
1968–69	Teaches at Jackson State University, Mississippi.
1969–70	Teaches at Tougaloo College, Mississippi.
1970	Publishes her first novel, *The Third Life of George Copeland*.
1971–73	Radcliffe Institute Fellowship, Harvard University.
1973	Publishes *In Love and Trouble: Stories of Black Women*, and *Revolutionary Petunias*, a book of poetry. Receives the Lillian Smith Award. Finds and marks Zora Neale Hurston's burial site in Fort Pierce, Florida, with a gravestone.
1974	Publishes *Langston Hughes*, a biography for young people. Receives the National Institute of Arts and Letters Award.
1976	Publishes a second novel, *Meridian*.
1977	Divorces Melvyn Leventhal; moves to San Francisco.
1978	Receives the National Endowment for the Arts Award.
1979	Publishes *Goodnight Willie Lee, I'll See You in the Morning*, a collection of poems. Edits *I Love Myself When I Am Laughing . . . And Then Again When I Am Looking Mean and Impressive: A Zora Neale Hurston Reader*. Awarded a Guggenheim Fellowship.
1981	Publishes *You Can't Keep a Good Woman Down*, a book of stories.
1982	*The Color Purple*, a novel, published to critical acclaim; wins the American Book Award and the Pulitzer Prize for Literature.
1983	Publishes *In Search of Our Mothers' Gardens: Womanist Prose*, a collection of essays.
1984	Publishes a volume of poetry, *Horses Make a Landscape Look More Beautiful*.

1985	Film adaptation of *The Color Purple*, directed by Steven Spielberg and starring Whoopi Goldberg as Celie, released by Warner Brothers.
1989	Publishes *The Temple of My Familiar*, a novel.
1991	Publishes *Her Blue Body Everything We Knew: Earthling Poems, 1965–1990 Complete*.
1992	Publishes *Possessing the Secret of Joy*, a novel.

Bibliography

Alps, Sandra. "Concepts of Self-Hood in *Their Eyes Were Watching God* and *The Color Purple.*" *Pacific Review* 4 (Spring 1986): 106–12.

Awkward, Michael. *Inspiring Influences: Tradition, Revision, and Afro-American Women's Novels.* New York: Columbia University Press, 1991.

Babb, Valerie. "*The Color Purple:* Writing to Undo What Writing Has Done." *Phylon* 47 (June 1986): 107–16.

Banks, Erma Davis and Keith Byerman. *Alice Walker: An Annotated Bibliography 1968–86.* New York: Garland, 1989.

Barksdale, Richard K. "Castration Symbolism in Recent Black American Fiction." *CLA Journal* 29 (June 1986): 400–13.

Bates, Robin. "Getting Man off the Eyeball: Alice Walker's Utopian Project." In *Cross-Cultural Studies: American, Canadian and European Liteatures: 1945–1985,* edited by Mirko Jurak. Ljubljana, Slovenia: English Dept., Filozofska Fakulteta, 1988.

Bloom, Harold, ed. *Alice Walker.* New York: Chelsea, 1989.

Bob, Jacqueline, "*The Color Purple:* Black Women as Cultural Readers." In *Female Spectators: Looking at Film and Television,* edited and with an introduction by E. Deidre Pribram. London: Verso, 1988.

Brock, Sabine and Anne Koenen. "Alice Walker in Search of Zora Neale Hurston: Rediscovering a Black Female Tradition." In *History and Tradition in Afro-American Culture,* edited by Gunter H. Leenz. Frankfurt: Campus, 1984.

Brown, Joseph, "All Saints Should Walk Away: The Mystical Pilgrimmage of *Meridian*", *Callaloo* 12 (Spring 1989): 321–31.

Buncombe, Marie H. "Androgyny as Metaphor in Alice Walker's Novels." *CLA Journal* 30 (June 1987): 419–27.

Butler, Cheryle B., "The Color Purple Controversy: Black Woman Spectatorship." *Wide Angle: A Film Quarterly of Theory, Criticism, and Practice* 13 (1991): 62–69.

Butler, Robert James. "Making a Way Out of No Way: The Open Journey in Alice Walker's *The Third Life of Grange Copeland.*" *Black American Literature Forum* 22 (Spring 1988): 65–79.

Butler-Evans, Elliott, *Race, Gender, and Desire: Narrative Strategies in the Fiction of Toni Cade Bambara, Toni Morrison, and Alice Walker.* Philadelphia: Temple University Press, 1989.

Byerman, Keith. "Desire and Alice Walker: The Quest for a Womanist Narrative." *Callaloo* 12 (Spring 1989): 332–42.

Byerman, Keith, and Erma Banks. "Alice Walker: A Selected Bibliography 1968–88." *Callaloo* 12 (Spring 1989): 343–45.

Byrne, Mary Ellen. "Welty's 'A Worn Path' and Walker's 'Everyday Use': Companion Pieces." *Teaching English in Two-Year Colleges* 16 (May 1989): 129–33.

Chambers, Kimberly. "Right on Time: History and Religion in Alice Walker's *The Color Purple.*" *CLA Journal* 31 (Sept. 1987): 44–62.

Cheung, King-Kok. "'Don't Tell': Imposed Silences in *The Color Purple* and *The Woman Warrior.*" *PMLA: Publications of the Modern Language Association of America* 103 (March 1988): 162–74.

Christian, Barbara. "The Contrary Black Women of Alice Walker." *Black Scholar* 12 (March–April 1981): 21–30, 70–71.

————. "Alice Walker: The Black Woman Artist as Wayward." In *Black Women Writers (1950–1980): A Critical Evaluation*, edited by Mari Evans. Garden City, NY: Anchor-Doubleday, 1984.

————. "No More Buried Lives: The Theme of Lesbianism in Lorde, Naylor, Shange, Walker." *Feminist Issues* 5 (Spring 1985): 3–20.

Coleman, Viralene J. "Miss Celie's Song." *Publications of the Arkansas Philological Association* 11 (Spring 1985): 27–34.

Coles, Robert. "To Try Men's Souls." *The New Yorker* (February 27, 1971): 104–6.

Collins, Gina Michelle. "*The Color Purple:* What Feminism Can Learn from a Southern Tradition." In *Southern Literature and Literary Theory* edited by Jefferson Humphries. Athens, Ga.: University of Georgia Press, 1990.

Danielson, Susan. "Alice Walker's *Meridian*, Feminism, and the "Movement."" *Women's Studies* 16 (Oct. 1989). 317–31.

Davis, Jane. "*The Color Purple:* A Spiritual Descendant of Hurston's *Their Eyes Were Watching God.*" *Griot* 6 (Summer 1987): 79–96.

Davis, Thadious. "Alice Walker's Celebration of Self in Southern Generations." *The Southern Quarterly* 21 (Summer 1983): 39–53.

————. "Poetry as Preface to Fiction: Alice Walker's Recurrent Apprenticeship." *Mississippi Quarterly* 44 (Spring 1991): 133–42.

DeVeaux, Alexis et al. "Legends in Our Time." *Essence* 21 (May 1990) 101–22.

Dreifus, Claudia. "Alice Walker: Writing to Save My Life" (interview). *The Progressive* 53 (Aug. 1989) 29–32.

Duckworth, Victoria. "The Redemptive Impulse: *Wise Blood* and *The Color Purple.*" *The Flannery O'Connor Bulletin* 15 (1986): 51–56.

DuPlessis, Rachel Blau. *Writing Beyond the Ending: Narrative Strategies of Twentieth-Century Women Writers.* Bloomington: Indiana University Press, 1985.

Early, G. "*The Color Purple* as Everybody's Protest Art." *Antioch Review* 44 (Summer 1986): 261–75.

Elliott, Emory. "History and Will in *Dog Soldiers, Sabbatical* and *The Color Purple. Arizona Quarterly* 43 (Autumn 1987): 197–217.

El Saffar, Ruth. "Alice Walker's *The Color Purple.*" *International Fiction Review* 12 (Winter 1985): 11–17.

Ensslen, Klaus. "Collective Experience and Individual Responsibility: Alice Walker's *The Third Life of Grange Copeland.*" *The Afro-American Novel Since 1960,* edited by Peter Bruck and Wolfgang Karrer. Amsterdam: B. R. Gruner Publishing Co., 1982.

————. "History and Fiction in Alice Walker's *The Third Life of Grange Copeland* and Ernest Gaines' *The Autobiography of Miss Jane Pittman.*" In *History and Tradition in Afro-American Culture,* edited by Gunter H. Lenz. Frankfurt: Campus, 1984.

Fannin, Alice. "A Sense of Wonder: The Pattern for Psychic Survival in *Their Eyes Were Watching God* and *The Color Purple.*" *The Zora Neale Hurston Forum* 1 (Fall 1986).

Fifer, Elizabeth. "The Dialect and Letters of *The Color Purple.*" In *Contemporary American Women Writers: Narrative Strategies,* edited by Catherine Rainwater and William J. Scheick. Lexington: University Press of Kentucky, 1985.

Finn, J. "Alice Walker and Flight 007." *Christianity and Crisis* 43 (October 31, 1983): 397–8.

Fishman, Charles. "Naming Names: Three Recent Novels by Women Writers." *Journal of the American Name Society* 32 (March 1984): 33–44.

Fontenot, Chester J. "Alice Walker: 'The Diary of an African Nun' and DuBois' Double Consciousness." In *Sturdy Black Bridges: Visions of Black Women in Literature*, edited by Roseann P. Bell, Bettye J. Parker, Beverly Guy-Sheftall. Garden City, N.Y.: Anchor-Doubleday, 1979.

Fowler, Carolyn. "Solid at the Core." *Freedomways* 14 (1974): 59–62.

Freeman, Alma S. "Zora Neale Hurston and Alice Walker: A Spiritual Kinship." *SAGE*, 2 (Spring 1985): 37–40.

Friedman, Sandra and Alec Irwin. "Christian Feminism, Eros, and Power in Right Relation." *Cross Currents* 40 (Fall 1990) 387–405.

Froula, Christine. "The Daughter's Seducation: Sexual Violence and Literary History." *Signs* 2 (Summer 1986): 621–45.

Gaston, Karen C. "Women in the Lives of Grange Copeland." *CLA Journal* 24 (March 1981): 276–86.

Gerstenberger, Donna. "Revisioning Cultural Norms: The Fiction of Margaret Atwood and Alice Walker." In *Cross-Cultural Studies: American, Canadian and European Literatures: 1945–1985*, edited by Mirko Jurak. Ljubljana, Slovenia: English Dept., Filozofska Fakulteta, 1988.

Halio, Jay L. "First and Last Things." *The Southern Review* n.s. 9 (January 1973): 455–67.

Hallenbrand, Harold. "Speech after Silence: Alice Walker's *The Third Life of Grange Copeland*." *Black American Literature Forum* 20 (Spring/Summer 1986): 113–28.

Harris, Trudier. "Violence in *The Third Life of Grange Copeland*." *CLA Journal* 19 (December 1975): 238–47.

———. "Folklore in the Fiction of Alice Walker: A Perpetuation of Historical and Literary Traditions." *Black American Literature Forum* 11 (1977): 3–8.

———. "Three Black Women Writers and Humanism: A Folk Perspective." In *Black American Literature and Humanism*, edited by R. Baxter Miller. Lexington, Ky.: University Press of Kentucky, 1981.

———. "Tiptoeing Through Taboo: Incest in 'The Child Who Favored Daughter.'" *Modern Fiction Studies* 28 (Autumn 1982): 495–505.

———. "On *The Color Purple*, Stereotypes and Silence." *Black American Literature Forum* 18 (Winter 1984): 155–61.

———. "From Victimization to Free Enterprise: Alice Walker's *The Color Purple*." *Studies in American Fiction* 14 (Spring 1986): 1–17.

Hedges, Elaine, "The Needle or the Pen: The Literary Rediscovery of Women's Textile Work." In *Tradition and the Talents of Women*, edited and with an introduction by Florence Howe. Urbana, Ill.: University of Illinois Press, 1991.

Heirs, John T. "Creation Theology in Alice Walker's *The Color Purple*." *Notes on Contemporary Literature* 14 (September 1984): 2–3.

Hellenbrand, Harold. "Speech, after Silence: Alice Walker's *The Third Life of Grange Copeland*." *Black American Literature Forum* 20 (Spring/Summer 1986): 113–28.

Henderson, Mae G. "*The Color Purple:* Revisions and Redefinitions." *SAGE* 2 (Spring 1985): 14–18.

Hite, Molly. "Romance, Marginality, Matrilineage: Alice Walker's *The Color Purple* and Zora Neale Hurston's *Their Eyes Were Watching God*." *Novel* 22 (Spring 1989): 257–74.

———. *The Other Side of the Story: Structures and Strategies of Contemporary Feminist Narratives*. Ithaca, N.Y.: Cornell University Press, 1989.

Hogue, W. Lawrence. "History, the Feminist Discourse, and Alice Walker's *The Third Life of Grange Copeland*." *Melus* 12 (Summer 1985): 45–62.

Hollister, Michael. "Tradition in Alice Walker's 'To Hell with Dying.'" *Studies in Short Fiction* 26 (Winter 1989): 90–94.

Homans, Margaret. "'Her Very own Howl': The Ambiguities of Representation in Recent Women's Fiction." *Signs* 9 (Winter 1983): 186–205.

Hubert, Linda. "To Alice Walker: Carson McCullers' Legacy of Love." *Pembroke Magazine* 20 (1988) 89–95.

Hudson-Weem, Clenora. "The Tripartite Plight of African-American Women as Reflected in the Novels of Hurston and Walker." *Journal of Black Studies* 20 (Dec. 1989): 192–207.

Iannone, Carol. "A Turning of the Critical Tide?" *Commentary* 88 (Nov. 1989): 57–59.

Inge, Tonette Bond, ed. *Southern Women Writers: The New Generation.* Tuscaloosa: University of Alabama Press, 1990.

Irwin, Edward E. "Freedoms as Value in Three Popular Southern Novels," *Proteus* 6 (Spring 1989): 37–41.

Jump, Harriet Devine, ed. *Diverse Voices: Essays on Twentieth-Century Women Writers in English.* New York: St. Martin's Press, 1991.

Juneja, Om P. "The Purple Colour of Walker Women: Their Journey from Slavery to Liberation." *The Literary Criterion* 25 (1990): 66–76.

Kelly, Lori Duin. "Theology and Androgyny: The Role of Religion in *The Color Purple.*" *Notes on Contemporary Literature* 18 (March 1988): 7–8.

Kirschner, Susan. "Alice Walker's Nonfictional Prose: A Checklist, 1966–1984." *Black American Literature Forum* 18 (Winter 1984): 162–63.

Kubitschek, Missy Dehn. "Subjugated Knowledge: Toward a Feminist Exploration of Rape in Afro-American Fiction." In *Black Feminist Criticism and Critical Theory,* edited by Joe Weixlmann and Houston A. Baker, Jr. Greenwood, Fla.: Penkevill, 1988.

Lanker, Brian, and Maya Angelou. "I Dream a World." *National Geographic* 176 (Aug. 1989): 206–26.

Leder, Priscilla. "Alice Walker's American Quilt: *The Color Purple* and American Literary Tradition." *Journal of the American Studies Association of Texas* 20 (Oct. 1989): 79–94.

Lenhart, Georgann. "Inspired Purple?" *Notes on Contemporary Literature* 14 (May 1984): 2–3.

Lupton, Mary Jane. "Clothes and Closure in Three Novels by Black Women." *Black American Literature Forum* 20 (Winter 1986): 409–21.

Marshall, Paule. "Characterizations of Black Women in the American Novel." In *In the Memory of Frances, Zora, and Lorraine: Essays and Interviews on Black Women Writing,* edited by Juliette Bowles. Washington, D.C.: Institute for the Arts and Humanities, Howard University, 1979.

McDowell, Deborah E. "'The Changing Same': Generational Connections and Black Women Novelists." *New Literary History* 18 (Winter 1987): 281–302.

McDowell, Margaret B. "The Black Woman as Artist and Critic: Four Versions." *The Kentucky Review* 7 (Spring 1987): 19–41.

McGowen, Martha J. "Atonement and Release in Alice Walker's *Meridian.*" *Critique.* 23 (1981): 25–35.

McKenzie, Tammie. "*The Color Purple*'s Celie: A Journey of Selfhood." *Conference of College Teachers of English Studies* 51 (Sept. 1986): 50–58.

Meese, Elizabeth A. "Defiance: The Body (of) Writing/The Writing (of) the Body." *Crossing the Double-Cross: The Practice of Feminist Criticism.* Chapel Hill, N.C.: University of North Carolina Press, 1986.

Nedelhaft, Ruth. "Domestic Violence in Literature: A Preliminary Study." *Mosaic* 17 (Spring 1984): 242–59.

Nowik, Ann. "Mixing Art and Politics: The Writings of Adrienne Rich, Marge Piercy, and Alice Walker." *The Centennial Review* 30 (Spring 1986): 208–18.

Parker-Smith, Bettye J. "Alice Walker's Women: In Search of Some Peace of Mind." In *Black Women Writers*, edited by Mari Evans. Garden City, N.Y.: Anchor-Doubleday, 1984.

Pinckney, Darryl. "Black Victims, Black Villains." *The New York Review of Books* (January 29, 1987): 17–20.

Porter, Nancy. "Women's Interracial Friendships and Visions of Community in *Meridian, The Salt Eaters, Civil Wars*, and *Dessa Rose*." In *Tradition and the Talents of Women*, edited and with an introduction by Florence Howe. Urbana: University of Illinois Press, 1991.

Pratt, Louis H. "Alice Walker's Men: Profiles in the Quest for Love and Personal Values." *Studies in Popular Culture* 12 (1989): 42–55.

Pratt, Louis H., and Darnell P. Pratt. *Alice Malsenior Walker: An Annotated Bibliography 1968–86*. Westport Conn.: Meckler Publishers, 1988.

Proudfit, Charles L. "Celie's Search for Identity: A Psychoanalytic Developmental Reading of Alice Walker's *The Color Purple*." *Contemporary Literature* 32 (Spring 1991): 12–37.

Pryse, Margorie. "Zora Neale Hurston, Alice Walker, and the 'Ancient Power' of Black Women." *Conjuring: Black Women, Fiction, and the Literary Tradition*, edited by Marjorie Pryse and Hortense Spillers. Bloomington, Ind.: Indiana University Press, 1985.

Robinson, Daniel. "Problems in Form: Alice Walker's *The Color Purple*." *Notes on Contemporary Literature* 16 (Jan. 1986): 2.

Ross, Daniel M. "Celie in the Looking Glass: The Desire for Selfhood in *The Color Purple*." *Modern Fiction Studies* 34 (Spring 1988): 69–84.

Royster, Philip M. "In Search of Our Fathers' Arms: Alice Walker's Persona of the Alienated Darling." *Black American Literature Forum* 20 (Winter 1986): 347–70.

Sadoff, Dianne F. "Black Matrilineage: The Case of Alice Walker and Zora Neale Hurston." *Signs* 11 (Autumn 1985): 4–26.

Sandes, Cheryl J., Katie G. Cannon, Emilie M. Townes, M. Shawn Copeland, Bell Hooks, and Cheryl Townsend Gilkes. "Christian Ethics and Theology in Womanist Perspective." *Journal of Feminist Studies in Religion* 5 (Fall 1989) 83–113.

Saunders, James Robert. "Womanism as the Key to Understanding Zora Neale Hurston's *Their Eyes Were Watching God* and Alice Walker's *The Color Purple*." *The Hollins Critic* 25 (Oct. 1988): 1–11.

Scholl, Diane Gabrielsen. "With Ears to Hear and Eyes to See: Alice Walker's Parable *The Color Purple*." *Christianity and Literature* 40 (Spring 1991): 255–66.

Shelton, F. W. "Alienation and Integration in Alice Walker's *The Color Purple*." *CLA Journal* 28 (June 1985): 382–92.

Smith-Wright, Geraldine. "Revision as Collaboration: Zora Neale Hurston's *Their Eyes Were Watching God* as Source for Alice Walker's *The Color Purple*." *SAGE* 4 (Fall 1987): 20–25.

Spillers, Hortense J. "'The Permanent Obliquity of an In(ph)llibly Straight': In the Time of the Daughters and the Fathers." In *Changing Our Own Words: Essays on Criticism, Theory, and Writing by Black Women*, edited by Cheryl A. Wall. New Brunswick: Rutgers University Press, 1989.

Stade, George. "Womanist Fiction and Male Characters." *Partisan Review* 52 (1985): 265–70.

Stein, Kara F. "*Meridian:* Alice Walker's Critique of Revolution." *Black American Literature Forum* 20 (Spring/Summer 1986): 129–41.

Steinem, Gloria. "Do You Know This Woman? She Knows You: A Profile of Alice Walker." *Ms. Magazine* (June 1982): 36–37, 89–94.

Tally, Justine. "Personal Development in the Fictional Women of Alice Walker." *Revista Canaria De Estudios Ingelses* 13–14 (April 1987): 181–95.

Tate, Claudia. "Alice Walker." In *Black Women Writers at Work*, edited by Claudia Tate. New York: Continuum, 1983.

Tavormina, M. Teresa. "Dressing the Spirit: Clothworking and Language in *The Color Purple*." *Journal of Narrative Technique* 16 (Fall 1986): 220–30.

Thomas, H. Nigel. "Alice Walker's Grange Copeland as a Trickster Figure." *Obsidian II* 6 (Spring 1991): 60–72.

Tucker, Lindsey. "Alice Walker's *The Color Purple:* Emergent Woman, Emergent Text." *Black American Literature Forum* 22 (Spring 1988): 81–95.

Turner, Darwin. "A Spectrum of Blackness." *Parnassus* 4 (Spring 1975): 202–18.

Vrettos, Athena. "Curative Domains: Women, Healing and History in Black Women's Narratives." *Women's Studies* 16 (Oct. 1989): 455–74.

Walker, Alice. "Turning into Love: Some Thoughts on Surviving and Meeting Langston Hughes." *Callaloo* 12 (Fall 1989): 663–66.

Walker, Robbie Jean, Janice W. Clemmer, Otis L. Scott, and Mary F. Sisney. "Implications for Survival: Coping Strategies of the Women in Alice Walker's Novels." *Explorations in Ethnic Studies* 10 (Jan. 1987): 9–24.

Walsh, Margaret. "The Enchanted World of *The Color Purple*." *The Southern Quarterly* 25 (Winter 1987): 89–101.

Walton, Priscilla L. "'What She Got to Sing About?': Comedy and *The Color Purple*." *Ariel* 21 (April 1990): 59–74.

Washington, J. Charles. "Positive Black Images in Alice Walker's Fiction." *Obsidian II* 3 (Spring 1988): 23–48.

Washington, Mary Helen. "I Sign My Mother's Name: Alice Walker, Dorothy West, Paule Marshall." In *Mothering the Mind: Twelve Studies of Writers and Their Silent Partners*, edited by Ruth Perry and Martine Watson Brownley. New York: Holmes and Meier, 1984: 142–63.

Watkins, Mel. "Sexism, Racism, and Black Women Writers." *The New York Times Book Review* (June 15, 1986): 1, 35–37.

Weston, Ruth. "Inversion of Patriarchal Mantle Images in Alice Walker's *Meridian*." *The Southern Quarterly* 25 (Winter 1987): 102–7.

Williams, Carolyn. "'Trying to Do Without God': The Revision of Epistolary Address in *The Color Purple*." In *Writing the Female Voice: Essays on Epistolary Literature*, edited by Elizabeth Goldsmith. Boston: Northeastern University Press, 1989.

Williams, Dolores S. "Black Women's Literature and the Task of Feminist Theology." In *Immaculate and Powerful: The Female in Sacred Image and Social Reality*, edited by Clarissa W. Atkinson, Constance H. Buchanan, and Margaret R. Miles. Boston: Beacon Press, 1985.

———. "The Color Purple." *Christianity and Crisis* 46 (July 14, 1986): 230–32.

Winchell, Donna Haisty. *Alice Walker*. New York: Twayne Publishers; Toronto, Canada: Macmillan; New York: Macmillan International, 1992.

Winchell, Mark Royden. "Fetching the Doctor: Shamanistic Housecalls in Alice Walker's 'Strong Horse Tea.'" *Mississippi Folklore Register* 25 (Fall 1981): 97–101.

Zeiger, William. "The Circular Journey and the Natural Authority of Form." *Rhetoric Review* 8 (Spring 1990): 208–19.

Acknowledgments

Untitled review of *The Third Life of Grange Copeland* by Josephine Hendin from *Saturday Review* (Aug. 22, 1970), ©1970 by the Saturday Review Associates. Reprinted with permission.

"To Try Men's Souls." Review of *The Third Life of Grange Copeland* by Robert Coles from *The New Yorker* (Feb. 27, 1971), ©1971 by Robert Coles. Reprinted with permission.

Untitled review of *Meridian* by Marge Piercy from *Liberty Journal* (May 1976), ©1976 by Reed Publishing, USA. Reprinted with permission.

"Limits." Review of *Meridian* by Greil Marcus from *The New Yorker* (June 7, 1976), ©1976 by Greil Marcus. Reprinted with permission.

"Some Letters Went to God." Review of *The Color Purple* by Mel Watkins from the *New York Times Book Review* (July 25, 1982), ©1982 by the New York Times Co. Reprinted with permission.

"'Celie, You a Tree.'" Review of *The Color Purple* by Dinitia Smith from *The Nation* 235 (Sept. 4, 1982), ©1982 by The Nation Associates, Inc. Reprinted with permission.

"All Those at the Banquet." Review of *Temple of My Familiar* by Ursula K. Le Guin from the *San Francisco Review of Books* 16 (Summer 1989), ©1989 by the San Francisco Review of Books. Reprinted with permission.

"The Beginnings of (Wo)man in Africa." Review of *Temple of My Familiar* by J. M. Coetzee from the *New York Times Book Review*, ©1989 by J. M. Coetzee. Reprinted with permission.

"Against the Tyranny of Tradition." Review of *Possessing the Secret of Joy* by Charles R. Larson from *Washington Post Book World* (July 5, 1992), ©1992 by the Washington Post Co. Reprinted with permission.

"What They Did to Tashi." Review of *Possessing the Secret of Joy* by Janette Turner Hospital from the *New York Times Book Review* (June 28, 1992), ©1992 by Janette Turner Hospital. Reprinted with permission.

"Walker: The Achievement of the Short Fiction" (originally entitled "Alice Walker: The Achievement of the Short Fiction) by Alice Hall Petry from *Modern Language Studies* 19 (Winter 1989), ©1989 by the Northeast Modern Language Association. Reprinted with permission.

"Race, Gender, and Nation in *The Color Purple*" by Lauren Berlant from *Critical Inquiry* 14 (Summer 1988), ©1988 by the University of Chicago. Reprinted with permission.

"Color Me Zora" (originally entitled "Color Me Zora: Alice Walker's (Re)-Writing of the Speakerly Text") from *The Signifying Monkey* by Henry Louis Gates, Jr., ©1988 by Henry Louis Gates, Jr. Reprinted with permission.

"Lettered Bodies and Corporeal Texts" (originally entitled "Lettered Bodies and Corporeal Texts in *The Color Purple*") by Wendy Wall, ©1990 by Wendy Wall. Printed with permission.

"Poetry as Preface to Fiction" (orginally entitled "Poetry as Preface to Fiction: Alice Walker's Recurrent Apprenticeship") by Thadious Davis from *The Mississippi Quarterly* 44 (Spring 1991), ©1991 by Mississippi State University. Reprinted with permission.

"Reading and Resistance: *The Color Purple*" by bell hooks, ©1990 by bell hooks. Printed with permission.

"Rewriting the Heroine's Story in *The Color Purple*" (originally entitled "A View from 'Elsewhere': Subversive Sexuality and the Rewriting of the Heroine's Story in *The Color Purple*") by Linda Abbandonato from *PMLA* 106 (Oct. 1991), ©1991 by the Modern Language Association of America. Reprinted with permission.

"Patches: Quilts and Community in Alice Walker's 'Everyday Use'" by Houston A. Baker, Jr., and Charlotte Pierce-Baker from *The Southern Review* 21 (July 1985), ©1985 by Houston A. Baker, Jr., and Charlotte Pierce-Baker. Reprinted with permission.

"A Conversation with Alice Walker" by Sharon Weightman (née Wilson) from *Kalliope* 6 (1984), ©1984 by Sharon Weightman. Reprinted with permission.

"Alice Walker: An Interview," from *Interviews with Black Writers*, edited by John O'Brien, ©1973 by Alice Walker. Reprinted with permission.

Index

This is one of six volumes of literary
criticism launching the
AMISTAD LITERARY SERIES
which is devoted to literary fiction
and criticism by and about African Americans.

◆

The typeface "AMISTAD" is based
on wood and stone symbols
and geometric patterns seen throughout
sixteenth-century Africa. These hand-carved
motifs were used to convey the diverse
cultural aspects evident among
the many African peoples.

◆

Amistad typeface was designed
by Maryam "Marne" Zafar.

◆

This book was published with the
assistance of March Tenth, Inc.
Printed and bound by Haddon Craftsmen, Inc.

◆

The paper is acid-free
55-pound Cross Pointe Odyssey Book.